# DIEGO MARADONA

This is the first book in English to closely examine the life of Diego Maradona from socio-cultural perspectives, exploring how his status as an icon, a popular sporting hero, and a political figurehead has been culturally constructed, reproduced, and manipulated.

The volume looks at representations of Maradona across a wide variety of media, including literature, cinema, popular music, printed and online press, and radio, and in different countries around the world, to cast new light on topics such as the instrumentality of sporting heroes and the links among sport, nationalism, and ideology. It shows how the life of Maradona – from his origins in the barrio through to his rise to god-like status in Naples and as a postcolonial symbol of courage and resistance against imperial powers across the global south, alongside scandal and his fall from grace – powerfully illustrates themes such as the dynamics of gender, justice, and affect that underpin the study of sport, culture, and society.

This is essential reading for anybody with an interest in football, sport studies, media studies, cultural studies, or sociology.

**Pablo Brescia** is a writer, critic, and Professor of Spanish at the University of South Florida, USA, where he directs the graduate program and teaches courses on contemporary Latin American literature and culture. His areas of research are the theory and history of short fiction and the intersection among science, technology, and literature in Latin America.

**Mariano Paz** is a Lecturer in Spanish and Subject Leader for Spanish at the University of Limerick, Republic of Ireland, where he is also an Associate Director of the Ralahine Centre for Utopian Studies. His research focuses on Latin American utopian and dystopian cinemas, science fiction, and popular culture.

## Critical Research in Football
### Series Editors:
*Pete Millward, Liverpool John Moores University, UK*
*Jamie Cleland, University of Southern Australia*
*Dan Parnell, University of Liverpool, UK*
*Stacey Pope, Durham University, UK*
*Paul Widdop, Manchester Metropolitan University, UK*

The *Critical Research in Football* book series was launched in 2017 to showcase the inter- and multi-disciplinary breadth of debate relating to "football". The series defines "football" as broader than association football, with research on rugby, Gaelic and gridiron codes also featured. Including monographs, edited collections, short books and textbooks, books in the series are written and/or edited by leading experts in the field whilst consciously also affording space to emerging voices in the area and are designed to appeal to students, postgraduate students, and scholars who are interested in the range of disciplines in which critical research in football connects. The series is published in association with the *Football Collective*, @FB_Collective.

Available in this series:

**Football, Politics and Identity**
*James Carr, Daniel Parnell, Paul Widdop, Martin J. Power and Stephen R. Millar*

**Football, Family, Gender and Identity**
The Football Self
*Hanya Pielichaty*

**Sport Mega-Events, Security and COVID-19**
Securing the Football World
*Jan Andre Lee Ludvigsen*

**Integrated Marketing Communications in Football**
*Argyro Elisavet Manoli*

**Football and Risk**
Trends and Perspectives
*Jan Andre Lee Ludvigsen*

**Diego Maradona**
A Socio-Cultural Study
*Edited by Pablo Brescia and Mariano Paz*

https://www.routledge.com/Critical-Research-in-Football/book-series/CFSFC

# DIEGO MARADONA

## A Socio-Cultural Study

*Edited by Pablo Brescia and Mariano Paz*

Routledge
Taylor & Francis Group

LONDON AND NEW YORK

Designed Cover Image: Marcos Brindicci/Stringer/Getty Images

First published 2023
by Routledge
4 Park Square, Milton Park, Abingdon, Oxon OX14 4RN

and by Routledge
605 Third Avenue, New York, NY 10158

*Routledge is an imprint of the Taylor & Francis Group, an informa business*

*British Library Cataloguing-in-Publication Data*
A catalogue record for this book is available from the British Library

*Library of Congress Cataloging-in-Publication Data*
Names: Brescia, Pablo, editor. | Paz, Mariano, editor.
Title: Diego Maradona : a socio-cultural study / edited by Pablo Brescia and Mariano Paz.
Description: Abingdon, Oxon ; New York City : Routledge, 2023. | Series: Critical research in football | Includes bibliographical references and index.
Identifiers: LCCN 2022025877 | ISBN 9781032052120 (hardback) | ISBN 9781032052090 (paperback) | ISBN 9781003196587 (ebook)
Subjects: LCSH: Maradona, Diego, 1960-2020. | Maradona, Diego, 1960-2020--In mass media. | Mass media and sports. | Sports and globalization. | Soccer players--Argentina--Biography.
Classification: LCC GV942.7.M32 D54 2023 | DDC 796.334092--dc23/eng/20220720
LC record available at https://lccn.loc.gov/2022025877

ISBN: 978-1-032-05212-0 (hbk)
ISBN: 978-1-032-05209-0 (pbk)
ISBN: 978-1-003-19658-7 (ebk)

DOI: 10.4324/9781003196587

Typeset in Bembo
by KnowledgeWorks Global Ltd.

# CONTENTS

# CONTRIBUTORS

**Luca Bifulco** teaches Sociology and Sociology of Sport at the University of Naples (Università degli Studi di Napoli Federico II), Italy. He is the General Editor of *Eracle. Journal of Sport and Social Sciences*. He has edited several volumes on the sociology of sports and on Maradona.

**Ksenija Bilbija** is a Professor of Spanish American Literatures at the University of Wisconsin – Madison, USA, specialising in cultural studies, gender criticism, post-traumatic memory, and *cartonera* publishing.

**Raymond Boyle** is a Professor of Communication and Director of the Centre for Cultural Policy Research at the University of Glasgow, UK. He has published widely on media and sport. He is also co-managing Editor of *Media, Culture and Society*.

**David García Cames** has taught journalism, communication, and literature at Eafit University and the Universidad Pontificia Bolivariana, both in Medellín, Colombia.

**Gabriela Garton** is a Visiting Scholar and Sessional Lecturer at Victoria University, Australia. Her main areas of research include the social study of women's sport, representations of athletes in the media, gender studies, and ethnography.

**Julia Hang** is a postdoctoral fellow and Professor of Social Classical Theory II at the National University of La Plata (UNLP), Argentina. Her research involves the social studies of sport, culture, and gender. She investigates the links between politics, sport, and gender in Argentine clubs from an ethnographic perspective.

**Martín Kohan** is an Argentinian writer and cultural critic who teaches literary theory at the University of Buenos Aires, Argentina. He is the author of several novels and collections of short stories. He won the Premio Herralde in 2007.

**María Rosa Lojo** is an Argentinian writer and cultural critic who teaches at the Universidad del Salvador, Buenos Aires, Argentina. She has published several novels and books of literary criticism, as well as collections of short stories and poetry.

**Pedro Angel Palou** is a Mexican writer and cultural critic who teaches Mexican literature at Tufts University, Boston, USA. He has published several novels and books of essays and literary criticism, as well as collections of short stories.

**Patricio Pron** is an Argentinian writer and literary critic. He holds a PhD from the University of Göttingen, Germany. He is the author of several novels and collections of short stories and the winner of the Premio Alfaguara de Novela (2019).

**Pippo Russo** is Researcher in Territorial and Environmental Sociology at the University of Florence, Italy, specialising in sport sociology, cultural sociology, and the sociology of citizenship.

**Beatriz Sarlo** is an Argentinian cultural and literary critic who has taught at the University of Buenos Aires, Argentina, and has been a visiting professor at Columbia University, the University of California, Berkeley, and the University of Cambridge, among others. She has published on Argentinian literature, culture, media, politics, and society.

**Edgardo Scott** is an Argentinian writer, essayist, and translator. He has authored books of essays, novels, and collections of short stories.

**Fernando Segura M. Trejo** has taught sociology at the Federal University of Goiás, Brazil, and at the CIDE, Mexico. His research on football is focused on social inclusion, the history of the World Cups, and the connections between sport and violence.

**Ana María Shua** is an Argentinian writer who has published books of poetry and several novels and short story collections. She is also a specialist in the genres of micro-fiction and children's literature. She obtained the Guggenheim Fellowship in 1993.

**Alan Tomlinson** is an Emeritus Professor of Leisure Studies at the University of Brighton, UK. His primary research areas cover leisure theory and the history/sociology of spectacle.

**Martín Virgili** is a teacher, guitarist, composer, and sound documentary maker. He directs the Center for Art and Science at the National Technological University (UTN), Argentina. His current research focuses on sound studies and soundscapes.

**John Williams** is an Associate Professor in the School of Media, Communication and Sociology at the University of Leicester, UK. His research is focused on issues of equality around class, gender, and ethnicity in sport, on the sociology of football and football fan culture and on spectator behaviour in football.

# PREFACE AND ACKNOWLEDGEMENTS

One afternoon in October of 2017 two scholars met at the University of South Florida, Tampa, in front of the library building. Dr. Pablo Brescia, professor of Latin American Studies at USF, was hosting the visit of Dr. Mariano Paz, a specialist on Latin American Literature and Film at the University of Limerick, Republic of Ireland. Over coffee, they discussed various topics. Football was one of them.

There was one problem however: their football sympathies put them on opposite sides of the fence. Dr. Brescia is a fan of Boca Juniors, and Dr. Paz of River Plate, the two most popular football clubs, and historic archrivals, in Argentina. They were about to go their separate ways but, as it has been the case in so many other instances, Diego Armando Maradona came to the rescue. They discovered they shared a passion for Maradona and for all that he encompassed.

And so *Diego Maradona: A Socio-cultural Study* was born. The email exchanges became longer and longer, the WhatsApp messages more and more frequent and, by the end of 2019, a book proposal was drafted. Many things happened in the following three years: Routledge accepted the proposal; Brescia and Paz built a team of standout contributors to the volume, a devastating pandemic hit the globe and Maradona passed away on November 25, 2020. The book became not only the first academic volume in English dedicated to the study of Maradona's cultural significance but also a tribute to a most relevant footballer. After his death, the Argentinian government declared three days of national mourning and opened the Casa Rosada (House of Government) for the people to come and pay their respects to their idol. Out of the many photos that went viral on that occasion, one became typically allegorical: a fan from Boca and a fan from River in a warm embrace. Just like the editors of this volume had done five years before. This is only one of the possible *Maradonian* effects this book explores.

Both Pablo and Mariano would like to thank Simon Whitmore and Rebecca Connor from Routledge for their unwavering support, the authors for their dedication and enthusiasm and the translators of several chapters and sections: David Atkinson, Emma Byrne, Allison Febo, Dolores Gadler, Muireann Prendergast, and Ana Terrazas Calero.

Pablo would like to thank María Victoria Torres, Adriana Novoa, Fernando Segura Trejo, and Edgardo Scott for the dialogue around Maradona. He appreciates the efforts of his sister Laura, and his friends Julia Martínez Pesqueira, Ariela Parisi and Andrea Aquino, who ran after books on Maradona in Argentina and Uruguay. He also would like to thank his family – Sonia, Lucía, and his parents – for listening to him speak incessantly about Maradona.

Mariano would like to thank the Royal Irish Academy, which funded the above-mentioned trip to Tampa through a Charlemont Grant, as well as the Faculty of Arts, Humanities and Social Sciences and the School of Modern Languages and Applied Linguistics, both at the University of Limerick, for supporting the development of this volume. He also thanks his colleagues James Carr and Martin J. Power in Limerick, Emanuele D'Onofrio in Rome, Pedro Rodríguez Pagani in Buenos Aires, and, last but not least, Lola and Magda.

And thanks to football.

# GLOSSARY

The following terms are used frequently in Argentinian Spanish — some of them are specific to the world of football but most belong to ordinary, everyday vocabulary.

**Aguante:** a collective practice based on steadfast support for a football club. The duty of fans is to attend the games, braving the elements if necessary, chanting and shouting passionately to back the team. From the 1980s onwards, the *aguante* becomes associated with physical clashes in the increasingly violent context of Argentine football, in which support must also be expressed through confrontation with the fans of rival teams. The practice is informed by the exacerbated cult of masculinity known as *machismo*.

**Cabecita negra:** literally "little black head", a derogatory and racist term used to refer to the poor and marginalised peoples of Argentina. Associated to darker skin tone and dark hair.

**Gambeta:** for convenience, usually translated as "dribble" ("to dribble" is used for the verb form *gambetear*). The original term in Spanish comes from dance, denoting a movement of the legs being crossed in the air. *Gambetas* therefore belong not only to sport but can also be seen in tango dancing. In football, the *gambeta* refers to a sudden movement of the body that allows the player to elude an opponent. It may also involve deceit, when the player pretends to move in one direction and then goes into another one. This is the foremost skill of talented footballers, usually attacking midfielders playing in the "number 10" position.

**La nuestra:** the style that defined the golden-age of Argentinian football in the 1940s and 1950s, favouring free-flowing, attacking tactics in which rigorous defending is not the key priority. It could be translated as "our style", connoting an opposition to the more organised and less spontaneous approach favoured by Europeans. For this view of football, entertainment is the main goal, and spectacle is more important than control and order.

**Pibe:** child or adolescent. In football, a *pibe* is a young, skilful, and astute player who comes from a low-class background and plays in a creative attacking position.

**Potrero:** an empty patch of untended earth used as a pitch, usually located in lower class neighbourhoods and slums. *Potreros* have no demarcations and no goals (goalposts can be improvised with almost any object). Thus, *potreros* are makeshift pitches in which football is played without the constraints imposed by the regulations of professionalised sport. As such, they are one of the defining spaces in which football is played in Argentina.

**Villa:** in Spanish, this refers to a usually picturesque small town. In Argentina, it is also a shorthand for "villa miseria", the term given to slums or shantytowns. The name of the town where Maradona grew up, Villa Fiorito, echoes the first meaning. However, economic crises and downward social mobility in Argentina from the 1960s onwards meant that some areas of Villa Fiorito could be considered a shantytown.

**Villero:** the inhabitant of a *villa*. Additionally, as an adjective form: of or relating to a *villa*. For example, *villero* football – i.e., football as played in a *villa*.

# INTRODUCTION

## The Cultural Significance of Maradona

*Pablo Brescia and Mariano Paz*

### Diego Maradona superstar

It is not possible to determine who has been the world's best footballer. Like any sport, football changes over time, so it is extremely complicated – and perhaps futile – to compare players across different historical periods. Thus, for some, the top spot may belong to Pelé, the Brazilian legend from the 1950s and 1960s and the only player to have won three World Cups. Younger fans might opt instead for Lionel Messi or Cristiano Ronaldo. However, there can be no argument as to who is the footballer who reached the highest peaks of stardom and mythification. A footballer whose fame stretched to most corners of the world with an intensity that transcended the realm of sport, transforming him into a cultural icon. A footballer who was regarded by so many not only as a celebrity and star but also as a hero, a legend, a redeemer, a martyr, and, even, literally, a god. This person was Diego Armando Maradona.

Maradona was a major figure in what is the most popular sport around the world: football (or soccer in American English, a term that will be avoided in this volume). The sports star is a subcategory within the world of stardom and celebrity, of which Maradona was a prime example. Contemporary celebrities – a product of late modernity rooted in consumer capitalism and mass media (Andrews and Jackson, 2001) – are dependent on their images being disseminated by the media, in a complex network which involves the production and circulation of images as commodities and as texts on the one hand, and the ways in which audiences and consumers receive, and respond to, those images on the other hand (Elliott and Boyd, 2018). For this reason, celebrities are particularly susceptible to be studied as social and cultural products. Stars do not exist outside texts (not only books and films, but also newspaper stories, TV programmes, advertisements, and so on), so in order to understand them, attention must be

DOI: 10.4324/9781003196587-1

paid to the social and cultural texts through which stars are produced and reproduced (Dyer 1998).

No footballer other than Maradona has had so many books written about him, so many films and television programmes revolving around his presence, and so many popular songs composed. No others have been the object of so many debates that exceeded the world of football and spilled over onto the spheres of politics, economics, law, culture, and art. If, as Dyer suggests, starts should be approached through the texts that talk about them, this book explores for the first time the ways in which Maradona has been constructed as a global icon in print and visual media, in literature, in fiction and documentary film, in biographies and autobiographies, and in music. But the volume also goes beyond these representations to discuss aspects of Maradona that are connected to social practices, such as religion (through the partially ironic, but also partially serious, Church of Maradona, which has thousands of international followers), feminism, and his legacy in the countries and football leagues in which he played or, in the case of the UK, in which he becomes a controversial figure.

## Why study Maradona?

Is it an exaggeration to claim that Maradona was such an important figure? His death was reported on the front page of printed and online versions of dozens of newspapers across the world. The list goes much further that the main national newspapers of countries in Latin America and Europe; it includes, for example, *The New York Times*, and dailies in China, Saudi Arabia, India, and Japan, to mention only a few non-Western countries. Is this sufficient evidence of his renown?

One incident could help us answer this question. Following Maradona's death on November 25, 2020, French President Emmanuel Macron wrote a public letter in which he paid an emotional homage to the player, saying that, more than a player, he was a dancer in cleats, and a true artist (*Infobae*, 2020). It is true that many people posted similar messages on social media, from former colleagues and teammates to journalists and ordinary fans. However, at that time, Europe was not only facing the second wave of the Covid-19 pandemic but, moreover, the official exit of Great Britain from the European Union was imminent, yet Macron still felt it necessary to take out time in his agenda to produce that letter whose significance rises even further when one considers that Maradona never played or coached in France. This was by no means the only example of a politician responding to Maradona's passing. Both the Israeli Prime Minister at the time, Benjamin Netanyahu, and the president of the Palestinian National Authority, Mahmoud Abbas, released press statements praising the footballer and offering their condolences.

Focusing on the impact that followed Maradona's death, as much as it affected millions of people, would not do full justice to his trajectory. Maradona's agency as a footballer, as a coach, and as a celebrity and star need to be understood alongside the larger economic, legal, political, sporting, and ideological structures that conditioned his personal life and his professional career. The object of *Diego Maradona: A Socio-cultural Study* is not only to comprehend Maradona and the different vectors that played out in the making of his status of hero, myth, or legend (and a hated enemy of many) but also to see how these very roles were constructed by cultural producers and the media.

## Who was Maradona?

The person who achieved global recognition and the unconditional adoration of millions of people was born on October 30, 1960, in the impoverished neighbourhood of Villa Fiorito, in the suburbs of Buenos Aires, Argentina. Maradona was the first son and fifth child of internal migrants who had arrived from the province of Corrientes, in north-eastern Argentina, in the search for a better life, but had to settle in a *villa*, or shantytown: Fiorito, where streets were unpaved, and houses often lacked running water and sewerage systems. The entire family would sleep in the only available bedroom in the house, under a roof that leaked when it rained, until as a teenager Maradona was given a professional contract by Argentinos Juniors, and all the family moved to a big house close to the stadium, located in a lower middle class neighbourhood in Buenos Aires. These details are essential to understand some aspects of Maradona's life and career, from his playing style to his political sympathies; indeed, they are also the key to understand the processes of self-fashioning and cultural representations that followed his football career and life.

In Argentina, Maradona is considered a national hero who symbolically redeemed the nation in the sporting arena, after the country was defeated by the UK in the Malvinas/Falklands war in 1982. As Simon Critchley has argued, "football is the place where the drama of national identity and non-identity plays itself faithfully out against a history of violence and war" (2018: 66). The two notable goals that Maradona scored in the game against England on June 22, 1986, during a quarterfinal game in the Mexico World Cup, cast him as a redeemer. This image rapidly crossed national borders and made Maradona a global symbol of anti-colonial struggle, of courage and resistance against imperial powers. Most importantly, Maradona became also a purveyor of happiness. In a period of a severe economic and political crisis as Argentina was emerging from a period of seven years of brutal dictatorship, he gave joy to millions of Argentinians when he led the national team to the championship in that same World Cup.

The image of Maradona as redeemer was further cemented in Italy, where he gained acclaim playing for SSC Napoli in Naples, where he fought yet another iteration of the biblical battle between David and Goliath. Naples, a city in the relegated Italian South, and its football club, had never experienced the scale of success brought about by the team that was built around Maradona from 1984 onwards, which included winning two Serie A championships and the UEFA

Cup. Never before the arrival of Maradona had Napoli (or any other team in the south of Italy, for that matter) been able to obtain the *scudetto*, the first division league title; never did Napoli win another tournament again after Maradona's departure. For the citizens of Naples, still today, decades after Maradona left the club in 1991, worshipping him contributes to the promotion of social solidarity and feelings of local and regional pride. Immediately after this death, the San Paolo stadium of Naples was renamed "Diego Armando Maradona".

## Studying Maradona; or Maradonian studies

That Maradona elicited the love and admiration of many is evident in films, documentaries, songs, dozens of murals that decorate the walls of Buenos Aires and Naples (some painted on the sides of buildings several stories high), and even altars in which he becomes almost a religious icon, comparable to the Virgin Mary or *San Gennaro*, a catholic martyr and patron saint of Naples. After he retired from football, he was hired as manager by teams in Argentina, in Mexico, and in the United Arab Emirates; he hosted the successful TV show *La Noche del Diez* in 2005; he coached Argentina's national team from 2008 to 2010; he was sought for endorsement by political figures such as Cuban leader Fidel Castro and Venezuelan presidents Hugo Chávez and Nicolás Maduro; and he was approached for advertisements and merchandising of dozens of products across the world.

This status of global star did not come without controversies as well, expressed across the different cultures and geographies in which his career and life developed. Maradona as a player, icon, public figure, and private person is deeply embedded in a series of complex discourses and meanings. Some of the phenomena described above have, of course, their own problematic undersides, from the nationalist and autocratic narratives that underlie Maradona's adoration in Argentina to the alleged links between the footballer and Neapolitan criminal networks. Some of his political connections put him close to non-democratic leaders with questionable human rights records, something at odds with his image of a tireless fighter for freedom and equality.

As relevant as Maradona has been for football and politics, as a sporting star, as a popular hero, and as a controversial celebrity who was constantly present in the media, no academic books in English have been published about him. There are several biographies and autobiographies, and dozens of books about him in other languages, but they tend to approach Maradona from a journalistic or, at best, an essayistic perspective that lacks the rigour and comprehensive latitude of academic enquiry. There is a significant *corpus* of scholarly literature on Maradona made up mostly of individual articles and book chapters, with some exceptions in the form of essay anthologies (in Spanish and Italian). This volume provides a systematic list of such sources which, although meticulous, can ultimately never aspire to be exhaustive.

However relevant these mostly isolated chapters and articles are, Maradona's importance as cultural icon deserves a more systematic inquiry. *Diego Maradona:*

*A Socio-cultural Study* is the first edited collection to approach the study of Maradona from several perspectives springing from diverse disciplinary fields. They include approaching him as a cultural artefact that has been constructed through art, from literature to cinema to popular music; discussing the ways in which his professional and personal biography have been represented in mass media; and reflecting on the ways in which his life intersected with specific areas of social life, such as politics, economics, religion, and the law. None of these themes can be studied in isolation, and readers will find how such approaches are interconnected to different degrees in the chapters that make up this collection.

This book is not only about football, in terms of history, its strategies, and its tactics, but mainly about contemporary culture and the making of heroes and stars. It is addressed at those who may or may not have specialised knowledge of who Maradona was and why he remains a central figure in popular culture. Our aim is two-fold. In the first place, to provide a rigorous, academic approach to understanding the cultural significance of a person who happened to be a football player, and whose exploits on the pitch contributed to define not just himself but the myriad of social interpretations made about him. These processes, in turn, resulted in the elevation of a person to a status of myth and legend. Studying these social phenomena requires the mobilisation of a theoretical toolbox from several disciplines in the humanities, including cultural studies, philosophy, sport studies, media studies, musicology, literary criticism, sociology, and anthropology.

Our second aim derives from the literature already mentioned: we argue that it is possible to define a niche field at the intersection of cultural sociology, cultural studies, and sport studies: that of Maradona studies. The multiplicity of meanings surrounding him, the sheer quantity of texts that have been produced about his figure (journalistic writing, novels and short stories, comics, cinema and television, music, and increasingly communications in social media), the political and sociological dimensions of the Maradonian phenomenon (including an entire religion, the Church of Maradona), all prove that the footballer cannot be fully accounted for by a series of articles, chapters, or indeed by the existing monographs. Even this collection, entirely dedicated to his study, will not be sufficient and the editors hope it will function as a gateway to themes and topics that could be explored further.

## Our chapters

The book is divided into three different sections. The first one, Global Maradona, presents five chapters focused on the connections between Maradona and the five countries that marked his career in the most significant ways: Argentina, Spain, Italy, Mexico, and the UK.

Chapter 1, by Pablo Brescia and Mariano Paz, focuses on Maradona and Argentina, the country where he was born, grew up, and initiated his playing career, and whose national team he led to victory in the 1986 Mexico World

Cup. The chapter approaches Maradona from four key angles, or takes: as a football player and manager, as a celebrity and media personality, as a political signifier, and as an object of academic study. The chapter acts both as an introduction for academics interested in Maradona and as an overview of the key moments and texts that contributed to defining each of these four spheres.

In Chapter 2, Maradona and Spain: Mythologies of the Hero Narrative, David García Cames discusses Maradona's first destination outside of Argentina: his two intense years playing for Barcelona. García Cames argues from the theoretical perspective of the hero narrative that, in a career that clearly mirrors the "rise and fall" formula of the hero, Spain was the stage that completed Maradona's departure from home in a path to further glory and adventure. Thus, Spain was (twice) an instrumental moment in the life of the player, since it was also a subsequent step in the return journey, as Maradona closed his European footballing career playing one season for Sevilla FC in Seville.

In Chapter 3, Maradona and Italy: The Rise and Fall of the Man on His Own, Pippo Russo turns his attention to the country where Maradona enjoyed his most successful spell as a footballer: Italy. Maradona's years at SSC Napoli, between 1984 and 1991, saw the player at his peak, not only leading a team to historical triumphs and being transformed into a legend, but also ending in dramatic and tragic form. Russo proposes that the links between Italy and Maradona are so profound that the player can be defined as Italian as much as Argentinian, challenging national territorial models. Reviewing the way in which he was represented in Italian media up to 1990, Russo argues that Maradona stands for the major and final emblem of the individual footballer, a figure that can be defined as the Man on His Own.

In Chapter 4, Maradona and Mexico: The Ecstasy and the Agony, Fernando Segura Trejo and John Williams demonstrate that Mexico is an important place in the making of the Maradona legend. What was his most significant performance in a single game took place at the Azteca Stadium in Mexico City: the Argentina-England game in which he scored two goals so notable and transcendent that they eventually were given names by pundits and journalists: the Hand of God goal and The Goal of the Century. But player and country, the authors argue, are not limited to that game or even that world cup, as they trace further connections between the two across time, examining testimonies on Maradona from the Mexican press and various journalists, and include Maradona's one-year spell as a manager of the second-division football club Dorados de Sinaloa.

In the final chapter of this section, Maradona and Britain: An Unforgettable Affair, Raymond Boyle compares the ways in which the player was presented in British media, specifically in England and Scotland, as the latter was a key location in Maradona's international career (as an 18-year-old, he scored his first international goal for Argentina against Scotland in 1979 at Hampden Park stadium in Glasgow). In Britain, opinions about the player would eventually evolve as they followed Maradona's career. Boyle shows here how the infamous Hand of God goal cast a shadow on the discourses about Maradona produced by English media, while at the same time it intersected with diverse political and cultural attitudes in Scotland, where reactions to it were much more sympathetic. However, Boyle concludes that, with the passage of time and in the aftermath of Maradona's death, English attitudes became more nuanced.

The second section in the volume is titled Representing Maradona, and it studies three forms of cultural production: literature, cinema, and music, showing the multiple interconnection between art and the figure of Maradona.

Chapter 6, Maradona and Literature: God is only Human, by Pablo Brescia, identifies and surveys an extensive *corpus* made of short stories, novels, poems, and a fragment of a play centred on Maradona which evoke, re-create, and replicate the peaks and valleys of his career and life. The chapter aims to show how this literary discourse lays bare a web of repetitive themes around Maradona's symbolic value both on and beyond the pitch (Maradona the footballing prodigy, the hero, the national redeemer, the unique genius, etc.). Following Roland Barthes, Brescia analyses the ways writers have sought to make Maradona a mode of signification and explores what this language reveals about national and global dynamics linking sport, identity, and cultural politics.

Chapter 7, Maradona and Cinema: Biopic, Documentary, Art Film, by Mariano Paz, is an introduction to Maradonian cinema. The chapter provides a map of the key works in the corpus, which includes mainstream biopics and sophisticated art films, independent documentaries and popular comedies, among other works. Most of these films are less about football than about a gamut of themes, in which Maradona becomes an allegorical or symbolical presence that eludes easy classification. Paz shows how the films construct different versions of Maradona (the political revolutionary, the fallen idol, the myth), while dealing with the complex intersection between the apparatus of cinema, memory, the use of archival images, and mythmaking.

In Chapter 8, Maradona and Music: Soundscapes and Echoes of the Maradonian Song, Martín Virgili discusses Maradona from the area of musicology and sound studies. Maradona's life, for Virgili, has been marked by the production of very specific sounds, ranging from fans chanting his name at stadiums and celebrating his goals, to rock and pop musicians writing songs about him. The chapter offers a reflection on the noises, the melodies, the shouts, and the singing that have enveloped Maradona. The footballer, argues Virgili, was adept not only at juggling the ball, but also at receiving the mass sounds that were produced around him. In fact, his relationship with the ball could be compared to a highly skilled musician improvising as he plays an instrument. As is the case with literature and cinema, more and more bands continue to record songs about Maradona.

The third and final section, Reading and Writing Maradona, examines Maradonian discourses – those produced by him and the ones who speak of him – from a multiplicity of perspectives including justice, autobiographical and biographical tropes, feminism, and religion. In addition, a final chapter includes shorter pieces by renowned Latin American writers and cultural critics, who provide insight of yet other aspects of the Maradonian dimension.

In Chapter 9, Spectres of Maradona: Chronicle/Fiction/Autobiography/Film, Ksenija Bilbija addresses Maradona's presence as a "ghost", conjured up by an archive of texts and films that point towards a complex intersection of memory, autobiography, and the concept of justice. For the author, neither Maradona's autobiography, nor the semi-fictional accounts, nor the affective narrative and cinematographic texts that tried to capture him can represent the footballer comprehensively, an impossible task indeed. Nonetheless, the emotional community formed in the "sharing" of Maradona speaks loudly about the Argentinian player's apparitions in cultural discourse.

In Chapter 10, The Maradona Story: Tropes in Biography and Autobiography, Alan Tomlinson compares Maradona's autobiography *El Diego* with the first biography of the player published in English: Jimmy Burns' *Maradona: The Hand of God*. Following Virginia Woolf's "granite and rainbow" conceptual dimensions when writing a life, the chapter examines these accounts *cum* narratives and identifies tropes such as "The Hand of God" and the idea of home in the balance between reality and fiction that shaped the renditions of the life of a sporting celebrity and the diversity of factors that created the Maradona persona.

Chapter 11, Argentinian Feminisms in the Light (and Shadow) of Maradona, considers an aspect that had been mostly neglected in Maradonian studies until very recently: feminist readings. Gabriela Garton and Julia Hang focus on the specific context of Argentina, where two interpretations have developed: in one, associated with traditional feminist movements, Maradona – given his conflictive relations with women, his often chauvinistic and patriarchal opinions and behaviours, and his refusal to recognise and support children born out of several affairs – should be condemned as an enemy of what feminism stands for; in a different view, traceable to more recent currents within feminism, such a dismissive attitude should be mitigated by other factors, such as Maradona's poor origin and his stance as a perpetual rebel which can inspire people to fight inequality in any realm of life.

In Chapter 12, Deifying Diego: The Church of Maradona and Beyond, Luca Bifulco explains the many similarities between sporting and religious experiences in order to focus on the mechanisms of the Church of Maradona, established in 1998. Between parody and authenticity, the church imitates several principles from Christianity to ultimately posit an idea of a "Maradonian sacred" relating to meaning, morality, and memory. For its committed followers, the Argentinian footballer is a "God" in so far as he stands as a symbol of collective identification, inspiration, and regional/national pride.

Finally, the last chapter, Writing Maradona, provides brief explorations in an essayistic form about Maradona as an icon. The short pieces it contains have been produced by prestigious fiction writers and cultural critics from Latin America. Martín Kohan, in "One and All", speaks about the many faces of Maradona and his resemblance of an "iconicity machine"; in "D10S: His Era, His Epic", Ana María Shua gathers testimonies from the Argentinian people to understand how the era and the epic of Maradona nurtured an idea of divinity surrounding his figure; Edgardo Scott speaks of "The Language of Tears", made up not only of Maradona's playing style but also of his words and lash-outs; in María Rosa Lojo's "Saint?", there is a reflection about why Maradona could be joining the ensemble of Argentinian popular saints; Patricio Pron's "M and M: To See or Not to See" details a comparison between Maradona and Messi and considers the ideas of "exceptionality" and "normalcy" linked to Argentinian history and society; in "Number 10 in Ten", Pedro Angel Palou details Maradona's career in ten quick flashes; and in "Children of Maradona", Beatriz Sarlo speaks of Maradonian mythology and theology to define the Argentinian footballer's life as an epic tale of transgression.

In his autobiography *Yo soy el Diego … de la gente* [translated first as *El Diego* and then as *Maradona. The Autobiography of Soccer's Greatest and Most Controversial Star*], Maradona speaks of his first steps in the sport and says that he started out as a defender: "As a *libero* [sweeper], you see everything from the back … You're the owner of the team" (Maradona 2011: 1). Just as Maradona's beginnings as a footballer, this book aims to provide a vantage point from where those interested in Diego Maradona can see an open field.

## References

Andrews, David L. and Steven J. Jackson. 2001. "Introduction: Sport Celebrities, Public Culture, and Private Experience". *Sport Stars: The Cultural Politics of Sporting Celebrity*. Eds. David L. Andrews and Steven J. Jackson. London and New York: Routledge, 1–19.

Critchley, Simon. 2018. *What We Think About When We Think About Football*. London: Profile Books.

Dyer, Richard. 1998. *Stars*. London: BFI Publishing.

Elliott, Anthony and Ross Boyd. 2018. "Celebrity and Contemporary Culture: A Critical Analysis of Some Theoretical Accounts". *Routledge Handbook of Celebrity Studies*. Ed. Anthony Elliott. Abingdon, UK, and New York: Routledge, 3–25.

*Infobae*. 2020. "La sentida carta de Emmanuel Macron por la muerte de Diego Armando Maradona". November 25. Web: https://www.infobae.com/america/mundo/2020/11/26/emmanuel-macron-despidio-a-diego-maradona-la-mano-de-dios-habia-puesto-un-genio-del-futbol-sobre-la-tierra/ [Accessed March 4, 2022].

Maradona, Diego Armando. 2011. *Maradona. The Autobiography of Soccer's Greatest and Most Controversial Star*. Trans. Marcela Mora y Araujo. New York: Skyhorse Publishing.

# PART I
# Global Maradona

# 1

# MARADONA AND ARGENTINA

## Four Takes

*Pablo Brescia and Mariano Paz*

## 1960–∞[1]

The plethora of nicknames Diego Armando Maradona received during his career – Pelusa, el Pibe de Oro, Maradó, El Diego, Diegol, El Diez, Diegote, D10S – not only speaks of the attempts to capture his significance as a player and sports celebrity but also to the quantity of information and interpretations readily available about him. His autobiographies and biographies; the documentaries, TV series, and films covering various aspects of his life[2]; the journalistic writings dealing with him as a player, coach, and celebrity; and the scholarly interest he has drawn (cf. the bibliography included in this volume) underline the symbolic charge of his name. As we argue in our introduction, this charge begets an entire field of "Maradonian" studies conceived as an infinite source of cultural iconicity.

Within this field, Maradona's complex and enduring relationship to Argentina, his country of origin, continues to be mapped and interpreted. Following his death on November 25, 2020, an avalanche of obituaries and commemorative pieces was published on various media in Argentina and across the world, trying to summarise Maradona in a single meaningful sentence. For several Argentinian journalists, it was "the day that football died" (see, for example, https://www.youtube.com/watch?v=0kSt8avOtFA). Another common reaction was best encapsulated by writer Martín Caparrós, who wrote: "He was Argentina" (2020). Not "he represented Argentina" or "he was the most renowned person from Argentina". Can a football player be a country, even metaphorically? At the same time, Maradona was, and continues to be, celebrated and idolised all around the world. Where can we place him, then, amid the pull between national and international systems?

In many ways, Maradona is an expression of the glocal, that is, the interconnection between the local and the global in the current world order (Pieterse

DOI: 10.4324/9781003196587-3

2013; Roudometof 2015). Sports have been studied from this theoretical perspective where both forms of social existence converge (cf. Andrews and Ritzer 2007; Giulianotti 2016; Maguire *et al.* 2021). Maradona has been recognised by national and multinational companies wishing to hire him to advertise their products; political leaders and governments looking to legitimise certain policies or agendas; and local and global media which always benefited from telling and "selling" stories about him. He is also a product of specific conditions in a marginalised neighbourhood in Buenos Aires, Villa Fiorito – so much so that, to fully understand his figure, we need to analyse it in relation to the country in which he grew up and which framed and conditioned his style of playing, his media personality, his political views, and his treatment as an object of study. It all comes back to the source: Argentinian society and Argentinian football.

This chapter offers a reading of the Maradonian phenomenon in relation to Argentinian football, national identity, and cultural dynamics through four dimensions or "takes": Maradona as a player and manager in Argentinian clubs and for the Argentinian national team; his relationship to the Argentinian media; his connection to politics; and, ultimately, his constitution as an object of study. For each take, we study specific moments, media appearances, discourses, and texts that best capture his identity as a global phenomenon anchored to the country that not only shaped him but was also shaped by him. If, philosophically, football "is about the drama—about the tension and the emotions it provokes" (Borge 2019: 192), in our proposition Maradona is the leading actor[3] in that drama – that is, a participant in actions and processes – as a player, coach, and "discursive hero" in Argentina (Alabarces 2014: 116; all translations are ours unless indicated otherwise).

## Maradona on the pitch (player/manager)

The emergence of Maradona in Argentinian football in the 1970s was a watershed moment. In total, he played for three teams in the national leagues (Argentinos Juniors between 1976 and 1980; Boca Juniors in 1981 and again between 1995 and 1997; and Newell's Old Boys in 1993). He took Argentinos Juniors to the first vice-championship in its history in 1980 and won the Metropolitano league title with Boca (scoring 28 goals in 40 matches). While in Argentinos he scored 115 goals and had 65 assists in 167 games, becoming top scorer in five consecutive tournaments, a record that still stands today. His return to Argentine football in the 1990s was much less successful (5 games and no goals with Newell's; 30 games and 7 goals with Boca, with no titles). As for the national team, he played in three Copa América (Perú 1979, Argentina 1987, and Brazil 1989) and participated in four World Cups: Spain 1982, Mexico 1986, Italy 1990, and United States 1994. He famously led the team to victory in 1986 and obtained second place in Italy. He played in 91 matches and scored 34 goals for the national team.

These statistics speak for themselves, but do not fully answer this question: why is Maradona considered even to this day a synonym of Argentinian football?

In this section we analyse moments that cemented his status as the most significant representative of Argentine football's *ethos* and *pathos* of the 20th century. As a footballer, Maradona became linked to a notion of a national identity based on the ideas of football as *play*, trickery and inventiveness, and of football as an instrument for *revenge* (literal or symbolic; against football adversaries, more powerful countries, or random opponents).

Julio Frydenberg points out that in the first three decades of the 20th century, football not only had a place in the formation of "collective identities" in Argentina but was also a vessel for "emotional expression and production of meaning" as well as a site of "a permanent critical debate juxtaposed with expressions of fanaticism" (2011: 14). Concurrently, and as Jonathan Wilson explains, the shift from a primarily agrarian, rural society into an urban, more industrialised one in the 1920s meant also new, heroic archetypes were needed for the nation. Hence, "there was only one cultural mode with the general appeal to fill the breach: the space gauchos had occupied in the mid nineteenth century came to be occupied by soccer [*sic*] players" (2016: 25). And what were the characteristics of this surging, supposedly new "national" character? Eduardo Archetti states:

> The creolization process implied a change from the school to the streets, and from the British to the new hybrids, products of the non-British immigration. In this direction, against the value of courage and will power, the Argentinian football players represent almost the contrary; they were portrayed a sensitive, artistic and great improvisers. In the international landscape of the 1920s, the Argentinian players represented for the Europeans something different, as I have pointed out: the incarnation of dribbling and extreme individualism.
>
> *1999: 72*

Archetti's ideas are further discussed later in the chapter but for the moment it is important to understand that, under this theory, the Argentinian football player takes on a multifaceted, complex identity, going against the colonial model (in this case, British) and adopting a style based on individual creativity and freedom, which was at odds with the idea of a collective effort and end-oriented results. Archetti synthesises this style in the image of *pibes* playing in *potreros*. Why is this important to understand Maradona's place in the history of Argentinian football? Because, according to the critic, "the figure and performances of Maradona can be seen not only as a continuation of *el mito del pibe* [the myth of the *pibe*] but also as its most perfect historical realization" (1997: 40).[4]

How and when does Maradona reach this realisation? It was a process. He played professionally for five years in Argentina (1976–1981) before coming back in the mid-1990s, when he was much closer to a mediatic Maradona (cf. next section) than to the *pibe* figure. Of the many moments that defined this first phase, we highlight three here. The first takes place during his professional debut with

Argentinos Juniors on October 20, 1976, when as a 15-year-old he substituted Rubén Giacobetti in the second half (see https://www.elgrafico.com.ar/articulo/1105/33691/maradona-asi-fue-su-debut). He remembers in his autobiography *Yo soy el Diego de la gente* (translated as *Maradona. The Autobiography of Soccer's Greatest and Most Controversial Star*):

> Montes [Argentinos' manager at the time] said to me: "Go on, Diego, play like you know how … and if you can, nutmeg someone". I did as I was told: I received the ball with my back to my marker, Juan Domingo Patricio Cabrera. I dummied and kicked the ball between his legs. It went clean through and I immediately heard the *Ooooolé* of the crowd … like a welcome.
>
> *2011: 17*

The second moment happened four years later while Maradona was still playing for Argentinos, in a game against his future team Boca Juniors. Famed Boca goalkeeper Hugo Gatti had said to a regional newspaper that Maradona had to take care of himself because he was prone to gaining weight. *La Razón*, a widely circulating Buenos Aires newspaper, picked up the interview days later and run it the night before the match. Maradona interpreted Gatti's words – meant as advice – as an insult. The star's agent, Jorge Cyterszpiler, tried to rile him up and asked his protegee to score two goals. Cyterszpiler "had already noticed that the angrier I was the better I played", says Maradona (2011: 35). On November 9, 1980, the visiting Argentinos beat Boca 5-3 and Maradona scored four goals on Gatti, receiving an ovation from Boca fans (see Maradona recounting the experience: https://www.youtube.com/watch?v=5Az4fDGhJ9I; the two players would eventually become teammates the following year). And the third moment happened on the night of April 10, 1981. At Boca's Bombonera Stadium, Boca beat arch-rival River Plate 3-0 with Maradona scoring an unforgettable goal:

> I received his [teammate Córdoba's] cross, brought it down with my left foot and almost hit as Fillol [River's goalie] came out. But instead I cut inside and left Pato [Fillol] crawling … I was going to walk the ball into the net when I saw Conejo Tarantini … closing me down. I decided I'd better get a move on. My shot squeezed inside the post.
>
> *2011: 47*

He became an idol for Boca fans especially because of that match and that goal (see https://www.youtube.com/watch?v=bnCK2FZW09k).

The three plays discussed encapsulate the traits that came to define Maradona's style: on the one side, not only ability, inventiveness, and explosiveness, but also guile when on the field; and, on the other, the need for a challenge from outside that elicits a mental attitude of a "me against the world" magnitude, sometimes directed against an individual, others against a collective. Two aspects of his way of playing became associated with Argentinian football: the *gambeta*, or dribble, and a trial where the odds are stacked against one side, fuelling a performative need for *revenge*. The word *gambeta* comes from an Argentinian dialect, *lunfardo*, that incorporated words from languages other than Spanish; *gamba* means leg in Italian, and *gambeta* refers to a tango movement made with the legs that involved velocity, beauty, and an element of surprise. So, both in Maradona's debut in Argentinian professional football and in his goal against River, there's an element of creation and *jouissance* – in nutmegging a rival, or in leaving opposing players crawling or "humiliated" in sports terms – that will become trademarks of Argentinian football. Of course, there were many Argentinian players who used the *gambeta* before Maradona, but none as culturally significant as him. To this, a psychological mechanism must be factored in: the need for an affront, such as the one fabricated in the "Gatti affair", to rise up to the occasion and show courage and value. In this case, an established player from one of the most popular Argentinian clubs "challenged" a younger and inexperienced opponent. The "weaker" team, through football ability and mental fortitude, was able to overcome the situation and win the "duel".[5]

The second phase of the identification of Maradona with Argentinian football is based on his forays with the national team. We again focus on three instances. First, his two famous goals (the "Hand of God" and "The Goal of the Century") in the Argentina *vs.* England Mexico World Cup quarterfinal game on June 22, 1986. Argentina would eventually become champions, beating Germany 3-2. Secondly, the play he makes against Brazil on June 24, 1990, in the round of 16 during the Italy World Cup. His assist to forward Claudio Paul Caniggia allowed him to score the single goal of that game (https://www.youtube.com/watch?v=wu0FfcdZQ18). Argentina would once again reach the final, losing to Germany 1-0. Lastly, the goal Maradona scored on June 21, 1994, in the United States World Cup. It was the third goal of a 4-0 victory against Greece during the group stage (https://www.youtube.com/watch?v=jyekACZBMeU). He would play in one more match, against Nigeria, before being expelled from the competition when he tested positive for pseudoephedrine, a banned substance by FIFA sold over the counter in the United States.

How do these moments happen to be linked to a national football style and identity and, in turn, become *Maradonian*? The 1986 game against England and Maradona's two goals are arguably the most discussed aspects of Maradona's career (https://www.youtube.com/watch?v=KCYC8aBOcBw; cf. also Chapters 4, 5, and 10 in this volume). The goals have been characterised as the two-sided trait of Argentinian football: on the other hand, the "cheating" nature of the first goal, when Maradona jumped high and hit the ball into the net using his left fist; on the other, a sublime expression of individual prowess for his second goal, a run from midfield in which he leaves several English defenders behind before pushing the ball past the goalkeeper. Uruguayan broadcaster Víctor Hugo Morales is left in awe and, in his famed narration, declares the play "a memorable run ... the best play of all time" (2013: Segundo Tiempo 8-9).[6] Maradona himself states that it was "the goal you dream of as a kid" (2011: 128). If this goal opens to memorability and aesthetic considerations about beauty, the first one interpellates a different area of philosophy: sport ethics.[7] In his book *México 86. Mi mundial. Mi verdad. Así ganamos la copa* (translated as *Touched by God. How We Won the Mexico '86 World Cup*), Maradona indicates that he is not sorry for having scored with his hand. Why? He first offers a footballing reason: "Because I grew up with this, because as a kid in Fiorito I would score goals with my hands all the time" (2016: 151).

But there is an additional reason which transforms him into a national and political actor. In retrospect, the result, according to Maradona, was "more than defeating a football team it was defeating a country" (2011: 127), echoing the symbolic "revenge by other means" for the Argentinean defeat by the United Kingdom in the Malvinas/Falkland war in 1982.[8] In the press conference after the match, a journalist asks him about his feelings as he was finishing the move and he responds: "I thought that I had fallen to two Englishmen, but was lifting a country" (Signorini *et al.* 2021: 125). This is the interpretation that has endured in the Argentinian football imaginary, so much so, that even today during an Argentina match one of the obligatory fan chants is: "If you don't jump, you are an Englishman!"[9] Together with the football skills – the *gambeta* and the trickery – this revenge-vengeance-duel-surmount the odds-triumph against adversity attitude, is there since the beginning of his career for Maradona, and in the Mexico 1986 World Cup it reaches his zenith. He remembers how adversity made the team stronger: "What nobody has understood, ever, was that our strength and our togetherness were born from just that, from our *bronca* [anger] ... the *bronca* we felt from having to fight against everything" (2011: 104).

The next two moments in his career with the national team exemplify other instances of the inventiveness-revenge dyad. In the Italy 1990 World Cup, Maradona was injured in the last group game against Rumania, which left him with a badly swollen left ankle. Before the knockout rounds, he declared that he would play "even in a cast" and also sentenced: "I believe in miracles" (2011: 160). In the round of 16 match against Brazil, Argentina was overwhelmed for the first 55 minutes and then Maradona, starting in midfield, used his *gambeta* to leave four players behind and pass with his right foot to Caniggia, who scored and gave Argentina the victory. Even though the motivating "revenge" framework was present – "in football, I want to beat them to the death. They're My Rivals, with capital letters", Maradona says of the Brazilians in his autobiography (2011: 164) – what remains is the epic sentiment: the legend may have begun to be sculpted in Mexico 1986 but was completed in Italy 1990. With a diminished team – Argentina had lost its starting goalkeeper and, as mentioned, Maradona had a serious injury – and facing a superior squad, the genie rubbed the lamp to produce beauty and victory against all odds one more time.

By 1994, conditions were much different for Maradona. An anti-doping control following an SSC Napoli game in April 1991 found traces of cocaine in his urine banning him from playing football for 15 months by the Italian federation; the ban was extended to anywhere in the world by FIFA. A month after returning to Buenos Aires, Maradona was arrested and charged with possession of a small amount of cocaine after the police raided an apartment in the city. His playing career seemed over. The Argentinian team, without its star, went on to obtain two Copa América titles (Chile 1991 and Ecuador 1993) and was on course for a comfortable qualification for the upcoming World Cup. However, a disastrous 0-5 defeat against Colombia in Buenos Aires on September 5, 1993 (with Maradona in the stands and the fans chanting *Maradoooo, Maradoooo*) changed things. Argentina's qualification now rested on a play-off round against Australia. This resulted in Maradona being recalled to the team, amid growing popular and political pressure. Argentina made it to United States 1994 World Cup with a notably slimmed down Maradona as its captain. In the first game against Greece, he scores after a combination with Abel Balbo, Fernando Redondo, and Caniggia. The *gambeta* – which requires speed and explosiveness – had been replaced here by precise passing, a common transition for veteran players: "one touch, *tac, tac, tac*, like a machine gun, one-two" is how Maradona describes it (2011: 215). Maradona's celebration of the goal is widely remembered: a purposeful run from the middle of the box to one of the corners as he yells *goaaaal!* straight up at the camera with a dishevelled, angry-looking expression. It was an emotional *catharsis*. This Argentinian recreation of Edvard Munch's "The Scream" (as it is known in football circles) can be placed squarely in the "me against the world" revenge mode that came to characterise Argentine football. It was the last goal Maradona scored with Argentina's jersey, but not his last image with it: that would be the walk off the field, holding the hand of a FIFA helper after Argentina's win 2-1 against Nigeria, being taken to the urine doping test that would prove his downfall after another positive result – this time for pseudoephedrine, a drug that would not be considered illicit today.

Very briefly, we must now turn to Maradona a club manager. His numbers are not impressive: one win, six draws, and five losses with Mandiyú, a club from the Corrientes province (October 1994–December 1994); two wins, six draws, and three losses in Racing Club (January 1995–April 1995); and eight wins, four draws, and nine losses in Gimnasia y Esgrima La Plata (September 2019–November 2020). However, with the Argentinian national team his record is better, 18 wins and 6 losses (November 2008–July 2010), having reached the quarterfinals of the 2010 South Africa World Cup. But again, the numbers do not tell the whole story. His stints as a club coach in Argentina were forgettable in sporting terms, while his tenure as manager of the national team was respectable in those same terms, but fraught with conflict between him and the Argentinian Football Association president Julio Grondona, and the national media. His last coaching job with Gimnasia allowed for both warm welcomes in all the stadiums he visited and the recognition of his increasing physical and mental deterioration (cf. Nelson Castro's *La salud de Diego* [Diego's Health] 2021, an entire book dedicated to the history of Maradona's health).

Three main images as a manager in/for Argentina remain embedded in the memory of fans. The first is an unfortunate one. On October 14, 2009, after Argentina's qualification to the 2010 South Africa World Cup with a 1-0 victory against Uruguay in Montevideo, Maradona held a raucous post-match press conference where he thanked the players, the fans, and his family but said that there were people who did not deserve his thanks: "those who did not believe—ladies, forgive me—they can suck it … you treated me so [badly], then keep sucking it" https://www.youtube.com/watch?v=LRpK9tc-xkA). Later he would confront a particular journalist, Passman: "You too Passman, you have it inside" again using a homophobic sexual metaphor to denigrate his interlocutors. These offensive expressions – that came to be part of a wider Maradonian discursive repertoire – cost him a two-month FIFA sanction and his absence in the World Cup draw. The inventiveness and play from his time as a player had yielded to the tenor of his discourse, a rhetoric that could be creative and spontaneous but was also inhabited by sentiments of impatience, resentment, and paranoia.[10]

However, the next "scene" reveals the emotional, mythical place Maradona occupied in the Argentinian football imaginary. His team was beaten soundly by the German squad in the 2010 South Africa World Cup; upon its return home, it is estimated that 20,000 people welcomed the bus carrying the players and the coaching staff. It is not far-fetched to assume that most of them went to see and support Maradona, still the football receptacle for the collective dreams, hopes, and aspirations of a nation (https://www.youtube.com/watch?v=_GwZsx0UFsQ). This Argentinian *aguante* football culture – the support for a team or player no matter the result – reached unthinkable levels when he was announced as new manager by Gimnasia: the club instantly added 3,000 new members; 25,000 people and 700 journalists were at the stadium the day of his presentation. In each game he coached, the opposing team prepared for him a special chair, or "throne", where he sat. His identification with Argentinian football at that time had less to do with a *gambeta,* the need for revenge, or his rhetoric (it was increasingly difficult for him to speak continuously) and more with his symbolic value as an enthroned icon. This last scene showed him, once again, on the pitch.

## Maradona on/and/in the media

Curiously enough, it is *after* Maradona reached his zenith as a national player (obtaining the Youth Football World Cup in Japan in 1979; reaching two World Cup finals and becoming in the process the best player in the world; returning to the national team in 1994) that the pervasiveness of TV and other visual media specialised in football penetrates not only the quotidian activities of Argentine households but also the national and global imaginaries. Maradona's trajectory as a player can be seen as a graph of peaks (1979–1981, 1986–1990) and valleys (1978, 1982, 1994), but his incarnation of an intense and complex collective national and cultural identity began between 1978 and 1982, solidified and reached its apex in 1986, intensified during the 1990s, and, after having finished his stint on the football field, became more controversial and conflictive during the 2000s. Concurrently, the legitimisation of football as an appropriate lens to view social and cultural dynamics was fuelled by an explosion of sports programming at the end of the 20th century around the world, particularly with the emergence of cable and satellite television and a pointed transition in the way athletes went from being celebrated to being celebrities. In Argentina, the launching of the sports channel Torneos y Competencias Sports (TyC Sports) on September 3, 1994, is a significant milestone in this regard, as it is, much later, the state-sponsored transmissions of the football show *Fútbol para Todos* (Football for Everyone) that begun in 2009. In this process, the relationship between Maradona and all media was essential.[11]

Born in a time without social media or even 24/7 TV news coverage, his figure may be analysed in the context of sport celebrity culture and through concepts such as "idol of consumption", "idol of promotion", and "vortextuality", an approach that exceeds the goals of this chapter.[12] Nonetheless, without a doubt, synchronically Maradona is the first and biggest football media celebrity both in Argentina and the world stage. It is an arch that goes from his "I have two dreams" speech in a TV interview in 1971 when he was ten years old and expressed his desires to play in the World Cup and to win the championship in the youth eighth division with his team at the time (see https://www.youtube.com/watch?v=Ee2On4lZ3e4) to his death at 60, when the Argentinian government opened up the Casa Rosada – the government's house – to allow the public to mourn and pay their respects to their idol. He proved to be the historical hinge between mass media, football, and celebrity culture and created in the process the character Maradona. Such character both used media and was used by media (see the excellent reflections by Rodríguez 1996). In this section, we point out key Maradonian media moments related to Argentina and focus on a scene of his 2005 television show *La noche del Diez* (#10's Night).

The first appearance on Maradona in a media outlet occurs very early and relates to the image of the *pibe* already discussed. While playing in the youth divisions of Argentinos Juniors, he would entertain spectators at half-time by juggling the ball in the centre circle. The popularity of this performance was described by the newspaper *Clarín* in September of 1971: "Diego Caradona [*sic*] earned the applause of the spectators during the Argentinos Juniors vs. Independiente halftime". The brief article states that "Dieguito seems to have escaped from those fields from the past [the *potreros*]" and although he "does not look like a pibe of our time though he is; and with that very Argentinian love for the ball our football will never cease to be nurtured by great talents" (qtd. in Fernández and Nagy 1994: 27). The curious mistaken identity – perhaps inadvertently pointing to Maradona's future charisma, since "cara" means "face" in Spanish – gives way to a well-known equation: at ten years old, the *pibe* Maradona is deemed a representative of *criollo* (creole) football. Fast forward to 1981. Maradona is the new Argentinean (football) hope. The country's biggest clubs, Boca Juniors and River Plate, are vying for him. He prefers Boca, which did not have the financial means to sign him. To force the issue, he talks to a journalist in the *Crónica* newspaper and tells him he is not going to River because Boca had already approached him. It was a lie. "That afternoon, *Crónica* came out with a headline that read: 'Maradona to Boca'. The operation was underway, we just needed the Boca directors to take the bait as well. They did", he says in his autobiography (2011: 38). Maradona was 21 years old. These two examples show that the attraction and exchanges between Maradona and the media were mutual.

Out of the many instances of his interaction with the media as a footballing superstar, three stand out. After the Argentina *vs.* England match during the Mexico 1986 World Cup, many questions are asked about the first goal. An Argentinian journalist, Héctor Ferrero, presses Maradona on the hand issue and when the player denies it, Ferrero says "perhaps it was God's hand", to which the Argentinian captain retorts: "Perhaps". This is how the phrase "the hand of God" becomes legendary; what is relevant to our discussion is that it originated as the result of an interchange between Maradona and the media. From this moment on, the association of Maradona to divinity has become commonplace, cleverly transformed into the acronym D10S (combining the word God in Spanish with the number Maradona wore on his jersey).

Another important instance in this context are Maradona's reactions during the Italy 1990 World Cup. During the final match against Germany, the Italian fans at the Olympic Stadium in Rome jeered Argentina's national anthem. Aware that his face would appear on close-up as the TV cameras focused on players lined up during the musical ceremony, Maradona made sure to famously swear "sons of bitches, sons of bitches" to retaliate for the Italian affront. Then, after the game ended with the defeat of Argentina, the disconsolate captain wept openly during the award ceremony and refused to shake hands with Joao Havelange, FIFA's president at the time. In both instances, there was no regard for sports "decorum"; he was consistent to a fault in his rebellious and spontaneous attitudes. Later, a distressed Maradona aired his grievances, being true to the emotive nature of his relationship to football and to Argentina (https://www.youtube.com/watch?v=Uj6eHdUvbCo).

Lastly, on November 10, 2001, after a dangerous health crisis that put him in the hospital, his former club Boca Juniors organised a tribute match between Argentina's national team (coached at the time by Marcelo Bielsa) and a "Stars team" made up of many active and retired footballers. Many more players – such as Pelé – and celebrities were in the stadium, filled with 50,000 fans. Maradona played for the national team which won 6-3, scoring two penalties. When the game was over, he delivered a short speech, thanking the fans and football. Two ideas are prominent in the speech. First, the love received. "I tried to make you happy, and I think I did", he said to the fans, "and I don't know how to repay you … this is too much for one person". Later, he would utter one of his famous phrases: "Just because one makes a mistake, football does not have to pay. I made a mistake and I paid. But ... the ball ... the ball does not get soiled" (https://www.youtube.com/watch?v=utU80lVfrbw). Besides the insistent references to "paying back" (for debts or sins), what stands out is, on the one hand, his continuation of a self-fashioning where he views himself – not only because of the skilful, joyful way he played but also because of what he achieved – as an instrument of happiness for the people and, on the other, the quasi-religious idea of the purity of football, which stands in a realm above individual mistakes (he is referring to his drug addiction) and above the machinations of the commercial network that robs the game of its authenticity (the fame, the money, the media). This communion with his most treasured object harkens back to that first appearance of Maradona in the media 40 years earlier: the "love for the ball" will always feed Argentinian football with unceasing talent; Maradona, as a standard bearer of that tradition, had come full circle.[13]

La Noche del Diez, a sort of late-night talk show, ran from August 15 to November 7, 2005, for 13 episodes. The high-end production (more than 200 people involved, a dozen or so cameras, numerous dancers dressed as angels), the media interest (hundreds of accredited journalists reported on the first episode), and the A-list of guests – in the context of Argentinian TV – that Maradona interviewed in situ or via satellite (including Raffaella Carrà, Thalia, Gabriela Sabatini, Mike Tyson, Fidel Castro – Maradona interviewed him in Cuba – Lionel Messi, and, very famously, Pelé, with whom he played an epic "head to head") made the programme a success, consistently beating the competition; the final show in the Luna Park stadium was transmitted live with 5,000 people in the audience (for more on the show cf. Zanoni, Alabarces 2007, Safirsztein 2021 and especially Gajnaj 2007). Perhaps all might be summarised in the catchphrase used by Channel 13 to promote the show: "God [D10S] chose our company to communicate".

On October 17, 2005, La Noche del Diez had a special guest: Maradona himself (the full interview here: https://www.youtube.com/watch?v=-JNtJuXm-Mzs). It was "Diego" interviewing "Maradona", a split that both recognises a process of self-fashioning initiated when, early on, he chose to refer to himself in the third person and also exploits a dual "Dr. Jekyll/Mr. Hide" nature (on the dualistic nature of Maradona popularised by former teammate Jorge Valdano and former physical trainer Fernando Signorini see Chapter 7 of this volume). In this episode of the show, Maradona becomes an actor who plays himself, fully aware of the image that has been created – together – by the media and himself, in a loop of autoreferentiality and interconnectedness which feedbacks the Maradonian web of meanings. Thus, all Maradonian topics are addressed. About politics, (the question that opens the interview) he says he is undecided who to vote for in upcoming elections; no candidate has managed to convince him. The audience notes a certain discontent with the state of Argentinian political affairs. When he talks about friends – specifically his former manager Guillermo Coppola – he reverts to the aggrieved Maradona, mentions the word "treason", and states that "one should not benefit [financially] from friendship". The audience sees disappointment. When it comes time to speak about drugs, "Diego" confesses his regrets to Diego, particularly about his addiction causing him to miss important moments in the lives of his daughters. He also turns the tables and clarifies that he did not gain any advantage by taking cocaine; if anything, the drug prevented him from reaching an even higher footballing potential, since he was often not fully fit for games. The audience claps when he says he has been "clean" for a year and a half. As for football, it gave Maradona everything: fame, money, glory, happiness, and "the people". Playing around with each other, both the interviewer and interviewee agree that they were "the best in the world". That is why his tombstone should read: "Thanks for playing football" and "thanks for the ball" (this wish became a reality). The audience chants throughout *Oleee oleee oleee… Diegooo, Diegooo*. Maradona asks Maradona about his family, and this is where he is at his most emotional: he wants his parents to live long lives to recover lost time in their company, speaks passionately about his daughters Dalma and Giannina, and dedicates a good chunk of the interview to "win back" his ex-wife Claudia Villafañe (a decade or so later he would accuse her of stealing money from him). He imagines himself a grandpa going to watch football matches and dying a serene death, and the audience shares in his sentiments. Finally, Diego and Maradona exchange gifts: tapes with the popular kid's show *El Chavo del Ocho* and a replica of Fidel Castro's army cap.

Diego, Maradona, and the audience all know the interview has been an ingenious *simulacrum*, a play with cameras and images; the "magic" of TV, an illusion of smoke and mirrors. However, the dialogue strives to be authentic. Several times the casually dressed Diego, with a sly smile, interrupts the more formally attired Maradona to amicably scold him with phrases like "You are asking this, Diego?" or "come on, we both know". This interplay points once again to the idea that, as with football, in his relationship to the Argentine media, Maradona knew how to play the game. The question is asked: "Could you live now if nobody recognized you?". The answer: "No, we are too used to it". This dependency on the recognition – of the people and of the media – is encapsulated in the last phrase uttered by Maradona to his TV self: "Whenever you need me, here I am".

## Maradona and politics

The Maradonian self-interview, with its references to the Argentinian elections and Fidel Castro, shows an important aspect that is often associated with the player: the field of politics. High profile footballers rarely get identified with specific political positions, but none has been more closely associated with (in theory) left-wing causes than Maradona. Not many athletes have the images of Castro and Ernesto "Che" Guevara tattooed on their bodies, so to a large extent the connection between Maradona and politics have been encouraged by the player. He never held an official post in government or political parties, although Carlos Menem – president of Argentina between 1989 and 1999 – designated him honorary "sports ambassador" prior to the Italy 1990 World Cup. His political interventions increased significantly after he retired from football.

The relationship between Maradona and politics is concerned with both political readings *of* Maradona and political views and pronouncements *by* Maradona over the years.[14] The discussion in this section involves, locally, Peronism, and globally, the socialist Latin American regimes epitomised by Castro's Cuba and, in the 21st century, by Venezuela governed by Hugo Chávez and Nicolás Maduro. Following Pablo Alabarces, we can distinguish two stages in the political trajectory of Maradona: a proto-political phase during his time as a player and later, as we have mentioned, a "discursive" stage (Alabarces 2014).

At the national level, Maradona has often been read as a symbol of Peronism, a movement that emerged in Argentina in the mid-1940s and has framed national politics ever since.[15] Juan Domingo Perón and his second wife Eva (who died in 1952) were charismatic, populist leaders, although it is challenging to situate the movement, and the political party that represents it, the *Partido Justicialista*, within a single political ideology. As Mariano Plotkin explains, Peronism

> divided Argentine society into two irreconcilable camps. During the years of his government, Perón had polarized Argentine society as no other political leader in the twentieth century had done. Moreover, the practical consequences of ten years of Peronist rule allowed for conflicting interpretations. For the vast majority of the working class, the ten years of Peronist rule had meant a real improvement in their living conditions through a notable redistribution of income, their incorporation into the political system and into the state apparatus, as well as the reformulation (in their favor) of old patterns of social relations with other sectors of society. But for those other sectors of society, and particularly for the middle class and non-Peronist intellectuals, Peronism had been a very traumatic experience.
>
> *1998: 30*

Maradona's parents were impoverished internal migrants from the province of Corrientes who travelled to Buenos Aires in search for a better life in the 1950s. They were also strong Peronist supporters; their oldest son would have learnt of his parents' sympathy from an early age, and he was old enough to understand the hopes generated by the return of Perón to Argentina in 1973, and the resulting disappointment because of his passing less than a year later.

These sympathies, however, did not translate into political activism for Maradona in the 1970s and 1980s. In his autobiography, the term "Peronism" appears just once, and Perón is not mentioned at all. On the other hand, the book is dedicated to, among others, Carlos Menem, whose neoliberal economic policies and alignment with the geopolitical interests of the United States have been attacked by left wing Peronist sectors that favour a populist or nationalist orientation (Fidel Castro is also on the list of dedicatees). Alabarces calls this period in Maradona's life "proto-political", defined ultimately by minor protestations, such as complaints about the scheduled times for some of the matches in the 1986 Mexico World Cup, played at noon under the scorching sun, and denunciations of a conspiracy against him in the Italy 1990 World Cup (Alabarces 2007: 146). It must be pointed out, however, that in 1983, before the general elections, he met with four candidates to the presidency, which was a clear signal of the significant influence and media power he already had for being a 23-year-old footballer (for more, see Fernández and Nagy 1994: 158). Maradona's most evident political statement during this phase, adds Alabarces, does not refer to Argentina: it is his endorsement of Castro and his socialist government in Cuba in 1987.

Alabarces' (2007, 2014, 2021) main political thesis proposes Maradona as the continuation of Peronism by other means. In a period in which Peronist policies and discourses were displaced from dominant positions in Argentina for several reasons (the death of Perón, the military government in 1976–1983, and the victory of the Radical Party candidate Raul Alfonsín with the return of democracy), Maradona turns into the myth that kept the popular mandate of Peronism alive: making "the people" happy. If Peronism is defined by giving a voice to the working classes and improving the living conditions of the poor, in the 1970s and 1980s Maradona symbolically attempted to recover that legacy. Thus, in a de-Peronised Argentina, he fulfilled the role of hero of the people, bringing them sporting if not economic joy, and reigniting a sense of patriotism and identity. Maradona was "a machine that fulfilled dreams and gave away popular happiness. That is to say, a Peronist machine" (Alabarces 2021: 5).[16]

This theory highlights points of contact between Perón and Eva Perón and Maradona, understood as charismatic figures who were loved by the people, and between Peronism and Maradona, understood as symbolic entities who were able to mobilise the working classes and provide meaning to their cultural and political practices. However, some of the complexities regarding local politics and the significance and appeal of Maradona would challenge this idea. For example, did the happiness brought about by his goals against England in 1986 not transcend the social class and cultural polarisation brought about by the Peronist project? At the same time, did the return of democracy and the early stages of the Raúl Alfonsín presidency (1983–1989) not appeal to the popular masses as a cause of rejoice? Even if such hope was undermined eventually by the severe economic crisis of the late 1980s, this view complicates rigid categorisations and univocal definitions of the popular. Although Peronism, in its different historical versions, always presented itself as a nationalist movement concerned with defending the "true interests" of the Argentinian people and willing to be the standard bearer of *Argentinidad* (Argentineness), Maradona, interestingly, became a definite emblem for the country when the victory against the English in the Mexico 1986 World Cup was read as a national vindication following the defeat in the Malvinas/Falklands War. The celebrations for obtaining the World Cup certainly undercut all sectors of Argentinian society, which had a non-Peronist party in government at the time.

When Maradona returns to Argentina in the 1990s, his political zigzags are tied to the ups and downs of his relationship with Menem: Maradona initially supports him and the head of the Ministry of Economy Domingo Cavallo, then attacks both, to finally end up backing Menem's bid for re-election. As Marcela Mora y Araujo writes, "Just like Menem cemented his strength in an alliance between the riches and the poorest, Diego walked that same tightrope: champagne with the world's aristocracy but an absolute and sincere identification with those who shared in his humble origins" (2021: 90).

After his stay in Cuba in the early 2000s, Maradona's identification with Peronism would be much more overt in the second decade of the 21st century. In his second work of autobiography, *Touched by God. How We Won the Mexico '86 World Cup*, he states that "I've been a Peronist all my whole life and I'll die a Peronist, because of my mother and because of Evita". He also expresses support for Cristina Kirchner, the Peronist president of Argentina between 2007 and 2015 (2016: 200).[17] In this book, the term "Peronism" or "Peronist" appear six times, and the volume is now dedicated to plenty of political figures: the brothers Castro, "Che" Guevara, Venezuelan president Nicolás Maduro, Hugo Chávez, Cristina Kirchner, and La Cámpora (a youth political organisation founded by Kirchner's son affiliated with Peronism), among others (interestingly, the name of Carlos Menem has been dropped from the list. None of these dedications appear in the English translation).

This turn towards a more outspoken attitude in party politics can be explained, according to Alabarces, because, unable to keep providing joy and uniting the people through his playing, Maradona shifts towards a discursive mode. A key example is his participation in a summit that took place in Argentina in 2005, where Maradona alongside Latin American political leaders such as Chávez and Bolivian president Evo Morales protested US commercial expansionism in Latin America. His political actions at this stage take the shape of public statements about a myriad of topics, mediatised through the multiple platforms (newspapers, radio, TV, cinema, digital and social media) that echo his opinions.

Alabarces claims that Maradona can be understood as "an empty signifier" available to all those who need to fill it with meaning (2007: 134). The same could be said about Peronism, a movement that has counted supporters on all sides of the ideological spectrum (from the far left to the far right) and whose leaders, when in power in Argentina, pursued divergent policies and agendas. Given these situational "inconsistencies", it might be misguided to criticise Maradona for his own contradictions on a political level (cf. Salazar-Sutil 2008: 450; Sebreli 2008: 201). Moreover, Jeffrey Tobin, discussing Sergio Levinsky's book *Maradona: rebelde con causa* (Maradona. Rebel with a Cause) (2006), makes a significant observation: "Maradona is rebellious without having a consistent political position. In effect, Levinsky's argument is that political coherence is a peculiarly bourgeois expectation, which Maradona effectively resists" (2002: 61).

This system of apparent unresolved contradictions is evident in Maradona's geopolitical sympathies and can be retrofitted to illuminate his political stances and alignments in Argentina. His admiration for Castro and Cuba's revolutionary government – perhaps Maradona's more consistent political view over the years – led to his endorsement of other leftist leaders in Latin America, such as Chávez and Morales. As it can be seen by shifting through the bibliography included in this book, it is commonplace to consider Maradona as an emancipatory figure who fought against powerful political and commercial organisations in the search for social justice and equality. However, this view overlooks his support for other authoritarian leaders, such as Lybia's Muammar Gaddafi and Belarus' Alexander Lukashenko (Makhovsky 2018), or regimes with questionable human rights records, such as the United Arab Emirates. A common denominator emerges: throughout his life, Maradona was attracted to authoritarian, charismatic, and personalist leaders and less inclined to adhere to a specific ideological political framework. At the same time, critics of the view that posits Maradona as an icon of anti-capitalist movements point out that he made millions out of advertising and publicity contracts with multinational companies, and that he always benefited financially from the political allegiances he cultivated, from the special treatment he received in Cuba to the lucrative contracts offered by Venezuela to host TV shows in the state channel Telesur during the 2014 and 2018 World Cups. Once again, we should tread with care: what are the underlying sociocultural assumptions of those who may censure a person who grew up in dire poverty and wanted to obtain above all financial security for himself and his family? Ultimately, it is impossible to locate Maradona within fixed political coordinates. He is as elusive in the political field as he was on the pitch.[18]

## Maradona as an academic object

Maradona's football feats, his media presence, and his connection to politics helped shape him as an object of study. He began to attract the attention of academics and intellectuals in the mid-1990s. A small group of scholars started publishing articles that went beyond the realm of sports journalism and football tactics at approximately the same time. Eduardo Archetti was, in many ways, the pioneer in this endeavour. An Argentinian cultural anthropologist who developed his career at the University of Oslo, he was interested in the study of popular cultures and masculinities in Argentina, expressed in two important forms of ritualised performance: tango dancing and football. The two involve skill in the movement of the body and are supported ideologically by specific views on masculinity and nationhood.

Archetti's approach was ethnographic, based on interviews with football fans, which allowed him to draw conclusions on social perceptions about football and Maradona. As stated, he recognised a football tradition founded on specific sociocultural roots and defined it in contraposition with the version of the sport introduced in the country by English immigrants. In 1996, he examined early writings in the sports magazine *El Gráfico* to extract a conclusion about Argentine football:

> The purity of the football player is not associated with the purity of the warrior and the emphasis on youth virility and sacrifice. One could say that the imaginary world of football reflects the power of freedom and creativity in the face of discipline, order and hierarchy. If men become men through discipline and a sense of responsibility inculcated in schools and military barracks, then football and the image of the *potrero* appear as counterpoint. The masculine ideal of football is the masculinity of those who never stop being children, who represent improvisation and play, and are in opposition to responsible men.
>
> *1996: 51–52*

*Criollo* football was forged in the *potrero*, a space free of institutionalised controls and regulations of sport where there are no referees, managers, and tactics; the pitch is made of earth, not grass, and there are no demarcations of any kind. In such space of improvisation, "a mythical territory to empowers those who belong to it", one figure stands out: Maradona represented perfectly the *pibe* from the potrero, with "freshness, spontaneity and freedom during play", childhood values that get "lost with the advent of maturity and adult responsibilities". Thus "the authentic Argentinian player will never stop being a child. Football allows a man to go on playing and remain a *pibe*" (2001: 156). Crucially, this not only applied to Maradona's skills but also to his whole personality. This conflation is deemed to be problematic: "In the case of a *pibe,* a lot of disorder is expected. Chaotic behaviour is the norm. They [the *pibes*] have a tendency to recompense, penalize or forgive others in an exaggerated way, to convey arbitrary judgements and choices ... Thus, a perfect *pibe* is creative, free of strong feelings of guilt, self-destructive and, eventually, a bad moral example to other players" (2001: 159). Thus, for Archetti, Maradona is the product of an enduring football tradition whose roots lie in the unequal realities of Argentina; these players emerge mostly out of the conditions of poverty and deprivation that exists in the marginal spaces of suburbs and urban centres. As a *pibe*, Maradona also belongs to "a mythical account which reproduces a tradition and a multiple and complex masculine world" (1999: 189).

It could be said that Argentinian sociologist Pablo Alabarces is Archetti's disciple within the field of Maradonian studies, even if working from a different point of view. He has worked extensively on the field of popular Argentinian culture, and on football in particular. He agrees with Archetti in reading Maradona as a national "hero", defining this heroic narrative model as la *épica del pobre* (the epic of the poor), which refers to the marginal conditions that allow for a redemptive story where the hero leaves his birthplace and triumphs in the outside world but never forgets his origins (2007: 134). Significantly, he adds two additional

categories of analysis: Maradona as a myth that transcended the national boundaries of Argentina, and which was, to a certain extent, self-created and, as we have
seen, Maradona as a political signifier, nationally and internationally. On the
national level, Maradona is the "surpassing" of Peronism. On the international
level, Maradona is a symbol of the subaltern – the disempowered, subjugated
peoples in the postcolonial world order.

Why did Maradona achieve this position? Following Peter Burke, Alabarces
explains that not all myths are created equal and reflects on this mythogenic
quality and the reasons why he is one of the "chosen ones". The answer can be
found in a "complex intersection" of several elements: "his exceptional quality
as a sports figure, his heroic condition, the narrative of the origin, the global
context of his performances, the new role of mass media, now central and in an
unstoppable expansion, the comings and goings of his ascent and fall, but also
the political conditions that made possible the production of the myth" (2007:
156). Interestingly enough, while in 2014 Alabarces sees Maradona's plebeian
identity "as a rictus without irreverence" and, as such, the ex-player "did not
question power anymore, but reproduced it" (2014: 120), in his last publications
this critical view is absent, as he prefers to tout Maradona as the "creator of the
impossible" with a "voice ostentatious and proud of its subalternity" (2021: 8–9).

Archetti and Alabarces are therefore the two scholars who have set the basis
for a critical study of Maradona as a cultural icon that can be localised, globalised, and glocalised in a series of interconnected meanings having to do with
nationhood, heroic popular narratives, masculinity, national and international
politics, postcolonialism, and the subaltern. María Graciela Rodríguez, in many
cases writing in collaboration with Alabarces (1996, 1999), agrees with their
coordinates to read and study Maradona and should be added to this first group.

Another voice that contributed to defining Maradona as an object comes from
a different methodological and ideological position. Juan José Sebreli, a prolific Argentinian public intellectual, has produced essayistic works of cultural
and social criticism grounded on modern philosophy and critical theory and
published by non-academic presses oriented to non-specialist readers. Sebreli's
position is critical of Maradona, systematically denouncing the processes of the
mythification and idolisation of the footballer that took place in Argentinian
society as misguided and problematic. Precisely because of this stance, Sebreli
provides a refreshing intervention on the subject, to whom he devoted chapters
in his books *La era del fútbol* (The Era of Football) (1998) and *Comediantes y mártires. Ensayo contra los mitos* (Comedians and Martyrs: Essay against Myth) (2008).

In this last volume, Sebreli focuses on debunking Maradona as an Argentinian
myth (he also discusses Carlos Gardel, Eva Perón, and "Che" Guevara). Perhaps
his most innovative contribution is to bring in a sexual perspective on the player.
In this sense, he first notes the pun between Madonna (The Virgin Mary) and
Maradona, found in references to the player by Napoli fans, which, alongside the
representations of Maradona as a Christlike figure, lead to a case of gender transgression implicit in speaking of the player as "Santa Maradona", *santa* being the

feminine version of *saint* in Spanish (2008: 165). Sebreli adds other elements from the player's biography, including his willingness to kiss his manager Cóppola and also his teammate Caniggia (on the mouth, publicly when celebrating goals), his occasional inclination to dress up as a woman in some of the wild parties he attended, and a supposed relationship between Maradona and Cris Miró, a trans woman in the 1990s, to further give weight to his argument. In this last case, even if the relation never took place, Maradona publicly defended Miró at the time, which was an uncommon stance in the Argentinian society of the 1990s as well as in the world of football (Firpo 2017). Sebreli situates Maradona's queerness mostly with his disregard for norms throughout his life and his interest in provocation and transgression. According to this critic, Maradona's attitudes towards sexuality and gender cannot be read as support for a more egalitarian and progressive stance, since they are undermined by other behaviours, such as his frequent use of homophobic terminology as insults, his mistreatment of women partners, including his failure (at the time) to recognise the son he had with Cristiana Sinagra (Sebreli, 2008: 189) and a public endorsement of boxer Mike Tyson after he was convicted for rape (200).

Sebreli's accounts on Maradona are highly problematic. Some of them are evidently biased, and he often makes assertions that lack evidence. For example, he mentions that without the support of the *camorra*, the Neapolitan mafia, the player would have had a very difficult time gaining the love of the city (2008: 169), a rather unlikely claim given how successful his spell with SSC Napoli turned out to be. Sebreli goes on to outline what he deems the apparent contradictions inherent in the actions of Maradona, an aspect already explored in this chapter. Sebreli's ideas inevitably led to controversy in a field in which even academics tend to speak of Maradona in often affective terms. Alabarces himself, for example, wrote that "Sebreli never understood or will understand my arguments" (2005a).

Maradona's status as an object continued to grow steadily even when he retired from playing football; alongside numerous biographies and journalistic works about him, some academic studies started to appear. In the 1990s, at around the same time of Archetti, Alabarces, and Rodríguez's contributions, two articles by non-Argentinian authors, Vittorio Dini and Ksenija Bilbija (who wrote Chapter 9 in this book), contributed to develop the field internationally. Dini (1994) sees Maradona in the framework of the Neapolitan hero, while for Bilbija (1995) Maradona is the embodiment of the postmodern. From the 2000 onwards, academic articles on Maradona have discussed specific aspects of his life and career from multiple points of view and disciplines, including how he has been interpreted as an actor in popular conspiracy theories (Tobin 2002); his performance as a polysemic signifier used in commercial and political communications (Salazar-Sutil 2008); his relationship to politics (Sibaja and Parrish 2014; Sarbajit and Naha 2017); and his cinematic representations (Acker 2012; Free 2014; Bauer 2018). A good number of academic works have been produced in Italy; among these, *Maradona: sociologia di un mito globale* (Maradona: Sociology of a Global Myth) (2014), edited by Luca Bifulco (author of Chapter 12 in this volume) and Vittorio Dini, is particularly relevant.

More recently, several edited collections have been produced in Argentina and in Spain, situated between an essayistic and an academic approach. Some of them seem to have been assembled somewhat hastily following Maradona's death (out of the more than 70 books on Maradona, almost half were published after his death; many wanted to honour him, but, in the process, converted him into a *cadavre exquis* that also became a Maradonian industry). Among them, *Todo Diego es político* (All Diego is Political) – a pun related to a song by the Argentinian rock group Patricio Rey y sus Redonditos de Ricota, "Every Prisoner is Political" – edited by Bárbara Pistoia (2021) stands out, as its ten chapters have all been written by women. It was published in digital form only a few days before Maradona's passing. Interestingly, none of them explore Maradona from feminist perspectives (see Chapter 11 in this volume for this). As with other anthologies, such as those by Gómez Villar (2021) and Zabala *et al.* (2021), several of the essays included are by and large hagiographic and impressionistic, reproducing the ideas that celebrate Maradona as a hero of people, political redeemer, and icon, but failing to study him with critical rigor (which admittedly was not their objective in the first place). Such approaches, then, lead to the replication and reproduction of the Maradona myth but do little to fully understand it. Still, some relevant arguments and observations are found in these collections. Significantly, the prolific production following Maradona's death points to the reinsertion and canonisation of the field of Maradona studies within the study of sport and popular culture.

## Maradona's heart

Can a football player be a country, even metaphorically? Indeed he can, and more. Speaking about H.G. Wells, Argentinian writer Jorge Luis Borges says that the work that endures "is always capable of an infinite and plastic ambiguity; it's everything for everyone" (1996, 76). The four "takes" this chapter has offered on the relationship between Maradona and Argentina prove, if nothing else, the infinite and plastic ambiguity of the subject and of his "work" and informs Argentinian cultural dynamics in the 20th century. Going back to two of his most famous phrases, "The ball doesn't get soiled" and "sons of bitches, sons of bitches", Maradona was the one who could attack with his football and his words, but who remained committed to the ball and the sport that made him.

Maradona was buried without his heart. After the autopsy was carried out, it was rumoured that a group of fans from Gimnasia y Esgrima wanted to raid a medical office that held the organ and steal it (Castro 2021: 358). It might seem like a fictional piece, but it is not. Speaking after a surgery to remove a blood clot in his brain, on October 2020, he said: "I am tired. I'd like to take a vacation from being Maradona". Is it any wonder that Maradona wanted to take a break from being Maradona? Leading actor in his own drama on and off the field, there is an essential irreducibility to his figure. In his self-interview during *La Noche del Diez* the informal Diego tells his formal self: "We speak the truth. I know who you are".

Perhaps we never will.

## Notes

1 The media started to use the symbol for infinity after the news of Maradona's death. See the video put together by his former club Boca Juniors, included in this article https://www.lanacion.com.ar/deportes/futbol/murio-diego-maradona-1960-al-infinito-emotivo-nid2520825/

2 Maradona's autobiography, *Maradona. The Autobiography of Soccer's Greatest and Most Controversial Star* (2001; English translations 2004 and 2011), is a product of his conversations with journalists Daniel Arcucci and Ernesto Cherquis Bialo. In addition, there are several biographies: Rodrigo Fernández y Denise Nagy's *De las manos de Dios a sus botines. Biografía pública de Diego Maradona no autorizada* (From the Hand of God to His Football Shoes. A Public, Non-Authorized Biography of Diego Maradona) (1994); Jimmy Burns' *Hand of God. The Life of Diego Maradona* (1996); Alexandre Juillard's *Maradona* (French; 2010); and Guillem Balagué's *Maradona. The Boy. The Rebel. The God* (2021). In Italian, out of the many available, we mention Cipriano Algore's *Diego Armando Maradona. Fango, oro e polvere* (Diego Maradona. Mud, Gold, and Dust) (2004) and Claudia Sapegno's *Diego da Buenos Aires* (2020).

3 Maradona himself begins his autobiography saying: "Sometimes I think that my whole life is on film, that my whole life is in print" (2011: 1).

4 Jim O'Brien explains that from 1920 to 1950 Argentine football developed a distinct style of play referred to as *la nuestra* which celebrated individualism "culturally rooted in the romantic escape of the poor boy, crafting the art of the Argentinian style of play in the urban wastelands of his neighborhood before escaping to enthrall the crowds by becoming a star" (2021: 94). Further discussion on *la nuestra* is beyond the scope of this chapter (cf. Wilson 2016).

5 In "México 86, nace el mito", Daniel Arcucci, one of the journalists that knew him best, explained this Maradonian-Argentinian attitude against adversity: "The Argentinian footballer becomes better in adversity and that is pure maradonismo. Maradonismo is explained when one fights against something or someone. When Maradona felt he was in a very favorable situation, he invented something unfavorable so he could fight against it" (Ferrer 2020: 63).

6 Borge states about the second goal: "[I]f there ever was such a thing as footballing beauty, this should be a prime example"; it is however an instance of *agon aesthetics* "whether the aesthetic experience in found within engagement in the football drama of competition" (2019: 198–199), also reinforcing the idea of a challenge.

7 Simone Magalhães Britto, Jorge Ventura de Morais, and Túlio Velho Barreto explain the sociological dimension of the "Hand of God" goal, stating that "Argentinean football was sacrificed in the name of national identity" and that "within the logic of dispute between two communities, Maradona's act might not be considered immoral" (2014: 679). Garry Whannel points out the opposite reactions from the Argentinian and the English press towards Maradona. For the Argentinians, he was the "Artful Dodger"; for the English a "dirty cheat". Whannel reminds us: "Morality is not only relative but also contingent upon power relations and upon positionalities—of national, class, gender and ethnic identities" (2002: 164).

8 The football animosity between Argentina and England has its own history prior to the Malvinas/Falklands war. At the Mexico 1986 World Cup, players from both teams had said before the encounter that it was only another match. According to Maradona, this was a lie: "Bollocks was it just another match!" (2011: 128). Burgo

goes through the testimony of some Argentine players of what transpired just before entering the field. Even though there are no specific details, the consensus is that the match was special. "We need to beat these sons of bitches!" was the cry in the tunnel and after the national anthems were played (2016: 84, 92).

9  We find a more nuanced approach in the book on Mexico 1986: "The truth is that the English had killed a bunch of kids. They were guilty, but the Argentines were just as guilty, sending those kids in *Flecha* tennis shoes (an affordable brand of Argentine tennis shoes at the time) to fight against the world's third largest military power". Later he explains that "I didn't play the game thinking we were going to win the war. All I wanted to do was to honor the memory of the dead" (2016: 136).

10  Archetti, anticipating Alabarces' ideas on the "oral Maradona" said: "Maradona talks about everything: rock, religion, politics, football, friendship, drugs, modernity, love, family, football authorities and managers, capitalism, poverty, money, women, men and children. He is kind of an erratic oracle ...." (1997: 47–48). An analysis of the Maradonian language is needed. Two volumes have gathered his phrases: Gatman and Burgo (2005) and Almada (2021). The Book and Language Museum in Buenos Aires put together 12 short videos entitled *Las verdades del diez* [#10 Truths] where different personalities comment Maradona's sayings https://www.youtube.com/watch?v=wC6Ibxb3p-k

11  For a general view on sports celebrity culture, cf. *Sport Stars: The Cultural Politics of Cultural Celebrity* (2001), and on Maradona specifically, cf. Archetti (2001), Alabarces (1996, 2014), and Leandro Zanoni's book dedicated to the "mediatic Maradona" which provides abundant information but only covers until 2006. It is aptly titled *Vivir en los medios. Maradona off the record* (Living in the Media. Maradona Off the Record), as the author crowns Maradona the "king of media" (Zanoni 2006: 243). From a global perspective, Burns states that "Maradona in fact became a key component in a giant money-spinning machine fueled by inflated transfer deals, TV rights, sponsorship and merchandising" (1996: vii). Ryu Spaeth, writing on the release of Asif Kapadia's documentary *Diego Maradona*, offers his take on the transition happening as the Argentine player is finishing his career: "This was when FIFA, the sport's governing body, became the corrupt mafia-like organization we know today; when European clubs were seized by oligarchs from around the world, turning players into fungible investments instead of hometown heroes; when the players themselves became steeped in the ways of commerce and trade and celebrity. When they learned, in other words, how to play the game: how to get the transfer to the right club, how to pose for social media, how to manipulate, as best they could, the coverage of the all-seeing tabloids" (2019). Uruguayan writer Eduardo Galeano puts it more poetically: "By Maradona's time, television and advertisement already held sway and things had changed. Maradona charged a high price and paid one as well. He charged for his legs, and paid with his soul" (2013: 247).

12  With regards to sport, media, and the heroic paradigm, Whannel speculates that "the related commercialization of sport would serve to heighten the tensions between a media-drive stardom and the romantic innocent expectations of heroism"; later, he coins the term "vortextuality" to explain rapid media exchanges "in an era of electronic and digital information" and its impact in the dynamics of sport (2002: 93, 206). Brooke Erin Duffy and Jefferson Pooley offer a useful framework to read contemporary "mass idols" stating that: "Just as Lowenthal understood mass idolatry as an expression of the dominant economic system, we contend that the stories our heroes tell—both in self-authored bios and in popular, third-person accounts—testify to larger anxieties in a precarious job economy ... In the face of uncertainty and against the backdrop of discourses and practices of neoliberalism, the guiding command is to orchestrate one's 'life project' in earnest ... With solids melted into air, responsibility for success or failure is the individual's alone, or so we come to believe" (2019: 28).

13  In 1995, Maradona was invited by a group of students to the Oxford Union Debating Chamber at Oxford University. There, he defined himself as a *pibe* product of the *potreros*. Of course, he had to end by playing keepie uppie. The video here: https://www.youtube.com/watch?v=j4IMsp3bAck

14  Those who may think politics and sports do not mix might do well to revise the controversies during the Argentina 1978 World Cup that took place with a military junta in power or the discontent of the Mexican people during the Mexico 1986 World Cup, after a strong earthquake devastated Mexico City in 1985. For a global analysis, cf. *Football, Politics and Identity* (Carr *et al.* 2021).

15  Juan Domingo Perón was in power in Argentina between 1946 and 1955 (his second term was interrupted by a military coup) and returned for a third period in 1973, cut short by his death in July 1974. Political leaders affiliated with Peronism have been in office in Argentina in 1989–1999, 2002–2003, 2003–2015, and 2019 to present.

16  It is truly amazing to see how Maradona's figure acquires diverse meanings. A young Maradona in the 1970s says he has "no time" for politics but the military Junta utilized him anyway as an example of national character and achievements and, for a while, his sale abroad was prohibited (cf. the chapter "The Junta's Boy" in Burns 1996). Decades later, Carlos Ares states that Maradona "is the Perón of the nineties, the only postmodern leader capable of continuing the fight for liberation and against dependency ... Maradona is also the Evita of the nineties" (qtd. in Levinsky 1996: 26).

17  Cristina Kirchner's government was, in ideological terms, completely at odds with Menem. Though the Kirchners endorsed his liberal economic policies in the 1990s, they later reversed many of them, renationalising companies that he had privatised, and reinitiating the trials of the members of the 1976–1983 military junta who had committed crimes and had been pardoned by Menem in 1989 and 1990.

18  To the political discussion on Maradona, we can add three books published in 2021: the hagiographic *Maradona. Fútbol y política*, by Julio Ferrer, and the more significant *Superdios. La construcción de Maradona como santo laico*, by Gabriela Saidon. See also Fernández Moores *et al.*

# References

Acker, Ana María. 2012. "Constructions of Power in the Documentary Film *Maradona*, by Emir Kusturica". *Verso e reverso* 26.63: 135–143.

Alabarces, Pablo. 1996. "Maradona revisitado. Apostillas a 'El fútbol no es la patria'". *Cuestión de pelotas. Fútbol, deporte, sociedad, cultura*. Buenos Aires: Atuel, 53–57.

———. 2005a. "Maradona, el fútbol, la patria, el peronismo y otros gremios paralelos. Un héroe en disponibilidad". *Encrucijadas* 33, s. p.

———. 2005b. "Santa Maradona, ascenso y caída de un mito futbolístico". *Delirios de grandeza. Los mitos argentinos: memoria, identidad, cultura*. Eds. María Cristina Pons and Claudia Soria. Rosario: Beatriz Viterbo, 41–53.

———. 2007. "Maradonismo, o la superación del peronismo por otros medios". *Fútbol y patria. El fútbol y las narrativas de la nación en la Argentina*. Buenos Aires: Prometeo, 133–160.

———. 2014. "La patria, Maradona y Messi: variaciones sobre el ser nacional". *Héroes, machos y patriotas. El fútbol entre la violencia y los medios*. Buenos Aires: Aguilar, 103–132.

———. 2021. "Maradona: mito popular, símbolo peronista, voz plebeya". *Papeles del CEIC* 249.1: 1–11.

Alabarces, Pablo and María Graciela Rodríguez. 1999. "Football and Fatherland: The Crisis of National Representation in Argentinean Soccer". *Sport in Society* 2.3: 118–133.

Algore, Cipriano. 2004. *Diego Armando Maradona. Fango, oro e polvere*. Milán: Bevivino Editore.

Almada, Lucas, ed. 2021. *La palabra de D10S. Maradona desde sus frases*. Buenos Aires: Librofutbol.com.

Andrews, David L. and Steven J. Jackson, eds. 2001. *Sport Stars: The Cultural Politics of Cultural Celebrity*. London and New York: Routledge.

Andrews, David L. and George Ritzer. 2007. "The Grobal in the Sporting Glocal". *Global Networks* 7.2: 113–153.

Archetti, Eduardo. 1996. "Playing Styles and Masculine Virtues in Argentine Football". *Machos, Mistresses, Madonnas: Contesting the Power of Latin American Gender Imagery*. Eds. Marit Melhuus and Kristi Anne Stolen. London: Verso, 34–55.

———. 1997. "And Give Joy to my Heart: Ideology and Emotions in the Argentinean Cult of Maradona". *Entering the Field. New Perspectives on World Football*. Eds. Gary Amstrong and Richard Giulianotti. Oxford and New York: Berg, 31–51.

———. 1998. "The Potrero and the Pibe. Territory and Belonging in the Mythical Account of Argentinean Football". *Locality and Belonging*. Ed. Nadia Lovell. London and New York: Routledge, 189–210.

———. 1999. *Masculinities. Football, Polo and the Tango in Argentina*. Oxford and New York: Berg.

———. 2001. "The Spectacle of a Heroic Life: The Case of Diego Maradona". *Sport Stars: The Cultural Politics of Cultural Celebrity*. Eds. David L. Andrews and Steven J. Jackson. London and New York: Routledge, 151–164.

Balagué, Guillem. 2021. *Maradona. The Boy. The Rebel. The God*. London: Weidenfeld & Nicolson.

Bauer, Thomas. 2018. "From Maradona to Jude Law: Sport in Paolo Sorrentino's Movies". *Studies in European Cinema* 18.1: 60–75.

Bifulco, Luca and Vittorio Dini, eds. 2014. *Maradona: sociología di un mito globale*. Caserta: Ipermedium.

Bilbija, Ksenija. 1995. "Maradona's Left: Postmodernity and National Identity in Argentina". *Studies in Latin American Popular Culture* 14: 199–208.

Borge, Steffen. 2019. *The Philosophy of Football*. Oxford and New York: Routledge.

Borges, Jorge Luis. 1996. "El primer Wells". *Obras completas*. Vol. 2. Buenos Aires: Emecé, 75–77.

Burgo, Andrés. 2016. *El partido. Argentina-Inglaterra 1986*. Buenos Aires: Tusquets.

Burgo, Andrés and Alejandro Wall. 2014. *El último Maradona: cuando a Diego le cortaron las piernas*. Buenos Aires: Aguilar.

Burns, Jimmy. 1996. *Hand of God. The Life of Diego Maradona*. New York, NY: The Lyons Press.

Caparrós, Martín. 2020. "Fue la Argentina". *El País*, November 26. https://elpais.com/deportes/2020-11-26/fue-la-argentina.html [Accessed March 21, 2022].

Carr, James, Daniel Parnell, Paul Widdop, Martin J. Power and Stephen R. Millar, eds. 2021. *Football, Politics and Identity*. Oxford and New York: Routledge.

Castro, Nelson. 2021. *La salud de Diego*. Buenos Aires: Sudamericana.

Dini, Vittorio. 1994. "Maradona: Héros Napolitain". *Actes de la recherche en sciences sociales* 103: 75–78.

Dini, Vittorio and Nicolaus Oscar. Eds. 1991. *Te Diegum: genio, sregolatezza e bacchettoni*. Milano: Leonardo editore [translated to Spanish as *Te Diegum. Maradona: genio y transgresión*. 2001. Trad. Roberto Raschella. Buenos Aires: Editorial Sudamericana].

Duffy, Brooke Erin and Jefferson Pooley. 2019. "Idols of Promotion: The Triumph of Self Branding in an Age of Precarity". *Journal of Communication* 69: 26–48.

Fernández, Rodrigo and Denise Nagy. 1994. *De las manos de Dios a sus botines. Biografía pública de Diego Maradona no autorizada*. Buenos Aires: Cangrejal Editores.

Fernández Moores, Ezequiel, Alejandro Wall and Andrés Burgo, eds. 2021. *Rey de Fiorito. Crónicas políticas y sociales de la vida de Diego Maradona.* Buenos Aires: Ediciones Carrascosa-SiPreBa.

Ferrer, Julio, ed. 2020. *D10S. Miradas sobre el mito Maradona.* Buenos Aires: Octubre.

_____. 2021. *Maradona. Fútbol y política.* Buenos Aires: Punto de encuentro.

Firpo, Hernán. 2017. "Carlos Sanzol. Periodista. 'Cris Miró fue un prólogo para la ley de Identidad de Género'". *Clarín*, January 23. https://www.clarin.com/espectaculos/fama/cris-miro-prologo-ley-identidad-genero_0_rJRVOg4wx.html [Accessed March 17, 2022].

Free, Marcus. 2014. "Diego Maradona and the Psychodynamics of Football Fandom in International Cinema". *Celebrity Studies* 5.1–1: 197–212.

Frydenberg, Julio. 2011. *Historia social del fútbol. Del amateurismo a la profesionalización.* Buenos Aires: Siglo XXI.

Galeano, Eduardo. 2013. *Soccer in Sun and Shadow.* Trans. Mark Fried. New York, NY: Bold Type Books.

Gatman, Marcelo and Andrés Burgo, eds. 2005. *Las mejores 1000 frases de toda la carrera del 10.* Buenos Aires: Distal.

Giulianotti, Richard. 2016. *Sport: A Critical Sociology.* 2nd ed. Cambridge: Polity Press.

Gómez Villar, Antonio, ed. 2021. *Maradona, un mito plebeyo.* Madrid: Ned.

Gajnaj, Ezequiel. 2007. *Medios y construcción de imagen. La construcción de la imagen de Maradona en el programa televisivo "La Noche del 10".* Córdoba: Universidad Empresarial Siglo 21.

Juillard, Alexandre. 2010. *Maradona.* París: Hugodocument.

Levinsky, Sergio. 1996. *Maradona, rebelde con causa.* Buenos Aires: Corregidor.

Magalhães Brittoa, Simone, Jorge Ventura de Moraisb and Túlio Velho Barretoc. 2014. "The Hand of God, the Hand of the Devil: A Sociological Interpretation of Maradona's Hand Goal". *Soccer and Society* 15.5: 671–684.

Maguire, Joseph, Katie Liston and Mark Falcous, eds. 2021. *The Palgrave Handbook of Globalization and Sport.* London: Palgrave Macmillan.

Makhovsky, Andrei. 2018. "From Buenos Aires to Brest – Maradona Takes Charge of Belarus club". *Reuters*, July 16. https://www.reuters.com/article/uk-soccer-belarus-maradona-idUKKBN1K62EL [Accessed March 21, 2022].

Maradona, Diego Armando. 2011. *Maradona. The Autobiography of Soccer's Greatest and Most Controversial Star.* Trans. Marcela Moray Araujo. New York, NY: Skyhorse Publishing.

Maradona, Diego Armando and Daniel Arcucci. 2016. *Touched by God. How We Won the Mexico '86 World Cup.* Trans. Jane Brodie and Wendy Gosselin. London: Constable.

Mora y Araujo, Marcela. 2011. "Hay fiesta en Olivos". *Rey de Fiorito. Crónicas políticas y sociales de la vida de Diego Maradona.* Eds. Ezequiel Fernández Moores, Alejandro Wall and Andrés Burgo. Buenos Aires: Ediciones Carrascosa-SiPreBa, 81–96.

Morales, Víctor Hugo. 2013. *Barrilete cósmico (el relato completo).* Idea y realización Ariel Magnus. Buenos Aires: Interzona.

O'Brien, Jim. 2021. "Enduring Passions: Football, Peronism and the Politics of National Identity in Argentina". *Football, Politics and Identity.* Eds. James Carr, Daniel Parnell, Paul Widdop, Martin J. Power and Stephen R. Millar. New York, NY: Routledge, 93–107.

Pieterse, Jan Nederveen. 2013. "What is Global Studies?" *Globalizations* 10.4: 499–514.

Pistoia, Bárbara, ed. 2021. *Todo Diego es político.* Buenos Aires: Síncopa.

Plotkin, Mariano. 1998. "The Changing Perceptions of Peronism: A Review Essay". *Peronism and Argentina.* Ed. James P. Brennan. Wilmington, DE: SR Books.

Rodríguez, María Graciela. 1996. "'El fútbol no es la patria' (pero se le parece)". *Cuestión de pelotas. Fútbol, deporte, sociedad, cultura*. Eds. Pablo Alabarces and María Graciela Rodríguez. Buenos Aires: Atuel, 37–57.

Roudometof, Victor. 2015. "The Glocal and Global Studies". *Globalizations* 12.5: 774–787.

Safirsztein, Yanina. 2021. "El armado de un nombre". *Todo Diego es político*. Ed. Bárbara Pistoia. Buenos Aires: Síncopa, 64–73.

Saidon, Gabriela. 2021. *Superdios. La construcción de Maradona como santo laico*. Buenos Aires: Capital Intelectual.

Salazar-Sutil, Nicolás. 2008. "Maradona inc: Performance Politics off the Pitch". *International Journal of Cultural Studies* 11.4: 441–458.

Sapegno, Claudia. 2020. *Diego da Buenos Aires*. Italia: Aliberti.

Sarbajit, Mitra and Souvik Naha. 2017. "Politics and International Fandom in a Fringe Nation: La Albiceleste, Maradona, and Marxist Kolkata". *Sport in Society* 20.5–6: 660–674.

Sebreli, Juan José. 2005. *La era del fútbol*. Buenos Aires: Sudamericana.

———. 2008. "Maradona". *Comediantes y mártires. Ensayos contra los mitos*. Barcelona: Debates, 165–202.

Sibaja, Rwany and Charles Parrish. 2014. "*Pibes, Cracks* and *Caudillos*: Argentina, the World Cup and Identity Politics". *Soccer & Society* 15.5: 655–670.

Signorini, Fernando, Luciano Wernicke and Fernando Molina. 2021. *Diego desde adentro. Cómo el mejor futbolista del mundo se convirtió en el mejor futbolista de la historia*. Buenos Aires: Planeta.

Spaeth, Ryan. 2019. "The Tragedy of Diego Maradona". *The New Republic*. October 10. https://newrepublic.com/article/155330/tragedy-diego-maradona.

Tobin, Jeffrey. 2002. "Soccer Conspiracies: Maradona, the CIA, and Populist Critique". *Sport in Latin America and the Caribbean*. Eds. Joseph L. Arbena and David G. LaFrance. London: Eurospan, 51–73.

Whannel, Garry. 2002. *Media Sports Stars. Masculinities and Moralities*. London and New York: Routledge.

Wilson, Jonathan. 2016. *Angels with Dirty Faces. How Argentinian Soccer Defined a Nation and Changed the Game Forever*. New York, NY: Nation Books.

Zabala, Santiago *et al.* 2021. *Fenomenología de Maradona*. Madrid: Altamarea Ediciones.

Zanoni, Leandro. 2006. *Vivir en los medios. Maradona off the record*. Buenos Aires: Marea.

# 2

# MARADONA AND SPAIN

## Mythologies of the Hero Narrative

*David García Cames*

*Translated by Muireann Prendergast*

### The trials

Diego Armando Maradona's time in Spain, both in his two years at FC Barcelona as well as in his short season at Seville FC, has always been considered a period of transition. The Spanish stage of his career is generally viewed as secondary to his greatest milestones, such as the Mexico 1986 World Cup victory and his titles with SSC Napoli. This chapter demonstrates, by analysing current documents as well as those of the time in question, that these two periods spent by Maradona in Spain, although not central to his greatest moments, nevertheless align perfectly with the mythical story built around him as a sports figure. Maradona's career allows us to follow, step-by-step, the narrative pattern explored by Joseph Campbell in his book *The Hero with a Thousand Faces* (1949). During his time in Spain, Maradona's journey makes evident the seduction of the "rise and fall" formula (*ánodos* and *káthodos*). The adventure of the hero to which Campbell attributed the term "monomyth", synthesised in the essential formula of "departure, initiation, and return", can be used as a map to trace the trajectory of Maradona and the ways in which his life has been understood, narrated, communicated, and commercialised.

Like every classical hero, Maradona occupies a liminal position. Halfway between the divine and the extremely human, an earthly hero overwhelmed by heaven, his destiny was to belong to everybody and to no one at the same time. Even so, the thousand faces of the mythical hero fail to account for the ficklest of sporting idols. Here, I will focus on some of the faces he showed in Spain and how these have been moulded over the years. Karl Kerényi (2009: 35) proposes that the mythology of heroes is based on the ability to weave a mythical with a historical time, a suggestion that is appropriate for an analysis of Maradona. His two periods in Spain occur at the beginning of the 1980s and 1990s, in two very

DOI: 10.4324/9781003196587-4

different socio-economic contexts separated, in addition, by drastic changes in the career of the footballer. The conflict between two worlds, the human and the divine, which always dominate the construction of the heroic figure, are expressed during the seasons at Barcelona and Seville through episodes essential to understand the fusion of chronicle and legend that gives meaning to the myth in its totality. This chapter follows the parallel path that is established between the player and the archetypal hero, highlighting among other aspects his departure from home, his trials at Barcelona, and his decline at Seville. The versatility of the mythical story allows, in this way, the insertion of his passage through Spain in the Maradona narrative.

## Leaving home (for Barcelona)

From Ulysses to Theseus, heroes must leave their land to reach the universal dimension that their myths grant them. The narrative of Maradona's arrival in Spain, and by extension in Europe, aligns precisely with this idea. The signing of the player by Barcelona FC was the result of sustained and sensationalised press attention in Argentina as well as in Spain over a number of years. From the first negotiations with Barcelona in 1978 until the definitive signing of the contract in 1982, the tug-of-war between the two sides was informed by economic issues and by pressures to prevent the departure of the country's (sporting) idol imposed by the military junta that ruled Argentina at the time. From this point onwards, Maradona was an essential, popular, and proletarian representation of the country (Alabarces, 2021). From his 1976 debut with Argentinos Juniors, his impact grew until he become in 1979 "an unprecedented media phenomenon in Argentinian sport. His surname was on the cover of *El Gráfico* at least once a month" (Zanoni, 2006: 49).

The dream of the *pibe*, a specifically Argentinian story where many of the phases of Campbell's hero are evident, was perfectly embodied in the young footballer. From the myth of his birth (Rank, 1961) in the impoverished *omphalós* of Villa Fiorito to his success in the 1979 Youth World Cup, Maradona fulfils, step-by-step, everything for which he seems predestined: to lift his family out of poverty, to triumph in the first division of Argentinian football, and to arouse the interest of foreign teams such as Sheffield United, Juventus, and Barcelona itself. However, his signing by an international club and the call to leave could not happen in a natural way in Argentina during those years. The Junta did not want to miss the opportunity of taking advantage of the country's most popular sporting figure, particularly following the success of the propaganda campaign they had orchestrated during the 1978 World Cup. As relayed in the documentary *Fútbol Club Maradona* (2019), it was Carlos Alberto Lacoste himself, once of the most feared military officials in Argentina and remembered for his role in organising that World Cup, who prevented Maradona from reaching an agreement with Barcelona in 1980. Vice admiral Lacoste demanded that the players remain in Argentina at least until the end of the 1982 World Cup to be held precisely in Spain, the same year in which the Argentinian invasion of the Malvinas/Falkland Islands would take place.

The fascination with the humble origins of this idol, an essential element of his status of legend, would soon be evident in the Spanish press. As early as December of 1978, in an article published in the *Marca* newspaper cited by Jimmy Burns in his book *The Hand of God,* the player was spoken about in the following terms: "He's short, stocky, with an Afro hairstyle which hasn't seen a scissors for months. He is a mere eighteen years old and yet he is potentially the most expensive player in Argentinian football" (Burns, 2011). Before disembarking in Barcelona, Maradona would have time to win his first club title with Boca Juniors in 1981 and become the leader of the Argentinian national team.

The modest performance by Argentina and Maradona in the 1982 World Cup was used by the Spanish press to question the competence of the future signing. Painful defeats against Italy and Brazil in the second phase of the championship, the latter compounded by the expulsion of the footballer in the match against Argentina's archrivals, were given significant coverage by the sports newspapers of the time. Here, he was spoken about in terms such as "expectación defrau- dada" (disappointed expectation) and "estrella opaca" (opaque star) (*El Mundo Deportivo*, 1982: 13). At that time, the label of *pibe de oro* also gained traction in the Spanish press in clear reference to his monetary value (Zanoni, 2006: 77). Doubts about the economic repercussions of the transfer even reached the main- stream media. Before the official announcement of Maradona's contract with Barcelona, the front page of the Spanish newspaper *El País* on May 24, 1982, carried the lines: "Maradona is not just a football player … to hire Maradona is to acquire a financial commitment with a multinational".

Maradona landed in Spain at a time when the country was trying to find itself and re-establish its identity. The failed *coup d'état* of February 23, 1981, instigated by the most reactionary sectors of the army, had revived all the ghosts of the 40 years of General Franco's dictatorship. The Spain of those years was an unstable country where the desire for freedom coexisted with threats to the young democracy coming from both extreme right and extreme left political forces. These were violent years, with the Basque terrorist group ETA (Euskadi Ta Askatasuna) planning and executing attacks which caused many victims, and the Spanish transition showing all its complexities. The elections of October of 1982 would give victory to the socialist party of Felipe González by a very large majority. A few months earlier, the World Cup had been the first show- case of that Spain, reflected in the opening ceremony held at the Camp Nou stadium in Barcelona. In this context, Maradona arrived in one of the great industrial centres of the country, a boiling point where a large migrant pop- ulation cohabited with a traditionalist ruling class. The contrast between the rebellious and foul-mouthed boy of Villa Fiorito and the bourgeois values of the city was to be a source of conflict during the two years that followed: "He was too much of a 'Southerner', too much the 'uncivilised outskirts' boy for those in Barcelona who were desperate to be considered European and orderly, respectful of the establishment" (Balagué, 2021). The player himself would recognise years later the difficulties he faced in adapting to the "idiosyncrasy of the Catalans" (Maradona, 2000: 69) and to a society that perceived itself as laborious, rigorous, and, above all, of sensible nature.[1]

In the years following the end of Franco's dictatorship, Barcelona continued to be a channel for Catalan nationalist aspirations, synthesised in its slogan of "Més que un club" ("More than a club"). It is important to note that Barcelona FC was not then the winning team of recent years. Despite its economic and social prowess, victories were scarce. The last League win dated back to Johan Cruyff's first year at Barça, in a distant 1974, while only victories in cup tournaments helped to alleviate the drought of major titles domestically or in Europe. From 1978, the team was chaired by José Luis Núñez, a construction entrepreneur who would hold complete control of the club until 2000. With the signing of Maradona for approximately US$7 million, President Núñez, a pragmatic and vain leader who was "obsessed with power" (Ludden, 2014), aspired to make profitable the expansion of the Camp Nou to 120,000 seats, which transformed it into the largest stadium in Europe. In addition, it was necessary to consider the inexhaustible media interest in football. As is still the case today, only Barcelona could boast two sports-themed newspapers (*El Mundo Deportivo* and *Sport*) published daily that devoted a minimum of ten pages to information about *culé* (fans of the Barcelona team). In addition to this, two Madrid-based sports newspapers (*Marca* and *As*) had millions of readers throughout the country. For journalists and readers alike, Maradona offered the promise of spectacle, a source of controversy, and, of course, cannon fodder as a young player of a mere 21 years old.

## Baptism by fires

The story of Maradona's two years in Barcelona fits the "trial roads" trope within his heroic journey. This idol had to leave his homeland to achieve the "macro-cosmic triumph" (Campbell, 2004: 35) that his myth demanded; accordingly, he had to face many difficulties such as a case of hepatitis, worldly temptations, disciplinary conflicts with club directors, and a career-threatening ankle injury. Those Barça years are presented as an incursion in the belly of the whale out of which the hero, although not fully aware at that time, would be completely reborn. Despite the problems, or precisely because of them, this phase of the Maradonian myth is undoubtedly part of his path of ascent (*ánodos*). In the following years, he would reach his apotheosis, both with his triumphs at Naples and in the Mexico 1986 World Cup. His enemies and antagonists in his two seasons at Barcelona represent, in this way, the tests of heroic adventure that precede the decisive confrontation.

His start at Barcelona was dazzling: 11 goals and only 1 defeat in 17 matches. In those first months, Maradona's play showed flashes of absolute beauty, like a goal of unparalleled perfection against Red Star Belgrade at Little Maracanã stadium.[2] However, the football hero would soon have his first major setback: a diagnosis of hepatitis in December of 1982 because of which he would be unable to play for three months. Soon, gossip began to circulate. Maradona's dissolute life in the city was *vox populi* and many wanted to create a link between this and a diagnosis other than hepatitis. Although the player always denied it, some observers such as journalist Fabián Ortiz interviewed for the documentary *Fútbol Club Maradona* (2019), claimed that what Maradona assured to be hepatitis was really a venereal disease. In any case, a club of the scale of Barcelona had to offer an alternative and tolerable version for its conservative supporters. Although no reliable documentation can confirm the veracity of these rumours, within the Maradona myth narrative, this has been classified as an "innocent" illness, which nevertheless removed the player away from the pitch shortly after his arrival at Barcelona.

His return to the team led to some of his finest moments at Barça. The dismissal of the rigorous German coach Udo Lattek and the arrival of the Argentinian César Luis Menotti, World Cup champion with Argentina in 1978 and in 1979 at the Youth World Cup (with Maradona a star in that team), undoubtedly motivated the player. Although Barça could not prevail in the League that year, won by Athletic Bilbao, the Catalan team would defeat its great rival, Real Madrid, in the finals of the Copa del Rey and Copa de la Liga. One of those matches displayed one of those typically Maradonian moments in which aesthetics and mischievousness prevailed over efficiency. It involved a goal where he overtook the goalkeeper before dribbling past defender Juan José causing him to hit the post; this led to a round of applause from Real Madrid fans, something rarely seen in matches between these two rival teams.[3]

Despite media pressure around him, Maradona was hopeful about his second season at the club. Within the squad, more and more teammates recognised his growth as a leader although, as Ramon Besa points out, the dressing room was divided according to each player's degree of affinity with the Argentinian player (Besa, 1998: 32–33). Nevertheless, the majority of the Barça players acknowledged his charisma and technical quality, as evinced in the testimonies of "Lobo" Carrasco, Julio Alberto, or Marcos Alonso, players featured in the documentary *Fútbol Club Maradona*. The end of that 1982–1983 season, despite his three-month absence, seemed to augur a successful future at Barcelona.

The hero is in essence a creature in permanent conflict, a "withered god", as Kirk calls him (2002: 208). Since classical times, his semi-divine condition (*hemítheoi*) fosters a clash between his sordid and sublime nature, both elevated and earthly. These contradictions, far from nullifying him, entail the hero's humanisation and consecration by public opinion. Like Achilles, heroes do not need to be exemplary but instead act as a mirror of their time. Juan José Sebreli says in this regard that Maradona is one of the contemporary idols who best demonstrates this dual nature: "He exemplified both aspects, one when he showed superhuman qualities in his sporting exploits; the other was evidenced by his scandals in the sordidness of the night" (Sebreli, 2008: 109). The inevitable clash with this two-faced or dual character of the hero would have its best expression in Spain in what was termed the "Maradona clan". The footballer, far from his homeland and the environment that saw him grow up, surrounded himself in Barcelona with a large group of friends, many of them former teammates of his first childhood team. The group included his representative Jorge Cyterszpiler, whom he had also met in those years. Propelled by nostalgia and overwhelmed by the possibilities of debauchery offered by a city like Barcelona, Maradona financially supported, fed, and welcomed his colleagues in his mansion located in the exclusive neighbourhood of Pedralbes. This group immediately aroused the suspicions and misgivings of the local press. Beyond the phagocytising nature of this environment, the qualifier of "clan" made evident the classism and latent racism towards Maradona both in the sports newspapers and in the stands of the Camp Nou.

Maradona remembered his group at Barcelona years later in his autobiography: "What was the clan? It was my people, my family, my friends, my employees … they were Argentinians who were in need of someone to protect them; and that someone was me" (2000: 80). The footballer presented himself as the protective hero of a group willing to "flatter him, pamper him, forgive him, thank him and never reproach him" (Besa, 1998: 62). The confrontation between the "clan" and the Catalan elite would only grow in the media, as detailed in the accounts of journalists and managers in the documentary *Fútbol Club Maradona*. President Núñez also took advantage of this controversy to attack the footballer repeatedly, claiming that he had to abandon his "Argentinian mentality" and adopt the "European mentality" if he wanted to succeed at the club (Zanoni, 2006: 87). These reproaches would help to exacerbate the classic Maradonian insubordination towards his leaders, something that would gradually increase until finally causing his departure from the team. The idol seemed to feel comfortable in the full expression of his double nature: unpredictable on the pitch, rebellious off the pitch, and proud of his status as a foreigner, showing at all times "the eternal battle between a free spirit and a censorious establishment" (Balagué, 2021).

Another issue – "proof" in this chaotic context – that continues to arouse controversy from Maradona's time at Barcelona is the starting point of his cocaine addiction. While some sources close to him have stated that he began to consume this drug in Buenos Aires when he played for Boca,[4] other direct witnesses affirm that this began in Spain. The truth is that Maradona himself always insisted that he met his particular "white goddess" during his stay at the Catalan club.[5]

He was on course to be consecrated the star player in Spain during the 1983–1984 season. However, the toughest test he would face during his time in Barcelona would come on September 24, 1983, the mere fourth day of the League. In a match at the Camp Nou against the reigning champions Athletic Bilbao, Maradona suffered the most serious injury of his career after a disproportionate tackle by Andoni Goikoetxea.[6] Before entering into the details of the injury, it is necessary to acknowledge the levels of violence tolerated in football during the 1980s, with the Argentinian midfielder as a scapegoat: "I am not complaining, I do not want to appear as a victim, but they fouled me a lot"

(Maradona, 2000: 68). In the World Cup in Spain, he had already experienced a paradigmatic episode in the game against Italy, where he was marked within (and sometimes beyond) the limits of the law by Claudio Gentile. The violence of some of these tackles is surprising by today's standards. The referees, particularly in the Spanish League, turned a blind eye to kicks at knee height or elbows to the face. If violence was a feature of daily life in Argentina and Spain during those years, the football pitch was also a hostile territory, an increasingly less playful reflection of wider political and social conflicts.

The Basque teams of Real Sociedad and Athletic Bilbao dominated the local competition in the early 1980s with their tough approaches to the game. The Bilbao team had won the League of the year of Maradona's arrival in Spain under the direction of one of the greatest defenders of contact football, Coach Javier Clemente. In its ranks was one of the most feared players in Spanish football, Goikoetxea, who in 1981 had seriously injured another Barça star, the German Bernd Schuster. While institutional relations between the Basque and Catalan clubs were on good terms because of their nationalist political affinity favouring independence from the Spanish state, they diverged in terms of their different understanding of football. This confrontation increased with the arrival at Barcelona of Menotti, a coach who defended football as a spectacle built around the figure of Maradona. These existing differences between the clubs exploded with the violent tackle of Goikoetxea in September of 1983 that caused a serious break in Maradona's left ankle. However, the referee only sanctioned the Basque with a yellow card. The Catalan press, *El Mundo Deportivo* and *Sport,* agreed to harmonise their September 26 covers with the same headlines: "El Crimen" (The Crime) and "Crimen Deportivo" (Sports Crime). At the end of the match, Menotti made a strong statement against violent play: "I'm not going to mess with the Basques but it seems that someone will have to die here for this to change"; Clemente replied by assuring that he felt "very proud" of his players (*Mundo Deportivo*, 1983: 8). The dialectical and discursive battle had only just begun.

The controversy generated by this incident lasted for months in the media. On the one hand, Goikoetxea was described as a "murderer", "Attila", "an anti-footballer", "butcher of Bilbao", and even "gudari" (Basque warrior), a name associated with ETA terrorists. The press, both Spanish and European, highlighted the persistently violent character of the player, calling for him to receive an exemplary sanction. Some demanded, like President Núñez, that the defender not play again until Maradona was able to do so, while newspapers such as the French *L'Équipe* asked for limits to be placed on violence in Spanish football (Carreño, 2018). Paradoxically, this supposed media campaign against Goikoetxea caused him to be received in the Basque Country as a true martyr and hero. From Bilbao, these offenses against the Athletic player were considered the result of an attack against the entire Basque people and against one of their representative institutions: "His popularity at home made it hard to imagine why Goiko would seek to find contrition for his more primitive displays at all when they were being celebrated by the Basques as vehemently as they were being condemned by the Catalans" (Sharp, 2017).

The initial sanction of 18 games was appealed by a group of Bilbao lawyers who, at the end of September, declared it "unconstitutional" (Benito, 1983: 8). Finally, Goikoetxea's punishment "was reduced with each appeal presented until it was seven matches" (Besa, 1998: 72). For his part, Maradona, following a period of recovery in Argentina described by many as miraculous, returned to the field of play in January, three months after that terrible foul that would continue to mark the careers of its two protagonists afterwards. The Basque defender was criticised as a violent player, so much so that even after Maradona's death he would continue to receive insults for having been one of his greatest antagonists (Herrán, 2020). Meanwhile, Maradona, as well as the media covering him, would remember that tackle as one of the greatest tests of his career. If, as Campbell asserts (2004: 84), serious setbacks contribute to the consolidation of the hero, the stories constructed in relation to the figure of Maradona identify this episode as a key point in his career: a challenge from which he would emerge stronger than before. At the same time, however, Maradona added an early enemy, and the conflict between both players did not end in that incident.

Maradona's injury pushed the clash between Athletic and Barcelona to its limits in the early 1980s. While the historic rivalry of the Catalans with Real Madrid was based on the opposition and resistance of the nationalist periphery against the central power, the duels with the Basque team responded essentially to sporting motivations, to two antagonistic ways of understanding and practising football. The bitter hatred of the fans and players transcended the separate identities of the two regions that found their common enemy in Madrid. This was arguably a question of aesthetics and Maradona, as always was the centre of the debate. The opposition between the theoretically "lyrical" football embodied by the Argentinian and the roughness of the Basques manifested itself in a hostility based on different styles of play, similar to that which many years later would occur between Pep Guardiola's Barça and José Mourinho's Real Madrid from 2010. In the clashes of the 1980s, Maradona, always eager to occupy centre stage, did not hesitate to present himself to the fans as the idol capable of saving the artistic values of football against violent play: "He has always required a tacit agreement with the public: for his art, he desires appreciation" (Balagué, 2021). The rivalry between Athletic and Barcelona also developed from the intolerant discourse of their two coaches. On the one hand, Clemente did not stop questioning Maradona, calling him an "utter imbecile" and, with an undisguised racism, referring to the "lack of education" of foreigners (Sirvent, 1984). For his part, Menotti asserted the theoretical moral superiority of his way of understanding football against the race of "anti-footballers" of the Basque team. The culmination of this confrontation would occur in spectacular style on May 5, 1984, with the dispute between the two teams at the final of the Copa del Rey.

## The need for exile

In what was supposed to be his season of success at Barcelona, Maradona and his club could only achieve third place in La Liga, behind Athletic and Real Madrid. His return to the football pitch after his injury was insufficient to improve the dynamics of the team. The final lifeline for the club, as in the previous year, was the Copa del Rey final. The clash against Athletic at the Santiago Bernabéu was predicted to be volatile, as the statements of players and officials before the match stirred up hatred to boiling point. Maradona was at the centre of the conflict. With a clear majority of Basque fans in the stands, Athletic Bilbao won 1-0 in a tense match that was plagued by fouls. The "Battle of the Bernabéu"[7] would reach its climax when, after the final whistle of the referee, Maradona capitulated to the provocations of his rivals and left the Bilbao player Miguel Ángel Solá unconscious following a knee to his head. The two teams engaged in a brawl broadcast live across the country. Martial arts kicks and punches flew on the grass, while the police prevented some members of the "Maradona clan" from entering the pitch. The Argentinian player left the field almost in shock, protected by his teammates and with the Barça shirt torn to pieces. He would never wear it again.

The "Bitter Final", so-called by the headline of *El Mundo Deportivo* on May 6, 1984, resulted in the shocking end of Maradona's period in Barcelona. The Maradona-hero emerged bruised but nevertheless alive from this last "test". There were many reasons that made his continuation at the club almost impossible. His clashes with the board of directors were reaching an untenable degree of hostility, as Maradona captured in his statements and autobiography: "They disrespected and doubted me" (*Mundo Deportivo*, 1984: 6); "The only thing I wanted was to leave there, to leave Spain, to leave Catalonia" (Maradona, 2000: 83). Attacks from the press for the excesses of his private life were also on the rise, and these reports generated a feeling of weariness, disaffection, and fatalism among many of the fans (Besa, 1998: 64). Compounding these issues was the player's poor financial situation. The uncontrolled expenses, both his own and that of his entire group in Barcelona, were bankrupting his company "Maradona Producciones", established by his representative Cyterszpiler to manage his contracts and image (Burns, 2011). When a modest team like Napoli knocked on Barça's door asking about the price of the Argentinian footballer, it was a timely opportunity to seal the divorce.

According to Campbell, "once having traversed the threshold, the hero moves in a dream landscape of curiously fluid, ambiguous forms, where he must survive a succession of trials. This is a favourite phase of the myth adventure" (2004: 89). Maradona's two seasons in Barcelona were nothing more than a continuous obstacle course. The departure from home, combined with the call of the adventure represented in the expectations generated by his signing, would announce the mythical reason for the sinking of the idol in the belly of the whale, from which later he would leave completely strengthened. In the Maradonian narrative, his

illness and the injury caused by Goikoetxea, to highlight some of these pit-
falls, had to be experienced and overcome before obtaining the triumph that
could only be achieved after battling against two archetypal monsters: England
in Mexico and northern Italy.

The passage of time has led to a widespread review of the significance of
those early years. Maradona's first experience in Europe is generally remembered with nostalgia and a sense of a lost opportunity. In *Fútbol Club Maradona*,
the testimonies speak of "frustrated project", "disagreement", or "story of what
could have been". In the same vein, the writer Carlos Zanón stated shortly after
the player's death: "There was no emotional bond created between the fans in
the stands and him. It was a cold and distant marriage based on the hope that
a League or European Cup win would give raise to the *culé* passion" (Zanón,
2020). The protagonist himself also voluntarily adopted and shared this view. In
his autobiography *Yo Soy el Diego*, the chapter dedicated to his years in Barcelona
bears the title of "Frustration", while his time in Naples is recalled with the symbolic title of "Resurrection" (a word that also reflects the journey of the hero
described by Campbell).

However, in his first period in Spain, despite long absences due to injury and
illness, the player performed well overall, as attested by his scoring of 38 goals in
58 games. Instead, high expectations following Maradona's arrival in Barcelona
lead critics and commentators to consider this period as an unproductive one in
this career. As a point of comparison, for example, in Barcelona Johan Cruyff's
excelled in his first year winning the League in 1974 but was only able to win
one Cup in his remaining five seasons in the team. In contrast, in his two years at
the club, Maradona won a Cup and a minor tournament (League Cup), although
it is true that he was not able to carry the weight of Barcelona on his shoulders
and make it his own, as he did later at Naples. We must also consider the difficulty of articulating, in a powerful group like Barça a plebeian story of rebellion,
so relevant to Maradona because of "his subaltern voice, a boastful voice proud
of his subalternity" (Alabarces, 2021: 4). Faced with the north-south dialectic
that Maradona was able to adopt from the start at Naples, the main opposition to
power that he managed to embody in Spain (unable to conform to the Catalan
nationalist discourse) was to represent and defend the idea of football as an aesthetic spectacle against the violent tactics of Athletic Bilbao. The footballer even
confessed in the days before the dispute of the Cup final of 1984 that he would
have preferred that Real Madrid win the League before Athletic Club. Although
Maradona justified this by stating that he considered himself a "football lover"
(Sirvent, 1984), it was a statement in favour of his team's great rival, both in
sporting and political terms, which would be considered a sacrilege by *culé* fans.

The dream of the *pibe* produced monsters in Barcelona but it was also the necessary prelude to the great milestones of the legend built around Maradona. The
city of Naples and its team then offered themselves as an exile that, before long,
would become a new home. The Neapolitan Mediterranean, so wild and similar
to the shantytowns of Buenos Aires, contrasted from the start with the restraint

and sensible nature claimed by the Catalans. Maradona was clear about his choice and the version that best suited his character. This is how the journalist Roberto Saviano summed it up: "He leaves Barcelona shattered, hungry and restless and that is exactly what has made him a Neapolitan" (Saviano, 2020). That player eager to vindicate himself, the unique leader of a minor team that flourished under him, will be the hero who would ultimately reach a universal dimension previously unknown in sport. As Gillo Dorfles affirms, "myth, once rooted and unleashed, works blindly: it aggravates the strength of the singular individual, turns him into an unarmed puppet tied to the thread of collective potentiality" (1973: 179). The football hero began to conceive the horizon of his apotheosis, but it was the tests at Barcelona that led him to his greatest achievements.

## Descent and decadence: The second Spanish spell

Maradona's second period in Spain would have little in common with the previous one. If the seasons at Barça, despite its difficulties, can be aligned with his path of ascent, his signing for Sevilla FC belongs within the heroic archetype of the path of descent or *káthodos*. The idol was plunged into an irreversible setback after his positive result for cocaine consumption in March of 1991, following an anti-doping test at the end of a Naples match. After having reached the peak of his glory between 1986 and 1990, the beginning of the decade in the immediate aftermath of the World Cup in Italy seems to signal the impossible reconciliation of mythical with historical time; that is, the demise of the outstanding footballer contrasts with the myth already built. Excess takes over, showing the constant seduction of the abyss. As an example of a classical hero, Maradona also succumbs to the sin of pride: "The essence of wealth is the lack of restraint; it is the form that *hybris* [hubris] takes in the world" (Vernant, 1992: 96–97). The mythological model is now Icarus, and the provocation of the gods condemns the character to a bottomless fall that translates into a painful decline.

The ensuing 15-month ban distanced Maradona from the pitch and his status as a footballer. His return to Buenos Aires, far from providing him with the peace he might have expected from home, brought with it his arrest for "drug possession" and many other scandals that titillated the Argentinian tabloid press (Zanoni, 2006: 141–151). When the sanction ended in July of 1992, very few teams seemed genuinely interested in signing him. Doubts about his physical condition, together with Napoli's resistance to letting him leave the club for financial reasons, set the scene for a "high-risk" signing. His primary wish to return to Boca Juniors clashed with his considerable financial demands. As a result, a "great soap opera" (Maradona, 2000: 220) ensued. Finally, the player was able to disassociate himself from Naples thanks to the intervention of FIFA, an institution motivated by its desire to see the world's most popular footballer recover his form for the 1994 World Cup (Balagué, 2021). The option of signing for Sevilla, a mid-table team in Spain whose best result in La Liga at that time was sixth place, was presented to Maradona as the most viable option due to the presence at the club of Carlos Bilardo, his friend and coach with whom he achieved his best performances. Most of the $7.5 million deal was financed by Mediaset, Silvio Berlusconi's media group that had just launched its private television channel in Spain.

Ten years after signing for Barcelona, Maradona returned to a very different Spain. The socialist government of Felipe González, after ten years in power, sought broad international exposure intending to consolidate and validate democratic Spain's entry into modernity. In 1992, there was a significant convergence of events and anniversaries: the 500th Centenary of the conquest of America, the Olympic Games of Barcelona, and the Universal Exhibition of Seville. The country, despite its economic problems and high unemployment rates, focused on renovating its infrastructural networks, exemplified in its high-speed train network. Like the rest of Spain, Seville faced 1992 conflicted between feeling pride at being the protagonist of this significant year and having doubts as to whether this would have any positive impact on daily life. As the capital of Andalusia and socio-economic centre of southern Spain, Seville is a city of 700,000 inhabitants. With fame-hungry leaders, such as President Luis Cuervas and his deputy José María del Nido, Maradona's signing for Sevilla became a real "media bombshell". As a result, the number of club members soared from 26,000 to 38,000, while on the day of his presentation at the club alone more than 150 foreign journalists were accredited for attendance, as noted in *Maradona in Seville* (2020), an Informe Robinson documentary directed by the former footballer and commentator Michael Robinson.

In sporting terms, Sevilla's hopes were placed in the symbiosis between Bilardo and Maradona. In the Argentinian imagination, the dispute between its two most famous managers – Menotti and Bilardo – has been represented as a quarrel between Apollo and Dionysus in the purest Nietzschean style. Maradona was under the orders of both, although his relationship was more intense with Bilardo, an obsessive and brilliant coach whose result-focused philosophy is usually summarised in his sentence: "Nobody remembers second place".[8] Seville assembled a tough and combative team, with outstanding players such as Diego Simeone and the Croatian striker Davor Suker. However, few observers expected Sevilla to compete with in-form Barcelona (more powerful at this point than in 1982) or Real Madrid, just as few believed that Maradona, then 31 years old, would be able to revive his miraculous periods of play with Napoli or Argentina's national team. Even if he was not in optimum physical shape, it was Maradona's return to the football pitch after 15 months of absence that was significant for his fans.

Maradona's official debut, on October 4, 1992, at the San Mamés Stadium against old enemy Athletic Bilbao, brought one of those crucial confrontations so common in his narrative. With shouts of "Goiko, Goiko" in the stands (Ludden, 2021), Bilbao's right-back player Andoni Lakabeg tackled Diego's right ankle in a way that reminded many of that infamous incident of a decade before. Fortunately, this time there was no serious injury. Wearing the captain's armband

and with the support of his teammates, Maradona concentrated on his football during his first four months at the club. His best game came at the end of the year against Real Madrid. Aware of the impact of playing against one of the great teams, and motivated by the challenge, many believed that the star footballer of previous years had returned. "Marvellous Maradona" was the headline of Marca following Sevilla's 2-0 victory on December 19th. However, this proved to be one of the few flashes of brilliance he displayed in the Andalusian capital.[9] From that point onwards, the situation would worsen, both on and off the pitch: "As the season continued, Maradona's ego continued to grow, and that was to form a divide between him, the fans and the hierarchy at the club" (Tejwani, 2018).

The dual nature of the hero could not be disguised in a city like Seville. The urban, metropolitan nature of Buenos Aires or the protective networks of Naples could be useful to stay out of the public eye; Seville left the player exposed. Faced with the backlash of public opinion, Maradona tried to maintain his subaltern discourse; for example, he participated in a cavalcade of the Magi where he represented Balthasar, the black king: "I wanted to be Balthasar because at this time, more than ever, blacks are being discriminated against all over the world" (*ABC*, 1993: 54). In his daily life, the idol succumbed to excess. Both in documentaries and in reports after his death, footage shows him driving his Porsche to buy drugs in the neighbourhood of Las 3000 Viviendas, one of the poorest in the country. Following an initial stage in which the club attempted to hide his scandals, he soon became the target of media investigations, which revelled in the life of an addict in the city of Don Juan that involved fights, prostitution, and an arrest for "reckless driving" (Méndez, 1993). To gather evidence of these activities, Sevilla FC "hired an agency to investigate the footballer's private life, building up a dossier for future legal battles" (Balagué, 2021). Talent was no longer sufficient for the Argentinian to hide the demons of his private life. Harassed by the media and unable to perform at the expected level, Maradona would take refuge again in the image of the genius whom, supposedly, only his own people could understand: "I got tired of it: once again I had made an enormous effort to return and nobody understood me. Only my people could, only those who were near me" (Maradona, 2000: 236).

The good physical condition that the player had reached at the end of the year deteriorated. The first big confrontation with the club board came when both Maradona and Diego Simeone attended two matches of the Argentinian National Team without permission from the club. The press and the fans supported the club against Maradona, who was jeered at by his home crowd at a match in the Sánchez Pizjuán stadium as a result. Another memorable episode was the so-called Battle of Tenerife (Ludden, 2021), a meeting in which the tension resulting from the confrontation between two coaches of opposing schools (Bilardo and Valdano, who responded to the "Menottista" school) ended with the dramatic expulsion of Maradona following his protests against the referee. The disagreements with the board and the fans did not abate until his final match for Sevilla. All the negativity and tension of the season culminated then. It was

June of 1993 and the clash against Burgos was to leave the team in seventh place in La Liga. According to the version presented in his autobiography, Maradona treated his knee with an injection during the break to continue playing the game, but, to his surprise, Bilardo replaced him shortly after starting the second half. This provoked a fit of anger from the Argentinian star, who left the pitch amid outrage and insults to his coach. "My problems are with Bilardo and I will solve this with him as men solve it, if Bilardo is a man, although I don't think he is" (Ávila, 1993: 87), he later told the press. The dispute progressed from words to a physical altercation the day after the match at Maradona's house. Although a reconciliation occurred at a team dinner, this public dispute with his former mentor evidenced the decline of the footballer.

That was the last time that Maradona wore the shirt of a European team in an official match: "He knew irredeemably he was no longer fit to play for the elite" (Balagué, 2021). As had happened in the Cup final played with Barcelona, the last image of the footballer on a field in Spain was linked to a brawl. Two grotesque endings marked two clear breaking points with no turning back. His short season in Seville was the product of the media gamble of a team that, although it managed to make the investment profitable in economic terms, could not improve its sporting dynamics. The Maradona who returned to the pitch after the 15-month ban was unable to lead a winning project. He did not even have the option of articulating his discourse of rebellion in a city where Sevilla's greatest rival was Betis, a more modest team traditionally associated with the popular classes. Sid Lowe summarised this stage of Maradona: "He spent just one season there, making twenty-nine appearances, and it didn't end as they would have liked, redemption becoming perdition" (2020). In the documentary *Maradona in Seville* (2020), a symbolic image summarises his time in the Andalusian city: Among testimonies of his companions, the camera lingers on images of the ruins of the Universal Exhibition of 92, focusing on a junkyard where figures of Curro, the multi-coloured beaked bird that was the mascot of the event, have been discarded. This is an effective metaphor for that year in the life of Maradona: the flight of an Icarus condemned to fall due to his sin of pride.

The only option for the football hero then was his return to his homeland, thereby closing the circle of the monomyth: "The first problem of the returning hero is to accept as real, after an experience of the soul-satisfying vision of fulfilment, the passing joys and sorrows, banalities and noisy obscenities of life. Why re-enter such a world?" (Campbell, 2004: 202). Despite the doubts involved, only Argentina could offer itself as a real destination for Maradona, as no European team would risk repeating the experience of Seville. As the decade of the 1990s progressed, the sports hero was being relegated in favour of the discursive hero (Alabarces, 2018: 33) and his memorable phrases would end up replacing his extraordinary dribbles. However, following his departure from Europe, the World Cup in the United States 1994 was presented as Maradona's last hope for redemption. For this, he needed to play competitively, and an unlikely opportunity appeared in Newell's Old Boys, in the city of Rosario. In his first match for Newell's, on October 7, 1993, a six-year-old boy named Lionel Messi was present in the stands. Many years later, he would evoke that day with a red-and-black number ten shirt under his own.[10]

## Spain in Maradona's hero narrative

This chapter focused on essential episodes that, either for their drama or for their cathartic nature, fostered and gave meaning to the Maradonian legend. The Maradona of Barcelona is a player who arrived for the first time in Europe and who, despite failing to meet the immense expectations placed on him, would deliver great moments of football. At Barça, Maradona could not, or would not, be the hero that the team and the city demanded. His rebellious and subaltern discourse and his fractious behaviour outside the field would not conform, as we have pointed out, to the rigorous idiosyncrasy of the Catalans and their ruling class. It would take many years for Barcelona FC to find its perfect idol in the figure of Messi, a quiet genius who embraced the values of the city and the team – stability, ambition, perseverance – until his forced departure to Paris Saint-Germain in the summer of 2021. Barcelona needed Messi, as Naples needed Maradona.

Faced with these two difficult years but linked to his hero's path of ascent, Maradona's season in Sevilla would embody the irrepressible fall to which the idol was doomed after his first sanction for doping. As a perfect setting for his circular and archetypal journey, Spain was the country that welcomed the footballer after his departure from Argentina and, later, the country that returned him to Argentina. Barcelona and Seville were two rungs on the ladder of his journey. The dual nature of the hero, licentious and exalted, virtuous and cruel, was another of the constants of his media treatment in Spain. The versatility of the mythical story found a perfect form of expression in the most protean of footballers.

Looking back, Maradona's faces remain inexhaustible.

## Notes

1 Catalans use the word seny to refer to their ability to evaluate problems with rationality, wisdom, judgement and sanity, something they consider their main virtue. The Catalan philosopher José Ferrater Mora, in his book *Les formes de la vida catalana* (1944), defined seny as "an experience with meaning, a personal vision with circumspection and prudence".
2 See https://www.youtube.com/watch?v=9jn9SRm6gYc
3 See https://www.youtube.com/watch?v=m0fZWqttRJs
4 The testimony of his former friend Carlos Fren on the topic of Maradona's cocaine addiction can be read here: https://www.sport.es/es/noticias/futbol-internacional/carlos-fren-maradona-empezo-consumir-cocaina-1981-cuando-jugaba-boca-8231839
5 An official campaign against the consumption of drugs in young people recorded by Maradona in 1984 for the Generalitat, the regional government of Catalonia, has become viral with the passage of time. See https://www.youtube.com/watch?v=Z_DWo_HqXws. He would make a similar recording some years later in another

anti-drug campaign when in 1996 he joined the "Sol sin Droga" (Sun without drugs) initiative promoted by the government of Carlos Menem. At the same time, he confessed to his own addiction. See https://lalozanoni.com/2021/03/02/sol-sin-drogas
6  See https://www.youtube.com/watch?v=MAMJceWS0Lo
7  A summary of Maradona's last game for Barcelona can be found here, including the final fight: https://www.youtube.com/watch?v=AlCzdmYmpIY
8  Bilardo's period in Spanish football is remembered above all for an incident that took place in the Riazor stadium. When one of his masseuses attended an opponent who had received an involuntary kick from Maradona, Bilardo shouted: "What the fuck do I care about the other! On the contrary, step on him". The chant of "Pisalo, pisalo" (step on him) was immediately incorporated into the repertoire of the Spanish fans.
9  Despite some good matches, Maradona's poor performance in Sevilla is perhaps exemplified by one of his most remembered moments at the club: going to take a corner, he found a ball of aluminium foil on the pitch and began juggling with his feet. See https://www.youtube.com/watch?v=DYqD17p9Ex0
10  See https://www.youtube.com/watch?v=JVmMvDxCGO0

## References

*ABC*. 1993. "Maradona, Diego y Simeone, llevaron ayer la ilusión a los niños del hospital San Juan de Dios". January 7, p. 54.

Alabarces, Pablo. 2018. "De Maradona a Messi: viejos y nuevos argumentos sobre el héroe deportivo y la patria". *Imago. A Journal of the Social Imaginary*, 11.4: 26–43.

———. 2021. "Maradona: mito popular, símbolo peronista, voz plebeya". *Papeles del CEIC*, 1: 1–11.

Ávila, Juan Manuel. 1993. "Maradona, tras ser sustituido, puso en duda la hombría de Bilardo". *ABC*, June 14, p. 87.

Balagué, Guillem. 2021. *Maradona. The Boy. The Rebel. The God*. London: Weidenfeld & Nicolson. Ebook.

Benito, Joaquín. 1983. "La sanción es inconstitucional". *Marca*, September 30, p. 8.

Besa, Ramon. 1998. *Maradona, historia de un desencuentro*. Barcelona: Barcanova.

Burns, Jimmy. 2011. *Maradona. The Hand of God*. London: Bloomsbury. E-book.

Campbell, Joseph. 2004. *The Hero with a Thousand Faces*. Princeton: Princeton University Press.

Carreño, Fernando. 2018. "Goikoetxea y Maradona: la entrada que hace 35 años cambió el fútbol español". *Marca*. https://www.marca.com/futbol/primera-division/2018/09/24/5ba8c9b9268e3e9b518b4586.html [Accessed June 24, 2021].

Dorfles, Gillo. 1973. *Nuevos ritos, nuevos mitos*. Barcelona: Lumen.

Ferrater Mora, José. 1944. *Les formes de la vida catalana*. Santiago, Chile: Agrupació Patriòtica Catalana.

*Fútbol Club Maradona*. 2019. Dir. by Roberto Rodríguez. Spain.

Herrán, Alfonso. 2020. "Goikoetxea estalla tras los ataques por su lesión a Maradona". *As*. https://as.com/futbol/2020/11/28/internacional/1606598635_246245.html [Accessed June 22, 2021].

*Informe Robinson: Maradona en Sevilla*. 2020. Produced by Movistarplus.

Kerényi, Karl. 2009. *Los héroes griegos*. Girona: Atalanta.

Kirk, Geoffrey Stephen. 2002. *La naturaleza de los mitos griegos*. Barcelona: Paidós.

Lowe, Sid. 2020. "Maradona's Time at Sevilla was Short, but Encapsulated his Talent, Generosity and Inescapable Demons". *ESPN*. https://www.espn.com/soccer/sevilla-fc/story/4247152/maradonas-time-at-sevilla-was-shortbut-encapsulated-his-talent-generosity-and-inescapable-demons [Accessed June 30, 2021].

Ludden, John. 2014. *Maradona in Barcelona*. South Carolina: Author edition.
_____. 2021. *Diego Maradona's Lost Season at Sevilla*. South Carolina: Author edition.
Maradona, Diego Armando. 2000. *Yo soy el Diego*. Buenos Aires: Planeta.
Méndez, Juan. 1993. "Maradona, citado ante un juez de Sevilla por conducción temeraria". *El País*. https://elpais.com/diario/1993/05/19/deportes/737762403_850215. html [Accessed May 18, 2021].
*Mundo Deportivo*. 1982. "Estrellas opacas". July 4, p. 13.
_____. 1983. "Estoy muy orgulloso de mis jugadores". September 25, p. 8.
_____. 1984. "Los directivos del Barcelona han pecado de soberbios". July 7, p. 6.
Rank, Otto. 1961. *El mito del nacimiento del héroe*. Buenos Aires: Paidós.
Saviano, Roberto. 2020. "Maradona siempre estaba allí, nunca traicionaba". *El País*. https:// elpais.com/deportes/2020-11-28/diego-siempre-estaba-alli-nunca-traicionaba. html [Accessed August 24, 2021].
Sebreli, Juan José. 2008. *Comediantes y mártires. Ensayo contra los mitos*. Barcelona: Debate.
Sharp, Will. 2017. "Andoni Goikoetxea: The Butcher of Bilbao". *These Football Times*. https://thesefootballtimes.co/2017/12/14/andoni-goikoetxea-the-butcher-of-bilbao/ [Accessed June 24, 2021].
Sirvent, José María. 1984. "Clemente y Maradona se insultan ante la final de la Copa del Rey". *El País*. https://elpais.com/diario/1984/05/01/deportes/452210413_850215. html [Accessed April 18, 2021].
Tejwani, Karan. 2018. "Diego Maradona: The Sevilla Diaries". *These Football Times*. https://thesefootballtimes.co/2018/12/04/diego-maradona-the-disastrous-sevilla-diaries/ [Accessed June 24, 2021].
Vernant, Jean-Pierre. 1992. *Los orígenes del pensamiento griego*. Barcelona: Paidós.
Zanón, Carlos. 2020. "Maradona en Barcelona: demasiado roto, demasiado pronto". *La Vanguardia*. https://www.lavanguardia.com/deportes/fcbarcelona/20201129/ 49774231581/diego-armando-maradona-fc-barcelona.html [Accessed June 29, 2021].
Zanoni, Leandro. 2006. *Vivir en los medios. Maradona off the record*. Buenos Aires: Marea.

# 3

# MARADONA AND ITALY

## The Rise and Fall of the Man on His Own

*Pippo Russo*

*Translated by Dolores Gadler*

### A methodological individualist: The construction of the sports champion

Diego Armando Maradona never left Naples and never left Italy. Italian culture has never ceased to deal with this presence, which morphed into a myth when Maradona was alive, and has become even more legendary since his passing, with the layers of time and a polyphonic narrative produced through many channels of cultural communication. Such a narrative displays an extraordinary cultural transversalism found in the voices of the people and of the elite and in traditional and new media, converging into an open narrative fabric. Maradona as an Italian cultural object can be perceived as a watermark when reviewing his representations in Italian culture and media. From daily newspapers to magazines, from old to new television programming, from art to digital technologies and carriers of a new language that has allowed for a deconstruction and redefinition of the sport myth, Maradona continues to be a remarkable object of attention.

Maradona's Italian years were crucial for affirming both his greatness and his fall from grace and were also indicative of profound social and cultural changes in Italian society. The encounter between player and country changed both, marking their zenith and decadence during the 1980s and 1990s. This period can be traced through the narrative that the media created and continue to create about Maradona. The media ecosystem at that time was still traditional – printed press, over-the-air TV, radio, and the traditional forms of cultural representation such as cinema, theatre, book publishing, figurative arts, and comics. This was an era that had not yet seen the transition to a fully integrated and interconnected communication. Nowadays, Maradona's narrative by the new media suppresses this temporal rift and the need to draw on languages and repertoires that are not their own. But this does not in any way

DOI: 10.4324/9781003196587-5

compromise the possibility that the figure of arguably the greatest footballer of all times can be deconstructed and reconstructed also through novel techniques and languages.

This chapter aims to review the representations of Maradona's playing career in Italian media up to 1990, understanding the player to be of the greatest examples of the individualist footballer – a figure defined as the Man on His Own. Scholarly criticism on the representation of the sports champion is abundant, from the relationship between the champion's biography and their time (Andrews and Jackson 2001; Rojek 2006; Russo 2017) to the celebrity dimension that speaks to his/her popularity (Nalapat and Parker 2005; Smart 2005; Cashmore 2006), to the morality constraints of a famous athlete's public profile (Lines 2010; Melin 2014) to the construction of the sports myth (Bifulco and Tirino 2018; Parry 2020). Each of these contributions provides a framework of knowledge, interpretation, and representation when analysing both the relationship between the sports champion and his/her era and the different personal and historical stratifications in which this relationship is inscribed.

By *personal stratification*, I mean the multidimensionality that must be considered when analysing individuals with very high cultural, communicative, and emotional impact on the sociocultural systems to which they belong. This multidimensionality can be described as a stratification system that exists between the fully public dimension that sees the sports champion being on stage with almost uninterrupted continuity and a private dimension known only to people of his/her most immediate social circle. By *historical stratification*, I refer to the processes of construction and deconstruction of the public image of the sports champion, modulated according to the different phases of his/her personal and professional life, to the changing social and historical context, to continuous retrospective judgements about behaviours, and finally to the historicisation triggered around the public figure after a crucial event (most importantly death, but also key events in life that had a significant impact on public opinion).

I argue here that to analyse Maradona in an Italian context we must consider an individualistic dimension. The Argentinian football player became a fundamental figure, culturally and sociologically, for understanding the times in which he lived in Italy because of his being completely individualistic, both in his way of building a relationship with the external world and in the way in which the external world defined his public profile. In this case, the concept of individualism must be stripped of the negative connotations of selfishness and egocentrism usually associated with the term. Instead, "individualism" here refers, on the one hand, to the ethical inclination to assume individual responsibility for oneself and for the social group that one considers representing, and, on the other hand, to methodological individualism that is especially appropriate when analysing the public representations of Maradona as a cultural object.

Maradona's individualism defines his public figure, but it stands out equally if it is compared to one element of *historical stratification*: the great stylistic and sociocultural change that affected Italian football between the end of the 1980s and the beginning of the 1990s – the contrast between man-to-man *vs.* zonal marking. The implications this change had in terms of sociopolitical culture would only be understood in the years to come. During those years, Maradona is the ultimate representative on the field of a football philosophy that focuses on the individual and shows how imperfect football itself can be as a team game.

## Structure and agency: Arrival and great expectations

In the summer of 1984, Italian football was enjoying a dominant position globally. The Italian national team led by Enzo Bearzot had unexpectedly won the 1982 World Cup in Spain and that victory had marked a historical and cultural turning point in the country. Italy had emerged from the period known as the "Years of Lead" (*anni di piombo*), which had permeated the entire 1970s and was characterised by a wave of both far-left and far-right incidents of political terrorism. That tense atmosphere suddenly vanished and winning the World Cup became a symbol of changing times. For Italy, the closure of the Years of Lead meant the end of a long period of crisis and the start of a second economic boom, after the one that had significantly modernised the country between the late 1950s and first half of the 1960s.

As Maradona was signed by SSC Napoli in 1984, Italian football had only been open to foreign players for four years. Following the 1966 World Cup in England, when the Italian national team was eliminated in the first round by North Korea, Italian football closed itself to the world and banned foreign players. The first, cautious opening of this sport policy took place in the summer of 1980 when only teams in the first division, the Serie A, were allowed to employ a single player of a foreign nationality. This quota was raised in the summer of 1982 to two foreign players per team. Despite these restrictions, when Maradona arrived, the Serie A was already hosting the best players in the world. For example, in 1983, Udinese signed Brazilian footballer Arthur Antunes Coimbra, better known as Zico, who was considered the best player of the world at that moment. The fact that a small club like Udinese could hire a footballer of Zico's calibre demonstrated the economic power of Italian football in that historical period. In the summer of 1982, a year before Zico's arrival, Juventus had procured Michel Platini, also in the shortlist for greatest footballer in activity. Therefore, when Maradona was signed, this meant the arrival of another world-class footballer in Serie A for the third consecutive summer.

In 1982, Maradona had no doubt the potential to become one of the top footballers but he had yet to live up to the high expectations he had raised among fans and pundits. He had disappointed as part of the Argentinian national team eliminated in the second round of the 1982 World Cup. Following that experience, his two seasons in the ranks of Barcelona were also considered underwhelming, albeit marred by illness (a case of hepatitis) and the serious injury he sustained in a game against Athletic Bilbao. In a reckless tackle, defender Andoni Goikoetxea broke Maradona's left ankle; he was not able to play for over three months. This led Michel Platini to denounce the violence of the Spanish league, and, through statements to the Italian press, he invited Maradona to come and play in Serie A, a league that was considered more skilful and therefore more protective towards talented footballers.[1]

The *historical stratification* perspective introduced above is essential here to understand this point. In May of 1984, the best players in world considered the Italian league as the most favourable for the game, given not only the quality of the footballers but also the protection offered to their well-being and skills. Conversely, the Spanish league was labelled as particularly violent and therefore scarcely protective of talent. Almost 40 years later, this perspective seems to have been inverted: those who pay attention to football in both countries know how heated this controversy became, fuelled above all by the Spanish media (*El País* 2018; *Marca* 2020). The new view posits the Italian style of play as overly defensive, meagre, and anti-spectacular – antithesis to the Spanish style at that time (Dalai 2013). The controversy was at its peak in April 2003, when on the eve of the Champions League semi-final between the Internazionale and AC Milan clubs the Spanish press invited readers to go to the cinema instead of watching a match on TV that foreshadowed a mediocre spectacle (Russo 2016). The Spanish public opinion about Italian football has not significantly changed since.

In terms of methodological individualism, the figure of the champion can be used to interpret these changes. Eight years later, in 1992, Maradona reversed the journey that had brought him to Naples and returned to Spain to play for Sevilla. Then, like in 1984, the transfer offered a sense of liberation, both for the player and to SSC Napoli, given that their relationship had deteriorated. In terms of *historical stratification*, the slow changes that would lead to the current order in Italian society began at this time. In fact, the decline of Maradona coincided with the slow descent of Italian football, gradually eclipsed by the English Premier League, which has become the richest and most coveted league by footballers in the second decade of the 21st century. In addition, at the time of the writing of this chapter, Spain is a more sought-after destination than Italy for top footballers.

When Maradona landed in Naples on July 5, 1984, he was the object of a double and emphatic welcome. On the one hand, there were the Neapolitan people, who for decades had been hoping to win the *scudetto* (a badge awarded to the team that wins the Italian championship) for the first time ever, and now saw in Maradona a means to achieve that desired end. On the other hand, there was the field of Italian football, which, after Zico and Platini, saw the coming of a third footballer also legitimately aspiring to the title of greatest player in the world. This was yet another confirmation of world leadership for Italian football. Maradona produced a "feel-good effect" for the country and for its national sport, a feeling usually reserved for major sporting events, such as winning the World Cup or hosting a large international event (Kavetzos and Szymanski 2010; Mutz 2019). In this case, however, the "feel-good effect" can be attributed to the fact that Maradona's arrival was interpreted as the ultimate confirmation of the competitive power of Italian football of that time.

Football is a powerful component of Italian identity, culture, and economy. It is an essential component of Italianness. The media attention given to the long process that would bring Maradona to play in Italy is indicative of this: the beginning of a negotiation that lasted about two months; Barcelona's doubts about selling Maradona; the multiple meetings and discussions, and finally the happy outcome that brought him to Naples for a figure just under 8 million US dollars, a low amount in today's transfer market but a record sum at the time. The newspaper headlines chronicling the deal reflect the emotions at stake during the process. The first headlines describe the disrupted negotiations between May and June and reported the player's thoughts and, at a certain moment, his clear wishes to leave Spain for Italy. The tension is effectively represented in a front-page headline in *Corriere dello Sport-Stadio* on June 8, 1984: "Maradona Blurts Out: This Wait is Killing Me".[2]

The way in which the Italian press described the eventual outcome – Maradona becoming a Napoli player – points to two main ideas that help us understand the phenomenon in Italy. The first has to do with methodological individualism. Maradona was expected and perceived as a messiah and in turn took on this role of charismatic leader because he needed to state his greatness, announced many times but still not fully accomplished through the obtention of a league championship. The second point concerns the historical and cultural context of Italian football and society, a context that was undergoing a period of growth and expansion, and that was crucial to enable the figure of Maradona to become the cultural object we now know. Maradona is decisive to help develop Italian hegemony in world football and indirectly stimulates the positive image of Italy as a key country in the international context. Thus, a resulting mechanism of structure and agency acts effectively on these changes in Italian society and culture. The process is a complex one: the interaction between the context in which an individual social actor finds himself and is moved to action, and the act itself, which contributes to change the context in which the actor is located, disrupting in turn a stable situation to create a new order. Structure is given by Italian hegemony in world football at the time (not only due to the 1982 World Cup victory but also to the international success of Italian clubs in European championships). It is within this structure that Maradona finds himself and is called to demonstrate his status as the world's top footballer. In this, case structure, in relation to agency, provides the context that legitimates a specific social role – the footballing star wanting to be the best – as relevant. At the same time, Maradona's actions in Italian football confirm his ambitions and have an effect not only on him as an individual but also on the whole structure of Italian football. This change will be confirmed by dominant position of Italian clubs in world football, which will reinforce even further through Maradona's performances. This interaction between structure and agency can be traced by focusing on the material produced by the Italian media, both during the period in which Maradona lived in Italy and after the end of his career.

## The loneliness of the football player: Maradona as a Man on His Own

On July 5, 1984, Maradona was greeted by 80,000 people during his presentation at the San Paolo stadium in Naples, today renamed Diego Armando Maradona, while the Italian press reported exultantly on the event. Six years later, on July 8, 1990, Maradona was hissing angrily *hijos de puta* (sons of bitches) at the audience in the Olympic Stadium in Rome who was booing the Argentinian national anthem as it was played before kick-off in the World Cup Final against West Germany. Maradona's image, standing in line next to his fellow Argentinian national team players, travelled the world and symbolises the closure of an era. I define this era as that of the Man on His Own, the trope that Maradona had embodied during all his years in Italy, and which came to an end following the 1990 World Cup. In between his arrival and departure from Italian football, there is the story of Maradona the football player: even while his status as myth reached a global dimension (Bifulco and Dini 2014), his Italianism was clear.

Although Argentinian, his Italianness can be explained by considering what was, for a prolonged period, the dominant Italian footballing culture before the arrival of zonal marking. The founding idea of this culture was that matches would be resolved, and won, by players who had individual skills, and not necessarily by collective association. As a main competing strategy, teams should rely on individual inventive and genius, on the individual temperament of the single football player – *i.e.*, the Man on His Own. The individual skills of each player on the pitch would create the necessary collective action to play and win. Before zonal marking, the attention placed on the more or less scientific organisation of a football squad was very low. All of this was perfectly aligned with Maradona's personality and talents, given that he was a great individualist and improviser. He would be the single player to be trusted with the destiny of the squad, allowing him to play exclusively at his own will and pace. Ultimately, the zonal strategy would produce a cultural change, inscribed within Italy's evolution as a country, a socio-economic process that stops right on the night of the 1990 World Cup Final. Thereafter, the downfall begins (Russo 2006).

Maradona's farewell from Naples allows for the definitive historicisation of his image, a process that started as soon as the negotiation that brought him to city was finally closed. And at that point, it is as if the pieces of a puzzle were put together: a society (the Neapolitan one) finds a charismatic leader who will develop his leadership in the following years, and a socio-historical context – Italy in the mid-80s – reaches the peak of a period of economic, political, and cultural growth that appears to have no limits.

Not knowing the exact day of Maradona's arrival, the front page of the *Corriere dello Sport-Stadio* of July 2, 1984, tried to imagine what means would be used to transport the footballer. The front page of the newspaper assumed that he would land in a helicopter, while Napoli fans hoped that he would make the journey to the stadium aboard an open-air car, like a major political or religious figure.[3] The headlines all insisted on images of liberation and conquest. The local press stressed the idea "Maradona Is (Finally) Ours",[4] while the national press reported the arrival as "Naples, Maradona Is Yours".[5] The news went beyond sports reporting and spilled out to the general information sections. In terms of *historical stratification*, the language used by the national media provides useful insight for analysis from a contemporary perspective.

Among the audio-visual material found on the Internet, there is a fragment of the Tg2, the news bulletin of the Italian state television broadcaster network – RAI – from the day following the announcement of Maradona's transfer to Napoli, July 1, 1984. It shows the Neapolitan fans celebrating the news as if the club had won a championship or an international cup. That enthusiasm was the sign of a city that had finally found its idol and felt it was on the verge of making the final leap to glory and greatness. That irrepressible enthusiasm was represented in the RAI Tg2 report as a typical expression of the Neapolitan character, and in general of southern Italy. In the introduction to the broadcast, the speaker in the studio explains that "the city celebrated with picturesque manifestations typical of Southern people".[6] At that moment, the words did not draw any attention or created the slightest controversy but today, after 30 years of sociological scholarship (Bourdieu and Wacquant 1992; Melucci 1998; Goldthorpe 2004; Santoro 2007, 2014) and the spirit of political correctness, such a passage, loaded with stereotypes, would be hardly tolerated. This is also the case in present-day comments of some YouTube viewers, as can be seen in the following examples (set in italics):

> Nonno del Brucaliffo: *"the city celebrated with picturesque manifestations typical of Southern people" How racist these words are!!! But maybe it was because it was chapping his ass!!! Diego come back, this house is waiting for you!!!* (referencing the famous Neapolitan song "Torna")
>
> rosaria romano: *Always racists …. But Maradona made you suffer*
>
> Fabio Maiorano: *An ANTI-SOUTHERN service … and we are on RAI … public television*
>
> Marco D.: *picturesque manifestations typical of Southern people … what the fuck is this broadcast?*

These and many other similar reactions certainly highlight the changed sensitivity towards the North–South dichotomy in Italy. This divide is not only based on the economic gap between the wealthy Northern regions and the poorer Southern regions but also progressively reveals cultural differences and feeds a debate that is not always consistent. But the reaction of the Internet users cited above shows a cultural change that also reflects a political change – the rise of a strong Northern party, the North League, which took its first steps precisely during those years. This fact signals how much the North-South gap has become the subject of sociocultural tensions in public opinion. The figure of Maradona would often play out an important role within these tensions.

In Italy, football was (and continues to be) a faithful reflection of this territorial imbalance. When Maradona arrived in Naples, no team south of Rome (which in the Italian geo-political division is part of Central Italy) had ever won the *scudetto*. And after Napoli won its two league titles during Maradona's era, no other Southern team has won (or came close to winning) the Serie A tournament again. Thus, Naples dominated the forefront of a Southern region that was always considered "lacking", both in football and in other areas of Italian life (Daniele e Malanima 2011; Barbagallo 2013; Felice 2016).

As long as the dyad Maradona-Napoli did not clash with the idea of "Italian football as a whole", the pattern that saw Maradona as a property of the city of Naples and its football, and secondarily of Italian football, worked. Provided that such pattern did not reveal its contradictions, it enhanced the figure of Maradona and the idea of the Man on His Own, both of which challenged football conceived as a team sport. Methodological individualism consolidated at the same time as the player would lead his club to crucial football victories. On the one hand, SSC Napoli was growing in importance under its charismatic leader and was about to win the first championship in its history. On the other hand, in the 1986 World Cup in Mexico, Maradona's unique performance secured the Argentinian victory.

In 1986, Maradona's fame was growing significantly after having played two seasons in Serie A, which, in addition to being the most competitive football league in the world, was also the most challenging and demanding in terms of tactical sophistication. He adapted to such a demanding game almost immediately and began to build his greatness. In Italy, he proved to live up to the expectations of those who immediately saw him as the greatest footballer in the world. He knew how to impose himself in a team like Napoli that at that time included many top players such as Alemao, Bruno Giordano, and Salvatore Bagni. He did the same over an Argentinian national team made up of good but not particularly outstanding players.

In this sense, this World Cup achievement is singular in the history of football and symbolises the triumph of the Man on His Own trope. Among team sports, football is the one in which individual skill has a higher possibility of expression. No player can win a football game on his own, but under certain conditions, an outstanding player can drag an ordinary team to the top of the world. This is what happened with the 1986 Argentinian team led by Carlos Salvador Bilardo, which was turned into a legend by Maradona. If ever there was an exploit in football history that can be described as the victory of a single individual, it is the cup won by Argentina that year. It is no coincidence that the official FIFA film about the tournament bears an unequivocal title: *Hero*.[7]

The headlines of the Italian newspapers during the 1986 Mexico World Cup echoed the feelings in Italy, whose national team had been eliminated in the round of 16 by a French side led by another "Italian" champion, Michel Platini. The Italian press followed Maradona as if he, by virtue of his unique individuality that began to be consolidated in Italy, could fill in the void left by the elimination of the national team. The newspaper headlines emphasised Maradona's individualistic dimension in an increasing and uninterrupted glorification. It had already been clear at the time of the draws for the final rounds in November 1985, when Italy and Argentina were placed in the same opening group. The following day the *Gazzetta dello Sport* published on the front page: "Italy-Maradona!"[8]

The hyper-individualist representation of Maradona by the Italian media would characterise the footballer's progression in the tournament. After Argentina's victory against England in the quarter-finals, it was the only Latin American team left among three other European semi-finalists (Belgium, France, and West Germany). The headline of the *Corriere dello Sport-Stadio* illustrated the mood in Italy: "Only Maradona Against Europe".[9] The front page of the *Gazzetta dello Sport* follows this trend. After the 2-0 Argentinian victory in the semi-final against Belgium, where Maradona scored two goals, the title read: "Diegoooal".[10] On the evening before the final against West Germany, the words used were: "Maradona Puts the World on His Shoulders".[11] And the next day, to celebrate the victory of the Argentinian national team, the chosen formula was: "Maradona is King of the World".[12]

## A Man on His Own (against an entire country)

The 1986 Mexico World Cup granted Maradona the status of the greatest footballer in the world and anticipated Napoli's first championship, sealed the following spring for the 1986–1987 season. Considering, as mentioned, the club's history, location, and the fact that it had never obtained a *scudetto*, such a victory can be compared to winning the World Cup. A long television programme, conducted by the famous journalist Gianni Minà (Maradona's long-time friend), illustrated the significance of Napoli's success.[13] For Maradona, the 1986–1987 championship was another milestone that added to a series of achievements that would include the 1988–1989 UEFA Cup and the second *scudetto* in 1989–1990. In addition, there were two second places in the Italian Serie A, placing Napoli as one of the dominant clubs in Italian football.

At the same time, both Maradona and the context in which he was operating changed, transforming the relationship between structure and agency. Why? We can identify three main reasons. First, securing a position in the top ranks of the Serie A, Napoli was not an outsider any longer, so it also began to generate dislikes, as it always happens to those who win. Second, shadows began to be cast on Maradona. His disorderly private life and the lack of discipline expected of a top athlete produced a sense of bafflement among the fans, the press, and his colleagues. Finally, there was the other element that, together with Maradona, culturally changed Italian football: the arrival of media mogul Silvio Berlusconi and the establishment of AC Milan led by Arrigo Sacchi.

The acquisition of Milan by Berlusconi took place during the 1985–1986 football season. The 1986–1987 was the first complete football season of Milan under his ownership, and Napoli won its first Championship. The 1987–1988 season was the first in which the team, under Sacchi, snatched the Italian championship from Napoli. The rivalry that ensued between Milan and Naples was not only about football: but it also confronted two opposing ways of being. Milan represented a cultural and organisational innovation in Italian football. Under Berlusconi, the team became linked to a private TV empire run by a person who, shortly afterwards, was going to pursue a political career as well. Besides this new structural condition, in footballing terms, the squad became the standard bearer of zonal football, organised according to Taylorism: its principles were, on the one hand, a sharp division of labour inside the pitch and, on the other, the primacy of the collective over the individual. Conversely, Napoli was a football team that wanted to represent a specific group of fans and the city in which they lived, happy to group together around its charismatic leader who would lead it inside the field. It played a style of football founded on the basis of man-marking – that is to say, on individual responsibility expressed as the clash of two players from opposite sides (usually it would be the defender to chase up a forward up and down the pitch).[14]

The fact that this new opposition would spill over to other sectors of Italian society became evident in the first months of 1994, when Berlusconi entered politics and started using football language, beginning with the metaphor "to enter the field" (Dal Lago 1994; Porro and Russo 2000). Retrospectively, it can be said that Milan was not only a manifesto of Berlusconian football but also an introduction to Berlusconian politics. It was the example of the political party/business company that revolves around an absolute leader and promises an overhaul, starting from the cultural models that guide the behaviour of a nation. Thanks to his private television broadcasting empire, Berlusconi's effect on the hitherto stable world of Italian culture was undoubtedly novel. In fact, he changed the way of thinking of Italians. It did so first in the cultural industry sector, and later in the world of football, which in symbolic terms is one of the strongest fields in the Italian cultural system (Foot 2006).

The impact of these private TV networks, compared to the RAI channels, marked a turning point in media culture. Before the TV channels belonging to Fininvest (the commercial name of Berlusconi's holding group) entered the media market, television production was monopolised by RAI, associating the role of a public TV company with mass education. RAI's content was characterised by an institutional tone, and its programmes carefully avoided any transgression of customs. Berlusconi's stations disseminated a very different cultural message, focusing on unrestrained hedonism, materialism, consumerism, and modernisation. The artistic quality of the programmes may be questioned, but its effects cannot be denied: it was a sharp cultural innovation in the mediasphere.

The same process took place in football. For example, Berlusconi strongly lobbied for the caps on foreign players to be relaxed. The rationale for this measure was that football must be a spectacle as well as a sport — a spectacle, moreover, that can be turned into a television product to be further commercialised. Linked to this, money could be translated into success in the pitch.

It could be argued here that, like Maradona, Berlusconi was also a highly individualistic and charismatic figure. This may be the case, but it is important to underline that these men used their qualities very differently. Maradona, as the Man on His Own, fought for his team and his people (fans, fellows, Argentinians or Neapolitans), with the aim of giving them joy and sporting glories, with no further agendas. Berlusconi, on the other hand, was a leader whose aim was to accumulate political and financial power for himself, inspired by the model of the multinational business company which he successfully implemented both in football and in politics. He saw himself as a CEO in all these three fields. This *modus operandi* is perfectly described in the film *Il Caimano* (The Cayman) (2006), directed by Nanni Moretti. In the film, Moretti, whose political and intellectual positions are different from Berlusconi's, draws attention to Milan's owner when he stages himself as both CEO and leader in the scene that emulates his famous helicopter arrival at the Milan Arena, on the occasion of the 1986 pre-season summer training camp. I am convinced that Berlusconian politics were already being planned parallel to the construction of his football project, which was undertaken as a stepping stone for a political career.

As the 1980s were ending, the rivalry between Milan and Napoli became more intense, with a peak of tension reached towards the final stages of the 1989–1990 tournament. The two teams were running head-to-head, but with three games remaining a violent episode changed the equation. During the Atalanta-Napoli match, which ended 0-0, a coin thrown from the stands hit Napoli footballer Alemao in the head and the Brazilian midfielder had to be substituted. According to the rules of the time, which would be revised after this incident, the team on the receiving end of the violent act would be awarded a 2-0 victory, regardless of what had happened on the pitch. The new result changed the balance of the championship and created uneasiness in the Milanese camp. Alemao was accused of having put up a scene and exaggerated the injury. Moreover, two days before the final game, Milan unexpectedly lost in Verona 2-1 in a game that was mired by controversial refereeing decisions. Although Napoli would have probably won the title anyway, these two episodes also contributed to the club's triumph that season.

The contrast between Napoli and Milan brought about an interesting tactical development. Arrigo Sacchi was the standard bearer of a football approach that marked the definite establishment of zonal marking as opposed to the man-to-man marking, even though the latter tactics, at the time, more fully embodied the Italian tradition. Despite having several top players in his team such as Marco Van Basten, Ruud Guulit, and Roberto Donadoni, Sacchi definitively dropped the role of the Man on His Own from his tactics. Under this new approach to the game, Napoli was lined up on the opposite side of Milan in terms of style. If Milan was built around a fully collective spirit, Napoli had thrived through the role of an individual hero embodied in Maradona. At the end of the decade, however, Maradona's heroic status would begin to fall.

The point of no return was marked by the 1990 World Cup in Italy. In the Italian imaginary, this event was going to end with a national victory on home ground which would symbolise the greatness of the Italian nation. Instead, the team's defeat against, of all teams, Maradona's Argentina in the semi-finals signalled the country's decline, which would hit football more slowly than other cultural or economic sectors. Once again, Maradona, in the Man on His Own version, was at the centre of the World Cup and of the Argentina-Italy match. But this time, for many Italian football fans, Maradona had ceased to be "one of us", as it had been four years earlier in Mexico, to become "the enemy within". The route leading to that semi-final played in Naples was set up by the poor performance of Argentina in the group stage of the tournament, adding a strong dimension of drama and *pathos* – a drama, once again, represented by the media as the challenge of one against all.

The mood in the newspaper headlines followed the pattern used four years earlier. When the Italian national team reached the semi-final after beating Ireland, the front page of the *Gazzetta dello Sport* retrieved the formula used five years earlier, stating: "Now Italy-Maradona".[15] And the day of the semi-final the same newspaper carried the headline "Blue Fever for Maradona"[16] – a reference to the colour of the Italian players' kit. When these headlines were published, the debate over the appeal made by Maradona "to his people" had already been unleashed. The debate surrounding the North-South gap had in those months made a comeback thanks not only to the mentioned rivalry between Milan and Napoli in the sprint to the championship that had ended before the World Cup, but also to the first electoral successes of the North League. Maradona had declared: "You cannot ask Neapolitans to be Italians once a year and despise them for the rest of the time" (*La Repubblica* 2021). On the evening of the semi-final, Napoli fans largely supported their squad leader and not the Italian national team, opening the final crack in the relationship between Maradona and Italy. This divide was unpleasantly expressed by the crowd at Olimpico Stadium in Rome on the day of the match, when they heavily booed the Argentinian national anthem played before kick-off. This sort of behaviour was unprecedented in an international match.

In March of 1991, Maradona would be banned from playing football for 15 months after testing positive for cocaine following a Napoli-Bari match. The team finished that season in the seventh position, and Maradona would never play for Napoli again.

## Post-Maradona?

Maradona's Italianness continues to appear in many narratives about his path as a football idol. It is of interest to reflect on the post-Maradona period in Italy, keeping in sight those decisive aspects that help us understand the cultural significance of Maradona's Italian years: the fate of man-marking in Italy's football, the destinies of SSC Napoli after Maradona's departure, and the relationship between the footballer and Italy, which had ended acrimoniously in 1991.

After 1991, man-marking and individualism in Italian football were abandoned for good. In that historical phase, zonal football was considered to be more rational from an organisational point of view, as well as more spectacular. But other factors played a role in this: an extraordinary propaganda operation in favour of this system mounted by Berlusconi's media conglomerate (which underlined Berlusconi's image as an innovator and an efficient leader), also reproduced by independent and national media. At the time, the media described man-marking football in a mostly stereotyped way, as old, conservative, and essentially harmful. Little by little, zonal football has fully displaced individual football, which is now used sparsely by some managers in some isolated matches only. According to some experts, this is damaging Italian football because it prevents young players from learning the art of marking. One of these specialists is none other than Claudio Gentile, who became famous for his marking of Maradona during the Italy-Argentina match in the 1982 World Cup (*Il Giornale* 2020). Opinions such as this one raise alarms for the purported loss of the cultural and technical specificity of Italian football.

After Maradona's departure, Napoli underwent a period of dizzying decline. In 1998 and then in 2000, the team was relegated to Italian Serie B, and in 2004, the club went bankrupt. Aurelio De Laurentiis, a renowned film producer, took over the club and this enabled the team to restart from Serie C and return to Serie A in 2007. Progressively, Napoli has climbed to the top of Italian football and managed to qualify for European competitions as well, although it has never been able to return to the full splendour of the days when Maradona was its captain. The collective feeling of nostalgia for the Argentinian, which began to emerge almost immediately after his farewell in 1992, has grown continuously, feeding the myth even among the generations born after his achievements. Following his death, Napoli's stadium, formerly San Paolo, was renamed Diego Armando Maradona.

Italian football has also experienced a decline, more gradual than Napoli's but longer in its duration. Even though the Italian national team won the 2006 Germany World Cup, Italian clubs have clearly lost competitiveness at international level and Serie A now lags in international wealth and prestige compared to the English Premier League, the Spanish La Liga, and the German Bundesliga. Not only the top world footballers seek other national leagues as their preferred destination (unlike in the 1980s), but also many Italian players now look to a career abroad. The failure of the Italian national team to qualify for the 2018 World Cup in Russia (the first time this had happened in 60 years) marked the lowest point of decline from which Italian football began to recover with the victory at 2020 European Championships (played in 2021, after the tournament was suspended due to the Covid-19 pandemic).

Despite all these statistics, the feelings of greatness have not been dispelled, and they lead to a painful comparison for football fans, when they look at a golden past and see that those memories correspond with the time in which Serie A hosted Maradona, the greatest footballer of all time.

## Notes

1  The statements issued by Michel Platini were reported in the *La Repubblica* newspaper on May 11, 1984. An image and text can be found on the web page https://sport. sky.it/calcio/approfondimenti/maradona-storie-maranihttps://sport.sky.it/calcio/ approfondimenti/maradona-storie-marani (*Sky Sport Italia*, 2019).

2  The newspaper fragment is reproduced in https://sport.sky.it/calcio/approfondimenti/ maradona-storie-marani (*Sky Sport Italia* 2019). It is worth noting that another part of the title also refers to Barcelona's wishes not to accept the offer from Napoli.

3  https://lastoriadelnapoli.wordpress.com/1984/06/30/diego-maradona/#jp-carousel-6793 (*The History of Naples and Its City*, n/d).

4  https://www.calcissimo.com/amarcord/30-giugno-1984-maradona-e-del-napoli-ripercorriamo-la-trattativa-che-porto-il-pibe-in-azzurro-49452 (*Calcissimo Amarcord* 2020).

5  https://www.gazzetta.it/Calcio/Estero/25-11-2020/vita-rosa-maradona-suoi-trionfi-pagine-gazzetta-3901155173243.shtml (*Gazzetta.it* 2020).

6  https://www.youtube.com/watch?v=NNw9oQjGmKg ("Maradona è del Napoli!", in *Il passato è qui* – You Tube channel, September 19, 2016).

7  *Fifa Tv* (You Tube Channel), November 27, 2020, https://www.youtube.com/ watch?v=3eDZV-p9DiI.

8  "15 dicembre 1985: il sorteggio Mondiale mette di fronte l'Italia Campione del Mondo e l'Argentina di Maradona", *Gli eroi del calcio*, December 15, 2020, https:// www.glieroidelcalcio.com/2020/12/15/15-dicembre-1985-il-sorteggio-per-il-mondiale-mette-di-fronte-litalia-campione-del-mondo-e-largentina-di-maradona/.

9  "La Storia – Quarti di finale Argentina 2 Inghilterra 1-Coppa del Mondo 1986", *Il Napoli online*, March 24, 2020, https://www.ilnapolionline.com/2020/03/24/la-storia-quarti-di-finale-argentina-2-inghilterra-1-coppa-del-mondo-1986-i-video-di-maradona/.

10  *Collezione Gazzetta*, Prime pagine, https://collezioni.gazzetta.it/it/prime-pagine/ foto/gazzetta-dello-sport/1986-06-23.

11  *Gazzetta.it*, Photo Gallery, Mondiale 1986, https://www.gazzetta.it/Foto-Gallery/ Calcio/23-05-2014/mondiale-1986-gazzetta-80739309559.shtml, May 23, 2014.

12  *Ibidem*.

13  *Napoli per uni scudetto – Napoli campione d'Italia*, Rai Uno – 17 maggio 1987, https:// www.youtube.com/watch?v=hUBW43EsfmU&t=1721s, June 20, 2018.

14  I develop this point elsewhere (Russo 2005, 2006, 2017).

15  Trent'anni di Italia 90. Appunti (molto sparsi) per un romanzo, https://liberementi libri.com/2020/06/01/trentanni-di-italia-90-appunti-molto-sparsi-per-un-romanzo/, *Liberementi*, June 1, 2020.

16  "La vita in rosa di Maradona, i suoi trionfi nelle pagine della Gazzetta", *Gazzetta.it*, https://www.gazzetta.it/Calcio/Estero/25-11-2020/vita-rosa-maradona-suoi-trionfi-pagine-gazzetta-3901155173243.shtml, November 25, 2020.

## References

Andrews, David L. and Steven J. Jackson, eds. 2001. *Sport Stars. The Cultural Politics of Sport Celebrities*. London and New York: Routledge.

Barbagallo, Francesco. 2013. *La Questione Italiana. Il Nord e il Sud dal 1860 a Oggi*. Roma and Bari: Laterza.

Bifulco, Luca and Vittorio Dini. 2014. *Maradona. Sociologia di un Mito Globale*. Santa Maria Capua Vetere: Ipermedium.

Bifulco, Luca and Mario Tirino. 2018. "The Sports Hero in the Social Imaginary. Identity, Community, Ritual and Myth". *Im@go*, VII:11, 9–25.

Bourdieu, Pierre and Loïc Wacquant. 1992. *An Invitation to Reflexive Sociology*. Cambridge: Polity Press.

Cashmore, Ellis. 2006. *Celebrity/Culture*. London and New York: Routledge.

Dalai, Michele. 2013. *Contro il Tiqui Taca. Come ho Imparato a Odiare il Barcellona*. Milano: Mondadori.

Dal Lago, Alessandro. 1994. "Il Voto e il Circo". *Micromega*, 1, 138–145.

Daniele, Vittorio e Paolo Malanima. 2011. *Il Divario Nord-Sud in Italia. 1861-2011*. Soveria Mannelli: Rubettino.

El País. 2018. "El 'catenaccio' como estado de ánimo". April 9. https://elpais.com/deportes/2018/04/09/actualidad/1523263706_639226.html [Accessed September 25, 2021].

Felice, Emanuele. 2016. *Perché il Sud è Rimasto Indietro*. Bologna: Il Mulino.

Foot, John. 2006. *Calcio: A History of Italian Football*. London: Harper Collins.

Giornale, Il. 2020. "Il pallone rovinato da troppi raccomandati. Mi hanno fatto fuori". April 29. https://www.ilgiornale.it/news/sport/pallone-rovinato-troppi-raccomandati-mi-hanno-fatto-fuori-1858969.html [Accessed October 3, 2021].

Goldthorpe, John Henry. 2004. "Sociology as Social Science and Cameral Science: Some Further Thoughts". *European Sociological Review*, 20:2, 97–105.

Kavetzos, Georgios and Stefan Szymanski. 2010. "National Well-Being and International Sports Events". *Journal of Economic Psychology*, 31:2, 158–171.

La Repubblica. 2021. "La geniale provocazione di Maradona ai Mondiali del '90: 'Gli italiani devono capire che i napoletani sono anche italiani …'". July 3. https://napoli.repubblica.it/cronaca/2021/07/03/news/la_geniale_provocazione_di_maradona_ai_mondiali_del_90_gli_italiani_devono_capire_che_i_napoletani_sono_anche_italiani_-308782780/ [Accessed October 19, 2021].

Lines, Gill. 2010. "Villains, Fools or Heroes? Sports Stars as Role Models for Young People". *Leisure Studies*, 20:4, 285–303.

Marca. 2020. "El *catenaccio* español: 'Es un ciclo triste y una mala noticia para el espectáculo: si nos lo dicen hace 20 años no nos lo creemos'". November 16. https://www.marca.com/futbol/2020/11/16/5fae9e05e2704e8e758b45a9.html [Accessed October 19, 2021].

Melin, Roger. 2014. "Are Sportpersons Good Moral Role Models?" *Physical Culture and Sport: Studies and Research*, 64:1, 5–16.

Melucci, Alberto. 1998. *Verso una Sociologia Riflessiva. Ricerca Qualitativa e Cultura*. Bologna: Il Mulino.

Mutz, Michael. 2019. "Life Satisfaction and the UEFA EURO 2016: Findings from a Nation-Wide Longitudinal Study in Germany". *Applied Research in Quality Life*, 14, 375–391.

Nalapat, Abilash and Andrew Parker. 2005. "Sport, Celebrity and Popular Culture. Sachin Tendulkar, Cricket and Indian Nationalism". *International Review for the Sociology of Sport*, 40:4, 433–446.

Parry, Keith D. 2020. "The Formation of Heroes and the Myth of National Identity". *Sport in Society*, 24:6, 886–903.

Porro, Nicola and Pippo Russo. 2000. "Berlusconi and Other Matters: The Era of Football Politics". *Journal of Modern Italian Studies*, 5:3, 348–371.

Rojek, Chris. 2006. "Sport, Celebrity and the Civilizing Process". *Sport in Society*, 9:4, 674–690.

Russo, Pippo. 2005. *L'Invasione dell'Ultracalcio: Anatomia di uno Sport Mutante*. Verona: Ombre Corte.

_____. 2006. *Il mio nome è Nedo Ludi*. Milano: Baldini Castoldi Dalai.

_____. 2016. "Italia, Spagna e il Cinema dell'incomprensione". *Panenka*. https://www. panenka.org/euro-2016/italia-spagna-e-il-cinema-dellincomprensione/

_____. 2017. *Filippide al Pit Stop. Performance e Spettacolo nello Sport Postmoderno*. Firenze: Editpress.

Santoro, Marco. 2007. "Per una Sociologia Professionale e Riflessiva (Solo Così Anche Pubblica". *Sociologica*, 1, 1–19.

_____. 2014. "Effetto Bourdieu: La Sociologia come Pratica Riflessiva e la Trasformazione del Campo Sociologico". *Rassegna Italiana di Sociologia*, 1, 5–20.

Smart, Barry. 2005. *The Sport Star: Modern Sport and the Cultural Economy of Sporting Celebrity*. London and New Delhi: Sage.

# 4

## MARADONA AND MEXICO

## The Ecstasy and the Agony

*Fernando Segura M. Trejo and John Williams*

### A Mexican affair

As Eduardo Archetti (2001) once said, the qualities of Diego Armando Maradona transcend the limits of his nationality and, in this sense, his figure posited multiple ways of being a sporting hero. Maradona continues to be the focus of an ongoing, ever-changing narrative, one that is publicly performed and differently read by a diffused global audience (Salazar-Sutil, 2008). It was in Mexico that the footballer experienced some of the most significant moments of his professional life. He reached the peak of his playing power by captaining the Argentina team to victory in the 1986 World Cup. In his autobiography *El Diego,* he refers to this tournament as *La Gloria* (The Glory); a moment when he felt that in his body, heart, and soul he was living the most sublime and productive episode of his career (Maradona, 2000). On June 29, 1986, Argentina defeated Germany 3-2 to win the country's second World Cup, after an intense, highly scrutinised, and controversial competition. Thirty-two years later, Maradona would return to Mexico in another role, much less celebrated but both intriguing and unexpected, as the coach/manager of the local second division club Dorados de Sinaloa. This would represent his longest and most consistent experience as a football manager. By the time of his arrival at the airport of Culiacán, capital of the state of Sinaloa, Maradona's life had become akin to a reality TV show, one marked by enormous media interest and exposure and regular falls from grace, followed by inevitable resurgences. During these years, his health was severely compromised on more than one occasion. As Leandro Zanoni (2006) points out, the media circus surrounding Maradona began to transform his performative gestures, seemingly, into affairs of state.

What makes Maradona's cult status so secure today, and perhaps unique in sport, was his extraordinary capacity to emerge from the pain of everyday

DOI: 10.4324/9781003196587-6

life and produce moments of joy for the people. His life had long become a multi-layered identity pastiche of the kind that problematises the modern conceptualisation of the sports hero (Salazar-Sutil, 2008: 442). In Mexico, Maradona not only enjoyed both the public celebration of his remarkable skills and powers of motivation but also arose suspicion and negative reactions due to his well-documented troubles off the field, as he moved along what seemed to have become an increasingly unstable path, routinely articulated via the sort of media vortex often generated around global sports stars (Whannel, 2010).

To better assess the impact that Maradona produced in a generation of sporting, media, and journalism commentators in Mexico, we have interviewed a selected number of people, including football journalists and commentators, media producers, and academics. The list includes Heriberto Murrieta, a well-known sport analyst who commented the 1986 World Cup on radio and TV for Televisa, the largest media communications company in Mexico; Francisco Gabriel De Anda, former first division footballer and now football commentator for ESPN Mexico; Ciro Procuna, also an analyst for ESPN Mexico; two female journalists, Erendira Palma, who works for *La Jornada* in Mexico City, and Cristian Díaz, correspondent of the same newspaper for the state of Sinaloa; Diego Mancera, sport journalist of the Mexican edition of *El País*; Adriana Islas Govea, a sociologist specialising in football; Jonathan Aldana, a sports news producer for a range of different media outlets; and Jorge Silva, an independent political and football analyst from the state of Veracruz.

In this chapter, we analyse specifically how the "Maradona narrative" was constructed in/from Mexico, as seen mainly through the eyes and voices of local journalists, and particularly in tabloid news coverage and documentary films. The structure of the chapter reflects the three pillars on which Maradona's relationship with Mexico stands: his performance in the 1986 World Cup; a series of occasional encounters with renowned Mexican figures; and his period as football manager of Dorados.

## The 1986 World Cup: Ecstasy and glory

On November 25, 2020, the death of Maradona had an immediate impact on local and national media in Mexico. Sport TV and radio shows covered the event thoroughly and the national press, as in many other countries, paid fulsome tribute to a player once widely considered the world's best. Most of the images produced in commemoration were naturally related to a mesmerising young player frozen in his prime: a diminutive but stocky 25-year-old smiling as he held up the FIFA World Cup trophy in the Azteca Stadium, the spiritual home of Mexican football and the international landscape for the 1970 and 1986 World Cup finals. The narratives linking Maradona to the World Cup in 1986 have been rather different elsewhere, of course, especially in England (Williams and Holt, 2020), but key features of the story of Maradona's sporting prowess and of his mythical status in global football are deeply rooted within those images of ultimate success and unconfined joy in Mexico.

Mexico first hosted a World Cup in 1970. The state offered minimal financial support at the time, so a network of Mexican businessmen not only became involved in funding the event but also used the opportunity to consolidate their control of football and television broadcasting rights in Mexico, a link which would have repercussions around the world for decades to come (Jiménez, 2020). Mexico 1970 was the first World Cup competition to be broadcast globally and the first staged outside of Europe or South America. For FIFA and its president, João Havelange, this was a signal for a future model of competition that would now market the sport globally, selling "a product called football" to states, sponsors, and stakeholders (Jiménez, 2020). A 2007 readers' poll in *World Soccer* magazine hailed the Brazilian team that won the 1970 World Cup as the greatest of all time, "a myth, a team to be held up as the ultimate exponents of the beautiful game" (Williams and Holt, 2020: 148). The Brazilian game was already enthroned and worshipped in Mexico too. Nevertheless, the exceptional Maradona was on the horizon in the 1980s, as Murrieta recalls:

> In Mexico, we had fresh memories of the 1970 performance and in the sport newsrooms, to which I already belonged. We all considered the brilliant Brazilian team that played in Spain in 1982. For 1986, with players such as Socrates and Zico, we clearly thought they had everything to become champions. We also listed other contenders, such as Italy or Germany. And Argentina was on the radar too, mainly because we knew Maradona could make a difference. I personally thought that he was already the most talented player of the times, but we would place the Brazilian squad above the others.[1]

It is also worth remembering that when Colombia withdrew its hosting rights for the 1986 tournament, the United States rolled in some heavy artillery – Ronald Reagan and Henry Kissinger, no less – to try to press FIFA to host the finals, but commercial and cultural connections secured the repeat event for Mexico (Kioussis, 2020). If the tournament ended up being, according to Havelange, "a resounding success", this positive outcome was not always assured, because the Mexican context in the mid-1980s was hardly ideal. The country was still reeling in emotional and physical torment from a strong earthquake that had struck on September 19, 1985, and had caused over 5,000 deaths in addition to significant material damage (Islas, 2018). Despite the suffering and destruction involved, members of the World Cup organising committee, *Televisa*'s spokespersons, and other government officials quickly reassured the public that the football event was "still on". This was widely read as a political gesture to distract the people in the aftermath of the nat-ural disaster and in the context of a crippling economic recession (Ridge, 2019: 962). Indeed, the inauguration of the tournament brought popular expressions of excitement and celebration, as well as relief. The Mexican team played its first matches at the Azteca with more than 120,000 spectators attending each game.

Argentina played at the Olympic Stadium of Mexico City and in Puebla, where Maradona defied climatic conditions and scored his first goal of the tournament. Procuna remembers: "During that first phase, it appeared that Maradona was not affected by the altitude. Mexico City and Puebla are cities located more than 2,000 metres above sea level, and he seemed to play at a different speed than the others. The goal against Italy was just one example of what he was capable of". In the round of 16, Argentina met old rivals Uruguay and won by a tight 1-0 at the Neza Stadium. This meant in the quarter-finals Argentina would face England at the Azteca on June 22nd. This would be the game to enthrone Maradona and act as a founding stage of his status as leg-end (Burgo, 2016). The Malvinas/Falklands war between Argentina and the United Kingdom that took place between April and June 1982 loomed in the background. In comments made in the documentary *Hazaña. El deporte vive: México 86*, Mexican journalist Gerardo Peña argued that this football fixture had taken on a very different resonance: "The stupidity of the Military Junta of Argentina, sending 18-year-olds to fight the British Army in 1982. Facing a government like Margaret Thatcher's, inflexible as few were, [was] a com-plete madness. Argentina needed desperately to win that match in Mexico". The local sport newspaper *Esto* agreed, offering the headline "The Ghosts of Malvinas Torture the Argentineans" (Burgo, 2016: 246). Murrieta explained that: "In the press, the morbid features of the war and how that episode could affect the game was more commented upon than the football tactics that each team could deploy".

The game was set for a noon start on a blistering, sunny day. Maradona had already publicly complained to FIFA about the scheduling, thus reinforcing his image as somebody who would be willing to stand up against the corporate power of FIFA and the broadcasting companies. The start time was obviously not changed, and the first half of the game ended in a nil-nil draw. In the second half, Maradona would produce the two goals that most significantly defined his career and his global image. Six minutes into the second half he famously scored using his left hand to beat the English goalkeeper, Peter Shilton. Only a short time later, Maradona scored his most famous goal, carrying the ball solo for over 50 meters and dribbling past four English outfield players and the goalkeeper. It was a performance that made Eduardo Camarena, who was com-mentating for Televisa and who appears in the documentary *Hazaña, El deporte vive: México 86*, exclaim: "Golazo! Golazo [Great goal!]! Portentous, very nice, remarkable goal by Diego Armando Maradona". His two goals in that game – one deceitful and the other magisterial – effectively wrote the story of this

World Cup. Murrieta, more than 34 years later, discerning sport from religious spirituality in Mexico, remembers:

> It was a particularly hot afternoon and the action that led to this second incredible goal went so fast that I did not have the time to mention all the names of the English players left behind. When it happened, I knew I was witnessing something historic. The [Hand of God] goal has been celebrated by his supporters and also for the cunning, but it constituted a severe infringement. Moreover, naming it as the Hand of God is a pure blasphemy and I cannot agree with that, even if I have always admired his skills.

These comments shared in an interview for this chapter by one of the most renowned football pundits in Mexico exhibit not only an admiration for Maradona's talent, but also a clear disapproval of his transgressive behaviour including what seems to be a curious religious censure. Archetti (2003) has argued in that vein that Maradona often placed a unique emphasis on the infantile nature of football, while stressing the importance of the natural street guile of the *pibe*, in a game laced with spontaneity and freedom. So, too, is the Argentinian style of play defined as *la nuestra,* derived from how creoles and immigrants from southern Europe creatively adapted and played football. Thus, in some quarters, the Argentinian game came to be seen, unjustly, as a series of ongoing pretences and fake intentions, with victory best achieved not through domination but through deceit (Brach, 2011: 418). This – and a very real sense of a symbolic revenge through sport following defeat in the South Atlantic conflict – only added to the reasons why Maradona was so lauded at home for his illegal goal (Rodríguez, 1996).

However, it is unclear who really created that expression "Hand of God" in the first place. Was it an Argentinian correspondent in Mexico who asked the player about the goal? Or the Mexican press when defining the action, long before it was adopted as a global motif? Or was it Maradona himself (Burgo, 2016: 250)? The footballer has willingly reflected on this goal on numerous occasions. In his book on the 1986 World Cup – translated into English precisely as *Touched by God: How We Won the Mexico '86* – Maradona stressed: "I do not regret scoring the goal with my hand. With respect for the fans, players and managers, I do not regret it, simply because I grew up doing these sorts of actions in Villa Fiorito and I did the same thing in Mexico before more than 100,000 people" (Maradona, 2016: 104).

The following day, the Mexican newspaper *El Excelsior* ran the headline: "Maradona Proved that It Is Possible to Weave with Feet" (Burgo, 2016: 246).[2]. With Mexico, Brazil, and Spain already eliminated, Mexicans now began to show more identification with Argentina and Maradona. De Anda, who was already training and dreaming about becoming a professional footballer, and would later become a football analyst, conveyed in his autobiography: "I watched the quarter-finals on TV with my brother and we could not believe what Maradona did, he was just brilliant. For the semi-final we went with our father to the Azteca and [Maradona] was again the absolute king against Belgium. Not only that he scored two marvelous goals, but he managed his team and the match in a remarkable way" (2020: 45).

When we interviewed him for this piece, De Anda reflected on what he took to be the mood in Mexico in 1986: "After the quarters against England we really wanted to see Argentina and this great captain holding the trophy". As a more general example of how the Mexican press had now "adopted" the Argentinian hero and his country, the front page of *Esto* showed its support on the day of the final with the unequivocal headline: "Come on Argentina!" For Silva, who was only six years old and who lived out this sporting saga with his family at home in Veracruz, the World Cup for them had four very intense moments: "Manuel Negrete's goal for Mexico against Bulgaria; the sadness of seeing the Mexican team beaten by Germany; Maradona's goals during the quarters; and, finally, Argentina celebrating the triumph in the last game".

The 1986 World Cup finals could now be tied to a single individual, and he would not disappoint. Nevertheless, Maradona, a man always very sensitive to unconditional signs of affection, felt that part (or most) of the locals in the stadium during the final were supporting Germany instead of Argentina. In his first biography he declared: "Those who celebrated our victory at the stadium were the Argentineans" (Maradona, 2000: 135). As a matter of fact, hundreds of Argentineans had recently emigrated to Mexico, seeking asylum from the repressive 1976–1983 dictatorship (Yankelevich, 2020). Notwithstanding the impressions of the captain, according to Murrieta, the *Azteca* paid fulsome tribute to the winning team after the final whistle.

The influence left by Maradona's exploits in 1986 would be deeply felt in Mexico. Procuna was just 12 years old, but he was so moved by the sheer audacity of this single player that he dreamt of becoming a sport journalist one day. Palma, on the other hand, was born in 1986 and she only started hearing about Maradona later, when she was six years old, but she was inexorably drawn to Maradona's contradictory life narrative and, as a journalist, she would follow closely the life of both the player and the man. Aldana was born in 1989, but as a young video analyst for TV Azteca and ESPN Mexico, more than 20 years later, he admitted to being "hypnotized by Maradona. He became a myth in Mexico, because his most famous actions happened here and many people kept those memories forever". The sociologist Islas was born in Mexico City in 1990, and as a young child, she watched her mother playing football with her younger brother. Her uncles considered Pelé to be the greatest player of all time, dismissing Maradona for his character and demons: "They thought he was a good player, but he was not a positive example, because they considered him a cheater". She, instead, was drawn to Maradona's deviant complexities. These remembrances and traces passed down from the 1986 World Cup games, nourished divergent images and debates about Maradona in Mexico for many years that followed.

## Between 1986 and 2018: The Mexican connection

Before 1986, Maradona had visited Mexico on several occasions, playing friendly matches with Argentinos Juniors in 1980 and with Boca Juniors in 1982. Over eight years after the 1986 World Cup, with his AS Napoli days behind him, Maradona was going through the second suspension of his career, after testing positive for ephedrine at the 1994 World Cup finals hosted by the United States. In December 1994, he was invited to take part in an indoor-football tournament in the city of Pachuca, capital of the state of Hidalgo. Now widely considered a tarnished and spent force, Maradona was in surprisingly good shape since he was training to resume his playing career in Argentina the following year. In Pachuca, Maradona shared the money he was paid for participating in the tournament with the rest of his teammates. Murrieta, already established as one of the main faces of sport at Televisa, played one game during the event. He found Maradona a committed teammate, describing this experience to us: "I played one match and I scored four times after marvelous assists by Maradona. He was very generous in many ways. After that game, we went to the TV studio in Mexico City, where I could interview him. I remember he was really motivated by the possibility of returning to Boca Juniors".

Ten months later, Maradona appeared for Boca at La Bombonera Stadium in Buenos Aires, in what would be the final resurgence in his playing career. In October 1997, he tested positive for cocaine use and was forced to retire as a player. While he was recuperating from drug addiction and struggling against obesity in Cuba in 2002, he was invited to the farewell match of Carlos Hermosillo, an iconic Mexican footballer. De Anda attended the game and was startled by what he witnessed: "We could not believe Maradona was in such bad shape. Although he had kept some of his skills when he touched the ball, he practically could not run. It was shocking to realize this was the same man that had shone in Mexico 16 years before". Maradona was reluctant to talk with the press during that trip. Islas watched the media coverage, which was narrowly focused on Maradona's poor condition: "I'd had always heard many negative opinions about him and when I saw those appearances, they just reinforced this obscure, damaging image, until I discovered years later about his life story when I was studying sociology at the UNAM". Here was a man clearly haunted by deep psychological crises and struggles with his own body.

But Maradona's personal situation improved in 2005, when he was offered a contract to host a new TV show called *La Noche del 10* (The Night of # 10) for Argentina's Canal 13. The show was aired in Buenos Aires and rebroadcast by Televisa in Mexico. Many Mexicans, among them all our interviewees for this chapter, eagerly tuned in and were surprised to see a slim, vigorous, smiling, articulate, and charming Maradona, a man reborn hosting a show replete with celebrities. Between August and November of 2005, 13 episodes were aired. One of them included a highly anticipated and respectful meeting with Pelé, whom a young Diego had first met in Rio in 1979. Mexico supplied important guests, including the actor and comedian Roberto Gómez Bolaños, alias *Chespirito* (Little Shakespeare). Although little known in the Anglophone world, Chespirito was a famous and beloved comedian across Latin America, whose influence in Hispanic popular culture cannot be overestimated. He wrote and created a highly successful and long-running TV show in the 1970s and 1980s, in which he portrayed a variety of comic characters, such as *El Chavo del 8* and *El Chapulín Colorado*, idolised by several generations of children. Mexican newspaper *El Universal* described the meeting between Maradona and Bolaños as "De ídolo a ídolo" ("From Idol to Idol"). When Maradona travelled to Mexico to support Boca Juniors against Club America for the 2000 Copa Libertadores semi-final, he had declared Chespirito to be one of his most cherished comedic entertainers. Everywhere he travelled, in fact, Maradona claimed he always carried videotapes of the series. When talking to Gómez Bolaños in *La Noche del 10*, he thanked the comic for making him so happy for so many years, demonstrating Maradona's always nostalgic and rather sentimentalised memories of childhood, a consistent feature of his character (Archetti, 2003: 217). Maradona also invited to his show a number of Mexican singers and actresses, including the Latin actress and pop singer Thalia and the singer-songwriter Paulina Rubio. The fact that he should attract such major figures, who would be willing to travel all the way to Buenos Aires to record the show, attests to the appeal that Maradona continued to have in Mexico.

During this time, when neoliberalism was gaining ground, Maradona was also becoming something of a symbolic expression of the Peronist heritage in Argentina, as Pablo Alabarces (2002) has claimed. His relationship with Cuban leader Fidel Castro contributed to what became a more constant and open support for left-wing regimes in Latin America. In November 2005, the former footballer shared a platform with Hugo Chávez and Néstor Kirchner in a demonstration in Mar del Plata against the free trade agreement proposed by President George W. Bush. The president of Mexico at the time, the conservative Vicente Fox, was in favour of the agreement and he criticised the Argentine sporting figure for his interference: "There is great paraphernalia about an athlete involved in politics who is making a lot of noise, but as presidents we are serious. Our debates are not guided by ideologies" (*Medio Tiempo*, 2005). Maradona did not respond immediately, but he addressed Fox the following year, when he was about to travel to Mexico for a series of indoor exhibition matches. He was concerned about the dangerous travails of Mexican nationals trying to cross the border into the United States: "Don't let the Americans build a wall and kill Mexicans on the border with the United States. You must take care of that, because the undocumented are killed like flies. And I say this to your face, Mr. Fox" (*Expansión*, 2020). Maradona's unusually outspoken political inclinations produced mixed reactions in

Mexico. While other, more conservative, newspapers took a different view, some young journalists such as Palma, for example, celebrated his political stance: "Here at *La Jornada*, we have always valued Maradona's positions and statements. What was very disturbing for other journalists in Mexico was fantastic for us; he is one of the very few footballers to make his opinions and ideas about social justice public".

Despite the success of *La Noche del Diez,* Maradona declined to do a second season. He would not return to host a TV show until the 2014 World Cup finals in Brazil. This time he was hired by the Venezuelan public network Telesur to host the daily show *De Zurda*. This title, which can be translated into English as "Lefty", is a pun that refers both to Maradona's footballing skills and to his (and the broadcaster's) left-wing political ideology. The show, broadcast every evening during the tournament, was an analysis of each day's football action and it was co-hosted with Víctor Hugo Morales, the renowned Uruguayan journalist and commentator whose radio commentary of Maradona's goals against England in 1986 (most notably the extraordinary second one) achieved emblematic status. Morales later transitioned into political journalism and is now well known for defending governments aligned with the left in Latin America. Criticism directed by Maradona at FIFA and particularly criticisms aimed towards the corrupt Joseph Blatter made Maradona claim that FIFA officials turned him away from the Maracanã stadium when he tried to attend Argentina's first fixture against Bosnia (Segura, 2018).

*De Zurda*'s broadcasts reached some cable channels live in Mexico and Hugo Sánchez, a national football hero, visited the show. Maradona praised the former Mexican striker and recalled the goals and outstanding performances he was internationally known for at Real Madrid, especially his spectacular *chilenas* (scissor-kicks). The latter made a point, in turn, of recognising the importance of fighting for players' rights and he stressed that there was no real union or coalition to defend them against the abuses of club owners in Mexico. Crucially, in this highly public forum, Sánchez highlighted the fact that Maradona had always been a pioneer in standing up to authority figures and paving the way for better protection for future players.

Four years later, Maradona and Morales hosted a reprise of *De Zurda*, also for Telesur, at the 2018 World Cup in Russia. In Mexican circles, Maradona was to become something of a controversial figure during the tournament. He first celebrated Mexico's triumph against the favourites, Germany, but later criticised the awarding of the 2026 World Cup to the United States, Canada, and Mexico, saying that the three countries did not have the levels of football excellence required to host such a prestigious event. However, ever loyal to his rather iconoclastic global political positions, Maradona cherished the election of Andrés Manuel López Obrador in June 2018 (*Expansión*, 2020). The new Mexican president would publicly welcome the footballer two months later when the latter was unexpectedly hired as a football manager in the Mexican second division. Yet a new Mexican adventure was afoot.

## Golden age: Maradona and Dorados of Sinaloa

On September 5, 2018, the Mexican media widely reported that Maradona had apparently signed a contract to manage Dorados in the second division of the domestic league. Within a socio-economic scenario where football clubs in Mexico are franchises that can be bought and sold, where only the biggest clubs can maintain their status as associations, some cities in Mexico have seen their professional clubs disappear, while others have received a brand new one. Dorados was founded in 2003 in the city of Culiacán, where no other professional football club competed, and it was immediately incorporated into the Mexican second division. A year later the new club won the play-offs and was promoted to the first division. Players of international prestige, such as Pep Guardiola, passed through the ranks of Dorados. However, their spell in the top flight was short lived. They were relegated in 2006 and they continued to play in the second division ever since, with the only exception being the 2015 season.

The announcement of Maradona's arrival in Dorados produced a world-wide echo. The stages that led to this signing remain a mystery. The initial link between Maradona and the Sinaloa team allegedly came out of an "idea" from an Argentinian football agent with strong connections in Mexico. Christian Bragarnik mentioned Maradona's name to Jorge Hank, a leading member of the family which owns Dorados and Xolos of Tijuana, among other important businesses in the country (Barbier, 2021). Among our group of journalists, Palma, Silva, Mancera, and Díaz all agree that the environment of Dorados fitted an ageing football celebrity with so much personal and professional baggage to contend with. At Dorados, Maradona was likely to find a hospitable atmosphere in which to coach. The club, though part of a competitive league, would not face the sort of media scrutiny one might find in the first division (be it in Mexico or elsewhere), and public pressure would be less marked. But for some football analysts in the country, Maradona represented a problematic character, a man long fallen from grace. In fact, many disbelieved the initial reports that he would take charge of the team.

Murrieta, Procuna, and De Anda were together running their morning show on ESPN when the news broke. Procuna, who had admired the Argentinian during his own childhood, nevertheless said live: "I hope this is a joke". De Anda was even more severe: "Maradona has nothing to contribute to Mexican football". Murrieta reasoned that, despite his controversial image, the presence of Maradona in the Mexican second division would be a magnet for global attention, for Mexican football in general and for Dorados in particular. But he also showed concern about the physical and mental health of the Argentine former footballer. De Anda, consulted in January 2021 on his scepticism on Dorados' new appointment, believed that the Argentine probably lacked the qualities required to manage a professional club. An enthralled Palma had a rather different feeling at her office of *La Jornada*: "We could not believe that Maradona was coming to live and coach in Mexico!"

When Maradona landed in the small airport of Culiacán, the place had never been so packed with journalists, observers, and the simply curious. Fans and local and international sports correspondents were present in numbers. On the day of his presentation to the press, Díaz and Mancera were in the room of an elegant hotel chosen for the occasion. The former remembers that the song La Mano de Dios (The Hand of God), by the Argentine popular singer Rodrigo, was playing everywhere. Mancera was impressed by the excitement of hardened journalists in the backstage area. Then, the media manager of Dorados showed up and made the unusual request of asking his colleagues to stand and applaud. "I'd never seen that", said Mancera, "the club treated us as fans and they only allowed three questions in total, obviously taken by TV correspondents".

However, collective expressions of popular affection were moderate in Culiacán. At the local stadium, around 5,000 people gathered to cheer him up during his initial presentation. When interviewing local people on the street, Mancera realised that many simply did not believe that Maradona's arrival was serious. They thought it was a public relations stunt or a marketing ploy and that, very soon, the famous Argentine would leave the city in the same unexpected way he had arrived. Díaz had the same view, reasoning that Culiacán is a city where football, though still important, is not as significant as baseball. Dorados' stadium was rarely at full capacity during home games. Other comments and rumours appeared on social networks, claiming there was a hidden link between Maradona's long-established addiction to drugs, and the reputation of the state of Sinaloa for its powerful and unforgiving drugs cartels. Such rumours echoed Maradona's dubious links with criminal associations during his time in Naples, but in this case no evidence was provided.

The first Dorados match played under coach Maradona was against Cafetaleros of Tapachula. It was exclusively broadcast by ESPN for Mexico and was shown live in many countries, including in Argentina. Predictably, Maradona's emphatic gestures and dances on the technical area seemed to matter as much – or more – to the broadcasters than the actions of his team and the game *per se*. The goals in a home win came towards the end of the match, with the new coach exploding with joy and running wildly along the touchline, a perfect image for television. The anticipated "Maradona effect" was already kicking in.

The extraordinary and unlikely saga of Maradona's Mexican coaching adventure can be tracked in a Netflix documentary entitled *Maradona in Sinaloa* in the local version of the platform, and *Maradona in Mexico* in all other national versions of Netflix. As Zanoni (2006) explains, Maradona's life had become public property, TV gold, and this latest Mexican episode was no exception. The show covers the two seasons that Maradona spent as manager of Dorados, portraying the daily training routines of the team, and the sacrifices made by a handful of fans who followed them across thousands of kilometres for away games. Of course, the emblematic coach came out to games amid major fanfares, not only in the home stadium in Culiacán, but also in every venue where his team performed. For example, he was wildly celebrated in places where his presence would have been simply unthinkable before, such as in Zacatepec, in the state of Morelos. Maradona left his mark away from the sporting arena, too. At the end of October 2018, a vicious hurricane hit the state of Sinaloa and the city of Culiacán hard, causing severe flooding and mass evacuations. Maradona quickly called the authorities to see how he could help the victims. The club held a benefit dinner for those whose homes had been lost or damaged.

Without spectacular performances but with an effective and organised brand of football, Dorados reached the play-offs in Maradona's first season, beating the favourites Indios of Ciudad Juárez in the quarter-finals, and then Mineros of Zacatecas to advance to the final against Atlético San Luis, a Mexican subsidiary of Spain's Atlético Madrid. During this run, an exuberant, apparently stress-free Maradona was filmed celebrating in the locker room with his wide-eyed players, dancing and singing to cumbia rhythms. De Anda commentated for ESPN on several of those decisive games, and he began to recognise the Argentine's achievement and his successful collaboration with coaches: "Maradona proved to be a great motivator, but we should not forget the role of his staff, with Luis Islas the main assistant and the third coach, the Mexican Mario García, who provided key knowledge about the local championship".

Dorados lost the final, and Maradona suffered verbal abuse from the fans at the San Luis stadium; he became furious and had to be restrained. The press story, inevitably, was the emotional reaction of the coach more than the game itself or the insults he received. Soon after, he travelled back to Argentina to undergo surgery on his knees. He would not be fully healed by the start of the following season, and the Dorados campaign began without him on the bench. The Netflix series shows the anxiety of the Dorados president and the radio commentators when it was not yet certain that Maradona would return to Culiacán.

A demoralised Dorados team lost the first four games without Maradona. When he finally returned, his team was still disjointed and could not put together a winning sequence. The media reaction was severe. The same journalists who had celebrated reaching the play-off final the year before now assured their audience, in heated debates reproduced by Netflix, that Maradona was a spent force, a man incapable of leading a struggling team. However, Maradona managed to stage a comeback. Dorados fought out a valuable victory in the tournament Copa Mx against the first division club Atlas. Revitalised, the team went into a winning streak and reached the play-offs once again, defeating Cimarrones and Mineros of Zacatecas, thus reaching the final for the second year in a row. However, Dorados lost again. This time, Maradona did not react to the insults of his opponents, but the atmosphere in the Dorados' dressing room, as portrayed in the Netflix series, was very dark. These images announced the end of an extraordinary Mexican adventure for Maradona: two seasons full of hype, emotion, carnival, and occasional vitriol.

For Díaz, it was the modest Mexican football club scene what brought fresh air into the failing lungs of Maradona. The respect he received from the people of Culiacán, the opportunity he was given to pass on his knowledge of football to a group of average young players, and a local media not obsessed with his personal life kept Maradona happy and calm, at least for about an entire year. Perhaps the feeling that a cycle had ended, or else the nostalgia he felt for his home country, led him to accept yet another new challenge: coaching Gimnasia y Esgrima de la Plata in Argentina, a traditional, mid-table first division club, which he joined only a few weeks after leaving Dorados. He would never return to Mexico.

## The Mexican frame and the legend

Amid the restrictions triggered by the Covid-19 pandemic, the Argentinian football league resumed playing in the second half of 2020, but fans were not allowed in stadiums. On October 30th, Maradona was honoured for his 60th birthday at the stadium of Gimnasia, but he appeared so fragile and deteriorated that he generated significant public concern. He could barely stand on his own and had to be assisted by two men walking alongside him. He looked seriously ill and only a few days later, on November 3rd, he was admitted to a hospital, where he underwent surgery for a haematoma on the brain. On the morning of November 25th, at around 10:30 in Mexico City, an online rumour began to spread over social media claiming that Maradona had died. By 11:00, the story was confirmed by all broadcasters, with official information coming directly from Argentina. The global nature of this figure was true in death as well as in life. Cable news channels in Mexico made the announcement of his passing as if Maradona had been a head of state. On the Televisa sports channel, in a generally gloomy climate, the former international Chilean player Ivan Zamorano was the main interviewee and he was asked to share his memories of Maradona. That night, national newscasts in Mexico opened with the stark and simple headline: "Maradona is dead".

The Mexican press framed Maradona's passing as a story rooted in a grand national narrative that was both divine – his passing was defined as a spiritual loss – and also historic in a sporting sense. It typically represented the Argentine at the very height of his powers, frozen in time, and in some ways even as a "gift" for/from the Mexican people back in the Azteca Stadium in 1986, when Maradona had stood joyously triumphant astride the football world. Borrowing a phrase that Uruguayan writer Eduardo Galeano had used a few years before, the cover of *La Jornada* on November 26th run the headline "Goodbye to the most human of the Gods", together with a photograph of Maradona holding the emblematic World Cup trophy in Mexico. *El Sol de México* went with a picture of his farewell game at La Bombonera in 2001, with a headline stressing that the world was mourning the departure of a great sporting idol. *Milenio*, another national tabloid, chose a photograph of Maradona as the 1986 World Cup captain, carried on the shoulders of a teammate, with the words: "Diego Armando Maradona, 1960-2020. From the hand of God: Shock, pain, mourning …. The world cries and pays tribute to the Argentine football star, who will lay in state at the Casa Rosada before a million devotees". *El Universal* went with a cartoon of the player jumping to score his first goal against England in 1986, with the playful caption: "Hand in hand with God".

*El Excelsior* chose a photograph of Maradona's beatific smile as he cradled the trophy at the Azteca, accompanied by the word single word "Heavenly". Writer Juan Villoro published a piece in *Reforma* under the title "The Death of God", in which he remembered the ways in which Maradona himself spoke about God as the "El Barba" (The Bearded One), a close presence, almost a personal friend. Thus, in the company of El Barba, Villoro concluded that Diego will kick the ball again, for myths do not die (2020). Fourteen years before, in his book *Dios es Redondo* (*God is Round*), Villoro had foreseen that, upon the death of this iconic player, there would be unity in the world of football. Only on one occasion could one man be all men, and that collective feeling would be embodied in the passing of Maradona (Villoro, 2006). Back in 2013, one of the authors of this chapter wrote, rather differently, that all analyses which imagined Maradona's departure would be faced with reflecting on his intense and troubled personal life, as well as on the tributes and the profound mourning his playing status would obviously demand (Segura, 2013).

José Ramón Fernández, a seasoned journalist and leading commentator for TV Azteca and ESPN Mexico, was so shocked at the news of Maradona's death that he shed tears on live television when remembering several moving anecdotes about the player. David Faitelson, one of the main analysts for ESPN Mexico, explained on November 26th that he had seen no other player who had exuded as much passion for the game as Maradona. Procuna, writing on his weekly platform for the ESPN website, called him "Genius of the football world. I have never seen a player more valuable, more important than Maradona in the World Cup of 1986" (Procuna, 2020). The rather sensationalist Mexican tabloid *Metro DF* featured three images on its cover of November 26th: an ageing Maradona holding a replica of the World Cup trophy in 2016 (the 30th anniversary of the achievement); a picture of cheering fans at the Dorados stadium in 2018; and the most repeated image on those days in Mexico: Maradona celebrating at the Azteca in 1986, along with the headline: "Dust, You Are: The Year 2020 also took Maradona". Amongst the various tributes that came out in the days that followed, it is worth noting that current affairs and political television programming in Mexico featured the Argentinian's departure as part of their main news agenda. For instance, the TV edition of *El Octágono* on November 27th had the former Chancellor of Argentina, Rafael Bielsa (brother of the football manager Marcelo Bielsa), interviewed on Skype to speak about the importance of the player for his country, his people, and for the world game.

As Salazar-Sutil (2008: 445) has argued, in a mediascape fuelled by criticism, cynicism, and scandalmongering, it is no surprise that Maradona has become the most important cult figure in football on account of his neo-spiritual power in a sacred domain: the football stadium. He was an anointed "football-saint" who could still feed audiences with "miracles" on the pitch, and fuel tabloid narratives about heroism, scandals, and remarkable comebacks. In interviews for this chapter, Palma reasoned that Maradona had provided a vital dose of romanticism in the otherwise overly mercantile world of football. Murrieta remembered, rather, not only the great, combative, and skilful player Maradona had once been, but also the fragile and sensitive human being he worked hard at trying to become later in Mexico, when he was off the field and away from the press glare, distant from adoring and questioning crowds, and free from draining hangers-on.

Memories of the iconic player will forever be associated with the 1986 World Cup in Mexico. In a corridor of the Azteca Stadium in Mexico City, there is a statue of Maradona jumping to score that Hand of God goal in the match against England. How many sporting idols might be so fondly recalled in this way for what is, after all, a highly transgressive act? However, there is also a plaque outside the same stadium commemorating his spectacular second goal in that game; arguably, like all great public symbols, Maradona lived simultaneously within and outside conventional laws. On Dorados' ground, a mural painted on his arrival in 2018 still depicts his celebration of the latter goal and the message in Spanish "Welcome Diego!"

Maradona's symbolic association with Mexico was also well expressed in February 2021 when the Argentine President Alberto Fernández visited his Mexican counterpart Andrés Manuel López Obrador. On February 24th, one of the national days of Mexico, López Obrador celebrated with Fernández the commemoration of the 200th anniversary of the Iguala Plan, signalling the formal independence of the country. In thanking the Argentine president for the visit, López Obrador mentioned the importance to the world of Argentine figures who had produced timeless images of beauty, such as Jorge Luis Borges, one of the greatest writers of the twentieth century. And, of course, there were approving words for Maradona, now considered a legend "shared" forever by these two countries.

On June 29, 2021, a new mural was inaugurated at the entrance of the Azteca with two images: Maradona wearing a Mexican *sombrero* and the Argentina football shirt, a representation reproduced from a picture taken from *El Gráfico* magazine a few days before the start of the 1986 World Cup, and a second one of the captain holding the trophy aloft. The mural was painted by the artist Jorge Alderete and was commissioned by the Argentine Embassy in Mexico and the Ministry of Tourism and Sports in Argentina (*As.com*, 2021). The Ambassador, Carlos Tomada, explained to the authors of this chapter that the Argentinian state wanted to pay a tribute to the player in Mexico, on the first anniversary of the 1986 triumph after Maradona had passed. On that same date, 35 years on from his highest consecration, a subsidiary of the Maradonian Church was opened in the city of Cholula, in the state of Puebla. It was the first representation of the Maradonian Church outside of Argentina (*Proceso*, 2021). As Archetti (2001) has put it, the cult of Maradona is global and local at the same time, and Mexico remains one of the most important countries for pilgrimages in his honour in this extraordinary, unique story which melds sporting prowess with personal crises, and media hyperbole with spirituality.

## Notes

1  Personal interview with the authors (our translation).
2  The original Spanish title of the article in the Mexican newspaper was "Maradona demostró que es posible coser con los pies" (Burgo 2016).

## References

Alabarces, Pablo. 2002. *Fútbol y Patria. El fútbol y las narrativas de la nación en Argentina*. Buenos Aires: Prometeo.

Archetti, Eduardo. 2001. "The Spectacle of a Heroic Life: The Case of Diego Maradona". *Sport Stars: The Cultural Politics of Sporting Celebrity*. Eds. David L. Andrews & Steven J. Jackson. London: Routledge.

_____. 2003. *Masculinidades: fútbol, tango y polo en Argentina*. Buenos Aires: Antropofagia.

*As.com*. 2021. "Inauguran mural en honor a Maradona en el Azteca". https://mexico.as.com/mexico/2021/06/30/futbol/1625023404_451771.html [Accessed June 29, 2021].

Barbier, Joachim. 2021. "L'Eldorado de D10S". *So-Foot*, 18.H, December 2020-January 2021: 428–435.

Brach, Bartlomiej. 2011. "Who is Lionel Messi? A Comparative Study of Diego Maradona and Lionel Messi". *International Journal of Cultural Studies*, 15:4, 415–428.

Burgo, Andrés. 2016. *El partido. Argentina-Inglaterra 1986*. Buenos Aires: Tusquets.

De Anda, Francisco. 2020. *De tu mano. José Francisco Gabriel de Anda*. México: ETM.

*Expansión*. 2020. "Las otras jugadas de Maradona en México: críticas a Fox y aplausos a AMLO". https://politica.expansion.mx/mexico/2020/11/25/las-otras-jugadas-de-maradona-en-mexico-criticas-a-fox-y-aplausos-a-amlo [Accessed November 26, 2020].

Islas, Adriana. 2018. "El Mundial que sanó la tragedia. México frente a la crisis del terremoto". *Istor*, 72, 163–168.

Jiménez, Axel. 2020. "Mexico 1970: Football and Multiple Forms of Modern Nation-Building during the 1970 World Cup". *Soccer & Society*, 21:8, 876–888.

Kioussis, George. 2020. "A Bid Denied: The U.S. Application Host the 1986 World Cup". *Soccer & Society*, 21:8, 946–959.

Maradona, Diego. 2016. *México 86. Mi mundial. Mi verdad: Así ganamos la Copa*. Buenos Aires: Sudamericana.

_____. 2000. *Yo soy el Diego. Diego Armando Maradona*. Buenos Aires: Planeta.

*Medio Tiempo*. 2005. "Critica Vicente Fox a Maradona por meterse en política". November 4. https://www.mediotiempo.com/futbol/liga-mx/critica-vicente-fox-maradona-meterse-politica [Accessed March 28, 2021].

*Proceso*. 2021. "Abren en Cholula la primera Iglesia Maradoniana en México". https://www.proceso.com.mx/deportes/2021/7/12/abren-en-cholula-la-primera-iglesia-maradoniana-de-mexico-267676.html [Accessed July 12, 2021].

Procuna, Ciro. 2020. "Maradona: genio del fútbol mundial". *ESPN Mexico online*. https://www.espn.com.mx/futbol/mexico/nota/_/id/7799961/diego-maradona-mexico-86-genio-del-futbol [Accessed July 12, 2021].

Ridge, Patrick. 2019. "*El desmadre*: Counter-hegemonic Fervour in Carlos Monsiváis's 1986 World Cup Chronicles". *Soccer & Society*, 20:7–8, 960–972.

Rodríguez, María. 1996. "Maradona revisitado". *Cuestión de pelotas: fútbol, deporte, sociedad y cultura*. Eds. Pablo Alabarces and María Rodríguez. Buenos Aires: Atuel.

Salazar-Sutil, Nicolás. 2008. "Maradona Inc. Performance Politics off the Pitch". *International Journal of Cultural Studies*, 11:4, 441–458.

Segura, Fernando. 2013. "Diego Armando Maradona: vers une interprétation de la vie de l´icône". *Spectacles sportifs, dispositifs d´écriture*. Ed. Jean-François Diana. Nancy: Université de Lorraine.

———. 2018. "Diego Armando Maradona: los Mundiales y la política". *Istor*, 72, 227–236.

Villoro, Juan. 2006. *Dios es Redondo*. México: Planeta.

———. 2020. "La Muerte de Dios". *Reforma*. November 26. https://www.reforma.com/libre/acceso/accesofb.htm?urlredirect=/la-muerte-de-dios-2020-11-26/op193562 [Accessed July 12, 2021].

Whannel, Garry. 2010. "News, Celebrity, and Vortextuality: A Study of the Media Coverage of the Michael Jackson Verdict". *Cultural Politics*, 6:1, 65–84.

Williams, John and Richard Holt. 2020. "*The Beautiful Game?* The FIFA World Cup and English Perceptions of Brazil and Argentina, 1958-1986". *Contemporary British History*, 34:1, 140–162.

Yankelevich, Pablo. 2020. "Argenmex: itineraries del exilo agentino en México". *Istor*, 80, 77–104.

Zanoni, Leandro. 2006. *Vivir en los medios: Maradona off the record*. Buenos Aires: Editorial Marea.

# 5

# MARADONA AND BRITAIN

## An Unforgettable Affair

*Raymond Boyle*

### British media systems and the age of Maradona

This chapter examines the range of representations of Maradona found over the decades in the British media. The British public first took an interest in Maradona when, as an 18 year old, he played for Argentina against Scotland at Hampden Park, Glasgow, on June 2, 1979, scoring his first international goal. He won rave reviews from the Scottish newspaper media for his performance. Over the next decades, the relationship between the player and his image in the British media would change reflecting not only his evolving career, but also the political context against which the player and international sport would be reported. Representations would also reflect internal tensions within the British media, with differing images of the player found in the Scottish- and English-based media. Within Britain, the English and Scottish media markets are by far the largest and hence the focus of this chapter. It does not focus on Wales or Northern Ireland, the latter of the United Kingdom (UK), rather than Great Britain.

In order to understand the discourses that surrounded Maradona, we need to acknowledge the highly political nature of mediated sport. Despite the idea that sport and politics do not mix, sport, and international sport particularly, is immersed in politics (O'Brien, Holden and Ginesta, 2021). Politics in this sense establishes powerful cultural narratives that are often bound in up in wider national and cultural identities (Boyle, Blain and O'Donnell, 1993). The mediation of sport is crucial in helping to shape the dominant narratives that become embedded in wider everyday discourses of ethnicity, race, and identity. By this we mean the ways in which the media transform discourses already embedded in sport and select, amplify, and construct these for wider public consumption. International sport offers a particularly rich site for such media

DOI: 10.4324/9781003196587-7

transformation (Alabarces *et al*, 2001; Sugden and Tomlinson, 2002; Boyle and Haynes, 2009) related to aspects of national identity formation through sporting representations.

The media era of Maradona the player was an analogue age. The abundance of often competing representations offered in the contemporary digital age of plenty may have shaped the Maradona story in more recent years, but as a player he was at his prime in a time dominated by strictly limited media in Britain. Maradona the player was defined by the newspapers and the narratives they shaped about him and by televised mega events such as the FIFA World Cup that brought the player into millions of homes every four years and played a central role in telling – and constructing – the story of Maradona the player (Archetti, 2001).

In this context, it is also important to understand the specific structural dimensions of the British media market in the 1980s and 1990s. Broadly, there were two tiers in the newspaper marketplace. The tabloids, or popular press – such as the London-based nationals like *The Mirror* and *The Sun*, or in Scotland, the Glasgow-based *Daily Record* – enjoyed significant circulation figures and aimed at a mass market. They carried a low cover price and were sustained by sensationalism, celebrity, scandal, sport, and a combination of soft and hard news. They were opinion-driven newspapers and so, in particular, were the sports desks at these papers. They were also characterised by large headlines (or splashes), and by the 1980s, an increase in sporting stories or celebrities crossing over from the back page (sport) to be covered on the front page (news) as an intense circulation battle between tabloids became a feature of this decade (Boyle, 2006). The Broadsheet market or quality press – examples being the London-based *Times*, or the *Guardian*, or the then *Glasgow Herald*, or the Edinburgh-based *Scotsman* – tended to be more restrained in their coverage of news and politics, carried less sport, and was aimed at a more affluent market. Again, this was not only an era of strictly limited media in Britain, but also a highly competitive newspaper market at a time of extensive newspaper readerships across Britain.

The complexities of the British state are reflected in the rather disorientating media system which characterises aspects of the British media (Curran and Seaton, 2018). Britain has a London-dominated media system, with various degrees of regional and national devolution. By this we mean that while there is a London-based UK press, there is also distinct Scottish newspaper market with titles aimed specifically at Scotland. There is a large BBC programme opt-out for Scotland that means that certain programmes are only shown in Scotland on BBC Scotland. Meanwhile, STV (Scottish Television) carries many London-based programmes on its channel, and it also has opt-out programming which shows, for example Scottish news, sport, and current affairs, to its Scottish audience. During the 1980s, for example, the semi-autonomous Scottish newspaper sector was an important carrier of Scottish national identity at a time of limited specific Scottish based television production. While the London-based national newspaper titles carried Scottish content, during the 1980s, a change that allowed customised and more regionalised editions of newspapers saw these London titles now offering a Scottish edition, usually with some Scottish news and sport added at the expense of English content, competing with the Scottish-based newspapers, such as *The Glasgow Herald, The Scotsman,* and the *Daily Record*, which sold few copies in England and created a distinctive Scottish public sphere in both politics and sport. In short, newspapers in Scotland marked out a distinctive territory particularly in Scottish sports journalism and reporting and carried UK-wide content (Blain and Hutchison, 2008). London-based UK dailies carried little or no Scottish content or sport. Typically, a sports journalist working out of London would have little knowledge or understanding of the distinctive media and sporting culture that existed in Scotland. Hence, there were two clearly diverging sporting and political agendas in existence during the high point of Maradona's playing career during the 1980s, and this helps to explain the very different discourses around the player that circulated in the sports journalism across the British press at this time. By 2008, when Maradona returned to Britain as manager of the Argentinian national team, two deeply rooted narratives around his story had already become well established in the sports media in Britain. In England, there was grudging admiration for him as an outstanding footballing talent, always underscored by the perception that he had cheated England at the 1986 World Cup finals in Mexico. In Scotland, he was portrayed as a maverick, footballing genius, whom the Scots were lucky enough to first see play for the Argentinian national team on his debut. To add to his lustre with the Scottish sporting and media sector, he had played a key role in helping to defeat that traditional Scottish sporting foe, the "Auld Enemy", England.

## A saint ordained: Maradona the genius

For many in the British media, the Maradona story began on that beguiling sunny afternoon at Hampden Park in Glasgow with an international football friendly played in front of a paying audience of 62,000 Scottish supporters and the transfixed Scottish media. Glasgow based sports journalist Hugh Macdonald reflects on this important sporting moment by arguing that: "Hampden of 1979 also offered the first stanza of a heroic poem that had glory, failure, redemption, more failure, weakening glory and redemption … Hampden '79 was my baptism into the benign cult of Diego. I subsequently spent the next four decades jumping at his goals, wincing at his excesses, and occasionally praying for his well-being" (Macdonald, 2020: 34).

The city of Glasgow is more than a footnote in the story of Maradona. It was there in 1979 and then 2008 that he marked his debut as both an Argentinian international player and, almost 30 years later, as the manager of the national team.[1] Hence, while Hampden Park, Glasgow, may be all but invisible in the Maradona story, it was significant as it signalled for many his arrival on the radar of the Scottish – and to a lesser extent the English – footballing media and public. It also began a love affair between the player and the Scottish footballing public (and the Scottish media) that would be consummated in the 1986 World Cup with his role in the defeat of England in the quarterfinal and would remain undiminished until his passing in 2020.

The arrival of world champions Argentina in Glasgow in 1979 was always going to be a major story in a football mad city. However, rumours in the Scottish press abounded about a new player, Diego Maradona, who was being tipped to become a global star. The Scottish footballing media in the late 1970s were a notoriously cynical and hard-nosed group of journalists, not easily impressed. The fact that they left Hampden that June day raving enthusiastically about what they had seen helped kick-start an affection for the footballing genius of Maradona that would remain undiminished within the Scotland media until his death. Scottish journalist Patrick Glenn, writing in the *Observer* under the head-line "Prima Maradona!" stated that:

> Diego Maradona left his mark on Hampden Park yesterday with a goal and a performance which destroyed Scotland and confirmed his claim to be called the new Pele … It is probably the first time in history that most of the infantrymen in the militant Hampden hordes had come prepared to marvel at a member of the opposition. Everybody, it seemed, wanted to see Diego Maradona. The genius of the 18-year-old Argentinian prodigy had preceded him throughout the world champion's tour of Europe, like a herald proclaiming the arrival of some great monarch.
>
> *The Observer, June 3, 1979: 32*

Hence, initial media engagement with Maradona by the Scottish and English sporting media was framed around unqualified admiration for someone the journalists were already recognising as a footballing genius. He was a player, they argued, who would be capable of sitting alongside the greats of the game such as Pele or Cruyff and who would dominate world football for many years to come. Of course, by the time Maradona appeared at his first World Cup in Spain in 1982, the framing of both player and country within the British media would be very different and inextricably linked to the military conflict between the two countries that took place in the South Atlantic between April and June of that year.

## Maradona and the "Hand of God"

Two newspaper headlines serve as examples of the content of this section: TANKS OUT FOR WORLD CUP CLASH (front page, *The Mirror,* June 20, 1986) and DIEGO THE CHEAT (*The Sun,* June 21, 1986).

The Falklands war of 1982, as it was called in Britain, centred on the disputed Falkland Isles or Islas Malvinas as they are called in Argentina and shaped the political narratives through which sporting clashes between the two countries were often framed. The conflict between Britain and Argentina was refracted through differing media and political lens. What was not in dispute was the deaths suffered during 74 days of conflict, with Argentinian losses over double of those of Britain. In both countries, the popular press rallied behind their respective troops, heightening tension and helping to harden attitudes on both sides. The war was in its dying embers as the 1982 World Cup in Spain started with Argentina, the defending champions, defeated by Belgium on the 13th of June. The conflict in the South Atlantic ended the following day and its legacy would shape both countries for many years to come. While they avoided each other in the tournament, this would not be case four years later in the 1986 World Cup in Mexico in a clash that would help determine the perception of Maradona in the British media until his untimely death 34 years later.

After the disappointment of 1982, Maradona arrived in Mexico in 1986 surrounded by media controversy centred on doubts with regard to his fitness and the supposed internal team tensions as he was named captain of a team tasked with securing another title. England had also qualified for the tournament and, as it became a possibility that the two teams might meet in the quarterfinals, the British tabloids made much of the concerns that some supporters might use the occasion as a platform for politically motivated violence, with *The Mirror* (20th of June) reporting that "[t]roops and riot police (were being) called in for England *vs*. Argentina game". Despite Maradona downplaying the nationalistic overtones that framed the pre-match reporting of the game, he would later admit in his autobiography: "In the pre-match interviews we all had said that football and politics shouldn't be confused, but that was a lie. We did nothing but think about that. Bollocks was it just another match!" (Maradona, 2004: 127–128). In any case, most of the British media had not believed Maradona's dismissal of the political implications at the time. There was a very real concern about violence occurring at the game, in part due to the presence of far-right English National Front members travelling with the England fans. Of course, the tabloid press loved nothing better than to stoke up the nationalistic temperature and rhetoric around such a symbolically loaded sporting event and then become condemnatory when this spilled over into actual violence (or football hooliganism as it was termed in the 1980s) in and around the match itself. However, it would be unbalanced to characterise the British media solely through the eyes of the highly influential London-based tabloids. It is also the case that insightful and reflective forms of sports journalism could be found in the newspaper market as the game grew ever closer.

In the build-up to the match, the legendary Scottish sportswriter Hugh McIlvanney, writing in the London-based *Observer* newspaper on June 22, 1986, was unstinting in his praise for Maradona and clear that he would be the deciding factor in the forthcoming quarter-final. Given the second goal that Maradona would score in that match, picking up the ball initially with his back to the England goal in his own half before embarking on a mazy and mesmerising run, McIlvanney's pre-match piece would prove to be unnervingly accurate. In "At the Mercy of the Prima Maradona", published on the morning of the game, the journalist compared the player to a high-end sports car:

> [He] is a Formula One machine all right, a phenomenon capable of reducing the best and swiftest defenders to impotent pursuit, of leaving them as miserable stragglers baffled by astonishing surges of acceleration and the most remarkable power steering in sport. Maradona's changes of direction are so devastatingly sudden and extreme that they must impose a huge strain on his lower body. Surely there has not been such a pelvis since Elvis Presley was in his prime.
>
> *The Observer, June 22, 1986; McIlvanney, 1995: 257*

The game was eventually won by Argentina by two (Maradona) goals to one. It would be the first of those goals scored six minutes into the second half that would define him in the eyes of much of British media – viewed as the actions of a cheat by the London-based newspapers, and with an element of admiration by some in the Scottish footballing media.

His handball, later christened the "Hand of God", made headlines after the match: "Hand it to Diego", The *Daily Mail*, June 23, 1986; "Fists Fly as England Go Out", *The Mirror*, June 23, 1986; "Cheats Prosper in Professional Sport", *The Daily Telegraph*, June 27, 1986.

Perhaps the most explicit linking of politics and sport came with the headline in the London-based *Sun* newspaper (at the time the largest selling newspaper in Britain) that splashed with "OUTCHA! Argies Get Their Own Back on Us", *The Sun*, June 23, 1986. The headline was clearly aimed at its English readership, since in editions of the paper on sale in Scotland the headline was changed from "on us" to "as England tumble out". It was a play on the infamous headline carried during the Falklands conflict when it reported the Royal Navy crippling the Argentinian cruiser General Belgrano with the front-page splash "Gotcha: Our Lads Sink Gunboat and Hole Cruiser" (*The Sun,* May 4, 1982). The populist, jingoistic language mobilised during the Falklands conflict by large sections of the British press was, in this case simply translated across into the sporting arena, often by non-sports tabloid journalists, as an easy form of cultural shorthand that revelled in the boundaries between "them" and "us".

As the game was being broadcast live on both major television channels in Britain, the BBC and ITV (STV in Scotland), it was also clear, through the numerous television slow-motion action replays and freeze frames for the watching public that the hand of Maradona had played a key role in the goal. Yet, if the first goal displayed an element of streetwise cunning within the game that the English-based tabloids liked to attribute to cheating when carried out by foreigner players but were always more reticent about condemning when committed by English players, the second goal cemented Maradona's reputation as one of the greatest players to ever grace the world stage. The goal, so accurately predicted by McIlvanney and described as a "miracle" by

England's manager Bobby Robson, offset somewhat the vitriol that parts of the English media were ready to unleash around the injustice of Maradona's initial goal.

For the British media, 1986 became a defining year in their treatment of Maradona and the narratives that helped frame his representation for the remainder of his life. It was a polarising moment in the media coverage of his life and times, despite him being only 25 years old at the time. For some he was cheat, for others a footballing genius, and for many more, he was in fact both of these things. His complex character and identity were forever captured in these two iconic moments witnessed live on British television by an audience of 23.7 million viewers (15.3 million on the BBC and 8.4 million on ITV) (www.barb.co.uk). It remains the third largest British television audience for an England World Cup match, with the second largest also featuring Argentina and their clash with England at the 1998 World Cup finals in France.

As is often the case with high-profile sportspeople, Maradona became a lightning rod for debate around a multitude of issues from ethics in sport to the growing influence of money and the media in the sport. In hindsight, these interventions seem faintly old-fashioned, given the changes in the football and media relationship that have transformed the game in the last few decades (Boyle, 2019). At the height of his footballing powers, Maradona existed in a pre-digital media age influenced and shaped by traditional newspaper, radio, and TV journalism and strictly limited television coverage of live club football. Yet, it is also true that he was the first global footballing superstar, projected around the world through the platform of the FIFA World Cup, who would experience both the growing power of media celebrity and a growing commercial shift in media values and content.

Distinct from their Scottish counterparts, the English media always viewed Maradona through the 1986 handball incident. Journalist Jason Burt acknowledged the degree that this puzzles others in the footballing world: "To the rest of the world it may seem churlish to examine his career through the prism of one match, but for England and England supporters no memory of him can be complete without recollections of that vivid World Cup quarter-final inside the vast cavern of the Azteca Stadium in Mexico City 34 years ago and in front of 114,580 fans" (Burt, 2020).

The defeat of the English team and the role played by Maradona in this defeat had different repercussions in the Scottish media and specifically among football fans, often to the chagrin of English journalists and football fans. For a stateless nation such as Scotland, the sporting arena has over the years been one of the few platforms through which a Scottish identity, as distinct from an English/British one, can be projected on the world stage. For many living in Scotland during the 1980s, the country felt politically and culturally invisible within the wider political discourses that often wrongly substituted England for Britain. The British media system of the 1980s (with the then exception of the Scottish newspaper industry) was a London-centric driven entity, which often failed to recognise the distinctive difference in Scotland's political, legal, and educational culture from that of the rest of the UK. The antecedents of Scottish political devolution (which finally occurred with the restoration of the Scottish Parliament in 1999) and the growing nationalist movement for Scottish independence that dominates the contemporary Scottish and British politics scene were being established in this decade, when the country felt it was suffering from a democratic deficit, as it had a London government that Scotland consistently did not vote for. It is against this wider backdrop that the hero worship associated with Maradona reached a sustained peak with the Scottish media and its footballing public and differentiated it from the reaction of English media and footballing supporters.

Yet even among the battle-hardened sports journalists of the London tabloids, time has added some long overdue reflection to the framing of Maradona. Andy Dunn, chief sportswriter with *The Mirror*, on looking back at the life of Maradona, noted that:

> Yes, the Hand of God goal in that quarterfinal was illegal but it is easy to forget how England had physically targeted him in that game. Remember him as a cheat if you want, but remember England, like every other opponent, were never bothered about legalities when it came to trying to stop Maradona. And that is what made his greatest goal all the more remarkable, that is what made this player all the more remarkable … No genius will ever be as flawed, no one flawed will ever possess his genius. Diego Armando Maradona. The greatest of all time? Probably. The most remarkable one-off? Without a doubt.
>
> *Dunn, 2020: 66*

Maradona drew publicity towards him like a vortex, yet journalists also highlight that for many football fans, including the English, he was always regarded as first and foremost an outstanding player. As Henry Winter, of *The Times* argues: "Three years ago, Maradona was presented on the Wembley field at half time of a Tottenham Hotspur game against Liverpool, and the reception was rapturous. English fans appreciate class, and are prepared to put past anger behind them to acknowledge greatness. If you love football, you love Maradona. Rest in peace" (Winter, 2020: 70). So, he would be "forgiven" by many (but not all) in the English game for first goal in the 1986 World Cup; the second of course has become embedded in World Cup history as one of the greatest of all time.

## A hero returns

Maradona returned to Hampden in 2008 as manager of Argentina for a friendly match against Scotland. He was given a hero's welcome by supporters and the Scottish media alike. Supporters displayed "Thank you for 1986" flags at the match referencing the role he played in the defeat of England. Maradona himself was acutely aware of his status in Scotland. Speaking to the Scottish newspaper *Daily Record* he stated:

> I am really happy to start my career as Argentina's manager in Scotland. The Scottish people love me because of the goals I scored against England. The Scots have a great rivalry with the English and will remember the goals I scored against them. The people will be friendly to us … I have great memories of Hampden. I played my first game for the national team there. We won 3-1 and I scored a goal. I have never forgotten it.
>
> *Daily Record, November 1, 2008*

The impact of his return to Glasgow was not only felt by footballing supporters in the city; the Scottish media were also in awe of him. As Graham Spiers, writing for *The Times*, noted the journalists "gathered in hushed tones around the entrance to an hotel in the centre of Glasgow yesterday. From the ever-growing kerfuffle that developed, any innocent passer-by might have thought that the Second Coming was imminent. "Have you seen him?" someone asked. "Yes, yes … he passed by that doorway five minutes ago." When Diego Maradona is in town, the natives evidently stir (*The Times*, November 8, 2008). The night before the game, the Argentinian squad trained at Celtic Park in the city, home of Celtic Football Club. Mathew Lindsay of the Glasgow *Evening Times* commented that:

> Most of football's greats have passed through Parkhead's gates' Celtic supporters can now add another name to the anthem they belt out lustily at home and away games alike. For Diego Maradona, who fleetingly graced the hallowed turf at Celtic Park for a training session with Argentina last night, is as great as they get. Admittedly, Diego, the man many believe to be the beautiful game's most talented ever exponent, was not at the world-famous Glasgow ground to play a match himself. He was there to put the national team which he represented with such distinction in his playing days, and has recently agreed to manage, through their paces. Yet, judging by the massive media interest in such a low-key event, you would have thought the great man was taking part in another World Cup Final.
>
> *Evening Times, November 18, 2008*

To characterise the standing Maradona had among the Scottish footballing public and media simply as an expression of an anti-English sentiment is also to misunderstand the Scottish psyche. Stephen McGowan, chief football writer of the Scottish edition of the *Daily Mail*, captured this connection when reflecting on the 2008 visit. He noted that knocking England out of a World Cup was always going to guarantee a warm welcome in Scotland, but it went further than that:

> In this country [Scotland], sports fans adhere to an old truth: brilliance and individual application may be admirable, but a sportsman often garners

greater appeal when he reveals his darker side … In this country, we like our heroes to come with a health warning. Our football, like our boxing, has thrown up some tragic figures. In Scotland we have witnessed all too many who, allowed half an opportunity, will find the most contrived method by which to waste their privileged lifestyles … Scotland has borne witness to no shortage of flawed maestros over the years. Never again, though, will we see another Diego Armando Maradona, the greatest footballer of all time.

*McGowan, 2020*

Maradona – the working class flawed footballing maverick – struck a chord with the Scottish sporting public who recognised in him the traits of many previous Scottish footballers and sportsmen of the past such as maverick footballers like Jim Baxter and Celtic's Jimmy Johnstone and working-class sporting heroes such as world champion flyweight boxer, Benny Lynch. In this sense, the success of Maradona in giving the English a metaphorical bloody nose over the years was only part of his appeal in Scotland.[2] He also tapped into a deeper part of the sporting psyche of the public rooted in aspects of a cultural and national identity that recognised and idolised the sporting outsider, the maverick, the flawed footballer from the streets. In 2008, Richard Williams, chief sportswriter of *The Guardian* observed astutely in "Glasgow Hails the Hand of God":

Apart from Buenos Aires, his home city, and Naples, where he performed miracles in the 1980s while falling under the influence of the Camorra and cocaine, there is possibly no city on earth that would give him a warmer welcome than Glasgow, where his hand-ball goal in Mexico 22 years ago was fervently acclaimed and where he will make his debut as Argentina's head coach in tonight's friendly match against Scotland.

*The Guardian, November 18, 2008*

The Scottish love affair with Maradona remained undiminished.

## Maradona and the British through time: Death and reconciliation?

As noted from the outset of this chapter, to understand the nature and tenor of the British media reporting of Maradona media context is crucial. The 1980s were a time of strictly limited television in Britain, and the wall-to-wall coverage of football on television (across free-to-air and pay-TV platforms) so enjoyed by footballing fans today would only develop towards the latter part of that decade and grow in the 1990s. This meant that for footballing fans in Britain in the 1980s, there was virtually no coverage of international club football shown on British television, and certainly no coverage of the major European leagues in Italy or Spain. For most football fans living in Britain in the 1980s, the opportunities to see Maradona during his time at FC Barcelona (1982–1984) or SSC Napoli (1984–1991) were limited or non-existent.

In Britain, the free-to-air Channel 4 (launched in 1982) did not start broadcasting its ground-breaking coverage of Italian football with its *Football Italia* programme until 1992, while British Satellite Broadcasting (BSB), one of the early movers in the Pay-TV market in Britain, only launched in 1990, with its Italian football coverage (watched by a tiny subscription-based audience) as one of its attractions. Even then, this consisted of around one live match every week, a situation unthinkable in the contemporary age of rolling live matches on Pay-TV. For the vast majority of football fans in Britain, the FIFA World Cups of 1982, 1986, 1990, and 1994 were their appointments to watch Maradona live on television, and as result these events, rather than his club playing career is what has tended to shape media coverage of the player in terms of the British media. In the late 1980s and into the 1990s, media coverage of Maradona in Britain begins to increase, but it tends to focus on his off-the-field issues which increasingly overshadow any sporting exploits. From reports of links with organised crime in Italy, to stories of addiction and weight gain, through to run-ins with the Italian tax authorities, the central narratives around the player shift from the sporting back pages to the sensationalist news sections of the popular press particularly when he tested positive for cocaine and was banned in April 1991. The merging in media coverage of his off-the-field issues with his on-field playing persona was stripped bare for the British footballing public at the 1994 United States World Cup. Here was a troubled genius, attempting at the age of 33 to return to the world stage and then falling spectacularly from grace following the post-match positive doping test that would lead to his expulsion from the competition.

His death will put Maradona back in the spotlight. In "Mesmerising Maradona Was Untouchable", Scottish sportswriter Graham Spiers writes: "For some reason, when great footballers die, you feel another milestone in your life passing. It is almost as if they represented a part of you —your youth, your middle years— and so your own chapters are passing and closing. I've felt my own mortality this week with the death of Maradona. But I feel so privileged to have watched him" (*The Times,* November 28, 2020). On his death in 2020, there was much focus from the British media around the 1986 World Cup and the "Hand of God" moment. And while it's true this was the prism through which much of the media began to make sense of his life, there were also plenty of reflective considerations of Maradona's wider political and cultural impact beyond simply that game with many positive journalistic pieces that gave context to his impact as a global footballer and also a cultural icon and national hero in Argentina. An example can be found in *The Guardian*, where Jonathan Wilson wrote:

> In the 1920s, as Argentina, a booming immigrant nation, sought a sense of identity, it became apparent that football was one of the few things that bound its disparate population together. No matter what your background, you wanted the team in the blue and white striped shirts to win —and

that meant the way the national side played was of political and cultural significance … He (Maradona) was not merely a genius but one who came draped in symbolic importance.

*Wilson, 2020*

The dominant motif of the coverage was that of the flawed footballing genius, whose life was played out, both on and off the pitch in the glare of public and media scrutiny. In a piece with the headline, "Outrageous and Fearless – Diego Lived Ten Epic Lives", Matt Dickinson, chief football writer in *The Times*, noted: "And what a talent. Billions kick a football but Maradona could do it perhaps better than anyone who has ever tried. That, surely, is how we remember him … We should give thanks to Diego Maradona, and football's most epic life" (Dickinson, 2020). Perhaps the overarching themes of the media coverage of his death are best summed up by the Scottish edition of the popular tabloid *The Sun* and its column-ist Bill Leckie. In "Beaten by Age-Old Foe", he recognised not only Maradona's genius on the pitch but also the chaotic lifestyle away from the playing field: "At his best, he was a fantasy who could outrun the wind, sidestep tidal waves and leap higher than the clouds. At his worst, reality was always going to man-mark the life out of the incredible Diego Armando Maradona. Because you truly never did see a man more in control of the ball on the pitch yet less in control of his life off it". And then he concluded: "We watch them rise, then crash. But none soared quite so close to the sun and spiralled so spectacularly back to earth as Maradona" (Leckie, 2020).

On television, BBC re-screened a documentary from 2006, presented by for-mer England footballer and now broadcaster Gary Lineker. *When Lineker Met Maradona* was a highly sympathetic feature that centred around an interview with the player in Buenos Aires before the 2006 World Cup. And while the goals against England were discussed, the programme showed Maradona as a warm, articulate, and passionate person, keen to enjoy his new-found health and fitness and to show Lineker his involvement with his local club, Boca Juniors. Interestingly, the interview also highlighted the cultural differences between Argentinian and English footballers and the culture that surrounds the game in both countries. There was mutual respect throughout the programme. Despite some criticism of Lineker's tweet on hearing of the death of Maradona in 2020, he maintained he had nothing but respect for the player: "By some distance, the best player of my generation and arguably the greatest of all time. After a blessed but troubled life, hopefully he will finally find some comfort in the hands of God #RipDiego": tweeted @GaryLineker.

Such was the impact of his death on the news media in Britain that even an elite business newspaper such as the *Financial Times* (FT), not noted for its sports coverage, recognised the impact of Maradona: "Although Maradona embraced, and was embraced by, the political left in the region—he even died on the anni-versary of the death of one of the people he most admired, the late Cuban dicta-tor Fidel Castro—Argentinians of all political stripes were distraught" (*Financial Times*, November 26, 2020: 6).

As noted above, the Scottish newspapers in particular focused on his Hampden goal of 1979 and his return to Scotland in 2008 as national coach. In this way, all newspapers speak to their markets and their readers and frame narratives through a particularly specific local, region, or national lens, and the death of Maradona reflected this process in the British media.

## Maradona moments

The British media representation of Maradona broadly falls into distinct moments. The first one takes place in 1979 with his goal as Hampden Park which sees the player arrive on the radar of the Scottish- and London-based media. For the Scottish media, this is the start of a love affair and fascination with Maradona that will last the rest of his life. For the London-based media, this is the age of Maradona the footballing genius and the arrival a genuine world-class epoch defining player. The second moment lasts through the 1980s and is shaped by the wider political climate between the two countries ignited by events in the South Atlantic in 1982. The 1986 World Cup and Maradona's role in knocking England out of it cast a long shadow in terms of the attitude of much of the London-based media to the player. It recognises him not only as the great player he was (epitomised by his second goal in the quarter-final), but also as a cheat who manipulated the rules to secure victory (epitomised by his first goal). The popular press in Britain tends to deal in absolutes, hence the cultural differences that might exist between what is defined as cheating in European football and that of South American football were never explored. The "cheat" narrative also fitted with the broader discourse around Argentina as a country that was informed by the military conflict and wider cultural and national stereotypes. It is important to remember that this period (the 1980/early 1990s) is marked by the dominance of the popular press in setting and sustaining such narratives, an age of little coverage of club football and limited media. In the third Maradona moment, his off-the-field troubles would come to dominate media coverage culminating in his expulsion from the 1994 World Cup. Yet, the fourth and final moment for Maradona and his affair with the British media took place with his untimely death and was perhaps more nuanced than some would have you to believe. Yes, the "Hand of God" ran through the coverage of the player and his life, but alongside there were wholesome and heartfelt praise from journalists, ex-players, and sportswriters thanking him for the joy he had brought to footballing fans over the years, and recognition of his status as one of the greatest players ever to grace the world stage. In short, media coverage moved from representing Maradona as a footballing superstar, to a stage dominated by that 1986 World Cup match, through a troubled off-field existence in Italy and beyond, to one that enjoyed some sort of redemption in his later years.

It is wrong, as has been argued throughout this chapter, to unproblematically talk about the British media and Maradona as if they operated with one voice. The Scottish media specifically both inflected and reflected an alternative political, cultural, and sporting space that existed in Scotland and their treatment of Maradona is indicative of this difference. In Scotland, Maradona's "cheating" was less of an issue for the footballing public, not least as his role in defeating England gave him cult status with Scottish supporters, while his travails and difficulties as a flawed sporting genius also resonated with the Scottish sporting psyche and was reflected in more favourable media coverage that was the case in England. His status as a sporting superstar meant that Maradona's status and the respect in which he was held by much of the Scottish media remained undiminished throughout his life and was kickstarted by that electrifying performance by the 18-year-old at Hampden Park.

Another time, another life.

## Notes

1 An interesting, if chaotic, account of Maradona's two visits to Scotland can be found in John Ludden (2021).
2 María Graciela Rodríguez (2003) studies the relationship between Scottish Fans – specifically those identified with the Tartan Army – and Maradona. This group is known for singing to the tune of the Hokey Cokey: "You put your left arm in/your left arm out/In, out, in, out/you shake it all about/You do the Maradona/ and you score a goal/That's what it's all about/Oh, Diego Maradona, Oh, Diego Maradona, Oh, Diego Maradona!/He put the English out, out, out" (2003). See an example here: https://www.youtube.com/watch?v=Iz4RQXMbbf4. In his recounting of the 1986 Mexico World Cup, Maradona states that he became an idol in Scotland because of the first goal against England in 1986. He also reveals that he asked to have the Tartan Army's song written in a piece of paper and has kept it (Maradona 2016: 166–167).

## References

Archetti, Eduardo. 2001. "The Spectacle of a Heroic Life: The Case of Diego Maradona". *Sport Stars: The Cultural Politics of Cultural Celebrity*. Eds. David L. Andrews and Steven J. Jackson. London; New York: Routledge, 151–164.

Blain, Neil and David Hutchison, eds. 2008. *The Media in Scotland*. Edinburgh: Edinburgh University Press.

Boyle, Raymond, Neil Blain and Hugh O'Donnell. 1993. *Sport and National Identity in the European Media*. London: Pinter Press.

Boyle, Raymond. 2006. *Sports Journalism: Context and Issues*. London: Sage.

Boyle, Raymond and Richard Haynes. 2009. 2nd edition. *Power Play: Sport the Media and Popular Culture*. Edinburgh: Edinburgh University Press.

Boyle, Raymond, ed. 2019. *Changing Sports Journalism Practice in the Age of Digital Media*. London: Routledge.

Burt, Jason. 2020. "How the 'Hand of God' Earned a Special Place in English Folklore". *The Daily Telegraph,* November 26, 4.

Curran, James and Jean Seaton. 2018. 8th edition. *Power Without Responsibility: Press, Broadcasting and the Internet in Britain*. London: Routledge.

Dickinson, Matt. 2020. "Outrageous and Fearless – Diego Lived Ten Epic Lives". *The Times*. November 26, 72–73.

Dunn, Andy. 2020. "A Genius Touched by God … And the Devil". *The Mirror*. November 26, 66.

Glenn, Patrick. 1979. "Prima Maradona!" *The Observer*. June 3, 32.

Leckie, Bill. 2020. "Beaten By Age-Old Foe". *The Sun*. November 26, 97.

Ludden, John. 2021. *Maradona. Give My Regards to Hope Street*. South Carolina: Author edition.

Macdonald, Hugh. 2020. "A Saint Ordained at Hampden". *The Herald*. November 26, 34–35.

Maradona, Diego. 2004. *El Diego*. Yellow Jersey Press: London.

———. 2016. *México 86. Mi mundial. Mi verdad. Así ganamos la copa*. Buenos Aires: Sudamericana.

McGowan, Stephen. 2020. "Maverick Who Had Scotland Enraptured From the Beginning of His Odyssey Until the End". *Scottish Daily Mail*. November 26, 94–95.

McIlvanney, Hugh. 1995. *McIlvanney on Football*. Mainstream Press: Edinburgh.

O'Brien, John, Russell Holden and Xavier Ginesta, eds. 2021. *Sport, Globalisation and Identity: New Perspectives on Regions and Nations*. London: Routledge.

Rodríguez, María Graciela. 2003. "Los días en que Maradona usó kilt: intersección de identidades profundas con representaciones massmediáticas". *Futbologías. Fútbol, identidad y violencia en América Latina*. Comp. Pablo Alabarces. Buenos Aires: CLACSO, 181–197.

Williams, Richard. 2008. "Glasgow Hails the Hand of God". *The Guardian*, November 18.

Wilson, Jonathan. 2020. "From the Buenos Aires Slums or the World's Best, Child Genius who Fulfilled an Argentinian Prophecy". *The Guardian*, November 26, 46.

Winter, Henry. 2020. "Ignore the Cheating—If You Love Football Then You Love Maradona". *The Times*. November 26, 70.

# PART II
# Representing Maradona

# 6

# MARADONA AND LITERATURE

## God Is Only Human

*Pablo Brescia*

### Maradona's (hi)story

The stage is set. Lights.

On October 11, 2009, in the Monumental Stadium in Buenos Aires, Argentina, Martín Palermo – a player with a mythological nickname, Titan – scores in the second minute of added time to give Argentina's football team a 2-1 win against Peru's squad. The goal saves the local team's chances of qualifying for the South Africa 2010 World Cup, a qualification ultimately obtained three days later in Montevideo, Uruguay, with a 1-0 win against the home team. Under an unrelenting rain, Palermo, who had suffered a broken nose during the game, runs wildly and takes his shirt off in celebration. On the side line, wearing a tracksuit and in his new role as team manager, Diego Armando Maradona – former football symbol of the Argentinian team for more than a decade and considered by many to be the best player in the history of the sport – yells at the top of his lungs and dives chest first into the wet grass, hydroplaning in ecstasy. At the post-game press conference, he says: "San Palermo appeared, and we live once again". The dream is alive, like so many times before.

The next scene is a chronicle of a failure foretold.

On July 3, 2010, Germany beats Argentina 4-0 in the quarterfinals of the South Africa 2010 World Cup. Having Lionel Messi on the field, considered by many fans and pundits to be the best player in the world and Maradona's successor, had not been enough. Sporting a thick white and black beard, wearing a grey suit and a light blue tie, and carrying a rosary in his right hand – not "God's hand", not the left hand that scored the first goal against the English national team in the Mexico 1986 World Cup – the Argentinian coach can't make sense of what has just happened. Afterwards, at the press conference, he says: "I have no more strength". The dream is over, like so many times before.

DOI: 10.4324/9781003196587-9

As a player, manager, and first global media football celebrity, Maradona was a never-ending source of news and anecdotes because of his actions and words on and off the field. If we were to re-watch or re-live in our imagination the scenes described above, they would not be out of place in a literary tale. It has round characters, a dynamic plot, captivating trials and tribulations, and even an epic sentiment of triumph against adversity.[1] Arguably, showcasing those moments and not his most famous sport feats as a player – his performance in the Mexico 1986 World Cup or his wins with Italian club SSC Napoli – gives further support to the idea that Maradona's history has had the structure and feel of a story.[2]

## Football literature and the Maradona factor

Sports in general and particularly football have developed a longstanding relationship to literature (cf. Lee McGowan 2020).[3] Authors of Latin American origin have been major contributors to this area of studies – which we may call "football literature", following Roberto Santoro's *Literatura de la pelota* (1971) – that lately has received increased attention in academic scholarship (cf. David Wood 2017; David García Cames 2018b). In Argentina, from the stanzas of the *Martín Fierro*, the national poem, to the fictions of Jorge Luis Borges, literature has been part of the fabric of that country's modern society. Meanwhile, since its arrival to the shores of the River Plate football became part of the processes that have helped shape Argentinian national identity. Literature has provided a platform to discuss identity processes linked to nationhood since the 19th century (cf. among many others Doris Sommer 1991), and football was added to this equation – and thus to politics, culture, and the social imaginary – from the day the ball began rolling in the Argentinian fields at the beginning of the 20th century (cf. Eduardo Archetti 1998, 1999; Pablo Alabarces and María Graciela Rodríguez 1999, Pablo Alabarces 2000; Julio Frydenberg 2011; Jonathan Wilson 2016). In due time, the Argentinian distinct way of playing football, represented by the figure of the *pibe* that comes from the *potrero*, would become *la nuestra*, "our way", not only of performing a sport, but, perhaps, of being.[4]

Even though football eventually became part of the identity toolkit, and as Argentinian as *mate*, *asado*, tango, and *dulce de leche* (a green tea infusion, a barbecue, a famous dance, and milk jam), its development into an object of study faced obstacles in those intellectual circles reluctant to accept sports – a practice performed and consumed by the masses – as a legitimate subject of investigative inquiry. Sports began to be considered worthy of academic attention in Latin America in the mid-1990s (cf. Alabarces 2015). Meanwhile, a convergent phenomenon was taking place: The constitution of football studies coincided with the increasing "footballization" of Argentinian society during this time which meant that "everything could be discussed in sports terms" (Alabarces 2000: 17). Alongside these changes in cultural dynamics, from the 1990s on there was an output increase, not only in Argentina, but also in Latin America and Spain, of creative works linked to football.[5]

How does Maradona fit into all this? As María Graciela Rodríguez stated: "[I]n Argentina's national (his)story, [Maradona] was the last great football hero" (2003: 190). Following Alabarces' hypothesis about *footballization* to its logical conclusion, this football player was perhaps the last great Argentinian national "hero". After his passing at 60 years of age, such claim seems more and more plausible. Why? How? What does literature have to do with it? A *corpus* made of short stories, novels, poems, and a fragment of a play centred around the figure of Maradona shows how literary discourse lays bare a web of repetitive themes around his symbolic value beyond the pitch. My objective is to explore and analyse in what ways writers have sought to answer these questions, and what those answers reveal about national and global dynamics linking sport, identity, and cultural politics.

## Maradonian studies and the literary context

The relationship between Maradona and literature points to a sub-field within sport studies, which we may call "Maradonian studies", shaped by the intersection of the history of Argentinian and world football, the sociology of sports, the link between football and media, political dynamics at the national and international levels, and the presence of Maradona in music, art, literature, and cinema. Focusing on the Maradona-literature connection, this chapter has two main objectives. First, it offers a comprehensive overview of creative works by writers where Maradona's character and/or actions are the main subject.[6] Second, it focuses on two distinct strategies employed to portray him. I discuss first literary representations of what is the pivotal moment of the Argentinian's player career: his two goals against the English team in the 1986 World Cup, known as "The Hand of God" and "The Goal of the Century", respectively. I examine several texts that have as background that Argentina *vs.* England match in the 1986 World Cup quarterfinals and its symbolic ties to the national-international politics of the Malvinas/Falklands Islands War, an armed conflict that took place between those two countries during April and June of 1982.[7] In the next section, I consider more briefly the representations of Maradona as an exceptional figure beyond football. I divide these representations in two parts: on one side, Maradona as a being who affects and alters the lives of others, becoming both a symbol and a vessel of psychological containment; on the other, Maradona as someone who breaks the mould and becomes a Protean character in the process. These narrative strategies, it must be pointed out, are often intertwined in the *corpus*.

Maradona was (and will continue to be) frequently characterised in public – and literary – discourse as a "god", "hero", "legend", or "myth".[8] For my analytical framework, I follow Roland Barthes' assertion in *Mythologies* that a "myth is a system of communication, that it is a message ... it is a mode of signification, a form" (1991: 107).[9] My goal is, then, to unveil such *Maradonian* form, a language with a seemingly inexhaustible mythogenic output, as portrayed in literary works. My contention is two-fold: on the one hand, literary representations of Maradona fashion a being whose actions on the field and words and actions off the field place him in a plane of existence different from other "earthly" individuals, with an identity that is unchangeable but movable; on the other, these representations feed from a pool of existing signifying practices – frozen in time, but not petrified in meaning – both reinforcing them and establishing new ones, thus creating a feedback loop that make Maradona, as Barthes says, a "system of communication".

As a player, Maradona had a renowned sports career spanning 21 years and his influence went beyond the world of football; we would be hard pressed to find another sports celebrity who has received such significant literary attention.[10] This chapter offers a comprehensive list, although there surely is more fiction/poetry/drama waiting to be compiled and examined, since many of these texts do not circulate widely and several were first published in newspapers or small presses. I have identified four novels – *Inocente* (Innocent) (1994), by Argentinian journalist Fernando Niembro and Argentinian writer Julio Llinás; *Diego Armando Maradona. La vita e le imprese di Diego Armando Maradona raccontate a fumetti* (2012) (Diego Armando Maradona. The Hand of God, published in Italian and translated to the Spanish in 2014 as *Diego Armando Maradona. La mano de Dios*), by Italian graphic artist Paolo Castaldi; Amhed Ahmadi's *Strange and Incredible Story of Maradona* (2013; a more accurate title is *Maradona, Plastic Goalkeepers, And That Decisive Penalty … Did He Score It? Or Not? What Happened?*) published in Farsi[11]; and *Il retorno degli Dei* (The Return of the Gods) (2021), by Italian writer Marino Bartoletti. I also include 13 short stories, one by the Italian Gianfranco Pecchinenda, *Quel Tal Maradona* ("That Maradona") (2020), and 12 by Argentinian writers, some of them well-known: "Yo fui Maradona" (I was Maradona) (1984), by Enrique Medina; "Maradona sí, Galtieri no" (Maradona, Yes; Galtieri, no) (1987), by Osvaldo Soriano; "Aquel gol de Maradona a los ingleses" (That Maradona Goal Against the English) (1996), by Roberto Fontanarrosa; "Dieguito" (Little Diego) (1997; and a longer version in 2014), by José Pablo Feinmann; "Me van a tener que disculpar" (You Will Have to Forgive Me) (2000), by Eduardo Saccheri; "Vivir para contarlo" (Live to Tell) (2004), by Hernán Casciari; "Bautismos" (Baptisms) (2004), by Walter Vargas; "Recomendaciones para parir un hijo que salga Maradona" (also published as "La partera de Maradona" [Maradona's Midwife]) (2009), by Rodolfo Braceli; "10.6 segundos" (10.6 Seconds) (2013), by Casciari; "Todo mientras Diego" (All While Diego) and "A llorar se aprende" (One Learns How to Cry) (2018), by Ariel Scher, and my own "Dos tiempos distintos" (Two Different Times) (2022).[12] To these we can add a fragment of the play *After Sun* (2001), by Argentinian playwright Rodrigo García, and the poems "Maradona" (2008), by Uruguayan poet Mario Benedetti, and "La mano the Dios" (The Hand of God) (2012), by Argentinian poet Osvaldo Picardo. All in all, 20 works centred on Maradona.[13]

These texts can be classified based on the different phases and "readings" of the player's life and career: his exceptional birth (Braceli); his precocious talent and character (Vargas); the pivotal Argentina-England match in 1986 (Soriano,

Fontanarrosa, Saccheri, Castaldi, Casciari 2013, Scher's "All While Diego", Picardo); his career in Italy, "sprinkled" with his 1986 performance and the Italy 1990 World Cup and other moments in his life (Medina, Castaldi, Scher's "One Learns How to Cry", Bartoletti), the United States 1994 World Cup affair (Niembro and Llinás), a retrospective look at his life filled with sickness, wants and regrets (Casciari 2005, Benedetti, García) and, finally, duplication, parody, and the grotesque (Pecchinenda, Feinmann, Ahmadi). But the significant question to be asked is: In what way are they Maradonian? How do these texts reproduce and, at the same time, create and therefore contribute to Maradona's mythogenic qualities? To respond, a different classification may be needed, one that speaks to a language constituted by a plurality of modes of signification. In these literary representations, we see – following Joseph Campbell's *dictum* – the many faces of the idol[14]: the patriotic avenger, the mythic–redemptive–tragic hero/D10S, the miracle maker, the protagonist of the "rags to riches" story, the hero of the poor and the wretched of the Earth, the cheater, the victim of an international conspiracy, the eternal *pibe*, and so on.

## There was talk of cheating and of God

Many Maradonian literary pieces have focused on the Argentina *vs.* England game on June 22, 1986, and the Argentinian's famous goals: Castaldi, Soriano, Fontanarrosa, Saccheri, Casciari 2013, Scher's "All While Diego" Ahmadi, and Picardo comment on them. Almost all journalistic and scholarly production on Maradona refer to the game and the two goals as well.

The graphic novel by the Castaldi *Diego Armando Maradona. The Hand of God* provides a vantage point to explore the topic. It is divided into 11 chapters or "touches", based on how many times Maradona touched the ball before scoring the second goal (the actual number is 12). In the first chapter, in a series of eight black and white vignettes, Maradona is depicted dribbling through the English defence; the only colour present (blue) is on his shirt and the only word printed is "gol" (goal), repeated twice, with the "o" extended 8 times and then 13 times. The chapter ends with an image of Maradona's back showing the number 10 and an excerpt from the famous narration of the play by Uruguayan journalist and long-time Argentina's resident Víctor Hugo Morales, ending in: "Thank you, God. For football. For Maradona. For these tears. For this Argentina 2, England 0" (2014: 17). These expressions capture the Maradonian mode of signification activated by his feat: the mythic–redemptive hero/divine being has turned football into a sacred realm; those receiving his "gift" are thankful to God for being moved to tears by this sports act. Here, Borge's idea of a "staged but not scripted" activity gains force: Maradona becomes an actor engaging in a (football) monologue and a privileged member of the audience, a witness (Morales) engages in a monologue of his own.

In the ninth chapter, Castaldi activates a second mode, one of the most prevalent ones: Maradona becomes a patriotic avenger, obtaining symbolic retribution for Argentina's defeat in the 1982 Malvinas/Falkland Islands war. The graphic artist draws Maradona as he is about to enter the field and a reporter stops him and tries to bait him into relating the upcoming game with the armed conflict. Maradona answers: "We are only football players; we don't do politics" (107). This is the "real" version of events. But Castaldi takes advantage of the fictional context: as he exits the lockers, Maradona enters an alternate space/time where he finds an old, balding man with a glass of wine. It is, of course, God (Maradona nicknamed him *el barba* – the bearded one – although in Castaldi's sketch, he does not have much of a beard) who tells the player that this will not be just another match. Startled, the Argentinian captain comes back to "reality" and gives his pre-game speech. It is not plays, but words that matter for this second mode: "I will not play just to win a football match. I will not play only to win a World Cup. I will play to return dignity to our people ... We must do it [beating the English team] for all the Argentinians who died like dogs in an unjust war! We must do it for the islas Malvinas" (126–127).[15] The drawings focus on the number 10 on the shirt, the AFA (Argentinian Football Association) emblem, and Maradona's face, as his teammates listen.

In that same chapter, the Hand of God goal is drawn and narrated with very few words. The drawings juxtapose the play and God's – the old man who had met with Maradona before – habitat, in frame sequence: a wine glass, leaves, God working on the field, the TV on, God's face. The chapter ends with a blurry sketch of the Argentinian player in the air extending his left hand (which seems chopped) towards a ball-balloon, whereas the English goalkeeper tries to reach for it with is right hand. The text is taken from a journalist (not Morales) who is narrating the play: "It was a handball. But in my heart I feel it was the hand of justice" (Castaldi, 133). The journalist speaking through Castaldi is not referring to a sense of fairness in the field according to how the match was unfolding, but to a sense of "poetic justice" – which commonly occurs in a literary piece like the one we are reading – with regard to the armed conflict, mixing football prowess ("splendid play" 133) with the idea of symbolic political retribution.

How do the other pieces re-create these goals? After retiring in 1997, Maradona received a homage in the Boca Juniors' Bombonera Stadium in Buenos Aires in 2001. That same year, Rodrigo García in his play *After Sun* mentions the goals against the English national team within a monologue of a character who wants to be Maradona: "I want open all the doors of my brain and my heart and score two goals in the same game against the English: one with the left hand and one with the left foot, dribbling through everyone" (García 2001). The focus is on football, but the mentions of the English and the left have clear political connotations.[16] In some ways, this statement synthesises almost all other literary depictions of the game, activating the two modes already mentioned (I will discuss Scher's "All While Diego" in the next section).

Soriano's "Maradona yes, Galtieri no" (1st pub. 1987) imagines councilman Louis Clifton fainting with each of Maradona's goals in the 1986 match while living in the Malvinas/Falkland Islands: "Outside a freezing wind swept the deserted streets of Port Stanley and the British troops listened alarmed as the little devil from Naples ruined the festivities of the 4th anniversary of the re-taking of what they called the Falkland" (Soriano 2010). The narrator, a journalist and writer from the Buenos Aires La Boca neighbourhood, tries to call Clifton via short wave radio to explain to him that extraordinary goals like the Goal of the Century "counted double" and compensated for the hand goal. He ultimately desists, afraid of "provoking and international incident". The story loses focus, but two elements remain: football and politics. Future opponents of Argentina in the tournament (Belgium and Germany) are mentioned, as well as the rivalry between Maradona and Platini. The political content is unmistakably Argentinian: Besides the 1982-armed conflict, there is a reference to famed Argentinian football radio narrator José María Muñoz, "the same one who in 1979 incited the masses celebrating the Football Youth World Cup to repudiate the Interamerican Human Rights Commission visiting Buenos Aires" and another one to Luis, a neighbour who brandishes the Peronist flag and has pictures of Eva Perón and Maradona, pointing to two defining moments of Argentinian history in the 20th century: the advent of Peronism in the forties and the rule of the military dictatorship between 1976 and 1983. At the end of the story, the narrator's Italian neighbour, Salvatore, "asked why if Argentina had a player of Maradona's calibre we [the Argentinians] couldn't pay the debt with the International Monetary Fund", invoking well-known codes – the IMF and foreign debt – that have factored in the Argentinian economy for years. The title of the story itself points to the supposedly obligated preference for all Argentinians: Maradona, yes (he was able to beat the English and he is the right choice); Galtieri, no (the former military president oversaw the islands' invasion that ended in disastrous defeat; he is the wrong choice).

Politics and football resurface with Fontanarrosa's flash fiction "That Maradona Goal Against the English" (1st pub. 1996). Curiously enough, there are some machinic metaphors here that clash with the idea of a purely instinctive player. Fontanarrosa compares him to an almighty computer – "his last generation computer orders him to stick out his tongue" – and speaks about his "magnetic" left foot and ankle that become one with the ball. As he is about to score the Goal of the Century, Maradona's "computer memory" reminds him of a very similar play also against England in Wembley Stadium in 1981 – a real event – when his execution was deficient; this time, however, it will be different. The mythic footballer gives way to the political connotations when the writer recounts how Maradona "pulls again, so smoothly, the ball from the left to right to leave behind the goalkeeper who cries for forgiveness for having invaded the Malvinas". Then, as the footballer accelerates, he is taken down by "the tripping of the last pirate" and imagines "the bitter gesture of [Margaret] Thatcher in her kingdom"; thus, the narration associates England with a colonising empire. The ending of the tale, however, reverts to the perfection of the goal execution: "And that's when many, almost everyone, let's say everyone, we think that he never, ever, made a mistake during the play" (Fontanarrosa 2001).

We find more narrative sophistication in the stories by Saccheri and Casciari and a curious take in Ahmadi's novel.

"You Will Have to Forgive Me" by Saccheri calls upon the web of meanings in the Maradonian system of communication to make the reader understand who the narrator is referring to without naming him: "To talk about him, among Argentinians, is one of our national pastimes. To ascend him to the stratosphere, or condemn him to the grill of hell, we Argentinians seemingly like to evoke his name and his memory". This last word is important: Embedded in the popular imagination, by the time the story is published Maradona has retired from professional football and has already experienced his first serious health crisis, so what remains is the remembrance of his greatest hits (the past) and the anguish of his "profane present". When explaining the 1986 match against England, the narrator uses the present: "It's not a game. What I mean is: it's not only a game". Here again, we see the idea of football and/as politics: The pain and the anger felt by the narrative voice "do not come from football". The first handball goal is seen as a theft, yes, but justified because "you robbed somebody that robbed you first", referring to the English colonisation of the Malvinas/Falkland Islands. Nonetheless, "besides being a trickster the guy is also an artist", and so comes the description of the second goal, which goes straight into symbolic revenge: Maradona is wearing blue but "carries the [Argentinian] flag". Saccheri focuses on the impotence not only of the players, but also of an entire nation: "Not even when the guy gifts them a fraction of a second more, when the guy slows down the vertigo so he can get better positioned for his left foot, not even then they will avoid going into history as the humiliated ones, the eleven English men scattered and incredulous, the millions of English watching the telly without wanting to believe what they know it is true forever". The dichotomies South/North, First World/Third World, empire/colonies, top/bottom (also apparent in Maradona's stint in SSC Napoli) point to racial, historical and economic disparities and are synthesised precisely in those English spectators who, according to the narrator, "with silly expressions and an open mouth" still think that "this cannot happen, somebody will stop him, that dark-sinned Argentinian guy wearing blue will not enter the box with the ball ready for his whims … something will happen so history will be righted and things will be as God and the Queen demand". So, the defeat might be "small and belongs to football" but it is also "absolute, eternal and unforgettable" (Saccheri 2000: 35–42).

Casciari's "10.6 Seconds", on the other hand, elects to activate the mythic footballer mode through an amplifying technique that focuses on the characters involved in the match. There is, however, a slight mention to politics as Maradona faces the English goalkeeper: "In the rules of soccer [sic] this [the Hand of God goal] is an illegal move, but in the rules of another game, a game more inhumane than soccer [sic], justice had been served … Peter Shilton plans his retaliation on the player's previous revenge". The reference is, of course, to war, and the idea brought forth is that even though the Hand of God goal did not abide by football rules it almost did not have to, since it ultimately served as symbolic national retribution for Argentina's military defeat (note the emphasis on words like "retaliation" and "revenge"). Casciari uses a zooming in-and-out technique to tell what is happening at the Azteca Stadium during the second goal and then projecting back to the past and future of the protagonists. As Maradona – never mentioned by his name – is about to score, the focus is solely on him. Like a God or a superhuman being, he "sees" everything: Past, present, and future coincide to finally finish what he started: "He closes his eyes. He lets himself fall forward and the entire world goes silent". Casciari de-emphasises national identity and political connotations and instead focuses on Maradona's football genius – "the advance seems deceptively quick, but the player regulates his speed, slowing down and faking. There's a secret geometry in the precision of the zigzag" – and in how that singular moment, underlined by the time markers in the story, renders all other characters as merely human, while he is becoming a being forever embedded in the popular imagination: "He knows the play will last 10.6 seconds. He knows it's time to let everyone see who he is, who he has been, and who he will be until the end of time" (Casciari 2013).

Ahmadi's novel, published in Farsi, has not received, as far as I can tell, any critical attention. It introduces four protagonists – a contract killer, a prostitute, a casino owner, and a film director – who anchor four chapters. Their stories relate to each other and also to five penalty kicks shot by the Argentinian player. Up to a point, Maradona serves mainly as a frame of reference, a source of inspiration and remembrance. But the last chapter is narrated by a young Maradona who is teaching a football clinic on "how to become Maradona in nine days". The young Maradona flash-forwards to 1986. He gets asked by one of his pupils: "Diego, what were you thinking when you used your hand to send the ball into England's net?" His response is surprising because Ahmadi de-activates the political mode and the mythic footballer mode, making the Argentinian star, in a tongue-in-cheek way, a giver of happiness through a sexual metaphor: "At that moment", Maradona answers, "I wasn't thinking about my nation's hatred against the British people, nor was I thinking about cheating or the goalkeeper or the goal. I was only thinking about delay sprays" (2013: 113). He explains that he tried to lengthen the climax of a goal to provide fans with a longer sense of euphoria and joy. The use of the *delay spray* metaphor relates to a slew of links between (mostly) masculine sexuality and the scoring of a goal; the novel uses an openly sexual and at times vulgar language, which would probably have prevented it from being published in Iran. Was Ahmadi also referencing Maradona's well-known promiscuity and scandals off the field? Perhaps. But the author seems to justify the infraction of the first goal against the English by making his character not only a male player who symbolically satisfies his sexual desires with a goal but also a vehicle for others to experience pleasure in the freest way possible.

To close this section, I bring to the fore Picardo's poem dedicated to that same goal. "It was only/in one time and one place. The thing is/that the jump is still the air,/in the end of a tired muscle/contracted by a war and a defeat". The patriotic sentiment is blatant: "And in the hushed ovation, Maradona/over the

English soars". The short poem finishes referencing the outcome and the beginning of the Maradonian (his)tory: "Afterwards, it was another day, as the sun
came up/and there was talk of cheating and even of god" (Picardo 2012: 188).[17]

## What does it matter what he did with his life...?

"It matters what he did with mine". This is a phrase attributed to Fontanarrosa
about Maradona. It encapsulates perfectly the second most often used strategy
in Maradonian representation: his affective effect on the lives of others. A case
can be made that all fictions about Maradona have this characteristic. I will
briefly discuss some of them and then will focus on Castaldi's graphic novel and
Niembro and Llinás novel.

As we have seen, Soriano's and Fontanarrosa's stories have a parallel design
that re-creates the Goal of the Century. In Soriano's, besides the fictitious councilman, we are presented with real characters from the past (Galtieri, Muñoz) and
perhaps fictional ones in the 1986 present (the Italian neighbour, the Peronist,
a hairdresser, the narrator's wife), all thinking or speaking about politics and/
or football through Maradona's play. Meanwhile, Fontanarrosa not only follows
Maradona's dribbling but also takes advantage of the opportunity to attack world
and sport leaders: Mikhail Gorbachev, then leader of Russia, Joao Havelange,
then president of FIFA, "king" Pelé, Margaret Thatcher, then English Primer
Minister, and even the Pope. For Fontanarrosa, Maradona's goal symbolically
shuts up all those who speak nonsense. Casciari's "10.6 Seconds" bring us back
to the pitch and follows the destinies of those involved in the play mixing up
facts and fiction around Maradona's impact on others: the sad end of the Tunisian
referee of the match, whose last name, says the narrator "would become a synonym for blindness"; the humiliation suffered by the sons of Peter Reid and Peter
Beardsley in a London rave by a Scottish man who imitates Maradona's dribble;
the lamentations of Kenny Samson and Terry Butcher over glasses of whisky
years after the game; the destiny of Terry Fenwick, who ends up coaching football in Trinidad and Tobago and, during his daughter's 18th birthday party, sees
her kissing an Argentinian boy wearing a national team jersey with the number
"10" in the back. There is even a mention of Peter Shilton's children who will
end up playing a video game (invented in Britain in 1986), called "Peter Shilton's
Handball Maradona" (Casciari 2013).[18] Casciari also follows the lives of Héctor
Enrique, Jorge Burruchaga, and Jorge Valdano, three of Maradona's teammates in
1986, mostly sticking to real biographical events and anecdotes. Finally, the most
removed fiction from the Goal of the Century is Ahmadi's, but the "presence of
absence" is felt: As the documentary's director thinks: "Maradona's face could
not be seen; we could only see his juggling of the ball. He was sure that everyone
watching the game on TV could recognize Maradona without seeing his face or
jersey number" (Ahmadi 2013: 72). We find the idea of the Argentinian player as
an omnipresent figure who reaches across space and time to influence the actions
of other people in all these fictions, reinforcing this mode of signification.

Scher's stories and "Live to Tell" by Casciari (2005) can be grouped together since they present *costumbrista* takes full of depictions of daily life and urban folk-lore where Maradona is used to re-signify the lives of others. Scher's "All while Diego" uses the second goal as a backdrop: "What happened to you when Diego Maradona, in the best play in football history, score the second goal against the English in the Mexico World Cup?" asks rhetorically the main protagonist, el Gordo (Fatso) (Scher 2018: 9). Fatso, The Tall One, and The Broken One spend time telling tales in the "Saturdays Bar" and on this occasion the fat man speaks of the "miracles" that happened when the Goal of the Century was in process: a woman was tending clothes and they dried up instantly; a lonely man hugged a painting and someone from the painting hugged him back. Droughts ceased; students understood complex algebraic equations. When a woman who enters the bar "sends a direct look of love into Fatso's direction", Fatso enunciates a phrase that will be repeated many times in the web of Maradonian significations: "—Thanks again, Diego" (11). The bar is again the setting for Scher's "One Learns How to Cry". The main character, "el Pibe", sees Maradona cry at the end of the final of the 1990 Italy World Cup and comprehends that his tears "were not his tears, the crying was him". He then continues: "[H]e had the whole world watching him, but felt alone ... trapped by that human combination of loneliness, defeat and injustice, he seemed like any man, any day, in any place" (Scher 2018: 93). Thus, we see not only the capacity of Maradona to symbolise the exceptional but also the ordinary and provide a vessel for emotional connection; the protagonist also starts to cry and learns that "when the crying is more than tears, it calls other cries. And, consequently, those other cries accept [the call] and go" (93). In Casciari's "Live to Tell", 50-year-old housewife Mirta Bertotti writes a letter to Maradona while the Argentinian player lies in a hospital bed "breathing through a little tube" (Casciari 2005: 204). This reference to one of his many hospitalisations allows for a retrospective through a female voice who thinks Maradona is "a bragger and has a dirty mouth" (204). Even though this distance could allow for some critical/creative perspective, Casciari's story follows the usual pattern: Bertotti sees the player through the (mostly masculine) eyes of others – thus her husband's tears in 1986 and 1994 and her sons' fidelity to the Maradona myth. Berotti prays for Maradona because he "gave happiness" to her family (204) and later explains that she also prays so he "can take a break from the effort of being unique and find time to be a normal guy" (205).

Castaldi's novel provides the clearest example of the Maradonian affective effect. There are three relevant examples. Salvatore Lipari, a photographer present at Maradona's introduction to SSC Napoli fans in July of 1984 at the San Paolo Stadium (today renamed Diego Armando Maradona) narrates the third chapter, depicting the event as "a giant lay mass where everyone invoked a new god" (2014: 37). The author – through Lipari's voice – also recreates the press conference where Maradona stated his desire to become the idol of the disenfranchised Neapolitan children, thus starting to build his "hero of the poor and the wretched of the Earth" image. The fourth chapter introduces the story of

Neapolitan Francesco Coppola, a former worker in a fibre cement factory who "was treated like a dog" in the Italian North and ended up sick with asbestosis. The last frame shows Coppola bedridden and with an oxygen mask, listening to Maradona speak on TV after having obtained the 1986–1987 *scudetto* with his Napoli: "Our people need to understand ... that winners are not the ones with most money but the ones with most fighting spirit" (55). The fifth chapter captures the days when Maradona decided to play a charity match to collect funds for a sick child; against Napoli's wishes, Maradona – who paid the insurance fee out of his own pocket – plays. Carmine Gianfelice, who marked him in that game, narrates the second half of the chapter: "For us, Diego was a hero. A god. And he still is. I believe that day he knew it too" (60). This web of characters intersected by the aura of Maradona includes Castaldi himself: In the auto/metafictional turn of the second chapter, he draws a self-portrait drawing the novel as he explains not only the creative process but also the challenge of his artistic representation: "I don't know what you expect. Maradona is a whole universe. An extraordinary universe" (21). In the last chapter, the author invents an unnamed manager – Maradona himself? – who assigns all characters in the novel positions in an imaginary football team. God plays centre half.

The novel *Inocente* (1995) is examined in Chapter 9 in this volume and has received some critical attention (Tobin 2002). Within Maradonian literature, it presents several characters affected by Maradona. His figure and actions help advance an espionage sports thriller with a what-if "alternate history" of the Argentinian player expulsion from the United States 1994 World Cup. The plot is contrived and bordering on delirious, mixing facts – some life events and the behind-the-scenes of the tournament – with fiction to advance the hypothesis of a sport hero being framed. Here, then, it is not about how Maradona affect characters emotionally, but rather how these characters are shaped by a narrative design based on a premise: The United States' Central Intelligence Agency aims to prevent Argentina and Maradona – for, among other things admiring Fidel Castro and criticising the Pope, the Vatican and FIFA – and Colombia – because of its association with the drug trade – from winning the cup. The novel feeds from a mode of Maradonian signification absent in my discussion so far: the paranoic "victim of a conspiracy" trope,[19] a mantra that became stronger when Maradona (and some in the Argentinian sports media) denounced a *mano negra* (dark hand) after Argentina's 1-0 loss to Germany because of a dubious penalty call in the finals of the Italy 1990 World Cup. Most of the CIA men involved in the novel (Carl Johnson, Tony Carrasco, Mel Kennedy, Anthony Llás, Coco Cardo, Alan Clinton) know little about the Argentinian player or football. Code names such as "1-25-10" or "dwarf" are used instead of his name as we learn about Maradona through a secret file being read by Johnson, who is "fascinated" (Niembro and Llinás 1995: 55) with his subject. In other Chapters (7, 13, 14, 18, 19, 20), the player is at the centre, as a third person narrator reviews life and career episodes and the chaos, and divisions of the 1994 Argentinian team. The plot tests the boundaries of verisimilitude as the "trap" is revealed: given that

Maradona took communion before each game (not a fact), the conspirators get him a wafer contaminated with ephedrine before facing the Nigerian team in the second match of the group stage, therefore provoking his fall. In a nod to *noir*, the novel also introduces Argentinian femme fatale Rubra Robirosa, the owner of a public relations firm, who becomes involved in this web: she mistakenly thinks the CIA wants to assassinate Maradona and tries to prevent it. In the last chapter, she meets the player – who is reflecting on his actions and thinks himself "possessed by a ghost who got inside and made him do things" (274) – and whispers to him: "I believe in you … I don't know how they did it, but they framed you" (275). This reinforces both the conspiracy theory and the "Maradona as a victim" trope.

As we can see, the extra-ordinary dimension of the Maradonian form as portrayed in literary fiction runs through all the pieces I discussed, affecting characters' lives in unforgettable, significant ways. Somehow, he remains above the fray. As Castaldi says at the end of his book: "Diego, you are free to do what you want. As always" (165).

## Breaking the mould/building Diego

Some Maradonian fictions shift away from his sporting feats and look at other aspects of his career and life, casting a wider interpretative net. Here I will address (in two separate groups) a third mode of Maradonian signification: Maradona as an exceptional, breakout figure who is perpetually being constructed and re-constructed.

In a first group, beginning and (almost) end are the focus of Braceli's short story and Benedetti's poem, while Vargas and Medina's stories point to defining moments in Maradona's career and García's monologue serves a piercing testimony to his larger-than-life figure. Braceli's "Maradona's Midwife" imagines the birth of the myth, again using the *costumbrista* genre. Maradona's mother announces to her husband that after four girls, their next child "will be a boy. And will play football like God intended" (2009: 128). To get to that result, she will follow the advice of Pierina, her midwife friend, who sets rules and rituals: "watch the sun when you drink water"; "eat things that come from trees" (so the child is born "with a stick"); "eat garlic while fasting" (so he speaks *sin pelos en la lengua*, or freely); thread a needle with eyes closed and so on (129, 135). The *machismo* is quite rampant, but interestingly enough, a day before his birth Doña Tota juggles a falling light bulb, forecasting the ability of the future football prodigy. Maradona's birth is compared to Jesus Christ's and Che Guevara's, underlining the child' uniqueness and revolutionary nature. Meanwhile, probably inspired by Maradona's bouts with health issues, Benedetti's poem "Today Your Time Is Real" mentions the passage of time and its toll on the Argentinian player, who nonetheless still survives: "Your age feed from other ages/It does not matter what mirrors say/Your eyes are not old yet". The "miracle" is that Maradona keeps winning the battle against death: "Another year has passed, and another year/You have defeated your shadows, aleluya". This celebratory ending ties in with the exceptionality in Braceli's story, that is, the "you are your own kind" idea, but in this case claims the right to be Maradona to the end: "You will have your own life and our own death". That is why, as the first verse of the poem says, "Today your time is real/nobody should forge it for you" (2012: 52).

Vargas' and Medina's stories take specific moments in Maradona's life and re-imagine them. Vargas recounts an alternate story of Maradona's official debut in the Argentinian 1st Division with Argentinos Juniors (October 20, 1976) and refers to a forgotten friendly against Estudiantes de la Plata on September 5th of the same year. The backdrop of the story is the sexual awakening of two teenagers and the political repression during the 1976–1983 military dictatorship. The protagonists make it to the stadium; the game is boring. But then, Maradona – "More *pibito* [little kid] than us"! (Vargas 2004: 108) – enters the game. The humiliation he performs on two experienced defenders – "Pachamé was left with a knee to the ground, like Columbus ... in shorts" (109) – is a sign not only of things to come, but also of the free play and daring, rebellious nature that would become one of Maradona's modes of signification. Meanwhile, Medina's "I was Maradona" is the only story in the *corpus* which captures the player's voice. As he is about to make his debut with SSC Napoli, many characters parade in his head: Jorge Cyterszpiler, his first manager; César Luis Menotti, his coach with the Argentinian national team; Enrique Omar Sívori, a famed Argentinian player who played in Napoli in 1965; family and friends. The short tale presents a flash biography and describes the pressures of performing felt by the young Maradona while focusing on details like his football shoes – "I should have changed them" – and the emphasis on his essence: "I like to play, I like to play. Yes, I like to play football" (Medina 1984). Finally, García's fragment in his *After Sun* puts forth a wish – "I want to be Maradona" is the rhythmic mantra – which plays with the idea of a singularity without limits: "I want to be Maradona to, with the same debauchery, defend tradition and at the same time dress it with oil and salt and eat it all, break the world for me, empty my full bladder above all, and be the most human of all" (García 2001). Poetic and poignant, García's invented monologue touches on Maradona's life and career and gives voice (perhaps) to the Maradonian collective unconscious – "I want to die, not because of drugs, nor because of family pressures, nor because of the burden of the victories, nor because of the ghost of failure, but because of my weakness: because the body cannot take it anymore, cannot receive anymore and so it goes and throws itself from a high floor" (García 2001) – anticipating a death that was not as spectacular but was, nevertheless, dramatic.

In the second group of this section, Ahmadi's novel and Feinmann's "Little Diego" posit Maradona as an empty signifier subject to many interpretations; these authors de-construct and re-construct several existing Maradonian signifying practices. In *Maradona, Plastic Goalkeepers, And That Decisive Penalty ... Did He Score It? Or Not? What Happened?*, a young Maradona – in his 20s – leads a workshop for kids on "how to become Maradona in 9 days". The Iranian author parodies everything: football clinics, teaching methods and even Maradona, who accuses regular teachers of being stupid: "I did not teach with formulas. This was my key mantra: 'to be Maradona does not have a formula; it's not like math'" (2013: 97–98). On the second day, he teaches kids how to not pass the ball on the field because, he says, "the ball is always for Maradona, and no one else" (100). In another session, he teaches how to score goals with hands. By the eighth session, he sends the kids home, liberating them by telling them: "Go play football in your streets!". The narrator explains: "No one complained. They all knew that they were not going to become Maradona" (117). Besides the humour, what is apparent in this depiction of Maradona is his exceptional individuality as a football player, pointing out the impossibility of replicating him. When we arrive at Feinmann's story,[20] we see parody and the grotesque in full force. In a football re-writing of Horacio Quiroga's "The Decapitated Chicken", Dieguito, the protagonist, is an eight-year-old child deemed "an idiot" and "a fag" (because he plays with dolls in the attic) by his father (Feinmann 2003: 47). One day, he sees a train run over a car; he runs to the wreckage and find the car's driver: his idol, Maradona. He takes the body-corpse home. Meanwhile, the Argentinian media is hysterical: the famous Argentinian player has disappeared (legend has it he has escaped to Colombia to live a life of anonymity with Argentinian tango singer Carlos Gardel). Dieguito quits school, starts speaking in the gerund form, and works nonstop in the attic. By the end of the tale, his parents smell something rotten. When they come up, the truth is revealed: their son was reconstructing Maradona's corpse, sewing a hand to one of the arms. Horrified, his father asks him: "What are you doing you big idiot?" to which the boy ("darkly satisfied for having been elevated by his father to the realms of greatness") answers: "Dieguito armando [building] Maradona" (53). Many aspects of the story merit further attention but, for our purposes, the plotline and especially the ingenious combination of Maradona's middle name and its sempiternal reverberations encapsulates one of the most powerful obsession of the Argentinian social imaginary in the last 60 years: the de-constructing and re-constructing of the multiple meanings of Maradona, pointing to the inexhaustible potentialities of a name, figure, and iconicity that, whether in reality or fiction, plays dead but it is very much alive.[21]

## An aesthetics of resonance

Most Maradonian creative literary works evoke, re-create, and replicate his peaks and valleys, often suffusing the piece with a patina of nostalgia and sentimentality that stifles originality. However, some transcend or at least interrogate the Maradonian web of repetitive themes and symbolic values. Castaldi's graphic novel cannot help but be sentimental, but there is creativity in the mixing and matching between images and words proposed by the Italian author; Ahmed's perspective distances itself from the myth and, while recognising the global significance of Maradona's figure, paints an imagined Maradona closer to the figure of a rebellious and unique trickster. Saccheri's story has a patina of *costumbrismo* but his expert use of narrative voice and the dichotomy between guilt and debt surrounding Maradona saves the tale from oblivion, as the idea of a hero who cannot be measured or judged by normal standards comes forth: "You will have to forgive me, gentlemen. There's a guy I can't judge" (2000: 36). Casciari's contribution (2013) is his use of point of view as he re-creates the paragraph in Borges' story "The Aleph" with the syntax of the "I saw... I saw" construction to conveying a sense of absolute perception of all spaces and times converging in those 10.6 seconds – the Borgesian references are underlined when Casciari says that Maradona "sees the dead body of an old man who died in Geneva eight days prior to that midday in Mexico, a man who had also seen everything in the world in a single instant" (2013), referencing Borges' death that same 1986 year. And Feinmann's story provides a window to many other possible Maradonas: a corpse, perhaps symbolising the nation and its delusions of grandeur, and a monster – Frankenstein? – embedded in the use of the horror genre.

Maradona's name was always particular, unique. While reflecting on his labour, Castaldi asks his readers: "Concentrate on the sound. Armandomaradona .... Pronounce it like that, one time, accentuate the first two letters a bit more and then let the other letters go. Like they do it in Argentina. Arrmandommaradona. Do you feel it? Inside, I mean. Do you feel anything?" (Castaldi 2014: 22). Maradona is a feeling which resonates, creating in its multiple representations, a resonance.

And so, we come to one more Maradonian literary story:

> Maradona has the ball. Two men on him. He steps on the ball Maradona. He runs to the right the genius of world football. And he leaves everyone in the dust. He is going to pass it to Burruchaga. Always Maradona! Genius, genius, genius. Ta-ta-ta; ta-ta-ta. Gooooooooal, gooooooooal. I want to cry, Dear God. Long live football. What a goal Diegoal, Maradona. It's to cry for. Forgive me. In a memorable run, in the best play of all time. Cosmic kite, what planet did you come from to leave so many English behind? To turn the country into a clenched fist screaming for Argentina? Argentina two, England cero. ¡Diegoal! ¡Diegoal! Diego Armando Maradona. Thank you, God. For football. For Maradona. For these tears. For this Argentina two, England zero.
>
> *Morales 2013: Segundo Tiempo 8–9*

This oral prose piece of the Goal of the Century by Morales is perhaps the most accomplished entry of this *corpus*. Is it literature? It can certainly be read as such.[22] The beginning describes the play ("Maradona has the ball. Two men on him. He steps on the ball"). As the Argentinian captain accelerates, the broadcaster seems to lose sight of the fact that this is a football match. Logic ("He is going to pass it to Burruchaga") gives way to the impossibility of the feat. So, the narrator can only manage to repeat a word ("genius") three times before surrendering to the singularity of the moment. The emotional "excess" produces a catharsis of the sublime: like a painting, we have bodies in movement, the presence of nature (the sun and the grass on the field) and the objects needed – the goal, the ball, the net. There is an unstoppable desire and a request for clemency ("It's to cry for. Forgive me"). And thus, the invention of the metaphor ("Cosmic kite, where did you come from?") and, after recognising the political symbolism of the epic ("to turn the country into a clenched fist screaming for Argentina"), a return to the field, to the match, to Maradona, to leave testimony of the ineffable and eternal. Maradona has become "Diegoal" and the teller can only thank God and football. Or the new god of football. In all its resonances, Morales' narration brings forth several distinct Maradonian modes of significations.

"The reader lives the myth as a story at once true and unreal" says Barthes (1972: 127). Myth is above all, a way of telling which cuts across time, space, and culture. In the case of Maradona as a Barthesian "form", I hope to have shown that, even within a web of repetitive themes, the existing signifying practices might be suspended in time but are not petrified in meaning. The figure of Maradona still speaks to us, and the many re-significations of the Maradona phenomenon cannot forget that "the writer's language is not expected to *represent* reality, but to signify it" (136). The best examples of Maradonian literature attempt to do that and get close to the task of engaging with one of the method Barthes recognises to decipher myth: "to posit a reality which is *ultimately* impenetrable, irreducible, and, in this case, poetize" (159).

Maradona knew all too well that to be is to be perceived in football and that many things were, as Borge states, staged, and, in a way, a simulacrum. Nonetheless, he managed to be an idol of the popular masses in a time of scepticism, dribbling past rules and regulations, on and off the field. Uruguayan writer Eduardo Galeano famously posited Maradona as "the most human of the Gods".[23] This idea of escaping the norm, of being out of this world, gains force in this Maradonian form. In his narration, Morales asks: "What planet did you come from?" In a TV interview from 1979, seven years before the Mexico 1986 World Cup, a Maradona (not Diego) answers. The journalist asks younger brother Hugo if he aspires to be like Diego. "I never thought about that", he answers. "Why?" the reporter insists. "Because my brother is a Martian".

## Notes

1 Juan Villoro argues that the dynamics of the sport clashes with its literary re-creation: "The system of references in football is so strictly codified, and involves the emotions so totally, that it includes its own epic, its own tragedy and its own comedy. There isn't any need for parallel dramas and the writer's invention is left with very little space to work with" (2014: 19). Meanwhile, Steffen Borge speaks of football being akin to a theatre play: "Football is *staged, but not scripted*. The football match, a staged competition, contains a kind of performance—improvised within certain parameters and according to certain rules" (2019: 205). This concept of "staged but not scripted" can be applied to Maradona understood as a literary trope. Yvette Sanchez claims that the Maradona phenomenon is self-sufficient "given that his biography already offers

an excessive show and a cult of a stylized martyrdom around which the creation of more stories becomes superfluous" (2007: 136; all translations are mine unless otherwise indicated). Yet David García Cames argues that "against the expiring nature of the TV replay or the journalistic chronicle, fiction literature can contribute to the sports myth a memorability and permanent character that runs parallel to the *logos* of the primordial" (2018b: 147).

2  Daniel Arcucci's *Conocer al Diego. Relatos de fascinación maradoniana* (2001) and Sergio Domínguez's *Maradona 365 historias* (2019) prove the relationship between Maradona and story in its most elemental form. In this regard, Micaela Domínguez Prost's *La mano de Diego* (2021) is of interest as it recounts ten global tales where the name Maradona becomes a secret password or unofficial "passport". Other books reinforce this connection, more closely related to chronicles: *Crónicas Maradonianas* (2021) and *Rey de Fiorito. Crónicas políticas y sociales de la vida de Diego Maradona* (2021), edited by Ezequiel Fernández Moores *et al.*

3  The volume provides a comprehensive overview but keeps mixing up "football fiction" and "novel" without acknowledging that other literary genres (poems, drama, and short stories) also have represented the sport through literature. For McGowan, a work of football fiction "significantly relies on football as a central, pivotal or substantive element; this can and should include more than one of the following: narrative structure; narrative situation; point of view; voice; language use; setting; and character development" (5).

4  The components of this *criollo* style are not crystal-clear and the debate of what constitutes the Argentine national style continues well into the 21st century. Several works discuss *la nuestra*; besides Archetti's studies (1998, 1999) and the epilogue to Freydenberg's book (2011), cf. Wilson (2016).

5  Perhaps Jorge Valdano, former player for the Argentine national team and FC Real Madrid, gave the *puntapié inicial* (kick off) when in 1995 he "curated" the anthology *Cuentos de fútbol*, which included well-known Spanish and Latin American writers such as Mario Benedetti, Eduardo Galeano, Javier Marías, Miguel Delibes, Augusto Roa Bastos, Juan Villoro, and, perhaps surprisingly, Valdano himself. From an academic standpoint, and in reference to specific Hispanic contexts – including its distinct regional and national identities, the best work on the subject is found in Wood (2017) and García Cames' (2018b). McGowan offers an impressive catalog of 527 novels related to football, including some in Spanish.

6  This *corpus* awaits further critical attention. To date, we have Brescia (2021); Carlos Andrés Bertoglio (2021); García Cames (2018a); Jeffrey Tobin (2002) and some observations by Sánchez (2007). Wilson mentions Soriano's story (148). Gustavo Bernstein's meandering book (1997) views Maradona through literature and philosophy.

7  Many writings on Maradona comment on his performance in the game. For an account of the match, cf. Andrés Burgo (2016). Cf. also Chapters 5 and 7 in this volume.

8  The pervasiveness of these tropes can be seen in the first lines of Jimmy Burns' biography: "This is a story of a natural-born football talent *who grew up to believe he was God and suffered as a result*" (1996: vii; emphasis mine). Guillem Balagué's more recent *Maradona. The Boy. The Rebel. The God* also participates of this branding and even the translation of Maradona's recollection of the Mexico 1986 triumph forgoes the Spanish (which references the tournament and "truth" in the title *Mi mundial. Mi verdad. Así ganamos la copa*) and instead insists with the equivalency Maradona=God in the title: *Touched by God. How We Won the Mexico '86 World Cup*. The reference to God (*Dios*) sometimes cleverly transformed into the acronym D10S (combining the word God in Spanish with the number Maradona wore on his jersey) has been used for several years now. In addition, perhaps the most well-known song about Maradona is "La mano de Dios" ("Hand of God"), by Rodrigo Bueno. Another example is the existence of the Maradonian Church since 1998. For a whirlwind tour of this church, cf. José Caldeira (2007) and the chapter in this volume by Luca Bifulco.

9 Given that *mythos* in classical Greece meant story or plot, be it real or invented, here I focus narrowly on the narrative and epic aspects of myth as related to football literature and Maradona. García Cames' (2018b) and Bifulco (2014; ed. in Spanish 2020) have contributed to this area. Several publications on sport, football and Maradona have studied the relationship between sport and the "hero-myth" paradigm that usually follows a "rise and fall" trajectory. A fierce critic of Maradona, Juan José Sebreli, is baffled by the Maradonian analogies, having the footballer compared to "Christ, Don Quixote, Ulises, Saint Genaro, Virgin Mary, Napoleon, Mick Jagger and ... Baudelaire" (2008: 165). Archetti (1998, 2001), Alabarces (2007, 2014, 2018, 2021) and Alabarces and Rodríguez (1999) have analyzed Maradona as a myth linked to national identity, popular culture, politics, and masculinities.

10 Wood states that much football (fiction) writing in Latin America consists of "elaboration of historical episodes, characters or interviews written in a style that is more literary than journalistic, but which tend to be published first in newspapers" (149). The newspaper publications reveal the fleeting nature of the pieces, often of a dubious literary quality. Essays on Maradona penned by writers might be a genre of their own in the Maradona studies field and therefore need to be fully addressed elsewhere (cf. Brescia 2021).

11 I thank Delaram Rahimi for her invaluable contribution in understanding the content of this novel, as I do not read Farsi. The summary of the novel is hers; the analysis, mine.

12 I will not be commenting on my own story.

13 As this *corpus* continues to expand, I anticipate more studies on relationship between Maradona and his representation in art and literature. Anthologies published as a tribute after Maradona's passing (cf. *Maradona, uno de los nuestros* and *El fútbol te da vida. Homenaje a Diego Armando Maradona* which both mix chronicle and fiction, and *El 10 Maradona. Antología chilena de historias de fútbol en homenaje a Diego Armando Maradona*, compiled by Reinaldo Edmundo Marchant) will not be considered in this chapter. In addition, Pecchinenda's story and Bartoletti's novel have not yet been translated and I will not comment on them as my knowledge of Italian is insufficient. Rewording McGowan's definition, for our purposes, a work of *Maradonian* fiction significantly relies on Maradona as a central, pivotal, or substantive element. In some works, his presence is tangential, used as either a prop or a trigger. In Argentine fiction, Rodrigo Fresán's "Final" (End) (1997) is an excuse for some elucubrations by the protagonist. Sergio Olguín's novel *El equipo de los sueños* (The Dream Team) (2005) imagines the first ball that belonged to Maradona stolen and with this incident the plot moves forward. In "Tránsito" (Transit) (2010), by Guillermo Saccomano, the protagonist has a relationship with a Maradona poster and ends up destroying it. "Club Sportivo 6-Argentina 4, Humahuaca 10-1-86" (2018), by Vicent Chilet, imagines Maradona scoring goals during a friendly match in Jujuy, where the national team trained to adapt to Mexico's above-sea level conditions (Maradona was not there). Some other stories in Scher's book (2018) – "Lo que nos perdimos" (What We Missed) and "Clases de fútbol" (Football Classes) – mention Maradona but don't do much more. In Italian fiction, *Juve-Napoli 1-3. La presa di Torino* (Juventus-Napoli 1-3. The Taking of Torino) (2011), by Maurizio Di Giovanni, recounts a match from 1986, that pitted French footballer Michel Platini against Maradona, who is not named in the piece. Two novels with the same name – Antonio Gurrado's *Ho visto Maradona* (I Have Seen Maradona) (2014) and Fabio de Paulis' *Ho visto Maradona* (2020) – recount Maradona's important moments in Italian football within plots that gather four Neapolitan friends around the memories of Napoli and Italy in the 90s and the rivalry Napoli-Milan and the Italy 1990 World Cup (Gurrado) and intertwine the first championship for the Italian club to the history of the city, related by a "Professor De Crescenzo" to a fan named "F." in the bar Portorico (de Paulis).

14 The reference here is to Joseph Campbell's *The Hero with the Thousand Faces*. García Cames (2018b) engages extensively with Campbell's ideas. The same author ends his analysis of three short stories about Maradona by stating that "the dual nature of the hero, petty and sublime, fits the image of the Argentine player to perfection" (2018a: 430).

15 Argentine and English players' comments before the match tried to lower the "war" expectations (cf. Burgo 2016 and Chapter 1 in this volume).

16 The relationship between Maradona and politics cannot be addressed here (cf. Chapter 1 in this volume for a brief take). Alabarces has dedicated the most consistent attention to the topic (2007, 2014, 2021). Julio Ferrer's *Maradona. Fútbol y política* (2021) is of anecdotal value; a more compelling, if impressionistic, volume is *Todo Diego es político* (2021), edited by Bárbara Pistoia, as well as some material found in *Maradona, un mito plebeyo* (2021), edited by Antonio Gómez Villar. Gabriela Saidon's *Superdios. La construcción de Maradona como santo laico* (2021) provides insightful comments. Sebreli offers a summary of what Maradona symbolises for different social and political groups: "For populist nationalism, he incarnates the myth of national identity; for the lower classes without political conscience, the myth of the beggar who becomes a prince; for leftist intellectuals, the myth of the social rebel; for contracultural youth, the myth of the transgressor" (2008: 172). Three non-Argentinian, much needed, views on the topic can be found in Bilbija (1995), Tobin (2002), and Salazar-Sutil (2008).

17 Significantly, there are more academic articles on The Hand of God goal than on the Goal of the Century (cf. the bibliography in this volume). A curious book in this regard is *Processo a Diego Armando Maradona. La mano de Dios* by Claudio Botti *et al*, which engages in a mock trial to examine the goal from a legalistic point of view.

18 In his review of the game, and again invoking the patriotic Maradonian mode, John Gage says that the Hand of God goal was Maradona's revenge "for us [the English] sinking the Belgrano" (a ship attacked by the British armed forces during the Malvinas/Falkland Islands war). Then Gage laughs. 323 Argentine soldiers died because of that incident. See https://www.youtube.com/watch?v=p0fY1tJRGnk

19 An investigation of Maradona's participation in the United States 1994 World Cup can be found in Andrés Burgo's and Alejandro Wall's *El último Maradona: cuando a Diego le cortaron las piernas* (2014).

20 The original version of the story is from 1997 and had a few pages; by 2014, it had grown to 30. The longer version emphasises the parodic and grotesque effects to amplify the sense of ridicule. There are jibes to all aspects of Argentine political life, a decidedly crude and rude couple (Dieguito's parents) and even Lionel Messi appears, first as a suspect of killing Maradona and then as a victim of kidnapping. The story loses quality, strength, and internal coherence. The only felicitous moment in this expanded version takes place when the protagonist finds the talking head of Maradona in the wreckage. The head speaks: "Save me *pibe*. I don't want to die before Messi" (Feinmann 2014: 23).

21 Bartoletti's novel situates Maradona in heaven, having dinner with other characters; the player is given one day to come down to Earth to revisit Naples. The story by Pecchinenda is an interesting take: a doctor has a patient who claims to have supplanted Maradona: "They made me a proposal to be his double, and I accepted, I guess" (2021: 26).

22 The full narration of the whole game has been published as Víctor Hugo Morales. *Barrilete cósmico (el relato completo)*. It is also included in *90 minutos. Relatos de fútbol*, pp. 138–140. The second goal narrated by Morales is available here: https://www.youtube.com/watch?v=O8G9ytZg-bM. The embarrassment produced by revisiting this "emotional explosion" has been acknowledged by writers like Villoro and by Morales himself, as Ariel Magnus explains in the epilogue to the book (Morales 2013: V). Cames argues that "literature represents the goal as eternity incarnated in an image, an image where time is absolute" (2018b: 221).

23 See https://www.youtube.com/watch?v=OpvkmPiVfeE

# References

## Creative Works

Ahmadi, Amhed. 2013. *Strange and Incredible Story of Maradona [the correct title is Maradona, Plastic Goalkeepers, And That Decisive Penalty … Did He Score It? Or Not? What Happened? In Farsi].* London: H&S Media.

Bartoletti, Marino. 2021. *Il retorno degli Dei.* Rome: Galucci.

Benedetti, Mario. 2012 (first published 2008). "Maradona". *Un balón envenenado. Poesía y fútbol.* Eds. Luis García Montero y Jesús García Sánchez. Madrid: Visor, 52.

Braceli, Rodolfo. 2009. "La partera de Maradona" (originally published as "Recomendaciones para parir un hijo que salga Maradona". *Perfume de gol.* Buenos Aires: Planeta, 2009). *90 minutos. Relatos de fútbol.* Buenos Aires: Cultura Argentina, 127–137.

Brescia, Pablo. 2022. "Dos tiempos distintos". *Olfato de gol. Nuevos cuentos de fútbol.* Eds. Antonio Sánchez Jiménez and José Domínguez Búrdalo. Madrid: Reino de Cordelia, 65–75.

Casciari, Hernán. 2005. "Vivir para contarlo". *Más respeto que soy tu madre.* Buenos Aires: Ediciones Orsai, 203–205.

_____. 2013. "10.6 segundos". *Orsai* 11: 36–49. Available in English at https://hernancasciari.com/en/blog/106_seconds

Castaldi, Paolo. 2014. *La mano de Dios.* Madrid: Diábolo Ediciones.

Chilet, Vicent. 2018. "Club Sportivo 6-Argentina 4, Humahuaca 10-1-86". *Maradona en Humahuaca y otros goles con historia.* Madrid: La Caja Books, 17–22.

*Cuentos de fútbol.* 1995. Selecc. y prol. Jorge Valdano. Madrid: Alfaguara.

De Paulis, Fabio. 2020. *Ho visto Maradona.* Napoli: LFA Publisher.

Di Giovanni, Maurizio. 2009. *Juve-Napoli 1-3. La presa di Torino.* Italy: Cento Autore.

Feinmann, José Pablo. 2003. "Dieguito". *Cuentos de fútbol argentino.* Buenos Aires: Alfaguara, 2003, 47–53.

_____. 2014. "Dieguito". *Bongo. Infancia en Belgrano R y otros cuentos.* Buenos Aires: Planeta, 21–51.

Fontanarrosa, Roberto. 2001. "Aquel gol de Maradona a los ingleses". *Página* 12. April 30. https://www.pagina12.com.ar/2001/01-11/01-11-11/pag31.htm

Fresán, Rodrigo. 2009 (1st published 1997). "Final". *90 minutos. Relatos de fútbol.* Buenos Aires: Cultura Argentina, 71–74.

García, Rodrigo. 2001. *After Sun.* Available at http://redenasa.tv/web/uploads/biblioteca/arquivo/4bff9610b4e8d0.40577627.pdf

Gurrado, Antonio. 2014. *Ho visto Maradona.* Milano: Ediciclo Editore.

*Maradona, uno de los nuestros.* 2021. Sevilla: Peña Sevillista Coke Andújar.

Marchant, Reinaldo Edmundo, comp. 2021. *El 10 Maradona. Antología chilena de historias de fútbol en homenaje a Diego Armando Maradona.* Santiago de Chile: Mago.

Medina, Enrique. 1984. "Yo fui Maradona". *El Gráfico.* https://www.elgrafico.com.ar/articulo/1088/35645/yo-fui-maradona-por-enrique-medina.

Morales, Víctor Hugo. 2013. *Barrilete cósmico (el relato completo).* Idea y realización Ariel Magnus. Buenos Aires: Interzona.

Niembro, Fernando y Julio Llinás. 1995. *Inocente.* Barcelona: Grijalbo Mondadori.

Olguín, Sergio. 2004. *El equipo de los sueños.* Buenos Aires: Norma.

Pecchinenda, Gianfranco. 2020. *Quel Tal Maradona.* Napoli: Amigdala Edizioni.

Picardo, Osvaldo. 2012. "La mano de Dios". *Un balón envenenado. Poesía y fútbol.* Eds. Luis García Montero y Jesús García Sánchez. Madrid: Visor, 188.

Saccheri, Eduardo. 2000. "Me van a tener que disculpar". *Esperándolo a Tito y otros cuentos de fútbol.* Buenos Aires: Galerna, 35–42.

Saccomano, Guillermo. 2010. "Tránsito". *Cuentos de fútbol argentino*. Ed. Roberto Fontanarrosa. Buenos Aires: Alfaguara, 364–373.

Scher, Ariel. 2018. "Todo mientras Diego" and "A llorar se aprende". *Todos mientras Diego y otros cuentos mundiales*. Buenos Aires: Grupo Editorial Sur, 9–11; 92–93.

Soriano, Osvaldo. 2010. "Maradona sí, Galtieri no". *Fútbol. Relatos épicos sobre un deporte que despierta pasiones*. Barcelona: Seix Barral. Available at http://www.don-patadon.com/2016/10/maradona-si-galtieri-no-de-osvaldo.html

Vargas, Walter. 2004. "Bautismos". *Del diario íntimo de un chico rubio y otras historias futboleras*. Buenos Aires: Ediciones al Arco, 103–109.

## *Essay and Criticism*

Alabarces, Pablo. 1996. "Maradona revisitado. Apostillas a 'El fútbol no es la patria'". *Cuestión de pelotas. Fútbol, deporte, sociedad, cultura*. Buenos Aires: Atuel, 53–57.

_____. 2000. "Introducción. Los estudios sobre deporte y sociedad; objetos, miradas, agendas". *Peligro de gol: estudios sobre deporte y sociedad en América Latina*. Comp. Pablo Alabarces. Buenos Aires: CLACSO, 11–30.

_____. 2007. "Maradonismo, o la superación del peronismo por otros medios". *Fútbol y patria. El fútbol y las narrativas de la nación en la Argentina*. Buenos Aires: Prometeo, 133–160.

_____. 2014. "La patria, Maradona y Messi: variaciones sobre el ser nacional". *Héroes, machos y patriotas. El fútbol entre la violencia y los medios*. Buenos Aires: Aguilar, 103–132.

_____. 2015. "Deporte y sociedad en América Latina: un campo reciente, una agenda en construcción". *Anales de Antropología* 48.2: 11–28.

_____. 2021. "Maradona: mito popular, símbolo peronista, voz plebeya". *Papeles del CEIC* 249.1: 1–11.

Alabarces, Pablo and María Graciela Rodríguez. 1999. "Football and Fatherland: The Crisis of National Representation in Argentinean Soccer". *Sport in Society* 2.3: 118–133.

Archetti, Eduardo. 1997. "And Give Joy to my Heart: Ideology and Emotions in the Argentinean Cult of Maradona". *Entering the Field. New Perspectives on World Football*. Eds. Gary Amstrong and Richard Giulianotti. Oxford; New York: Berg, 31–51.

_____. 1998. "The Potrero and the Pibe. Territory and Belonging in the Mythical Account of Argentinean Football". *Locality and Belonging*. Ed. Nadia Lovell. Routledge: London; New York, 189–210.

_____. 1999. *Masculinities. Football, Polo and the Tango in Argentina*. Oxford; New York: Berg.

_____. 2001. "The Spectacle of a Heroic Life: The Case of Diego Maradona". *Sport Stars: The Cultural Politics of Cultural Celebrity*. Eds. David L. Andrews and Steven J. Jackson. London; New York: Routledge, 151–164.

Arcucci, Daniel. 2001. *Conocer al Diego. Relatos de fascinación maradoniana*. Buenos Aires: Prometeo.

Balagué, Guillem. 2021. *Maradona. The Boy. The Rebel. The God*. London: Weidenfeld & Nicolson.

Barthes, Roland. 1972 (1st ed. 1957). *Mythologies*. Trans. Jonathan Cape. New York: The Noonday Press.

Bernstein, Gustavo. 1997. *Maradona. Iconografía de la patria*. Buenos Aires: Biblos.

Bertoglio, Carlos. 2021. "Maradona's Ghost and Co.: Narrating Maradona in Argentine Football Literature". *Funes: Journal of Narrative and Social Sciences*. Special Issue: *Global Maradona: Man, Athlete, Celebrity, Idol, Hero, Myth* 5: 90–104.

Bifulco, Luca. 2020. *Maradona, un héroe deportivo. Tres estudios sociológicos de Italia*. Buenos Aires: Ediciones Godot.

Bilbija, Ksenija. 1995. "Maradona's Left: Postmodernity and National Identity in Argentina". *Studies in Latin American Popular Culture* 14: 199–208.

Borge, Steffen. 2019. *The Philosophy of Football*. Oxford; New York: Routledge.

Botti, Claudio *et al*. 2020. *Processo a Diego Armando Maradona. La mano de Dios*. Milano: Edizioni Le Lucerne.

Brescia, Pablo. 2021. "Efecto DAM: Diego Armando Maradona en algunas representaciones literarias". *Funes Journal of Narratives and Social Sciences*. Special Issue: *Global Maradona: Man, Athlete, Celebrity, Idol, Hero, Myth* 5: 43–54.

Burgo, Andrés. 2016. *El partido. Argentina-Inglaterra 1986*. Buenos Aires: Tusquets.

Burgo, Andrés and Alejandro Wall. 2014. *El último Maradona: cuando a Diego le cortaron las piernas*. Buenos Aires: Aguilar.

Burns, Jimmy. 1996. *Hand of God. The Life of Diego Maradona*. New York: The Lyons Press.

Caldeira, José. 2007. *Iglesia Maradoniana*. Mar del Plata, Argentina: Author's Edition.

Campbell, Joseph. 2008 (1st ed. 1949). *The Hero with the Thousand Faces*. Novato, California: New World Library.

*Crónicas maradonianas*. 2021. *Lástima a nadie maestro, blog*. Buenos Aires: Milena Cacerola.

Domínguez, Sergio, ed. 2019. *Maradona 365 historias*. Buenos Aires: Librofútbol.com.

Domínguez Prost, Micaela. 2021. *La mano de Diego*. Montevideo: Tajante.

Fernández Moores, Ezequiel, Alejandro Wall and Andrés Burgo, eds. 2021. *Rey de Fiorito. Crónicas políticas y sociales de la vida de Diego Maradona*. Buenos Aires: Ediciones Carrascosa-SiPreBa.

Ferrer, Julio. 2021. *Maradona. Fútbol y política*. Buenos Aires: Punto de encuentro.

Frydenberg, Julio. 2011. *Historia social del fútbol. Del amateurismo a la profesionalización*. Buenos Aires: Siglo XXI.

García Cames, David. 2018a. "El gol y el héroe. Aproximación mítica a Maradona en tres cuentos argentinos". *Pasavento. Revista de Estudios Hispánicos* 6.2: 413–431.

_____. 2018b. *La jugada de todos los tiempos. fútbol, mito y literatura*. Zaragoza, Spain: Prensas Universitarias de Zaragoza.

Gómez Villar, Antonio, ed. 2021. *Maradona, un mito plebeyo*. Madrid: Ned.

Maradona, Diego Armando. 2011. *Maradona. The Autobiography of Soccer's Greatest and Most Controversial Star*. Trans. Marcela Mora y Araujo. New York: Skyhorse Publishing.

Maradona, Diego Armando and Daniel Arcucci. 2016. *Touched by God. How We Won the Mexico '86 World Cup*. Trans. Jane Brodie and Wendy Gosselin. London: Constable.

McGowan, Lee. 2020. *Football in Fiction: A History*. Oxford; New York: Routledge.

Pistoia, Bárbara, ed. 2021. *Todo Diego es político*. Buenos Aires: Síncopa.

Rodríguez, María Graciela. 2003. "Los días en que Maradona usó kilt: intersección de identidades profundas con representaciones massmediáticas". *Futbologías. Fútbol, identidad y violencia en América Latina*. Comp. Pablo Alabarces. Buenos Aires: CLACSO, 181–197.

Saidon, Gabriela. 2021. *Superdios. La construcción de Maradona como santo laico*. Buenos Aires: Capital Intelectual.

Salazar Sutil, Nicolás. 2008. "Maradona Inc: Performance Politics off the Pitch". *International Journal of Cultural Studies* 11.4: 441–458.

Sánchez Yvette. 2007. "La literatura de fútbol, ¿metida en camisa de once varas?" *Iberromania* 7.27: 131–142.

Santoro, Roberto. *Literatura de la pelota*. Buenos Aires: Papeles de Buenos Aires, 1971.

Sebreli, Juan José. 2008. "Maradona". *Comediantes y mártires. Ensayos contra los mitos*. Barcelona: Debates, 165–202.

Sommer, Doris. 1991. *Foundational Fictions: The National Romances of Latin America*. Berkeley: University of Berkeley Press.

Tobin, Jeffrey. 2002. "Soccer Conspiracies: Maradona, the CIA, and Populist Critique". *Sport in Latin America and the Caribbean*. Eds. Joseph L. Arbena and David G. LaFrance. London: Eurospan, 51–73.

Villoro, Juan. 2014. *God Is Round*. Trans. Thomas Bunstead. New York: Restless Books.

Wilson, Jonathan. 2016. *Angels with Dirty Faces. How Argentinian Soccer Defined a Nation and Changed the Game Forever*. New York: Nation Books.

Wood, David. 2017. *Football and Literature in South America*. Oxford; New York: Routledge.

# 7

# MARADONA AND CINEMA

## Biopic, Documentary, Art Film

*Mariano Paz*

### Screening Diego

The Iranian film *Taste of Cherry* (1997), by Abbas Kiarostami, tells the story of Badii, a middle-aged man who is going through an unspecified life crisis and is contemplating suicide. He has not made up his mind yet, but he is looking for somebody to bury him if he does take his own life. The story follows Badii as he drives around Teheran and its barren suburbs trying to find a person who would be willing to help. He reaches a construction site atop a hill where an impoverished caretaker keeps watch over the machinery from an elevated shack. There is nothing there except for "earth and dust", as the watchman, an Afghan immigrant, puts it. He invites Badii to his single-room shack, although he has nothing to offer him except tea. His dwellings are bare, with no decorations or ornaments and only a chair for furniture. However, hanging on one of the decrepit walls is a poster of Diego Armando Maradona, photographed wearing the light blue and white Argentina kit, ball at his foot. It seems an image taken from a game, although only Maradona is visible in the frame.

The Argentinian player is never mentioned by name and has no relevance for the plot of the film, a naturalistic work concerned with the verisimilitude of its characters. His image, which may even go unnoticed as it remains in the background, is not there to attract attention or make a point; it is simply an element of the *mise-en-scène* that lends authenticity to a work of realism. This poor, forgotten man in a remote corner of Tehran is one of the millions of admirers of Maradona globally. This cinematic moment condenses two important elements that define the figure of Maradona in relation to cinema: his international reach, and his appeal to art-house filmmakers.

This chapter explores the representation of Maradona in world cinemas, mapping out the significant corpus of films in which the player appears in different

DOI: 10.4324/9781003196587-10

capacities, from small cameos to major roles. The list spans documentaries, traditional biopics, melodramas, art films, and even the fantastic, many of them made by renowned directors, such as Emir Kusturica and Paolo Sorrentino. Even allowing that narrative genres entail a degree of fluctuation and hybridity, the wide range of styles and types make it difficult to categorise these films. Some of them, for example, go well beyond what could be termed the football film, itself a subgenre of the sports film (Glynn 2018). Football, like cinema, provides spectacle, drama, and narrative and contributes to mythologising specific events and persons (Rowe 2008). Both cultural forms, therefore, converge around the figure of Maradona.

The variety of Maradonian films echoes the gamut of audiovisual texts that involve the footballer well beyond cinema: television programmes of all kinds (in some cases, hosted by the footballer himself), commercials, music videos, and others. This chapter is concerned specifically with representations of Maradona in feature-length films and is organised according to three sections. The first one studies the early representations of Maradona in Argentinian fiction cinema, discussing *¡Qué linda es mi familia!* (*What A Nice Family I Have!*) (dir. Ramón "Palito" Ortega 1980); *Te rompo el rating* (*I Break Your Ratings*) (dir. Hugo Sofovich 1981); and *El día que Maradona conoció a Gardel* (*The Day Maradona Met Gardel*) (dir. Rodolfo Pagliere 1995). These are the three first feature-length films in which the player is involved as an actor, and which set the scene for future cinematic presences. The second section discusses international documentaries focused on the player: *Maradona by Kusturica* (dir. Emir Kusturica 2008); *Maradonapoli* (*Maradonaples*) (dir. Alessio Maria Federici 2017); and *Diego Maradona* (dir. Asif Kapadia 2019). The three can be considered art-house documentaries that explore Maradona from different perspectives and styles. All of them are concerned with the attempt to define Maradona as an icon and myth. The final section focusses on fiction films that revolve around Maradona in more complex ways than the Argentinian films in the first section. They include the mainstream biopic *Maradona, la mano de Dios* (*Maradona, the Hand of God*) (dir. Mario Risi 2007); the minimalist *El camino de San Diego* (*The Road to San Diego*) (dir. Carlos Sorín 2006); and the baroque *Youth* (2015) and *È stata la mano di Dio* (*The Hand of God*) (2021), both by the prestigious Italian director Paolo Sorrentino.

## The early era

The connection between Maradona and cinema began when he was only 20-years old and was still playing in the national league for a relatively small club, Argentinos Juniors. It is revealing, then, that he attracted the attention of filmmakers even before becoming a global star. His first cinematic appearance is a cameo role in *What a Nice Family I Have!*, where he plays himself (though his name goes unmentioned) for under 2 minutes of screen time. The film is essentially a star vehicle for Ramón "Palito" Ortega, perhaps the most famous singer-songwriter in 1960s and 1970s Argentina, who also directs the film. At the time, Ortega would have been a much more popular celebrity than Maradona, but they do not have any screen time together. Instead, Maradona has a single scene alongside Luis Sandrini, a major comic actor of classic Argentinian cinema.

The plot revolves mostly around Ortega, who plays an aspiring actor and singer attempting to launch his career. His father, played by Sandrini, is the president of the football club where Maradona plays. The club is struggling financially, and its main hope for survival is the sale of its leading player, although the president is adamant he will not be sold. In the scene, the president attends a training session in which we see Maradona doing keepie-uppies. The two meet by the touchline and have a brief conversation. Maradona does not say much, and he is clearly not too comfortable in front of the cameras (this would eventually change). Sandrini tells his player (who is only referred to as *pibe*) that he will reject any offers for him until the World Cup, something that Maradona accepts happily, saying he is not keen on leaving since he would rather live close to his friends and family.

Although a minor plotline, this scene echoes what happened with Maradona in real life with his transfer to FC Barcelona (cf. Chapter 2 of this volume). The player would continue his career in Argentina until the 1982 World Cup, despite increasing interest from European clubs in acquiring him. To a large extent, the refusal of Argentinos Juniors to sell him was due to the pressure of the military government that was ruling the country at the time. The *de facto* government had already used football for political aims, by hosting the 1978 World Cup, which contributed to legitimise an unconstitutional administration. Keeping the rising star of world football in the country would be part of a nationalistic agenda (further emphasised if the national team were able to retain the World Cup in the 1982 tournament in Spain).

The similarity between real life and fictional storylines, however, could be more than a simple coincidence: after all, the films made by "Palito" Ortega in the late 1970s and early 1980s had close ties with the military. While they were not exclusively propaganda films, they very much voiced the ideologies and world views of the right-wing dictatorship (Finchelstein 2014: 151–152). Therefore, Maradona in this film becomes the instrument of two different forces: on the one hand, of a commercial production that relies on popular actors and singers to increase its appeal; on the other, of a more sinister political agenda underlining that Maradona should remain playing in Argentina even as his growing reputation made him a target of the biggest clubs in the world.

Only one year later, Maradona would have similar role in *I Break Your Ratings*, another popular film, in this case, an example of low-brow, vulgar comedy starring Jorge Porcel, a prolific comedian who featured in dozens of films and TV programmes in the 1970s and 1980s. Porcel plays an aspiring TV personality who gets a chance to become a news reporter. In a number of (supposedly) comic vignettes, he is seen engaging in increasingly sensationalist news reportage that will attract viewers. At one moment, he attends an Argentinos Juniors game to cover the footballing star of the moment. This time, Maradona is not just juggling the ball during training but playing a competitive game. The stands are packed with extras and his full name is used: the journalist addresses him as Diego, the coach as Maradona.

In the fictional match, Maradona gets the ball and dribbles past four or five players and the goalkeeper. He finds himself facing an open goal … and right before he can shoot, the journalist enters the field, embraces the player, puts a microphone to his mouth, and begins asking him shallow questions about the goal he is about to score (how he feels about it, who will he dedicate it to, and so on). Amid desperate shouts from the manager by the touchline and boos from the stands, the goalkeeper tracks back and catches the ball.

That is end of the comic sketch, and the film moves on. But now we have seen a Maradona who is somewhat more comfortable in front of the camera. The intention behind such sequence points out a strong trend in the national media at the time: its increasingly intrusive reporting in the search for scandalous news. Later in the film, a network executive will express his surprise at the high ratings this reporter is achieving, and the reply is that people have become attracted to sensationalist journalism. In relation to Maradona, the scene can also be read as a prophetic commentary on the relationship between the player and the media. Eventually, Maradona would become hostage to the paparazzi and the press in general, who would follow him wherever he went and constantly intrude into his private life.

Maradona's subsequent appearance as character in a fiction film would take longer to arrive, in another Argentinian production: *The Day Maradona Met Gardel*. By now, 1995, Maradona was already a global star, the peak of this career behind him. He had also gone through the most difficult moments as a player, including two bans from playing football after positive doping tests (the second one during the 1994 World Cup). In the film, thus, we have a completely different person than the Maradona of the two previous works. The player also has a much more important role in the story, a bizarre sort of fantasy tale – in fact, a subtitle that is seen in the opening credits (though not in the film's posters or other publicity material) describes it as a "fable about heroes". The plot is not strong on coherence, even when allowing for the estrangement that is characteristic of fantasy genres. It revolves around the following premise: Carlos Gardel, the most important singer in the history of tango, who died dramatically at the peak of his career in June 1935 in an aeroplane crash, is not dead. Gardel has instead been trapped in a timeless limbo by an evil spirit or demon, in the shape of a beautiful woman played by actress Esther Goris. She has tricked him into signing a Mephistophelian pact: Gardel would gain the eternal love of the people, and in turn, he would go on living and singing only for the pleasure of this devil. The pact had been signed the day before the fatal crash.

In 1995, a public homage to Gardel is being prepared for the 60th anniversary of his death. Maxi, a young film editor working on a clip of Gardel highlights to be used at the ceremony, stumbles upon the truth. He also realises that the spell can be broken only by somebody with a status equivalent to that of the singer. There is only one person who has achieved this: Maradona. Assisted by a good being, perhaps an angel, Maxi finds the footballer, who in real life was living in Buenos Aires and about to return to play for Boca Juniors, and asks him to join their quest in finding Gardel. Maradona, no stranger to the bizarre, accepts this task casually, without expressing any doubts. Eventually, they find the singer and the two legends have a short conversation (for some unexplained reason, Gardel knows perfectly well who Maradona is), and the evil spell is broken.

To a large extent, the film consists of documentary footage from Gardel's performances and his films. Maradona appears in the final third and has a few brief scenes. The final sequence, of about 5 minutes of running time, is made up of documentary footage of Maradona, suggesting he has now taken over Gardel as the main Argentine hero. It is clear from the settings and décor that this is a low-budget film. Visually, the repeated use of extreme close-ups of the actors' faces, alongside low-angle and tilted-angle shots, distorts the images and adds an uncanny, oneiric quality to the story. The film was a commercial flop and panned by critics in Argentina (Zucchi 2016). However, the attempt to build a parallel between Maradona and Gardel is not surprising, for they are two of the most important mass idols that Argentina, a country inclined to the construction and adoration of mythical figures, has produced. According to Horacio González, "as Gardel was to song, Maradona was to football" (2021: 102).[1] Ideologically, thus, the film supports a cultural nationalism that is characteristic of *costumbrismo* — an aesthetic trend that highlights local customs and practices. It could be certainly read as a celebration of Maradona's return to professional football in Boca Juniors, but, by conveying a romanticised vision of the player as an Argentinian hero, it also contributes to the mythologising of Maradona through the national media that deems him a being "out of this world". In a universe of angels and demons, Maradona's supernatural powers can help the side of good defeat evil.

This trio of Argentinian films, therefore, show Maradona at two stages of his professional career. On the one hand, the rising young star whose brilliant future is ahead of him. On the other, Maradona as having completed the path to stardom and glory — so much so that he has replaced Gardel in the pantheon of national myths. The first two films incorporate the player as one of many ingredients in a mix of popular tropes aimed at maximising the appeal of avowedly commercial productions, but they also reveal that Maradona was seen as a particularly special player, anticipating a successful future career. After all, it was not customary for Argentinian popular films to include cameos by footballers. The third film acknowledges that Maradona has gone beyond expectations to become an exceptional being, one who could match not only footballers but also spirits and devils. Altogether, the films crystalise the cinematic character of Maradona and his potential to contribute different meanings to an audiovisual story. Many more films would follow in the new century.

## Documenting Diego: From performance to archive

If the early films featuring Maradona make for a rather haphazard collection of lowbrow entertainment and nationalistic mythology, from the turn of the millennium onwards several major filmmakers came to be drawn to the footballer as a cinematic object. Unavoidably, given his status as a global celebrity and the controversies that constantly surrounded his professional and personal life, Maradona is the subject of dozens of documentaries, most of them made for TV stations across the world. This section is concerned with feature-length non-fiction cinema. Three films in particular stand out in this corpus: *Maradona by Kusturica* (dir. Emir Kusturica 2008), *Maradonaples* (dir. Alessio Maria Federici 2017), and *Diego Maradona* (dir. Asif Kapadia 2019).

It should be noted that non-fiction cinemas, although representing real events and real people, are also works that draw on many of the same conventions and aesthetic techniques of fiction as they present constructed narratives of events and specific characters (Aufderheide 2007; Waldron 2018). In fact, as Michael Chanan argues, documentary representation "is always already subject to the film-maker's angle, perspective and artistry" (2007: 4). The films discussed below are no exception to these intrinsic features of non-fiction cinema, although some of them make this approach more evident than others. They all offer, therefore, different visions of Maradona informed by factors ranging from the favoured aesthetic approach to the ideology of the filmmakers.

Emir Kusturica, one of the world's most renowned living filmmaker and winner in all major film festivals such as Cannes, Venice, and Berlin, is a controversial figure in his own right, as well as a football fan (Iordanova 2002, Bertellini 2014). It is, thus, not surprising that he chose to make a film on Maradona. The result, *Maradona by Kusturica*, is a clear example of performative documentary – a mode in which the director of the film is not only present in the story but deeply involved in it, making it evident that stories are always conditioned by a subjective point of view (Nichols 2001). In this case, Kusturica is not only the narrator but a character in his own film, often appearing alongside Maradona and sometimes on his own, walking around the streets of Buenos Aires and meditating on the cultural significance of the footballer. Shot over a two-year period, the film lacks a unifying backbone, and its meandering narrative may be due, in part, to the difficulty in having access to Maradona. In one scene Kusturica's frustration is evident: having recently arrived in Argentina, he travels to Maradona's house with his small crew for a shooting session only to find out, after waiting at the door for some time, that the player has changed his mind and has decided to go somewhere else instead.

Pablo Alabarces has described the film as the encounter of two "monumental narcissists" (2014: 60), and Ksenija Bilbija argues in Chapter 9 of this volume that Maradona is present in the film as a spectral figure. It is nonetheless clear that the film is more interested in Maradona the man than in Maradona the player. Though it contains some archival footage of Maradona's career, including the obligatory goals against England in the 1986 World Cup quarter-finals, and others that have been less revisited (such as his goal against Kusturica's beloved Red Star Belgrade club), the focus is placed on the life of the footballer at the time the film was shot. The player is invited to Belgrade, where he meets Kusturica's family, and they visit Red Star Stadium. Maradona is also followed during a trip to Naples, which shows the undiminished passion of the fans, who hurdle around him whenever he steps out on the street. Kusturica also interviews Maradona a few times in several settings, including his childhood home in the impoverished *Villa Fiorito* slum, and he captures a performance in which the player sings a famous song about him, "La mano de Dios" – a significant scene which is analysed by Martín Virgili in Chapter 8 of this volume.

As Bertellini states, Kusturica feels that Maradona is comparable to himself "in terms of biography, creativity, independence, and political affinity" (2014: 139). The director sees Serbia and Argentina as being very similar within the world order because both are peripheral countries that have been the victim of Western imperialism and the IMF. Moreover, Kusturica finds correspondences between the player and several characters in his films, such impoverished workers, and political dissidents, which he underlines by adding clips from those films. Perhaps for this reason the director chooses to emphasise a political view of Maradona, evident from early on, when he states that had Maradona not been a footballer he would have become a revolutionary. At several stages throughout the film, the narrative is interrupted by short, animated vignettes, scored by the Sex Pistols song "God Save the Queen". They show a cartoonish Maradona running on a football pitch, ball at his foot, while a series of figures – Maradona's enemies, real or imagined – attempt to stop him. These are not football players but political figures: Margaret Thatcher, Queen Elizabeth II of England and Prince Charles, Ronald Reagan, Tony Blair, and George W. Bush. Maradona is attacked by these powerful people in the same way Argentina and Serbia, in Kusturica's perspective, have been punished by the countries those people represent.

One of the key scenes in the film that supports Kusturica's vision is Maradona's role in the international political protests held in Argentina in November 2005. At the time, the IV Summit of the Americas was hosted in the coastal city of Mar del Plata (about 400 km south of Buenos Aires). It was attended by the heads of state of all nations in South and North America, including President Bush, and many others from Central America and the Caribbean. The summit turned out to be a chaotic event due to the sharp disagreement between the participating presidents, particularly in relation to the FTAA (Free Trade Area of the Americas; ALCA in Spanish), a free trade agreement proposed by the United States and favoured by Canada and Mexico, but which faced strong opposition from most countries in South America (Marridoriaga 2005; *The New York Times* 2005).

Against this background, a "counter-summit" denouncing the US agenda and the presence of Bush was planned at the same time and in the same city. One of the main organisers was Miguel Bonasso, a left-wing journalist and politician who secured the support of regional leaders such as the presidents of Venezuela and Bolivia, Hugo Chávez and Evo Morales. Maradona was a guest of honour. The organisers travelled from Buenos Aires to Mar del Plata by train, in a trip that become known as *Tren del Alba* (Dawn Train) (*The Guardian* 2005; Russo 2005). Travelling in the train, among hundreds of protesters, were several Argentine figures from the world of culture (actors, singers), Bonasso, Morales, and, most notably (followed by Kusturica and his crew) Maradona, who attracted more attention than any of the other passengers. For the organisers of the "counter-summit" the free trade agreement was simply an excuse to extend neoliberal policies across the region, to the benefit of the United States and the detriment of South American nations. Once in Mar del Plata, thousands of people gathered at the city stadium, where the regional leaders delivered speeches. Maradona did not take centre stage, but upon Chávez's invitation, he approached the main stand, wearing a T-shirt with photo of George W. Bush and the caption "War Criminal", and offered a few words advocating peaceful but firm protests aimed at "restoring our dignity" and calling to defend "what is ours" in the face of the US pressures for the FTTA treaty to be signed.

In the film, the train scenes are shot with a hand-held camera, offering shaky and fluid takes (understandable amid the train movement and the huge crowds) that convey a sense of realism and urgency to the images. As usual, Maradona is surrounded by fans, photographers, and police escorts. In the voice-over narration, Kusturica suggests that the train is not just headed for Mar del Plata, but towards better times in Latin America. Interviewed by one of the many journalists covering the event, Kusturica explains that "people need somebody to lead them because the leaders of the world today, they are not good enough". Naturally, he thinks that Maradona could be that leader.

According to Marcus Free, the political vision of the film expresses "Maradona's notionally Christ-like symbolism as a potentially redemptive, revolutionary figure for the geopolitical South" (Free 2014: 208). The view of Maradona as redeemer and radical is very much in line with one of the most widespread views about the player, whose victories with Argentina over England, and with SSC Napoli over the wealthier clubs of Northern Italy, epitomise such a position, later echoed by Maradona's declarations in favour of the Castro regime in Cuba and, as we can see in the film, his attacks on George W. Bush. This idea of Maradona as a utopian agent, widely shared by several thinkers and intellectuals, overlooks the player's association with other types of political figures and regimes, from the neoliberal administration of Carlos Menem in Argentina (1989–1999), a close ally of President George Bush, to his support for authoritarian leaders with poor human rights records around the world. In any case, it could be argued that Kusturica was as much attracted by the spectacle of the *Dawn Train* as he was by its political implications. The premise of Maradona embarking on multitudinous ride alongside political leaders and activists in a protest against the US President is yet another colourful episode in the life of the football player, but also one which could have come out of Kusturica's imagination.

The opposite approach to documenting Maradona in cinema can be seen in *Maradonapoli* (2017), by the Italian director Alessio Maria Federici. The film is devoted to the connection between Maradona and Naples, which, as the title suggests, can be considered intertwined entities. Player and city have become inextricable, perennially conflated, with Maradona imbued in the collective memory of the residents of Naples as much as in the materiality of its streets and buildings, as the travelling shots across the city show. Originally intended as a documentary about the Maradona murals that abound in the city, the director realised during location scouting and pre-production that every Neapolitan had their own stories about Maradona, based on a significant emotional investment in the star, and modified his approach to the film (Federici 2021).

Ultimately, it consists of a mosaic of interviews with over two dozen Neapolitans across a wide range of backgrounds and social classes. Most, though not all of them, are male. None of them are football experts, and none of them are personally related to Maradona in any capacity. They are simply representatives of the people of Naples: cooks, shop owners, a professor of robotics, an antiquarian, a medical doctor, a tattoo artist, a librarian, a priest, a journalist, a housewife, a taxi driver, and many others. The fact that these people are named only towards the end of the film reinforces the idea that here the collective experience is more important than individual identities. We never see the director and there is no voice-over narration; Maradona himself appears for only a few minutes and through archival footage recorded during his time as a Napoli player – one of them is a TV interview, the other one a rarely seen but impressive recording of Maradona in the cockpit of an aeroplane making its approach to Naples International Airport. There are no images of Maradona playing football.

Hence, unlike *Maradona by Kusturica*, in this film there is no attempt to capture the "real" Maradona, who appears briefly in the mentioned footage, but to explore the remembered and the imagined Maradona. Thus, the Maradona we see in this film is one that is reconstructed in the memories of fans; a multiplicity of people making up a large Maradonian collective. The use of medium and close-up shots of those interviewed reveal the emotion they feel when attempting to make sense of the feelings they have for Maradona, some of them coming close to tears. Admittedly, such feelings are reinforced by a haunting and melancholic musical score – but this is non-diegetic music added in post-production and does not change the affective value of the opinions given by the interviewees.

The statements and recollections offered can be classified according to several axes, three of which stand out in my view. The first one is related to "napoletantità" – i.e. Neapolitan identity, or the condition of being a Neapolitan. Maradona is seen as an authentic citizen of Naples, despite being Argentinian: "Maradona is a Neapolitan living abroad" says one of the interviewees. Another one mentions: "When he arrived in Naples, the city was ready to embrace him, and to breastfeed him". Maradona, therefore, becomes a son of Naples. The second trope is a more obvious one: Maradona as a redeemer, who changed the symbolic order of power in Italy and beyond: "He is a sports genius who comes over and changes history. For a while Naples becomes the capital of the world" states a fourth fan. The final trope is related to the player as a cultural and media phenomenon, which gave rise to a (black) market of Maradonian merchandise: magazines, books, shirts, balls, flags, keyrings, posters, action figures, and even food, among many other elements, were produced and commercialised in the streets of the city.

The scene that registers such merchandise is particularly interesting because it shows the materiality of memory, and how specific personal objects can acquire symbolical significance as markers of the past. Here, the editing picks up pace: shots are very short as the enumeration of objects by different people are cut together in what seems like a continuous sentence. The camera moves slightly away from its subjects to reveal more of their surroundings and the Maradonian possessions they treasure: a broken plastic figure of the player owned by a woman; a restaurant dessert, prepared by two chefs, that contains ten ingredients and is inscribed with the number 10; and the kiosk of a street vendor of memorabilia that shows his stock of scarves, flags, and cushions (among many other products) that evoke Maradona.

But there is an additional point to be made: this flow of objects, produced, and consumed within the streets of Naples, was, as mentioned, informal. No rights were ever paid to the player or the club for exploiting the image of Maradona, who was well aware of what was happening, but opted to look the other way and refused to take any actions to prevent these activities. The short TV interview with Maradona that the film includes is precisely about this issue, with the player stating that as long as the business is led by working-class people, who have simply found a way to make a living by producing and selling such merchandise, then he is happy with it. In fact, being able to help the people means more to him than being an object of their admiration. If one is to look for signs of Maradona as a progressive person who places the benefit of the people above profit, then such a stance on image rights could be a much better illustration of his ideology than his tattoos or his political statements.

*Maradonapoli* is, thus, a reflection on the affective dimension generated by the player, and of cinema itself as an instrument to record and reproduce the passions that Maradona instilled in the citizens of Naples. Invariably, their accounts show an admiration that reaches, or even surpasses, idolatry. It is also an original work which deliberately eschews the voice of the film director, of the player, of football experts, and of Maradona's family and friends. In this film, the medium is the message: Maradona was a popular idol, and *Maradonapoli* is most faithful to this premise by letting the people of Naples tell their own Maradonian stories.

The third main cinematic documentary is *Diego Maradona* which is markedly different to those discussed above. Its director, Asif Kapadia, is a British filmmaker responsible for two other renowned non-fiction films based on global stars. The first one is *Senna* (2010), about the Brazilian racing driver Ayrton Senna, and the second one is the Oscar-winning *Amy* (2015), about British singer Amy Winehouse. It could be argued that all three characters have several common traits: they were beloved and highly charismatic celebrities, as well as haunted figures (both Senna and Winehouse met untimely deaths, and the latter was plagued, like Maradona, by substance abuse). There are, moreover, several connections between all three documentaries. As Hannah Andrews (2017) notes, *Senna* and *Amy* avoid featuring talking heads giving opinions and stories about the characters, and the narrative is constructed through images and voice-over commentaries from friends and family. Both are also organised chronologically as a "rise and fall" story (Andrews 2017: 351). The same applies to *Diego Maradona*, with the main difference being that the player was alive when Kapadia produced his film, so one of the voices heard in the film is that of Maradona himself, who agreed to be interviewed by Kapadia.

As in *Maradonapoli*, we never see the director, or indeed Maradona himself outside of previously recorded images. But here Maradona is present in almost every shot, and the voiceover commentaries belong not to the fans but to a range of people who were close to the player in several capacities. While the interviews were specially conducted by Kapadia for the film, all the shots come entirely from pre-recorded footage. They are often home videos made by the Maradona family, or recovered from TV broadcasts and interviews, though the main source is a treasure trove of previously unseen footage that Kapadia was given access to – more than 500 hours of film that had been captured by a cameraman who was following Maradona around during his years at SSC Napoli (NPR 2019). Thus, the film is mostly focused on Maradona's career while in Naples, with only a few obvious additions (including Maradona's performances in the 1986 and 1990 World Cup tournaments). As with Kapadia's other two documentaries, the result is a meticulously edited work that very carefully weaves the Maradonian narrative through often unmatching visual and audio tracks.

The most important voices that narrate the story are those of Maradona, his Argentinian biographer Daniel Arcucci, football journalist Gonzalo Bonadeo, and Fernando Signorini, a fitness expert and the player's personal trainer. The film endorses a dualistic idea that Signorini had already expressed before a few times: there are two sides to the footballer, Diego and Maradona. Diego is the charismatic, good-natured family man who grew up in poverty, is loyal to his friends, and eager to help those in need. Maradona is the persona that Diego built around himself to be conveyed to the rest of the world through the media and contains all his negative traits. Famously, Signorini presented this view to Maradona, telling him that whereas he would follow Diego wherever he went, he would never go anywhere with Maradona. The footballer's reply was customarily sharp: "Sure, but without Maradona, Diego would still be living in Villa Fiorito [the slum where Maradona grew up]".

Thus, the film endorses a binary vision of the character of Maradona: a sort of Dr Jekyll and Mr Hyde, good and evil person contained in the same man. Such vision is conveyed almost exclusively through an extensive archaeology of archival material and precise editing. On the side of good (or Diego), we see Maradona laughing with teammates while his father cooks an asado (barbecue) during the Mexico 1986 World Cup; playing with, and hugging, his young daughters; spending time with his parents and wife, visibly fond of them. On the side of darkness (or Maradona), we see the player under the effects of drugs; attending parties of notable mafia bosses in Naples; and we are presented with Maradona's former lover Cristiana Sinagra and their newborn child (who Maradona refused to recognise and support until he was in his late 20s).

Discussing the film, Oscar Ariel Cabezas argues that this binary perspective obeys to a "Hollywood paradigm" which reduces the life of Maradona to a simple contradiction, leading to a "bourgeois moralising" that condemns the player without fully understanding him (2021: 178). While recognising that the film conveys a dichotomic view of Maradona, my reading here differs from Cabezas', whose division into plebeian and bourgeois spheres is no less dichotomic. We should not forget that the player himself seems to have embraced this dual existence. For example, he would usually talk about himself in the third person, invariably using his last name and not his first name in these occasions. And he interviewed himself in an episode of a TV programme he hosted in Argentina, with two Maradonas (thanks to a visual trick) sitting face to face at a table (this is analysed further in Chapter 1).

In my opinion, *Diego Maradona* could be considered an example of what Catherine Russell calls archiveology, a trend in contemporary film practice based on the recycling of archival footage to create new audiovisual texts, using "the image archive as a language" (2018: 12). The practice involves appropriation and translation, "from one medium to another, whether from film to video, analog to digital, narrative to nonnarrative, fiction to documentary" (219). At its best, Kapadia's film offers a collage of images from the unearthed archives of Maradonian footage that speaks for itself. In fact, the film often defends Maradona: for example, by showing the brutal treatment he received from the England team in the famous 1986 game: while moralists always remember the illegal "Hand of God" goal, they tend to ignore the violent fouls Maradona received, such as an elbowing on his face by English defender Terry Fenwick. On the other hand, showing some of the negative aspects of Maradona's life is also a way of refusing to mythologise the player and to acknowledge this was a man of contradictions.

## Maradona as fictional character: From biopic to art film

This section moves from documentary to fiction films made in the 21st century. The first major fictional film to represent the footballer is the biopic *Maradona: The Hand of God* an Italy-Argentina co-production released in 2007 directed by Marco Risi, an Italian filmmaker who does not enjoy a major reputation but is the son of celebrated director Dino Risi. It is the only feature-length biopic about the player – the Amazon Prime Video series *Maradona, sueño bendito* (*Maradona: Blessed Dream*) was released in 2021, and it follows many of the narrative strategies introduced in *Maradona: The Hand of God*. The film was shot for the most part in Buenos Aires and features Argentinian actors, with the major exception of the leading role: Maradona is played by the Italian Marco Leonardi (two other actors play the footballer as a child and a teenager).

Short for "biographical picture", the biopic is an enduring cinematic genre that, as Belén Vidal argues, "commands as much critical derision as industrial visibility" (2014: 2). Although biopics may be, as Cartmell and Polasek state, "routinely dismissed as bad art, shallow, formulaic, inauthentic, and disrespectful of history" (2020: 1), they are still a highly popular genre that continues to be widely produced and exhibited. Given Maradona's global celebrity on the one hand, and the level of spectacle and drama that his career and personal life entailed on the other, it is hardly surprising that a biopic was based on him.

*Maradona: The Hand of God* is a well-directed and technically competent work, supported by solid performances from the cast, while also following the conventions of the genre, but it fails to add novel perspectives on the player. The film is mostly chronological, although told as a flashback from the point of view of a convalescing Maradona in January 2000 (after suffering a severe health crisis following drug abuse), and it shows three versions of the player: as a boy, a teenager, and an adult.[2] It is focused on the melodramatic aspects of his life, in particular, his relationship with his girlfriend and later wife Claudia, and like in Kapadia's film, the narrative is framed by the rise-and-fall arch that marked Maradona's career (emphasising his years in Naples and concluding with his second ban from the sport during the United States 1994 World Cup). An elegiac, over-the-top score contributes much to this aesthetic approach.

It is impossible, as Paolo Sorrentino has argued (Sollazzo 2021: 106–107), to capture the entire life of Maradona in a single film. But *Maradona: The Hand of God* deliberately avoids showing the most conflictive aspects of the football player. For example, although he is portrayed as a womaniser, his affair with Cristiana Sinagra, and the child they had, is ignored. The overall account is not necessarily a fully whitewashed one, since his addictions and his extramarital relations are shown clearly, but the film takes care to add mitigating circumstances as well. This would seem to exculpate Maradona from his actions and denies him agency over his life. At the same time, the charismatic performance of Leonardi manages to be faithful to the original character, who rarely appears unlikeable throughout the story.

In what is, in my opinion, the most interesting scene of the film, the player gives his fiancée Claudia a luxurious diamond necklace and then, immediately, gives an identical one to his mother. Maradona then leaves the room; the two women face each other as they try on their necklaces, in silence, not sure of what to say. The scene adequately hints at many elements that characterised Maradona's life: the rivalry between his mother and Claudia, and the Oedipal parallel between mother and lover for Maradona. However, this level of subtlety is mostly absent from the film.

The next film to be analysed is completely different in style and approach. Carlos Sorín's *El camino de San Diego* (*The Road to San Diego*) (2006), an Argentinian film, is not technically about Maradona, although the story revolves entirely around the player. Sorín is a foremost auteur in contemporary Argentinian cinema, renowned for his minimalist and gentle works of realism and social realism, which sometimes include elements of genre, particularly the road movie (Tompkins 2013; Garibotto and Pérez 2016). *The Road to San Diego* is, ultimately, a road movie about the affective significance of Maradona in Argentinian society. The main character is Ignacio "Tati" Benítez, one of those millions of citizens for whom the player represents more than a sporting idol: Maradona justifies Tati's existence and gives sense to his life. He is, almost, a god to him.

Tati, a logger, lives in a small town in the north-eastern province of Misiones, one of the poorest regions of Argentina, in very humble conditions with his wife and young children. The plot is based on a comedic premise. Tati, walking through the local rainforest, stumbles upon the root of a tree that, for him, resembles Maradona. It is a big piece of wood, made up of part of the tree trunk with two branches going out at each end: the piece is supposed to look like the torso of Maradona, arms spread out upwards as if celebrating a goal, and a long-haired head at the top. The similitude is obvious only for Tati, who has the number 10 tattooed on his back, has taught his two parrots to shout "Maradona", and attempted to name his daughter Diega (a female form that does not exist in Spanish, and, therefore, was rejected by the registrar). But Tati carves the number 10 onto the piece of wood, and his faith that it represents Maradona seems to convince everybody else.

One day, a neighbour tells Tati (who does not own a radio or TV set) that Maradona has been admitted to hospital following health crisis (a real event that took place in April 2004). As the logger watches images of the crowds gathering outside the clinic where Maradona is fighting for his life, praying and chanting, he decides to go to Buenos Aires to bring him the statue as a gift. This is not a small feat for Tati: the distance to Buenos Aires is over 1,200 km, but he does not have any money or own a car. However, he still decides to make the trip, supported by his understanding wife. At this point, the film shifts into road movie territory, as it tells the story of Tati's long journey into the city, mostly hitchhiking.

Sorín draws on the techniques of realist aesthetics, such as the use of non-professional actors, location shooting, and natural lighting, to convey a sense of authenticity. But the film avoids the pessimism and grittiness often found in realism. A strong sense of social solidarity persists despite extreme poverty, with characters always willing to help Tati. The film shows the effects of years of economic crisis in the deprived interior of Argentina but does not dwell on any signs of violence and disintegration (social conflict is portrayed through a group of protesters, or picketers, that have blocked a motorway). Furthermore, as Free has argued, the film is laden with religious symbolism (2014: 207). The title itself is a reference to "El camino de Santiago" (the pilgrimage set of routes leading to the Spanish city of Santiago de Compostela) and, for Free, the tree root also connotes the crucifixion, thus suggesting a view of Maradona as a martyr. To this line of argument, we should add, as Tompkins notes (2013: 117), that the Maradona statue can perform miracles: when Tati encounters the road blocked by the picketers, showing the root is enough for the protesters to move aside and allow the vehicles to drive on.

Following another trope of social realism, the ending of the film is an open one. Tati finds out along the trip that Maradona is no longer in hospital: as soon as his condition stabilised, he characteristically escaped the clinic and retired to a country club to play golf. Tati makes his way to the country club, where hundreds of fans remain gathered outside the gates to show their support of the player. He manages to hand over the statue to a security guard, who assures him it will be delivered to Maradona. Sometime later, the player leaves the club in his SUV, escorted by the police, perhaps headed to the airport en route to a rehabilitation centre in Cuba. He may or may not have taken the gift with him. As the crowd and the press disperse, a lottery vendor gives Tati a ticket and tells him to make sure to check the result the following day. The final shot of the film shows a flock of birds flying in the sky, and then the screen fades to black.

Are those birds, which optimistically connote freedom, a sign that Tati will win the lottery? This would add a teleological subtext to the story, meaning that it was Tati's destiny to find his luck in Buenos Aires and would represent another indirect miracle performed by Maradona. On the other hand, such an ending would be at odds with the conventions of social realism by raising the possibility of individual salvation and would undermine the few instances of social criticism presented. Tompkins suggests that the presence of wild animals at the beginning of the film hint at the possibility of reading it, at least in part, as a fable (2013: 112). This may open the door for a more positive, perhaps magical, interpretation. Ultimately, Tati can be read as a symbol of the millions of destitute citizens of Argentina: people who lack even the most basic possessions, for whom Maradona may be the only source of happiness and of hope.

Whereas Sorín is a filmmaker who developed a solid career in independent Argentinian cinema, Paolo Sorrentino is the leading example of the film director as superstar in 21st century Italy. While Sorín's works tend to be understated, quiet films, Sorrentino's are lavish and exaggerated. In the words of Russel Kilbourn (2020), Sorrentino is a throwback to the golden age of Italian auteurs such as De Sica, Fellini, and Antonioni. Besides being a highly accomplished creator, whose works have obtained multiple awards, including an Academy Award for Best International Feature Film and the Jury Prize at Cannes, Sorrentino was born and raised in Naples and is an SSC Napoli supporter. He was a teenager when Maradona joined the club and was able to watch him play from the stands as he took the team to win its first ever Serie A title. Sorrentino's feelings for the player are no secret: when receiving the Oscar for *La grande bellezza* (*The Great Beauty*) (2013), the director thanked, as sources of inspiration, Federico Fellini, Martin Scorsese, and Maradona.[3] But the implications of fandom for Sorrentino go well beyond the affective level and, as it will be seen below, had major consequences in a tragic event that marked the director's life. Most of his works are Italian productions, but he has also made two English-language films and both rely heavily on the presence of Maradona and its symbolisms: *Youth* (2015) and *È stata la mano di Dio* (*The Hand of God*) (2021).

Sorrentino's second English-language film, *Youth*, stars Michael Caine, Harvey Keitel, and Rachel Weisz. The story is set for the most part in a luxurious resort located in the Swiss Alps. Two lifetime friends, Fred (Caine) and Mick (Keitel), are spending the summer holidays at the place, relaxing in a healthy way that includes exercise, diet, and regular check-ups – a yearly routine they have been doing for a long time. Fred is a renowned British composer and conductor, now retired, and Mick is an American film director writing what is going to be his final work and, according to him, a testament to his career. The film deals with a series of themes: the relentless passage of time and its consequences, nostalgia over things done or not done in the past, and love and friendship. All of this is told through Sorrentino's usual toolbox of sophisticated camera movements, careful shot composition, flamboyant mise-en-scène, and reliance on symbolism. According to Kilbourn, the film is a kind of oblique homage to Fellini's *8½* (2020).

The important point for the purposes of the present discussion is that this sumptuous spa is frequented, in addition to the main characters, by a host of other wealthy and famous guests. They include the current Miss Universe, a major Hollywood actor, and Diego Maradona (convincingly played by Roly Serrano, who had the role of Maradona's father in *Maradona: The Hand of God*). The Maradona we see here is an obese, severely out-of-form individual, who can barely walk on his own without help, and often needs to use an oxygen mask. Although towards the end of his life Maradona's health had deteriorated significantly, the fictional Maradona in *Youth* is in worse shape than the footballer would have been in 2015. He is never referred to by name, and instead of the tattoos of Fidel Castro and "Che" Guevara that the player had on his arm and calf, this cinematic version has a giant tattoo of the face of Karl Marx on his back. This is an obvious pun; the film leaves no doubt this is Maradona. Serrano, the actor, looks quite similar to the footballer, even when wearing sunglasses and a sports cap. At one moment, some of the hotel guests are at a swimming pool. Fred is talking to a young child who wants to play the violin and is left-handed. Maradona overhears the conversation from a distance and approaches the child to show his support. "I am also left-handed", he tells him. The American film star replies: "Christ! The whole world knows you are left-handed" – not only confirming that this man is Maradona but also associating him with God.

Maradona is not a central character in the film – he appears in seven short scenes in total – but he is nonetheless an important presence at the hotel. Whenever he is out in the gardens or swimming pools, the other guests (all of them famous people in their own right) seem drawn to his figure in awe and admiration. As Bauer argues, the film emulates Maradona's "virtually unaltered power to fascinate others" (2021: 67). Arguably the most moving scene involving the player takes place over two different moments. In the first one, we see Maradona, accompanied by a young, blond girlfriend, walking slowly and laboriously past a tennis court. The player looks towards the empty court and sees a tennis ball lying still on the red clay. A medium close-up of the actor's face manages to convey a sense of longing, reinforced by the non-diegetic soundtrack. As Maradona goes by, the song "Just (After Song of Songs)", by David Lang, is played back, with the lyrics repeating the chorus "And my beloved" over a point-of-view shot of the tennis ball. Maradona's true love has always been the ball.

This love affair is emphasised further in the following scene involving the player. Somehow, Maradona has made his way to the tennis court on his own. We see him wearing only a bathing suit, standing in the middle of the court, doing keepie-uppies with the tennis ball. This is not gentle ball play; however, he is kicking the ball strongly with his bare left foot, making it rise high above the air, and hitting it again before it touches the ground. Given the speed and height the ball is reaching, and the precision of the movement, the shot was completed by adding a digital ball (Hennessey 2017: 454). Only the real Maradona would have been capable of replicating this ball-juggling.

This scene is directly connected to the themes explored in the film, involving acceptance of the passage of time as much as redemption and perseverance. Here, Maradona presumably risks his life (he could suffer complications from such strong physical activity) for what is his ultimate passion: kicking a ball, even if it has to be a tennis one. It also shows that, despite his age and condition, his talent is not lost. A similar trajectory will be mirrored by the protagonist, who eventually accepts to come out of retirement to direct a performance of his own musical piece before the Queen of England. The lesson is clear: is it possible to overcome physical or psychological difficulties and find renewed meaning to one's own life.

Sorrentino's second film with a strong Maradonian presence was released at the end of 2021: *È stata la mano di Dio*. Literally, this should be translated as "It was the hand of God", although the film, produced by Netflix, has been released in English as *The Hand of God* (the same formula was used for the Spanish version – it is important not to mistake this film with the Risi biopic discussed previously). Though fictional, *The Hand of God* has a strong autobiographical core. It revolves around the life of Fabietto Schisa, a teenager who lives with his parents and two siblings in a middle-class home in Naples. The story begins in 1984, just before Maradona joined Napoli. Fabietto's main concern, like everybody else at the time, is whether Maradona would be indeed signed by Napoli. The negotiations for this transfer were complex and only resolved at the last moment (see Chapter 3 of this volume); during this time, the city was rife with suspense, expectations, and rumours about the player's potential arrival. At one point, Fabietto's elderly uncle Alfredo tells him: "If Maradona doesn't come to Naples, I'll kill myself".

The film is much more than a saga of Maradona in Naples, but the footballer acts as a grounding force for the more realistic elements of the plot, in a story that owes much to the work of Fellini and is laden with dreamlike sequences and allegory. The playful and often funny first half of the film, exploring Fabietto's life as a lonely teenager who is also very close to his parents and brother, takes a tragic turn halfway through the story. One weekend Fabietto's parents go on a trip to their recently acquired holiday home in the mountains in central Italy. Fabietto declines to join them because he prefers to go to see Napoli play. At the cottage, a carbon monoxide leak from a malfunctioning heating system intoxicates and kills Fabietto's parents, who lose consciousness and die without ever realising what is happening.

This plot point is completely autobiographical: this is what happened to Sorrentino's parents on April 5, 1987. Sorrentino had opted to go to see the Empoli-Naples match that weekend (Bilmes 2021). The film captures the infinite tragedy this represents for Fabietto, with the second part becoming much darker in tone, figuratively but also literally, through a more subdued colour palette, the use of low-contrast lighting, and an increase in night scenes. The narrative becomes also a coming-of-age tale at this point, for Fabietto is forced to grow up suddenly, and confront a future of uncertainty.

In happier times, the family had watched the 1986 World Cup, sitting together in the small balcony of the Schisa family home. Fabietto's uncle Alfredo, a communist, celebrated Maradona's hand-of-God goal against England as a political statement, as revenge against English imperialism a few years after the Malvinas/Falklands War. Now, when Alfredo finds out, at the funeral, that Fabietto was not with his parents because he wanted to see Maradona play, he is shocked, and declares immediately: "It was him! It was him! It was the hand of God" (this is the line that makes up the film's original title in Italian). Within the tragedy, Alfredo is grateful that Fabietto has been spared, and, in his eyes, it was a miracle performed by Maradona.

In some ways, *The Hand of God* is an indirect ode to Maradona, a personal homage from Sorrentino his idol. At the very beginning, the film opens with a white on black intertitle containing a phrase from the footballer: "I did what I could. I don't think I did so badly". For Fabietto, given the circumstances, plenty of things could have gone wrong. For example, he could have tried to follow in the footsteps of a (petty) criminal friend, later getting dragged into more serious crime networks. Or he could have suffered mental health issues, like her aunt Patrizia. Eventually, Fabietto decides he will not study philosophy at university, as he may have intended in the past, but will move instead to Rome and try to become a filmmaker. At the very end, on his way to the capital, Fabietto is sitting on a train and watches out of the window. As the train is leaving a station, the figure of a little monk appears on a platform. He takes off his hood, revealing he is a boy of about ten with fluffy, curvy hair, smiles, and waves goodbye at Fabietto. This is the "munaciello" or "little monk", a fantastic creature or spirit popular in the Neapolitan folkloric tradition.

The *munaciello* had already appeared, early in the film, before Aunt Patricia. When she later claimed to have encountered him, only Fabietto seemed to believe her. Now, by saying goodbye to the *munaciello*, who remains standing at the station, the film connotes that Fabietto has finally come of age, and will no longer believe such wild stories. But the *munaciello* also looks a bit like the boyhood Maradona, the one captured by a famous TV clip in black and white in which he mentioned that his dream was to play in the World Cup. Could this be a supernatural, Maradonian being, who in a way confirms he has helped Fabietto (Sorrentino's alter ego) and is wishing him well in his future? Like Maradona, Sorrentino has not done so badly either.

## Towards the Maradonian film

There are as many films about Maradona as there are Maradonas. For some, he is a political activist and a revolutionary — or a figure who, through the artifices of cinema, can be staged to appear as a fighter against real and perceived enemies of the people. For others, Maradona is a puzzle that can be reconstructed by putting together the millions of pieces that make up his story and his identity. Maradona is also a symbol and a myth, which allows for multiple readings and interpretations. In cinema (like in reality), Maradona can be a saviour, a redeemer, a misunderstood genius, a bedrock of collective memory, and a victim of obscure political and corporate powers.

It is evident that Maradona's legendary status did not need to be supported by the apparatus of cinema (although, on the other hand, audiovisual media such as television first, and social media later, did play an essential role in the construction of Maradona as a cultural icon). At the same time, it is also revealing that the player has been the subject of more films than any other footballer – or any other sports stars for that matter. These are not, for the most part, commercial works attempting to exploit the appeal of the player, but rather complex and elaborate works made by sophisticated filmmakers. Maradona appeals to directors around the world, becoming the object of independent domestic films and expensive international productions, of fiction and non-fiction films, as well as a literal cinematic subject and an allegorical, or even metaphysical, signifier.

At the same time, more audiovisual texts continue to engage with the Maradona, as football is now being increasingly revisited in series and documentaries produced by streaming services such as Netflix, Amazon, and Apple TV. For example, in 2019, Netflix released the series *Maradona in Mexico*, a documentary of seven episodes about the star's experience as manager of the Mexican second division team Dorados de Sinaloa. In 2021, Amazon Prime Video released the ambitious biopic *Maradona: Blessed Dream* (Amazon Prime Video): told over ten episodes, the series covers the life of the player until his World Cup success in 1986 (a second season is not officially confirmed but will apparently be produced).

If the "football film" can be considered a distinct subgenre, it is only by understanding it in combination with other genres such as comedy, drama, melodrama, and the biopic. However, many of the films discussed, such as *The Road to San Diego* and *Youth*, have very little, if anything, to do with football. Would it be possible, then, to speak of the Maradonian film (and TV series) as distinct subgenre or category within audio-visual production? Perhaps it is too early to tell. But if the growing engagement with Maradona in the field of cultural production that followed his death indicates a trend, then it is likely we will see many more audiovisual works dedicated to him in the future.

## Notes

1 My translation. In the original: "Como Gardel fue el canto, Maradona fue el fútbol".
2 Almost the same pattern is followed by the Amazon Prime Video biopic *Maradona: Blessed Dream*, which begins at exactly the same stage in the life of Maradona (his January 2000 health episode) and has four actors playing four different stages in the life of the footballer.
3 Sorrentino's Oscar speech can be seen here: https://www.youtube.com/watch?v=Zdu-Tqa2udk

## References

Alabarces, Pablo. 2014. *Héroes, machos y patriotas. El fútbol entre la violencia y los medios*. Buenos Aires: Aguilar.

Andrews, Hannah. 2017. "From Unwilling Celebrity to Authored Icon: Reading *Amy* (Kapadia, 2015)". *Celebrity Studies*, 8:2, 351–354.

Aufderheide, Patricia. 2007. *Documentary Film: A Very Short Introduction*. Oxford: Oxford University Press.

Bauer, Thomas. 2021. "From Maradona to Jude Law: Sport in Paolo Sorrentino's Movies". *Studies in European Cinema*, 18:1, 60–75.

Bertellini, Giorgio. 2014. *Emir Kusturica*. Urbana: University of Illinois Press.

Bilmes, Alex. 2021. "Paolo Sorrentino: How Diego Maradona Saved My Life". *Esquire*, November 19. Web: https://www.esquire.com/uk/culture/film/a38250611/paolo-sorrentino-interview-the-hand-of-god-diego-maradona/

Cabezas, Oscar Ariel. 2021. "'Maradoo', la imagen de un niño plebeyo". In Antonio Gómez Villar, ed. *Maradona, un mito plebeyo*. Madrid: Ned Ediciones, 175–184.

Cartmell, Deborah and Ashley D. Polasek, eds. 2020. *A Companion to The Biopic*. Hoboken: Wiley Blackwell.

Chanan, Michael. 2007. *The Politics of Documentary*. London: BFI and Palgrave Macmillan.

Federici, Alessio Maria. 2021. "Prefazione: Tanti film, tante storie, un solo Diego". In Boris Sollazzo, ed. *Non avremo un altro D10S: Diego Armando Maradona. Una vita da cinema*. Milan: Edizioni Bietti, 11–16.

Finchelstein, Federico. 2014. *The Ideological Origins of the Dirty War: Fascism, Populism, and Dictatorship in Twentieth Century Argentina*. Oxford: Oxford University Press.

Free, Marcus. 2014. "Diego Maradona and the Psychodynamics of Football Fandom in International Cinema". *Celebrity Studies*, 5:1–2, 197–212.

Garibotto, Verónica and Jorge Pérez, eds. 2016. *The Latin American Road Movie*. New York: Palgrave Macmillan.

Glynn, Stephen. 2018. *The British Football Film*. New York: Palgrave Macmillan.

González, Horacio. 2021. "Orfandad y gloria". In Antonio Gómez Villar, ed. *Maradona, un mito plebeyo*. Madrid: Ned Ediciones, 101–106.

*Guardian, The*. 2005. "10,000 Protest against Bush". November 4. Web: https://www.theguardian.com/world/2005/nov/04/usa.argentina

Hennessey, Brendan. 2017. "Reel Simulations: CGI and Special Effects in Two Films by Paolo Sorrentino". *The Italianist*, 37:3, 449–463.

Iordanova, Dina. 2002. *Emir Kusturica*. London: BFI Publishing.

Kilbourn, Russell J. A. 2020. *The Cinema of Paolo Sorrentino: Commitment to Style*. New York: Columbia University Press.

Marridoriaga, Jorge. 2005. "La Cumbre de las Américas se cierra sin poner en marcha un área de libre comercio". *El País*. November 5. Web: https://elpais.com/diario/2005/11/06/internacional/1131231607_850215.html

*New York Times, The*. 2005. "Negotiators Fail to Agree on Free Trade Proposal at Americas Summit". November 6. Web: https://www.nytimes.com/2005/11/06/world/americas/negotiators-fail-to-agree-on-free-trade-proposal-at-americas.html

Nichols, Bill. 2001. *Introduction to Documentary*. Bloomington: Indiana University Press.

NPR. 2019. "Kapadia's Latest Film 'Diego Maradona' Examines Soccer Legend". September 26. Web: https://www.npr.org/2019/09/26/764548422/kapadias-latest-film-examines-soccer-superstar-diego-maradona

Rowe, David. 2008. "Time and Timelessness in Sport Film". *Sport in Society*, 11:2–3, 146–158.

Russell, Catherine. 2018. *Archiveology: Walter Benjamin and Archival Film Practices.* Durham: Duke University Press.

Russo, Sandra. 2005. "El Tren del Alba". *Página 12.* November 5. Web: https://www.pagina12.com.ar/diario/elpais/subnotas/58860-19451-2005-11-05.html

Sollazzo, Boris, ed. 2021. *Non avremo un altro D10S: Diego Armando Maradona, Una vita da cinema.* Milan: Edizioni Bietti.

Tompkins, Cynthia. 2013. *Experimental Latin American Cinema: History and Aesthetics.* Austin: University of Texas Press.

Vidal, Belén and Todd Brown, eds. 2014. *The Biopic in Contemporary Film Culture.* New York and London: Routledge.

Waldron, Dara. 2018. *New Nonfiction Film: Art, Poetics, and Documentary Theory.* New York: Bloomsbury Academic.

Zucchi, Marina. 2016. "Un encuentro imposible: El día que Maradona conoció a Gardel". *Clarín.* October 26. Web: https://www.clarin.com/espectaculos/cine/dia-maradona-conocio-gardel_0_r19jkPAkl.html

# Filmography

*Diego Maradona.* Directed by Asif Kapadia. Film 4, Lorton Entertainment, On the Corner Films, 2019.

*È stata la mano di Dio.* Directed by Paolo Sorrentino. The Apartment Pictures, Netflix, 2021.

*El camino de San Diego.* Directed by Carlos Sorín. Guacamole Films, Kramer & Sigman, Wanda Vision, INCAA, TVE, 2006.

*El día que Maradona conoció a Gardel.* Directed by Rodolfo Pagliere. Multimedios América, Radiodifusora El Carmen, 1995.

*Maradona by Kusturica.* Directed by Emir Kusturica. Pentagrama Films, Telecinco Cinema, Wild Bunch, Fidélité Productions, Rasta Films, 2008.

*Maradona, la mano de Dios.* Directed by Mario Risi. Cosmo Production, Institut del Cinema Català (ICC), Pol-Ka Producciones, 2007.

*Maradonapoli.* Directed by Alessio Maria Federici. Cinemaundici, Rancilio Cube, 2017.

*¡Qué linda es mi familia!* Directed by Ramón "Palito" Ortega. Chango s.c.a., 1980.

*Taste of Cherry.* Directed by Abbas Kiarostami. Abbas Kiarostami Productions, CiBy 2000, Kanoon, 1997.

*Te rompo el rating.* Directed by Hugo Sofovich. Aries Cinematográfica Argentina, 1981.

*Youth.* Directed by Paolo Sorrentino. Medusa, Indigo Film, Barbary Films, Number 9 Films, C-Films, 2015.

# 8

# MARADONA AND MUSIC

## Soundscapes and Echoes of the Maradonian Song[1]

*Martín Virgili*

*Translated by Dolores Gadler*

### If I were Maradona

This chapter approaches the figure of Maradona from the perspective of sound studies, considering the footballer as a body that produces sounds and relationships between sounds. For this, we must accept the *inscriptions of sound in his body* and ask ourselves "what would things be like if one were (namely, felt, sensed, imagined, acted like, or became) a certain type of person?" (Feld, 2013: 218). How would things be if we were Maradona? In the same way, we should pay attention to the sound marks that he left in Argentinian society and think of the materiality in which those marks reverberate in culture and in the landscape. The echo seems to be the matter. Murray Schafer (1993) was the first to state that the sounds that people emit both in music and in language are always echoes of the surrounding landscape, establishing a deep and invisible connection. In addition, the songs dedicated to Maradona portray a landscape nourished by the booming daily life of a city: they are the echo of those times, like a background noise that is woven beyond stadiums.

The aim of this chapter is to reflect on the meanings behind the sounds we associate with Maradona. Are the roars celebrating Maradona's goals at the Azteca Stadium not analogous to the cries of protest in a popular mobilisation? Or to the lyrics "The fight, the fight/We're going to win!" by the Vj Awax?[2] I am picturing a sound image: Maradona as a *soundboard*, proved by the Neapolitan mantra "O mamma, mamma, mamma/sai perché mi batte il cuore?/Ho visto Maradona" (Oh mum, mum, mum/do you know why my heart beats?/I've seen Maradona). The following sections explore acoustemology, understood as the epistemological study of acoustics (Feld, 2013: 222), soundscape, and musical analysis to understand the connection between Maradona and sound.

DOI: 10.4324/9781003196587-11

## The sound and the fury: Screaming the name Maradona

I was born in Argentina, in the city of Buenos Aires. I did not grow up in a "football-loving" family; football, like tango and *lunfardo*, was a lurking force that I recognised by its sound. When I spent time with my maternal grandfather, he would tune in to tango stations. On Sundays, the sound dynamics got feverish as the radio broadcasts transmitted the local football championship and the airwaves were filled with movement and excitement. The football commentary was an in-between event; it was and it was not song. I knew by heart the cadences and stops, the pauses and vocal juxtapositions preceding the announcements, which required the same amount of energy as the lead voice. The sound action moved through the cadences of the Spanish word *gol* (goal) that was shouted and sung at the same time, stretching the "o" (*goooooool*) and in *crescendo* with the intention of embracing the listeners with the voice.

In the 1980s, Argentina returned to democracy after a violent period of dictatorship. That return brought with it a new disposition of sound relationships. A sound-cry resurfaced after years of silence, whispers, and murmurs. Once again, the street was occupied by bodies that made noise and that got together to produce sound with greater intensity. When I was ten years old, a new presence was born, which, even without a face, was also a sound, a story, an emotion: the 1986 World Cup in Mexico. It was not until the game between Argentina and Italy that I realised that the country was immersed in something emotionally unique. I was on a school bus with my classmates when the driver started yelling "gooool" frenziedly together with the teachers accompanying us. And they all started to sing: "Olé olé olé olé, Diegooo, Diegooo" repeatedly, like a mantra that we also joined. "Diego" became a cry associated with joy and amazement. I could hear that simple name at school, at the cinema, at the supermarket, everywhere.

Maradona was pierced, adored, and besieged by sounds throughout his life. It was an excess and a symptom. Fifty years elapsed from that "Que se quede, que se quede" (Let him stay, let him stay!) shouted in July 1970, when Maradona, barely nine years old, was doing his tricks with the ball in the centre of the pitch, to entertain the audience during half-time in an Argentinos Juniors-Boca Juniors match, to the "Maradooó, Maradoooó" cried during the tribute paid to him in 2020 in the Gimnasia y Esgrima La Plata Stadium. During this time, many, especially in Argentina and Italy, established an asymmetric relationship, from an acoustic point of view, with Maradona's body. His name has been cried out endlessly and sung by great monophonic choirs in many stadiums around the world. Maradona himself remembers when he debuted with the Argentinian national team at the beginning of 1977: "I started warming up and I heard the stands chanting my name: Maradooó, Maradooó! I don't know what came over me. My legs and hands were shaking. The crowd's roar was so loud … I'm not kidding, I was shitting myself" (Maradona, 2021: 20). During a football match playing for Barcelona against Seville in January of 1984, something similar happened to him:

> We beat them 3-1. I scored two goals, the second and the third. When we were 2-0 up, the people began to ask El Flaco [César Luis Menotti] to take me off so they could applaud me. It was then that Sevilla pulled one back and everyone shut up. I scored the third and they started again until Menotti took me off. The stadium went wild, they were all shouting and clapping, it was more than the classic "Maradoó, Maradooó!" I don't know … it was like a shriek: it's one of the ovations that I remember most clearly of my whole career. No one could believe it.
>
> *Maradona 2021: 72*

He was 24 years old at the time. He would still have to hear the "roar" during in Mexico 1986 and in Italy, over the 1987 and 1989 championships, the yells and whistles at the 1990 World Cup in Italy, and the ovations and cries in his farewell in Boca Juniors in 2001, to mention a few significant moments. The sound accompanied him till the end: on the day of his death, the mere presence of the coffin summoned his name.

Maradona was the constant receiver of a significant, acoustic, and symbolic sound flow, and he had to learn to live with those sounds and to endure them. He had to control the quivering these chants produced in him. He had to stabilise his body. In this sense, Bernhard Waldenfels talks about the capacity of bodily resonance, "which allows the voice of Another *to resonate* in one's own body (and vice versa)", determining a "response register" to dialogue with the world (quoted in Rosa, 2019: 88). So, if "hearing and sound production are embodied competences that place the actors and their acting capacity in specific historical worlds" (Feld, 2013: 222), where do we place Maradona's body? What reactions, what "reflex acts" do these sounds produce? And, also, what perceptions and emotions are felt by the people when they recognise themselves as part of the group that produces those sounds?[3] What happens to music when it discovers these sounds, when it perceives 100,000 people chanting "Maradooó, Maradooó …"? Stretching the "o" at the end, "Maradooó", is a football chant that encompasses a whole structure of sounds and attitudes, such as the *aguante* and different choreographic participatory gestures.[4] It is a compact and energetic sound, a simple chant of tribute and gratitude that over time has acquired other meanings. For example, it could become a protest, shouted by the public when an Argentinian national team was playing poorly, or a compliment, when someone did something outstanding (Soriano, 2020: 89).

Argentinian musicians and singers belonging to various genres (popular music, cumbia, rock) have used this chant: Pocho "La Pantera" (1993), in "Maradona no perdona"; Julio Lacarra, in "Dale 10" (1995); Los Piojos, in "Maradó" (1996); and Rodrigo, in "La mano de Dios" (2000), among many others. On the one hand, these songs amplify a public and mass sound/landscape, the sound of the stadium and the fans, with the intention of making it reverberate in the musical composition. On the other hand, it is Maradona who returns the inscriptions of the sound in his body to the musical community, by resisting that sound and by showing society that there is only one recipient for that sound load: him. And society listens to that resistance. When Maradona himself sings "La mano de Dios", as it can be seen in a scene in the 2008 film *Maradona by Kusturica*, he changes the personal pronouns in the original lyrics from the third person to the first person and never chants the chorus "Maradó, Maradó". He stays silent. He only knows how to receive that sound: his function in society is to be at the receiving end of this symbolic force, to assimilate it and give it back.

Along these lines, the use of the chant by Los Piojos, one of the most popular Argentinian rock bands in the 1990s, appears more like a cry of war and resistance. Pablo Alabarces considers that the band saw in Maradona the "symbol of a lost authenticity that links rock to football" (2002: 147) given the Argentinian social and political context in the 1990s. However, we also hear how Maradona gives back to his community *the control of those sounds*. By then, he had already reached the peak of his career and had also gone through several very critical moments. Those who chanted his name were not a homogeneous group[5]: Maradonians and also his detractors were beginning to emerge. Thus, the "Maradó" sung by Los Piojos is more spasmodic, with a different energy charge. The musical accompaniment is dizzying and anxious: it does not sound like the uproar of a football pitch as in the other songs. It is not a chant that everyone wants to sing, but rather it is a choir that summons those who feel called to the cause. It is an energetic and resistant chant, like the euphoria that precedes a confrontation.

Maradona's body is reactive to mass sound. He knows how to handle, accept, and negotiate that difference. In the 1990 World Cup final at the Olympic Stadium in Rome, Italy, the audience witnessed a moment of tension between the fans and Maradona for the first time. The Italian public began to jeer and boo the Argentinian National Anthem with the players lined up on the pitch before the match. The TV cameras captured each player in close-up, singing along, until it reached Maradona, the only player who reacted, shouting back "sons of bitches, sons of bitches". At this point in his career, the sound no longer intimidated him. It did not exercise its coercive function on him. His body knew and recognised the affective influences and the tremors of sound and could for that very reason engage in a duel with its forces. Los Piojos together with Mano Negra in "Santa Maradona" were the first bands to dedicate songs to Maradona which emphasised his critical position towards power and presented him as a model of resistance. That defiant bond will later reverberate on young trap, rap, and hip-hop artists from different countries, who will incorporate it and recycle it in their own contexts. In different ways, an attitude of rebellion, marginality, courage, position towards power, confrontation, and danger is heard in songs and described in videos such as "Maradona" (2017), by the Nigerian singer Niniola; "Maradona" (2018), by the French rapper Lacrim; "Maradona" (2019), by the Kosovo rapper Xhani; "Maradona" (2019), by the Italian rapper Colza; "O,

Płomień 81, Maradona" (2020), by Polish rappers Onar and Paweł Kapliński; and "Maradona" (2020) by Italians MC Kliton & Kido, to name a few. Here, the word "Maradona" once again invokes the echo of a safe response to a threatening situation, be it due to "street problems", "sexist violence", "the challenge of recovering from a childhood of deprivation and poverty", and "the daily dangers of suburban neighbourhoods". It is as if somehow the musical *underground* had found in Maradona's figure and word a robust sign to renew its content, or as if his presence had acted as a "sound tattoo" embodying many different meanings in a single gesture.

## Maradonian soundscapes: The Maradonian rhythm

As soon as Maradona's death was announced, at noon on November 25, 2020, the Maradonian resonance began to unfold. Radio stations, television, social networks, and news websites started to broadcast songs, footage from his playing career, with an emphasis on his renowned goals and dribbles, excerpts of interviews with his emblematic phrases, the clips in which he sang alone or accompanied by renowned artists, and all kinds of sound expressions added to his voice. People in the street shouted and sang his name; the wind brought and carried away "Diego did not die/Diego did not die/Diego lives in his people/fucking hell", "Olé, olé, olé olé/Diego, Diego". After his death, the sound that had accompanied him since his childhood re-emerged as a spectre that bore his name and his story. In death, he was different too.

When considering Maradona's relationship with sound, rhythm may be the first recognisable parameter. As a child, he stood out for his skills hitting the ball and his keepie uppies. He grew up listening to the rhythm produced by the sound of his foot hitting a ball: *tac, tac, tac, tac*. Modest but effective percussion, his listening regarded that sound of leather (or any of the other materials of his early improvised balls), in counterpoint with his inner heartbeat.[6] Rhythm functioned as his centre of gravity and a positional and levelling reference; above all, it determined the way he moved:

> Everything I did, every step I took, was because of the ball. If la Tota [Maradona's mother] sent me on an errand I would take with me anything that resembled a ball: it could be an orange, or scrumpled-up paper, or cloths. And I would go up the steps on to the bridge that crossed the railway, hopping on one foot, the right one, and taking whatever it was on the left, *tac, tac, tac* .... That's how I walked to school as well.
>
> *Maradona, 2021: 3*

Maradona had rhythm: his foot kept hitting any object he could find, with the regularity of a ticking clock. For this reason, he understood the inertial behaviour of rhythms, their speed, and markings. "A juggler doesn't spend the entire show throwing the balls up", says Michael Cerveris, Tony Award-winning actor and singer. "Half the time, the juggler is waiting for them to fall" (Biguenet, 2015: 75). Similarly, Maradona perceived an active time and a time on pause. His ability to deceive his opponents had to do with controlling the game as a whole and with the changes of pace (knowing how to see and feel the pause). César Luis Menotti, who coached him at the Youth World Cup in 1979 and again at the World Cup in 1982, explained those abilities: "He easily dribbles his way into the opposition's half. The goal is always in his sight. He consistently finds a pass to the best-placed teammate. His short passes and shots are pure wonder, *with a prodigious change of pace*" (Menotti, 2020; my emphasis).

Eduardo Archetti studied the exchange of bodily meanings between football and dance. He observed that the transformation of the tango in Argentina in the 1920s and 1930s coincided with the consolidation of a football playing style. The informants in his research believed that dribbling and dancing were related. In tango, the changes of rhythm in a step are expressed through the figures *cortes y quebradas* (literally cuts and breaks), which also invoke the great dribblers in Argentinian football. According to one of the informants:

> The *corte is* a sudden pause, an unexpected break in the dancing and in the figures; it is not movement. Much dribbling in football is a *corte*, a player stopping and at the same time controlling the ball. A *corte* can eliminate a defender and can help to change direction, as in tango. On the contrary, a *quebrada* is an athletic contortion, a dramatic movement, and a rapid improvisation with the legs and the waist, avoiding physical contact with the opponents. The essence of tango dancing was a combination of *cortes* and *quebradas*.
>
> The best Argentinian players, and Maradona is the most fantastic example, based their way of playing on *cortes* and *quebradas*.
>
> *2003: 225*

Maradona's relationship with the ball from the point of view of sound can be compared to that of a musician who improvises with his instrument. His skills are considered "an art"; according to Alejandro Apo, he was "the most artistic of all players in the world" (2020: 50), a genius of the corporal improvisation whose highest expression in football was dribbling – which, in the "creole style" of Argentinian football, was regarded as the fundamental identity trait of the sport (Archetti, 2003: 219).

The theorist and improviser Derek Bailey describes the link between the musician and the instrument as a generative bodily principle arising from an autonomous intelligence. Bailey recalls Curt Sachs' definition of the term instrumental in *The Wellsprings of Music*: "The original concepts of vocal and instrumental music are utterly different. The instrumental impulse is not melody in a 'melodious' sense, but an agile movement of the hands that seems to be under the control of a brain center totally different from that which inspires the vocal melody" (quoted in Bailey, 2010: 182). Bailey observes that it is the "attitude of the performer towards this tactile element", to the "physical experience of play-ing an instrument, to the instrumental impulse, what largely determines his way of playing" (2010: 183).

From a musical perspective, the ball was for Maradona the instrument and a source of material, of resources, of experimental options, in the same way that the guitar or the voice is for a musician who improvises. We can even go a little further and make the "instrument the theme", the "subject", as Steve Lacy once pointed out (Bailey, 2010: 183). When the energetic disposition is directed to the instrument, and especially when in the field of "free improvisation", the creative register gives in to the inventiveness of the moment, to the trance. The musician says, "I don't know how I did it". When we listen to a freely improvised passage, we are surprised.

These considerations on the nature of rhythm and musical improvisation present a clear connection with Maradona, both in the singularity of his tech-nique and in "the musical" form of his way of playing. He himself points out this fact when remembering his famous second goal against England in Mexico: "Whenever I see it again I can't believe I managed it, honestly. Not because I scored it but because it seems a goal like that just isn't possible, a goal that you can dream of but never actually scored" (Maradona, 2021: 128). Águeda Pereyra compares Maradona and art in a way that broadens Maradona's figure and places his achievements on an aesthetics level: "There is a poetics in his body language, that body that plays but also dances: and in the unpredictability of his move-ments … there is singularity, there is a break in what his body can do" (2021: 36). Alejandro Dolina also detected this trend not only in his rhythm but also in his singing: "Diego sings and intones very well, and it seems curious to me that he hasn't explored that atypical and natural side" (Dolina, 2020: 46). Maradona loved music, which was an essential part of his daily life, as he tells in his book on the 1986 World Cup:

> We always had to play the same songs too, of course: Bonnie Tyler's ballad "Total Eclipse of the Heart" and the Sergio Denis tune "Gigante chiquito", which made me cry like a baby; the theme from Rocky —my favourite— would make me feel stronger than Dal Monte's training sessions. If you didn't hit the field ready to rip the other team to shred after listening to that —plus all the rage and the enthusiasm we had inside— then you were made of stone and not fit for the team.
>
> *Maradona, 2016: 86*

Throughout his career, Maradona sang in several TV shows and appeared onstage next to many famous artists. He even composed memorable duo versions with popular Hispanic musicians – Hugo Marcel, Pimpinela, Soledad Pastorutti, Joaquin Sabina, Charly Garcia, Marco Antonio Solis, Rodrigo Bueno, Bersuit Vergarabat, Fito Páez, Andres Calamaro, Los Piojos, and others. At the same time, his voice produced words that exerted a direct cultural and social influence.

Maradona expressed himself in almost all social areas, certain that his voice would be heard and often employed as a political symbol. He was aware of both the weight of his speech and the rigor that music demands when it is subjected to a melody. In that sense, his singing was confident and consistent. In his melodic line, there are no excesses or forced coloratura, there are no superficial extravagances. Instead, there is canon and meaning. This can be seen in his version of the Carlos Vives song "Voy a olvidarme de mí" that he performed in his programme *La Noche del 10* in 2005.[7] Throughout the song, Maradona was always careful not to overdo things. He was not worried about a certain nasal tone, or that the ambitus was narrower – he always preferred the note to the register, the phrase to the pitch.

Results on the Internet for "Diego sings" or "Diego dances" show that, since Maradona is a container for sounds, they display their material condition on him. We can see him during a warm-up in Germany in April of 1989 while the stadium loudspeakers played "Live is life" (Opus). This confirms how, in one of the most emblematic moments as a footballer, he let the sound enter his body. According to the context, he could be dancing or doing artistic gymnastics. He could be a busker or a circus acrobat. But the decisive factor at this point is the consubstantiation between sound and body, the way in which that relationship was presented in his performances.

## The sound of music: The Maradonian song

Songs are one of the major and most efficient tools for social communication. They move from body to body like a good virus, and they mark them. Songs contain meanings and carry a part of the world under a format that protects them from being diluted in time and space. We know that a song structure usually contains verse, chorus, solo, and bridge sections that lead to new verse sections or back to the chorus section, and then to the end. And all these parts are linked by a theme and a context in which they fit (Byrne, 2012: 31). Songs can start with the chorus, or with an instrumental introduction. They can be long or short, with or without instruments, with additional parts or sections, or simply they can be a song where verse and chorus sections are not distinguishable, but they still work fine. Apart from these and other structural peculiarities, songs (should) reflect the relationship between the singer and the world, where the singer captures and experiences the *tone* of a situation and senses the echo of that *tone* again in his own life.

On Spotify, there are 199 playlists under "Maradona": "Canciones para Maradona" (Songs for Maradona) contains 139 songs; "Para siempre Diego Maradona" (Forever Diego Maradona) 68; "Gracias Diego" (Thanks Diego) 54; "Pibe de Oro" (The Golden Boy) 27. On Twitter, and especially after his death, there was a surge in vernacular rankings of the best songs written for Maradona. Major newspapers and broadcasters, national and international, including *La Nación*, *Infobae*, *Página 12*, *Olé*, *Marca*, and *CNN*, also provided lists of the best

Maradonian songs.[8] Maradona speaks about these lists in his autobiography. Out of the many songs, Maradona mentions those by Andrés Calamaro, Los Piojos, Mano Negra, and Julio Lacarra but goes on to add that his favourite is "La Mano de Dios", by Rodrigo, which he considers the most beautiful song about him ever done, and whose lyrics he knows by heart.

When does this relation between Maradona and the song begin? If we consider dates and places, the founding moment of the Maradonian song can be traced back to June 22, 1986, at the Azteca Stadium in Mexico City. Before that date in Argentina, there are no songs dedicated to Diego. During the World Cup quarter finals between Argentina and England, Maradona metaphorically transmutes from human to God.[9] There is no other goal that has been commented with so much emphasis and that is so linked to a sound since its conception. Its author has perceived this and comments: "In my view, that second goal is set to music. And the music is Víctor Hugo Morales's commentary. I've had to watch and hear that goal in English, Japanese, German … But Víctor Hugo's commentary is like no other" (Maradona, 2016: 172).[10]

That same day, before the game was even finished, Peteco Carabajal composed "La cancion del brujito" (The Little Wizard's Song), the first Maradonian song. In an interview, Carabajal recalls:

> I had a melody without a theme. When Argentina played against England during the 1986 World Cup, where Maradona scored two goals, one with the "Hand of God" and the other when he rushed off from midfield, I was watching the game on my own. For the second goal, when begins his run, I sat up on the bed, as if something great was about to happen …. That moment, I decided that the lyrics I was going to write for that melody would have to do with that particular skill that only some people have.
>
> *2020*

However, the Maradonian song precedes Maradona. The sounds of football had already preceded his own history. On May 20, 1942, Reinaldo Yiso and Juan Puey recorded in Buenos Aires the tango "El sueño del pibe" (The Dream of the Pibe). The song tells the story of a young football player who receives an invitation for a trial from a club he supports. That night he dreams of becoming a star. If we pay attention to the lyrics, Maradona and the *pibe* from the tango have almost everything in common: their humble origins, their desire to succeed in a big club, the need to earn money to help their families, and their dream of scoring a match-winning goal. The tango says: "Dribbling past everybody he faced the goalkeeper/and with a strong kick he opened the score".

In 1994, Maradona sang this tango on a television show called *La verdad de la milanesa* but he replaced the names of the football players in the song, mentioning instead Mario Kempes, Jorge Olguín, and himself.[11] In his autobiography, he says that this is one of his favourite tangos and adds: "I don't know why, maybe because it has a lot to do with me. In fact, when I sing it I change the names of the characters and I include myself" (Maradona, 2000: 267). The life of that *pibe* reverberates in Maradona's own life and both are joined by the same sounds: "The stadium packed, glorious Sunday/at last they were going to see him play in the first division". We already know how stadiums sound: the *pibe* and Maradona feel the same, they hear the same. This resonance multiplies and deepens in the lyrics of "La vida es una tómbola" [Life is a Lottery] by Manu Chao (2007). In the line "If I were Maradona" the singer puts himself in the footballer's place, trying to see the world like him. Maradona feels like the *pibe* in the tango and Manu Chao ... does he not feel like Maradona and the *pibe* at the same time? The three share the same situation in this song: the humble origin and the yearning for success dissociated from economic power and aimed at collective emotion and motivating passions and sound.

But the resonance game does not end here. The Argentinian rock group La Beriso presented in 2003 its album *Solo canciones* and included its own version of "El sueño del pibe". The arrangement begins with an electric guitar introduction with typical tango tempo markings, followed by the voice in the first verse. In the second one, the drums and bass are added, harmonising the initial line of the guitar. In the third verse "Mommy dear I'll make money", the band speeds up the *tempo* and takes the song into punk territory. The band also changes the lyrics and includes Maradona among the footballers that the child admires. Once again, a singer puts himself in Maradona's place. After a vertiginous bridge dominated by the guitar, the band lowers the decibels in the penultimate verse and in the last verse they release the musical intensity again. In this part, the famous commentary of Maradona's goal by Víctor Hugo Morales is added as part of the musical material. The same formula can be found in other Maradonian songs such as in "Homenaje al 10" (Homage to Number 10) (2005), by Antonio Ríos, and "El gol del siglo" (The Goal of the Century) (2020), by Daniel Devita, but in La Beriso's version the commentary is directly connected to the tango lyrics, showing that the *pibe* has always been Maradona.

Another important theme in the Maradonian song are the echoes of the Malvinas/Falklands war. It appears in several songs by Argentinian bands and artists that emerged in the 1990s as "Maradó", by Los Piojos; "Angel vengador" (Revengeful Angel) (2001), by Zumbadores; "La cueca de Maradona" (Maradona's Cueca) (2001), by Guillermo Guido; "Barrilete cósmico" (Cosmic Kite) (2006), by El Farolito; "¿Qué es Dios?" (What is God?) (2008), by Las Pastillas del Abuelo; and "Gloria al 10" (Glory to Number 10) (2011), by Pampa Yakuza, among others. In these lyrics, Maradona is portrayed as a peaceful redeemer. The question is: are the sounds of that war also inscribed in his body? The song "El gol del siglo" (The Goal of the Century) by rapper Daniel Devita puts together three types of soundscapes that reverberate on Maradona's body: (a) the war soundscape (gunshots, hymns, tears, euphoria, silences, and a shaking ground); (b) the football soundscape, since the artist, rather than describing the goal, evokes once more Víctor Hugo, who becomes part of the song with his commentary; and (c) the tango landscape, which is represented by the use of the bandoneon in the introduction and also alludes to the fact of "being Argentinian". The lyrics are about 700 words. Maradona's name, however, is never mentioned: he appears as a mirror of those intertwined landscapes, as an echo of war, football, and tango.

The last echo that I will discuss is the one I identify with the figure of the prayer. Before the Maradonian Church was created, music had already raised its prayers. Mano Negra in his "Santa Maradona" (1994) openly asked (in French): "Santa Maradona pray for us". But there are many further examples, especially among Argentinian musicians, most of them very popular. They include: "Y dale alegría, alegría a mi corazón/es lo único que te pido al menos hoy" (And joy to my heart/it's the only thing I ask of you, at least today) (Fito Paez, "Y dale alegría a mi corazón" [And Bring Joy to My Heart] 1991); "Cabeza de mi patria, pueblo, santo y pecador" (Head of my country, people, saint and sinner) (Ataque 77, "Francotirador" [Sniper], 1997); "Es verdad que el Diego es lo más grande que hay/es nuestra religión, nuestra identidad" (It is true that Diego is the greatest ever/he's our religion, our identity) (Ratones Paranoicos, "Para siempre Diego" [Forever Diego], 2001); "Hoy en Italia sos más que un santo/Está San Genaro y luego estás vos … No te mueras nunca/Diego Armando" (In Italy today you are more than a saint/There is Saint Genaro and then there is you … Don't ever die, Diego Armando) (Terminal Tango, "No te mueras nunca" [Don't Ever Die], 2001); "Ya más nadie iba a manguearle/milagros a San Genaro/porque entrabas a jugar" (Nobody asked anymore for/miracles by San Genaro/because you were on the field) (La Guardia Hereje, "Para verte gambetear" [To See You Dribble], 2004); "Por tus milagros a mano/Y el milagro de tus pies/Muchas gracias señor dios/Muchas gracias señor diez" (For your handy miracles/for the miracle of your feet/Many thanks Mr. God/Many thanks Mr. Ten) (Las Pastillas del Abuelo, "¿Qué es Dios?" [What is God?] 2008); "Nadie sabe bien con qué poderes/rezan hombres y mujeres/por una mano de dios" (Nobody knows well with what powers/pray men and women/for the Hand of God) (David de Gregorio, "Barrilete cósmico" [Cosmic Kite], 2017).

What does the sound of this obsession with the divine and religious tells us? Why the prayer? Popular culture has no doubts: the word "Maradona" is the centre of a prayer. To say it is to be protected. A war correspondent in Iraq relates that "in a trench the only existing photo was one of Diego wearing the Argentinian T-shirt … we are at war and this Iraqi felt protected by Diego, how can you explain it?" (Caldeira, 2007: 25). In this way: Maradona is like home, built by the everyday way of his sounds and his way of speaking and expressing himself. But above all, Maradona is a name and a sound that everyone can make their own.[12] Esquirol declares that "the essential thing in language is protection" and that deep down there is a prayer, "as when one places the hands in front of the body to avoid impact" (2015: 157). That gesture and the prayer are closely related because words are comforting: "The word acts like a coat and the text is its fabric" (Esquirol, 2015: 158). The prayer appears as a primordial sound, the cry for help before the unknown, the hand that is raised so that we can be rescued. Maradona was there to rescue us from the uncertainty. That is why people ask, pray, and worship Maradona. It could even be stated that the National Decree 936/2020 of November 25, 2020, which declared three days of National Mourning in Argentina following Maradona's death, perfected his word as a home and refuge, in addition to making his name the reverberation of a country: "Beyond his individual and group achievements as a footballer ... he has represented the Argentinian people before the world, in such a way that the word 'ARGENTINA' immediately brings back 'MARADONA'".[13]

## Final echo

Probably, in the next World Cup Maradona's name will be called out in a stadium, but he will no longer be there to receive the chants. What will happen to those sounds? What meanings will they evoke? They will give shape to two different spaces. First, they will emphasise a disembodied and deified Maradona turned into a saint, and, given the confusing circumstances of his death, into a martyr. Second, they will make us hear the sound of a nation. In July of 2021, the Argentinian team beat Brazil 1-0 in the Maracanã Stadium in the Copa América final. Several memes pictured Maradona like a good-natured God that had guided the Argentinian team from heaven. A few weeks earlier, a new sound event had taken place in Argentina. On Twitter, the AFA (Argentinian Football Association) invited fans to shout together to commemorate the 35th anniversary of Maradona's iconic second goal against England in 1986: "On June 22nd at 16:09 play the commentary of Diego's goal against the English at full volume. And when the ball goes into the net again, we're going to roar out into the sky. Let's celebrate it again!" Maradona was evoked not only by his name but through the fundamental sound of football: the goal cry. "Maradona" and "goal" merged into a common sound that bounced directly on the word/sound/concept Argentina. Maradona consubstantiated with the land. That, too, seems to be his destiny.

Sound and immanence and/or sound and transcendence. The Maradonian sonorous dithyramb leaves us at this critical point and perhaps the new musical generations will be able to assimilate this dialectical tension without much difficulty. Right now, new songs where Maradona acts as a sound "blow", like a tattoo, continue to emerge. "Diego Maradona" (2020) by the German pop band Provinz goes in that direction. The chorus, introduced by a long melisma that occupies five of the eight bars, repeats his name like a mantra: "Ah ... Diego Maradona/Ah Diego Maradona". The music is euphoric, instrumentally dizzying, and supported by open, catchy choruses. It is a different song from the listening point of view: Maradona is entangled in a sound that escapes the rhythms and styles typical of rock and Argentinian popular music, and the rudeness that the rap, trap, and hip-hop songs mentioned try to convey. In an interview with the band, Warner Music Germany says: "Provinz turns the analogy of the rise and fall of Diego Maradona into a hymn to sweet power and the sense of immortality of youth, behind which there is always a looming sense of emptiness and foolishness".[14] For this band coming from a town of shepherds and famers near Ravensburg, there is apparently nothing much to do or to fight for. They declare themselves numbed by the geography – although they also refer to youth in a wider sense.[15] The song says: "And I'm bored, because down here behind the hill/ There is usually nothing to celebrate, so shoot me in the head/I'm about to eat, which helps me to forget/But before we leave/Shoot me like Diego Maradona". Maradona emerges as a luminous reflection, as if his name were a bullet that immediately acts on our consciousness, a radical and mobilising presence.

Just as Maradona marked his body with symbols of contemporary culture, now he himself is a mark for the new generations. It remains to be seen what the future sounds and echoes his song will bring in the years to come.

## Notes

1  I would like to thank: Nicolás, Juan y Federico Zúberman for their time and affection. Ernesto Cherquis Bialo for animating my journey. Pablo Brescia for his trust. Laura Novoa and Camila Juárez, for everything always. Leonardo Salvini, Leopoldo Juanes, Pamela Guruciaga, and the group M40 for the talks about El Diego. Negra40. com and the CEAC (UTN-MDP) for collaborating with my research.

2  Vj Awax is a musician and producer from the island of Mayotte. In February of 2020, he released his single "Maradona" with the St Unit & McBox. The lyrics appeal to the rebellion of marginalised classes.

3  For an approach to mass behaviour in football, cf. Herrera.

4  The participatory sound of the stadium is synchronised with a choreography: "the most common gesture involves an arm extended diagonally towards the sky, accompanied by a forward and backward movement of the forearm and a fairly loose wrist" (Herrera, 2018: 482).

5  Around the year of the song by Los Piojos and in "his visits to the different places in Argentina, an interesting phenomenon occurred: (Maradona) was surrounded by the affection of the public outside the stadium, and thoroughly booed the pitch" (Alabarces, 2002: 154).

6  In the chapter "Rhythm and Time in the Soundscape", Schafer refers to the heart, the breathing, the pace, and the nervous system as rhythmic patterns of humanity, and develops the existing links between these rhythms and the creative practice. "At least Walter Benjamin has referred to the subject when suggesting that, in Proust, who was asthmatic, the reader experiences a syntax that insinuates a fear of suffocating" (Schafer, 1993: 313).

7  Available at https://www.youtube.com/watch?v=Jn8xiec7vpA&ab_channel=lalomunoz

8  See: *La Nación*: https://www.lanacion.com.ar/espectaculos/musica/10-canciones-dedicadas-diego-maradona-nid2520928/; *Infobae*: https://www.infobae.com/teleshow/infoshow/2020/11/27/maradona-la-maquina-de-inspirar-canciones-los-mejores-temas-que-le-compusieron-a-lo-largo-de-su-vida/; *Página 12*: https://www.pagina12.com.ar/308001-canciones-para-maradona; *Olé*: https://www.ole.com.ar/maradona/canciones-diego-maradona-todas_0_NcrHbxQ4B.html; *Marca*: https://www.marca.com/tiramillas/musica/2020/11/25/5fbe966dca474188478b45fe.html; *CNN*: https://cnnespanol.cnn.com/2020/11/25/maradona-y-la-musica-escucha-las-canciones-que-algunos-artistas-le-dedicaron-al-astro-del-futbol/

9  Andrés Burgo points out this change of status: "The ball buzzes out of Maradona's foot and crosses the line. It is not a goal, it is football alchemy, and is, also, as if an eternity lightning fell on the Azteca Stadium. Time speeds up and, at the same time, stops: it becomes marble, it is sealed in bronze, it is engraved in the memory of

millions of people around the world and that moment begins to be, forever, an eternal moment" (2016: 194–195; our translation). For the Maradonian Church, the "Maradonian Easter" is celebrated on June 22, the day of resurrection (Caldeira, 2007: 23).

10 The commentary for the entire match was published as a book, titled *Barrilete cósmico* [Cosmic Kite] (Morales, 2013). Over time, action and commentary became dependent on each other: when we watch the move, we hear the sounds. When we hear the sounds, we see the move.

11 Available at https://www.youtube.com/watch?v=sBiGYUb1b6Y.

12 For Deleuze, a "sound assemblage" occurs when a voice disregards the task of "sustaining the sound" and only relates to the timbre, that is, to itself. "With the timbre [the sung, spoken voice] discovers in itself a structure that makes it heterogeneous to itself and gives it a power of continuous variation" (Deleuze and Guattari, 2002: 100). Maradona's voice is enough to summon all the parts (parameters) that constitute a sound, to find the common sound, according to Thomas Mann, "a simple howl that passes through all the degrees" (*id.*).

13 Available at https://www.boletinoficial.gob.ar/detalleAviso/primera/5237540/20201125?suplemento=1.

14 Read the full interview at: https://www.warnermusic.de/news/2020-04-17/provinz-schiessen-sich-ab-wie-diego-maradona-seht-das-video-zum-neuen-song.

15 Referring to their latest production "*Zu spät um umzudrehen*" (Too Late to Turn Around, 2020), the band calls on the youth to get involved and commit to global politics: "the provinces are becoming political. Because even if 2020 was in a sense a year of social stagnation, it was also the most politically uneasy year …. Black Lives Matter, lateral thinker demonstrations, plus a long-simmering discussion on a nearing climate catastrophe: as a thoughtful, young person, you cannot be apolitical these days". https://provinzband.com/.

# References

Alabarces, Pablo. 2002. *Fútbol y patria: el fútbol y las narrativas de la nación en la Argentina*. Buenos Aires: Prometeo.

Apo, Alejandro. 2020. "El inventor de la pelota". *D10S: Miradas sobre el mito Maradona*. Ed. Julio Ferrer. Buenos Aires: Octubre, 49–50.

Archetti, Eduardo. 2003. "Playing Football and Dancing Tango: Embodying Argentina in Movement, Style and Identity". *Sport, Dance and Embodied Identities*. Eds. Noel Dyck and Eduardo P. Archetti. Oxford: Berg, 217–229.

Bailey, Derek. 2010. *Improvisación. Su naturaleza y su práctica musical*. Asturias: Ed. Trea.

Biguenet, John. 2015. *Silencio*. Buenos Aires: Godot.

Burgo, Andrés. 2016. *El partido. Argentina-Inglaterra 1986*. Buenos Aires: Tusquets.

Byrne, David. 2012. *Cómo funciona la música*. Spain: Ed. Random House, Inc.

Caldeira, Joseph. 2007. *Iglesia Maradoniana*. Mar del Plata Edición de autor.

Carabajal, Peteco. 2020. "'Peteco reveló cómo nació 'La canción del Brujito', tributo a Maradona". *El Liberal*. November 27. Web: https://www.elliberal.com.ar/noticia/pura-vida/548932/peteco-revelo-como-nacio-cancion-brujito-tributo-maradona?utm_campaign=ScrollInfinitoDesktop&utm_medium=scroll&utm_source=not

Deleuze, Gilles y Guattari, Félix. 2002. *Mil mesetas. Capitalismo y esquizofrenia*. Barcelona: Pre-Textos.

Dolina, Alejandro. 2020. "Entre el heroísmo y lo épico". *D10S. Miradas sobre el mito Maradona*. Ed. Julio Ferrer. Buenos Aires: Octubre, 46–48.

Esquirol, Joseph María. 2015. *La resistencia íntima. Ensayo para una filosofía de la proximidad*. Barcelona: Acantilado.

Feld, Steven. 2013. "Una acustemología de la selva tropical". *Revista Colombiana de Antropología*, 49.1: 217–239.

Herrera, Eduardo. 2018. "Masculinity, Violence, and Deindividuation in Argentine Soccer Chants: The Sonic Potentials of Participatory Sounding-in-Synchrony". *Ethnomusicology*, 62.3: 470–499.

Maradona, Diego Armando. 2000. *Yo soy el Diego de la gente*. Buenos Aires: Planeta.

———. 2016. *México 86. Mi mundial. Mi verdad. Así ganamos la copa*. Buenos Aires: Sudamericana.

———. 2021. *El Diego*. Trans. Marcela Mora y Araujo. London: Yellow Jersey Press.

Menotti, César Luis. 2020. "En Barcelona, en donde jugó dos años, Diego brilló y también sufrió". *Télam*. November 25. https://www.telam.com.ar/notas/202011/536458-en-barcelona-en-donde-jugo-dos-anos-diego-brillo-y-tambien-sufrio.html

Morales, Víctor Hugo. 2013. *Barrilete cósmico (El relato completo)*. Buenos Aires: Interzona.

Pereyra, Agueda. 2021. "La gruesa perla irregular". *Todo Diego es político*. Ed. Bárbara Pistoia. Buenos Aires: Síncopa, 34–44.

Rosa, Hartmut. 2019. *Resonancia. Una sociología de la relación con el mundo*. España: Conocimiento.

Soriano, Manuel. 2020. *¡Canten, putos!* Buenos Aires: El Gourmet Musical.

Schafer, Murray. 1993. *El paisaje sonoro y la afinación del mundo*. 2013. Barcelona: Intermedio.

# PART III

# Reading and Writing Maradona

# 9

# SPECTRES OF MARADONA

## Chronicle/Fiction/Autobiography/Film

*Ksenija Bilbija*

## … And justice for all?

This chapter will address Maradona as a ghost – an "other who is not present", in Derrida's sense – the one conjured up by texts that collectively constitute an archive of the footballer's innumerable spectral selves and that intend to foreground his engagement with societal justice.[1] Fair play in football roughly represents what justice in society is, "an ideal of truth beyond judicial power" (Arfuch, 2020: 43), and while striving to represent himself as a fighter for societal justice, Maradona is also known for saying that there is no justice in football (*El Gráfico*, 1996: 87). To do this, I will examine some of those cryptic archives: the chronicle *Maradona soy yo* (1993) (*Maradona Is Me*) by Alicia Dujovne Ortiz; the novel *Inocente* (*Innocent*) by Fernando Niembro and Julio Llinás (1995); the autobiography *Yo soy el Diego* (2000) (translated as *Maradona: The Autobiography of Soccer's Greatest and Most Controversial Star* (2005); and the documentary film *Maradona by Kusturica* (2008) by Emir Kusturica. Rather than seeking to judge the player as a human being, keeping in mind Arfuch's framework of memory, autobiography, and justice, I will reflect on the reaches of the hand of justice and ponder whether justice has been served in our engagement with the narrative spectres of Maradona.

## The spectre of a chronicle

On July 4, 1993, almost exactly three years after Argentina lost the World Cup trophy in Italy, Argentine author Alicia Dujovne Ortiz was writing an epilogue to the Spanish translation of her chronicle *Maradona Is Me*, originally published in France in 1992. Between the publication of the French original (written in the summer of 1991), the 1992 Italian translation and the forthcoming version in Spanish, the author managed to interview Maradona in his Seville home;

DOI: 10.4324/9781003196587-13

the book published by Emecé Editores in Buenos Aires in August of 1993 thus included an additional epilogue, and its back cover featured a black-and-white photograph of Dujovne Ortiz in familial conversation with the football star in his living room. The book's initial print run was 4,000 copies. It received virtually no critical response, and only a very limited readerly response in Argentina.[2] The French edition was well received by critics and was followed by translations in Italian, Spanish, and Japanese.

Dujovne Ortiz's Flaubertian incursion into the "spectral I" of Maradona, refracted through her own itinerant self, is an imaginative literary venture into the raw depths of the footballer's self. The project is risky, both for a woman author and for an author who does not define herself as a football enthusiast. I will focus my reading on the spectral Maradona conjured in the final pages of Dujovne Ortiz's chronicle, in the epilogue that appears only in the Argentine version of the book and has thus been written especially for the home-country audience.

Chronicle is a hybrid genre: its texts meander between fact and fiction, pairing the narrative flexibility and malleability we might expect to find in a novel with journalistic approach to truthful and ethical accounting. Chronicle probes the nature of fiction and nonfiction, especially in its constructions of the self as a spectre and a spectator. It not only tells the novelist's or journalist's truth but also encourages the reader to hear a voice that is not unlike her own and yet, not *really* her own. *Maradona Is Me* explores the tension between the self and the other beyond the public-private paradigm via a process in which identification with the chronicle's character – by both writer and reader – is elicited. "The spectator [in theater]" writes Freud in 1904, "is a 'poor wretch to whom nothing of importance can happen,' who has long been obliged to damp down, or rather displace, his ambition to stand at the hub of world affairs; he longs to feel and to act and to arrange things according to his own desires —in short, to be a hero. And the playwright and actor enable him to do this by allowing him to *identify himself* with the hero" (Freud, 1985: 122). We shall later see Maradona's connection to this Freudian idea.

In Dujovne Ortiz's empathic reimagining, she is even visited by the spectre of Virgil, who secretly leaves Maradona-related press clips at the Naples hotel where she is staying and guides her through infernal manipulations between the powerful Italian club owners Corrado Ferlaino (SSC Napoli) and Silvio Berlusconi (AC Milan), thus helping her to configure the truth – though here the heroic identification is of course with Dante who also visited hell guided by Virgil, in his *Divine Comedy*, and not with the main character of her own chronicle. The narrative is sustained by a second (and here, more directly relevant) heroic identification as Dujovne Ortiz ties her story of Argentina's national icon, a globally recognised footballer who always prioritised his Argentine identity, to questions about her own experiences as an emigrant. An Argentine who has herself lived in Paris for over twenty years, the author travels from Paris to Naples – seeking, she explains, the story behind the "portrait washed in tears and a neck extended towards the medal of defeat, while an ax, visible only to the eyes of the heart, looms over a suddenly fragile-looking cervix" (Dujovne Ortiz, 1993: 11; all translations from the Spanish are mine, unless otherwise indicated). It is the TV image of the star, under threat and crushed by Argentina's loss to West Germany in the finals of the 1990 World Cup, that haunts the author, propelling her to ask how and why the vision made her feel like an Argentine. The thesis she ventures in the initial pages of the chronicle's first, French, edition is the same one she confirms in the epilogue of the Argentine version of her book: Argentina is a gypsy nation. Dujovne Ortiz does not only use the fictionalised gypsy metaphor to portray her nation as marginalised in the neoliberal distribution of wealth and to position her compatriots as displaced due to the social and historical conditions that fuelled European migration to Argentina in the late nineteenth and early twentieth centuries. She also reverses this image of transience to apply it to the European exile into which the brutal military dictatorship (1976–1983) forced her and many Argentines, and to analogise the dispersal of that country's players across European clubs. She sees identity as cultural property and Maradona as a prime example of a passionate and essentially free soul who, when not living in his native country, always found his place in the disparaged south: in Naples, the south of Italy, or Seville, the south of Spain.

In the ending that originally concluded her book for French and Italian readers, Dujovne Ortiz describes herself, late in 1991, writing a letter to the ever-elusive Maradona, whom she has unsuccessfully pursued in Naples and who was by then living in Buenos Aires once again. The sad outcome of a 1990 World Cup final decided by a late penalty kick and his ultimate disappointment in Neapolitan fans were all behind him. In the Argentine edition published two years later, Dujovne Ortiz has managed to interview the footballer, and she closes with a scene in which she is sitting in the same room with the flesh-and-blood Maradona. They chit-chat about his rebellious nature and his fight against power, intimidation, and inequality, and he invokes his favourite metaphor of being a megaphone for the voiceless. He repeats a point he has often made to journalists that he never wanted to be a politician but says he could not remain apolitical as he watched his people go hungry. Author and character together cannot help talking about systemic injustice and corruption in the Argentina of President Carlos Menem,[3] about the half kilo  of cocaine found in the player's home that somehow ended up being just a few grams and the curious instance where the original judge in charge of the case was suddenly replaced by another less sympathetic one who happened to be President Menem's friend.[4] Maradona thanks the author for her courage in defending him when no one else did – when his drug addiction and alleged mafia relations were the top story – and she can't help but notice a slight provincial accent in his voice. They belong to different social classes; they have different backgrounds and different levels of education – and yet they share the same perception of injustice. "You believed me" (Dujovne Ortiz, 1993: 216), Maradona concludes, even though he has not actually read her book, that they had never met before that evening, and that Dujovne Ortiz had not even been sufficiently interested in football to follow his declarations of innocence and promises of reform related to drug problems in press. The truth he recognised and acknowledged was literary: it was, in other words, her story-telling that *did justice*.

In *Maradona Is Me* Dujovne Ortiz effectively articulated, on a symbolic level, Argentinians' widespread sense of injustice. The root of the problem is, of course, economic inequality, and in her narrative the author frequently circles back to that issue by invoking the image of Maradona's father working hard in a bone meal factory, and by describing the abysmal living conditions in Villa Fiorito, where Maradona grew up and first started kicking around a ball in streets filled with garbage and without sewage or running water. And, while it is in the real neighbourhoods that justice must be achieved, fiction – or in this case, chronicle – has a role in displaying general injustice through a character's personal claim to justice. There is no doubt that Dujovne Ortiz is subjective and self-conscious in her quest, openly recognising her identification with her footballer hero even in the very title of her book. But her choice of a *somewhat* fictional epistemology (and we should not forget that chronicle is a liminal genre encompassing elements of both fiction and nonfiction) allows her audience to look at the question of justice from the outside and judge. Nevertheless, Dujovne Ortiz also tests how pure fiction can operate to secure justice by recounting to her unique audience a story written by the Uruguayan writer Mario Benedetti in 1959, a year before Maradona was born. "Left Striker" is the monologue of a football player who was badly beaten up for scoring a goal in spite of taking a bribe to throw the game. Maradona says gravely: "Exactly. It fits with my situation. It is how it was" (Dujovne Ortiz, 1993: 217). He goes on to remember his days in Naples: threats from the mafia, the lingering fear about the safety for his daughters' lives. *Via* the story of a battered left striker, acted out by a Flaubertian author who had been moved by Maradona's own tears after the 1990 World Cup loss, the footballer – who is now transformed into a "spectator in theater" as Freud postulated – identifies with Benedetti's character and thus experiences catharsis. Dujovne Ortiz uses fiction to provide the aesthetic experience for the unsayable. And if that telling moment was not enough, she has also arranged to incorporate another instance of poetic justice in the final pages of her epilogue, indicating that SSC Napoli's owner Ferlaino was charged and arrested that very year (1993) in the sweeping anti-corruption campaign organised by Italian government. Blinded by the sense of justice emanating from her compassionate imagination and redemptive power of fiction, Dujovne Ortiz does not foresee Maradona's expulsion from the 1994 World Cup and the end of his career as a footballer, only a year into the future.

## The spectre of fiction

In March of 1995, sports journalist Fernando Niembro and fiction writer Julio Llinás published a novel titled *Innocent*. Under the unsourced epigraph "Reality is a hypothesis of imagination", the novel attempts to redeem Maradona from his

drug-related[5] expulsion from the 1994 World Cup in the US. Unlike biographical genres, which may linger at the frontier in the undefined space between
fiction and nonfiction, the novel has no responsibility to the facts and can employ
reparatory mechanisms to correct reality's many failures of justice. In the world
of readers' suspended disbelief, *Innocent* attempts to clear the name of the football
star accused of using performance-enhancing drugs and, of course, announces
its verdict in the title. "Innocent", as a title term, also implies the *naiveté* of a
footballer framed by his enemies, a character whose natural honesty and sense of
justice have activated the covert workings of powerful organisations including
FIFA, the CIA, and even the Vatican. The book's cover features a distinctive
number 10 on the iconic sky-blue and white stripes of the Argentine national
jersey stamped by an official-looking CIA logo with the words TOP SECRET;
half-opened multicoloured capsules spill a powdery substance over the shirt. An
Argentine reader can in fact judge this book by its cover, which unmistakably
indicates who the novel is about and what its storyline will be. The back cover
marketing blurb situates the narrative in the 1994 World Cup and stresses that
the host country is uneasy about the Colombian and Argentine teams. In the
former case, the unease is due to Colombia's association with the drug trade;
in the latter to the presence of Maradona in the team, who, according to the
blurb, is, "by many considered the best in the world, apparently unruly and
capricious", a player whose personal opinions have shaken up the football establishment. "The guy is famous and different", and "the CIA, the creator and the
keeper of the international order, doesn't like those who are different". The
player is never named, but the publicity for this conspiracy thriller treats him as
a modern Moloch, an idol demanding great sacrifices. Only nine months had
passed between Maradona's expulsion from the World Cup, having tested positive for ephedrine in a post-match control, and the publication of the book, and
Argentinians who were still reliving the national trauma of Maradona's humil-
iating debacle didn't need any additional prompting to understand what they
would find between the book's covers.

In the months since the star's removal from the World Cup, Argentinians had
already responded to the events as a tragedy. The well-known journalist Mariano
Grondona compared Maradona to Oedipus and Hamlet, characters who over-
stepped their bounds and were punished for others' wrongdoing (Grondona,
1994: 40). Much of the discussion that ensued among Argentines had to do with
their idiosyncrasy, as they saw the player through the lens of personal views about
justice and the rule of law. "Respecting the law does not have any prestige in
this country" wrote Argentinian writer Mempo Giardinelli in another editorial
on the topic: "One could even say that it is an Argentinian way of life. Believing
that happiness is eternal, that it is not so important to follow the rules, nor assume
responsibilities. It is easier to blame the others, imagine conspiracies, believe that
when one makes a mistake he becomes the victim of the other and not of his own
actions" (1994: 79). Giardinelli does not blame Maradona for anything, although
he wonders elliptically – "Did he know it?" – while watching the replay of the

moment when the smiling star is taken off the field to be tested and concludes the player is the victim of a society that believes everything can always be fixed. Another editorial sees Maradona as Argentina's *alter ego*, an embodiment of the nation, and projects his individual successes and wrongdoings onto a national scale.[6] Jorge Lanata, a prominent Argentine journalist who founded the daily *Página/12*, summarised the national quandary: "Can we really be a modern society that plays by the rules of modern countries, or are we just a boy from the poor barrio always thinking he can play by other rules, thinking he won't get caught?" (cited in Nash, 1994: 4).[7]

*Innocent* is a poorly written novel with a contrived plot. It never succeeds in spinning its hypothesis – that a hero of the sport has been framed – into a compelling narrative. Its heavy-handed writing advances every gripe that ever circulated regarding the misfortunes of the rebellious idol who had dared to reveal power games and corruption within football's governing body and who, at the same time, openly sympathised with Fidel Castro. This fact, it must be pointed out, was the sin that, according to this novel, the US would not tolerate. Because of the star's iconoclastic comments about the Vatican and the alleged "recommendation" Maradona made to Pope John Paul II to sell the gold ceilings at the Vatican if he wanted to help the poor, the authors of *Innocent* also felt entitled to add the Pope to their conspiracy. That the book was a runaway bestseller despite its many and obvious flaws may be partly due to not only its adrenaline-rush plot, but also – as, of course, the title suggests – the appeal of the novel's proclaimed intent to exonerate a national hero. Argentines didn't buy this novel because it made a strong case that Maradona was innocent. They bought it because they strongly wanted Maradona to be innocent.[8]

The novel opens with undercover CIA officer Anthony Llás on his way to Colombia to meet local agent Coco Cardo and arrange for the use of a special ointment, prepared by a witch doctor, to make Colombian players sluggish during their upcoming World Cup games. Argentine femme fatale Rubra Robirosa, owner of the biggest public relations firm in Latin America, accidentally meets Llás and Cardo in a resort hotel and reaches the mistaken conclusion that their plan is to assassinate Maradona, allowing the host country to win the World Cup. One has to wonder if the authors attached to their only female character – the single one who is emphatically not a football fan – the notion that the US, a country where in the 1990s (as well as now) the men's team is far from reaching the last stages of the tournament, could actually win the 1994 World Cup as an effort to underscore how ludicrous and implausible that idea was. Although not a fan, Rubra is Argentine and thus cannot allow such an injustice against her compatriot. She flies to New York to alert the sport's authorities, but Alan Rothenberg (the nonfictional president of the United States Soccer Federation, the governing body that oversaw the event, here borrowed as a character) does not take her warning seriously. Llás orders another CIA officer, Mel Kennedy, to somehow get an ephedrine-infused communion wafer to Maradona right before facing the Nigerian team in the second match of the group stage, since he is apparently known to receive communion ahead of major games, thus heading onto the field with sins forgiven. Luckily for the conspirators, Mel's childhood love Bill is now a priest, and he eventually agrees to offer Holy Communion to the player. A FIFA medical representative (who is also, somehow, part of the conspiracy) turns out to be an aficionado of magic tricks; thus no one notices foul play when he draws Maradona's name in what is supposed to be a random drug-testing selection process. In the end, Maradona is unjustly kicked off the tournament. In a reversal of the usual mechanics of suspense fiction, here the ending is no surprise to any of the readers since it coincides with the actual facts; the interest lies in the breathless handling of the conspiracy that leads to the inevitable ending that, as we've seen above, many Argentinians considered tragic and unjust.

Niembro and Llinás' novel engages in a reparative exercise with the irreparable by incorporating curious and numerous acts of poetic justice: most of the conspirators involved in framing Maradona die, some killed by their own partners and others by suicide, and none of them has a loving wife like the footballer does. Some conspirators are even killed because they come – in the course of writing intelligence reports – to empathise and even identify with the player whose career they are destroying. Yet in a deeper sense of the term "poetic justice", as posited by the philosopher Martha Nussbaum (1995), the literary imagination of *Innocent* fails to deliver any good, true reparation.

It is difficult to lay out the "argument" of this sloppy novel, which at one point even mixes up the names of Colombian midfielder Alex Escobar and defender Andrés Escobar, who was tragically assassinated by the drug cartels on returning home after scoring an own goal in the game against the US. It is interesting, however, to focus on the novel's short epilogue. Turning to this text from our reading of the Argentine version of Dujovne Ortiz's chronicle, there's an eerie similarity between the chronicle's epilogue – where the Argentine female uninterested in football meets with Maradona to settle a score of fictional justice – and the epilogue of *Innocent*. The novel's epilogue is narrated from the viewpoint of Maradona, who in a post-expulsion meeting with Rubra Robirosa ruminates about his life and a "phantasm inside him that makes him do the things he does and say the things he says" (Niembro and Llinás, 1995: 274).

The idea that a ghost has taken over Maradona's life decisions is repeated throughout the epilogue, with reiterated emphasis on a controlling force that time and again directed him towards "what was just". The fictional Maradona abdicates free will and submits to this power invested in him by some higher force, guiding him through life. Yet he retains his humility: "He had the same tastes, the same weaknesses, the same feelings, the same ideas. He liked women, cars, sports, empanadas, ravioli. He was bored by books, complicated movies, strange things" (Niembro and Llinás, 1995: 274). Maradona is at once superior (guided by a higher power towards good) and ordinary (a "typical" empanada-loving Argentine). Without really understanding why he is telling all this to an unknown "magnificent" woman who, again echoing Dujovne Ortiz's relationship to her subject, "was not from his [social] class", he hears her soft voice: "I came to tell you that I believe in you. I think that you didn't use drugs. I am not sure how they did it, but they set you up". While Maradona only wants to know her name, she finds it necessary to confess "that I also admire you although I don't know why. I don't care about football" (Niembro and Llinás, 1995: 275). Though she is a woman not interested in football, Rubra is an Argentine: nationality trumps gender, and she believes in Maradona. Despite the possible element of sexual attraction, the relationship of this "dazzling woman" to the football player seems instead – and again – to be one of identification. She has long lived with the secret of a childhood rape but now, though she still "had her ghost", she feels Maradona's monologue "could have been her own with some changes in origin and surroundings" (Niembro and Llinás, 1995: 275).

It could be argued that Argentines seem to share with Maradona the sense that they are inhabited by an apparition or spectre, an observer either internal or external (looking on at the self "from the bleachers"). The authors of *Innocent* reconfigured reality and constructed a plot, much desired by the national readership, in which a protagonist with a natural and unquestionable sense of justice was framed by an increasingly elusive system. However, Niembro and Llinás' reparative narrative exercise remains lodged in the sphere of individual justice and ultimately fails to inspire any meaningful debate in the arena of social justice. After all, proposing in its conclusion an unruly spectral presence that could be lurking in every Argentinian who – abused by male predators, poverty, or foreign institutions – *feels*, without ever *knowing*, what is just, seems to authorise claims for justice based on impulse and not on the application of the rules of the legal system. Spectres and ghosts alike demand our ear and action, but this novel does not make its call audible.

## The spectre of autobiography

Maradona's autobiography *Yo soy el Diego* [*I Am El Diego*] was originally published in September 2000 by the editorial conglomerate Planeta and rapidly translated into eighty-eight languages. The English version appeared in 2004 under the title *Maradona: The Autobiography of Soccer's Greatest and Most Controversial Star*. He had retired from football three years prior to the publication of his life story and began drafting his life narrative in February of 2000 in Cuba, where he was recovering from congestive heart failure caused by his serious cocaine addiction. As it is a common practice, Maradona is not the sole author; he instead put his story into the hands of two sports journalists who seem to admire him unconditionally, Ernesto Cherquis Bialo and Daniel Arcucci. They shaped into a narrative thirty-eight hours of recorded interviews conducted over forty-one days throughout February and March of 2000, at a time when Maradona was already seen as a *former* football player.

This is not a confessional biography on the model established by Saint Augustine. True, there is a trace of criminality in Maradona's self-narrative that echoes episodes in the life of Augustine, who admits he stole pears from an orchard not because of need but for the pleasure of doing wrong. And while Saint Augustine agonises over his unprovoked and hard-to-explain petty delinquency, Maradona takes pride in his offenses – like outsmarting the referees in the Mexico 1986 World Cup to score a goal against England with his hand. The resulting text – *I Am El Diego* – goes against the grain for these types of testimonies that many times aspire to be self-purging restitution narratives in which the recovering addict itemises his redeeming characteristics, looks back at the time when he was healthy, acknowledges his current condition as a roadblock, and mentally projects forward to recovery. Maradona offers no self-assessment that could yield insights into his condition and never reflects on the path that eventually led him to a rehab clinic on the outskirts of Havana.

While the (auto)biographical account does offer occasional glimpses of the footballer's wit and his vibrant, charismatic persona, it is a compilation of clichés and lacks the kind of imaginative or creative dialogues that might have revealed his inner world. It blends autobiography with the familiar genre of sports biography, where interviewers have designed the memory prompts, used their vast collection of press clippings to trigger the star's clever comments, and then transcribed and edited the final account. Thus rather than an act of self-revelation, as the autobiographical genre presupposes, *I Am El Diego* is a mostly chronological and restrictive version of memories already familiar to readers from Maradona's previous statements to the national and international press, emotion-laden events that gloss over the violent outbursts and family betrayals that repeatedly showed up in the news.

Maradona engages in a fictionalisation of the self that, guided by the interviewers, develops themes typical of celebrity life stories. The foundational framing of the (auto)biography constructs the world-renowned player as a passionate, undeterred pursuer of social justice who does not always play by the rules but will always cherish his nation and its working-class fans above all else. The framing is achieved through the customary retelling of the rags-to-riches life story of a proletarian who remains loyal to his humble roots, a man who like his fans is a mix of virtues and defects. Readers see Maradona's enduring love for football and his alleged honesty and dedication to the fight against establishment corruption. "Everything I say in this book is the truth, I swear on my daughters' lives" says Maradona in his last chapter, "I Am El Diego", envisioned as a concluding address to readers (the sentence is omitted from the English version). "I will continue to speak the truth until the end. I will not compromise, because I can't stand to, I can't stand injustice", he says in his passionate finale; he wants readers to understand that "[n]obody will ever make me believe that my mistakes with drugs or in business have changed my feelings. Nothing. I am the same as always. I'm me, Maradona. I am El Diego" (Maradona, 2005: 286). Maradona's truth is based on his emotional conviction that he is always acting honestly, for justice, and his emotion is the proof of that honesty: he waters that statement with rivers of tears that flow onto every page of the book.

Yet the story ultimately crafted by Bialo and Arcucci never engages critically with the social structure that created the life conditions in his birthplace
Villa Fiorito, nor the exploitative nature of his father's work in the bone meal
factory. Given that in the book Maradona constructs a self who is a fighter for
social justice, it is perhaps surprising that there is no further exploration of these
topics. In *I Am El Diego,* as in the tattoos of Marxist revolutionary icons Che
Guevara and Fidel Castro that Maradona proudly exhibited on his right arm and
left leg, he carries his socialism as a personality trait rather than a commitment
to enact socialist values or to engage in radical sociopolitical action. Maradona
was, in the end, more a narcissist and tattoo socialist than an activist working
to make life fairer. He was an extraordinary football player but not a fighter
for the collective good and the redistribution of wealth. As number of scholars
who brilliantly analysed Maradona as social construct and cultural icon suggest,
his embrace of socialism was contradictory.[9] For Maradona freedom meant not
being bound to moral and social responsibilities. And though he promises the
reader in the first paragraphs of his bestseller that he will "tell everything", he
does not actually expose himself in any way because he fails to offer anything
that was not already known.[10] Rather than getting to the heart of the matter
on hot-button issues like his secret links to cocaine and Neapolitan mafia, he
glosses over the details with casual assertions that "everyone knows what I am
talking about" – potentially embracing fans in an illusory friendship and sense
of shared inside knowledge, but not actually telling them anything else that they
may want (or not?) to know (the sentence is omitted from the English version).
While Maradona styles himself (here as elsewhere) as "the voice of those without
voice",[11] he does not actually speak for a community, whether Argentine, international, or even a broader community of workers.[12] In the original version in
Spanish, chapter seven, "Los amigos, los enemigos" ("Friends, enemies"), which
has been omitted in its entirety from the English translation, the claim to be a
voice for the voiceless is emphasised by mimicking the spectre of Evita, another
Argentinian populist icon with a rags-to-riches story. Maradona uses again the
megaphone metaphor to indicate that he sees himself as projecting the voices
of the voiceless working people of Argentina. But the sentence ends with an
unexpectedly ambivalent, and even possibly derogatory, note that without him
the "voiceless ones" would have never in their "fucking lives" be heard. One
can certainly speculate on the ambivalence here and propose that an irritated
Maradona is responding to the critics who, in saying he has not done enough for
the working people, forget that they would otherwise have nothing at all and
should be grateful for what he has done for the poor.

This same chapter clarifies that while he does not hate those whom he has
fought in the media, he does hate those who "put their hand into people's pockets, like some politicians do, ... or those who can kill people, like the Argentine
military did at one point (82)". The very image Maradona uses, "putting a hand
into people's pockets" is a common expression, but also one that appeared earlier
in the book, in the player's retrospective accounting of the unethical goal he had

scored with his hand: "The first [goal] was like sticking my hand in the pocket of an Englishman and getting a wallet which was not his" (Magalhães Britto, 2014: 680). He sees himself as a rightful avenger of the Argentine defeat in the 1982 Malvinas/Falklands War over British-governed territories in the South Atlantic. That this outcome in a tragic and unnecessary armed conflict brought the end of the Argentine military dictatorship does not enter into Maradona's assessment of the situation. His references to state terror are, in fact, sparse as he looks back at a career that took off in October of 1976 when, at age 15, he was promoted to the first team of Argentinos Juniors, six months into a brutal dictatorship that would eventually disappear thousands of citizens. When he looks at the 1979 infamous photo of him shaking hands with General Videla, head of the military junta, he says he did not have a choice (28).[13] He mentions that in exchange for a transfer from Argentinos Juniors to Boca Juniors he was paid in kind with "some apartments" (Maradona, 2005: 40) but never managed to obtain the ownership titles of those properties. Ultimately, they would prove impossible to sell. One of these apartments was directly opposite the clandestine torture centre ESMA [the Navy Mechanics School]; knowing the illegal methods used by the military to acquire land (methods that included abduction, torture, and murder), we can guess where these properties came from and why he would have been unable to sell them. Maradona comments generally about the infamous 1978 World Cup, mostly expressing his resentment that he ultimately was not part of the national team, but he urges his readers not to see the Argentine triumph as dirty if only because "Videla and his cronies, who made thirty thousand people disappear, don't deserve anything, least of all to tarnish the memory of the success of a group of lads" (Maradona, 2005: 27). For someone with so much insight into how both sports and politics worked at the time, it is perhaps surprising Maradona does not mention the rumours that the Argentine junta had sent a large transfer of grain to Peru on the understanding that their (already disqualified) national team would lose their next match by at least four goals, the number Argentina needed to qualify over Brazil (Koller and Brandle, 2015: 236). All he says about the apparently fixed game is, "[w]e thrashed Peru" (Maradona, 2005: 25).

Maradona received a million-dollar advance for his life account, and the publisher's marketing machine worked to build his reputation for social engagement. With the book's fifth printing, the original title *Yo soy el Diego* was enriched by an explicitly proletarian tagline: *de la gente* (of the people). Not "Diego of the football fans", but Maradona as a social champion of the people: *Yo soy el Diego de la gente* (*I am El Diego of the people*) is the persona behind this pseudo-autobiographical writing. Despite its branding, the book remains a fairy-tale account spiced up with picaresque insights about the workings of the football establishment, but any further sense of the need for social justice and its promotion is absent. Reading it, we see foregrounded instead a concept of divine justice manifested through his (in)famous hand goal (dubbed the "Hand of God") and his self-identification as a proud divine arbiter called upon to repair and revenge the outcome of the Malvinas/Falklands war. While Maradona extends his miraculous hand via sport as entertainment extravaganza to the demands of the global neoliberal market and invites his readers to the emotion-packed journey through his career, the question that remains is how much freedom in judging these readers actually have, given the presumption that messianic judgement cannot be unjust. One can only imagine that this is the reason his autobiography serves as a holy text on which new members of the actual cult called Church of Maradona (founded in 1998) swear their allegiance. Insofar as Maradona's (auto) biography constructs a narrative of triumph, it is an account of a footballer's meritocratic success, not the triumph of a life commitment to justice.[14]

## Spectre of a documentary film

In 2008, when the Bosnian-born Yugoslav and now Serbian director Emir Kusturica premiered his documentary film *Maradona by Kusturica* at the Cannes Film Festival, Maradona had already been out of football's official arena for more than a decade: he had suffered drug and alcohol addiction, obesity, "cardiac and criminal arrests",[15] football bans, a serious car accident, divorce, and the dissolution of his family. In 2005, when Kusturica announced his plans to portray a real Maradona, the former footballer was topping the Argentine media ratings as the host of a wildly popular weekly TV show *La Noche del 10* [The night with #10]. A renowned filmmaker whose work had been recognised by the prestigious Venice, Cannes, and Berlin film festivals, he had since been exploring other career paths as a film actor, musician, and city planner. Both Maradona and Kusturica had some key character traits in common: each was described as passionate, witty, stubborn, unpredictable, and sincere in his desire to act with fairness.

It would be hard to imagine Maradona choosing to watch any of Kusturica's allegorical and satirical art films about Balkan idiosyncrasies. It would be equally hard to imagine Kusturica, a huge football fan, choosing anything else on a Sunday afternoon over watching Maradona dribble and outsmart his opponents on the pitch. His desire to be close to the still-charismatic Maradona is palpable throughout the documentary. In making the film, the two had to rely on the constant murmuring of interpreters. But in another sense, their communication was conducted through a flow of energy emanating from the director's need to create a space where the two would coexist.[16] In that sense, the promise to make a film about the real Maradona leads back to Kusturica's creation of the world in which they converge and in which the idolised Maradona would acknowledge his existence. The film's poster reflects this psychodynamic: a human-sized, human-shaped (yet three-dimensional) Kusturica stands in front of huge painted mural – a two-dimensional Maradona in an iconic portrait. The "real Maradona" that Kusturica promised to bring to the screen is nothing but a spectre of his own desire to conjure up a more just world according to his vision. Placing Maradona in the centre of that vision helps him justify his own restorative project.

The film's original title, which the director had announced together with the footballer three years earlier at the Cannes Film Festival, was *Don't Forget*

*Fiorito*. But by the time the film was finished, he had not only forgotten Fiorito but had replaced the name of Maradona's birthplace with Maradona's own name. Furthermore, much as Dujovne Ortiz had done, Kusturica injects himself into the title emphasising his role as a creator of the footballer. While Dujovne Ortiz had been unable to resist the footballer's magnetism (and tears) in 1993, Kusturica in 2008 reimagines himself as a "Maradona of cinema". In the documentary's very first scene, the director is playing a guitar, performing with his band at a concert in Buenos Aires; he is introduced as "Señor Diego Armando Maradona from the world of cinema".[17] He later goes through his own filmography to conclude, rather forcefully, that Maradona could have been the hero of at least three of his films. Kusturica's documentary fuses what-has-been with what-could-have-been to transcend the spatio-temporal boundaries of his and Maradona's respective countries. By representing a series of geopolitical parallelisms and similar historical patterns of inequality sustained within each of their nations and their disadvantaged relationship with Western powers and the International Monetary Fund, Kusturica's use of the concept of justice seems to take the form of a call for an ever-elusive freedom and equality rather than to stress the responsibility of individuals.

*Maradona by Kusturica* repeatedly intercuts the documentary's fable of Maradona's political engagement with scenes from the remarkable anti-autocratic films that had originally made the director famous, including *When Father Was Away on Business* (1985). "It wouldn't be hard to imagine Diego playing the father who atones for his adultery in prison during politically turbulent times" (Kusturica, 2008: 1.43), he contends in a voiceover as his band welcomes onstage the real Maradona with the ethno music that is their signature sound. While there is a romantic betrayal in the plot of the film, the narrator's father is not a political rebel; he has been condemned to a harsh internment camp because he had once made a laconic negative comment about an anti-Stalinist cartoon, back when the Tito-led Yugoslav Federation had distanced itself from the Soviet Union to pursue a more independent political and economic path. Later in the documentary, when Maradona and Kusturica are riding a private train headed to Mar del Plata for the protest against the Summit of the Americas, where a US-backed free market agreement was to be signed, the scene of the father returning from the gulag-like camp is interjected. The Yugoslavs' historic "No" to the Stalinist Soviet Union in 1948, background to Kusturica's feature film, is in no way comparable to Maradona's performative and highly rhetorical "No" to the superpowers arriving to sign the treaty portrayed in the documentary. And although during the train ride Kusturica nostalgically remembers his childhood, there is no real comparison between the imaginary poverty of his Sarajevo neighbourhood in the 1970s and Maradona's slum of Fiorito, where kids are forced to search through mountains of garbage looking for something to eat.

Kusturica's film on Maradona is a fantasy project that strives to intersect their professional and family lives. The director is not only eager to incorporate Maradona as a character in his cinematic fictions but also to connect their private spheres: he brings the footballer into his family and is thrilled that his mother gets a chance to talk to Maradona on the phone the day before she dies. While in Buenos Aires, Kusturica is introduced to the footballer's parents, daughters, and former wife. He further embeds himself into the footballer's story by bringing him to the Red Star stadium and restaging the goal Maradona scored against the Belgrade team in 1982. The director neglects to foreground that nine-year-old Maradona's first football team was called Estrella Roja [Red Star], but he does bring Maradona to recount every move he made before scoring for Barcelona, in a game he played a quarter of a century earlier: as Maradona remembers how he entered the box, how he dummied a defender and went past the goalkeeper, the doppelgänger-like director mimics his gestures in awe. Maradona then assists the director by tapping the ball ever so perfectly that Kusturica strikes and clips the ball into the back of the net (Kusturica, 2008: 37.13). Over the ethno-Balkan rhythms of his band's music of the soundtrack, Kusturica becomes Maradona! And when the two sit down on the empty bleachers where once spectators had been unable to contain their roaring excitement, Maradona kisses Kusturica's hand and the director kisses him back, thus sealing the celluloid moment.

Kusturica's desire to edit and direct his own vision of reality does not end with this documentary. Maradona tattooed on his body two-dimensional images of Che Guevara and Castro, but Kusturica has built an entire town (named after himself) and created a three-dimensional world of the very same fighters for social justice. The streets and squares in Küstendorf reflect the founder's personal (and quite patriarchal) mythology of the just world: there is a Maradona square, a Che Guevara Street, and a Castro housing complex. Kusturica is the sole demi-urge of this ethno-nationalist Disney/Hollywoodesque town that grew out of an illusion, a set he constructed in 2004 for the film *Life is a Miracle*. The town of Küstendorf intends to display Serbian identity as it would have been without five centuries of Ottoman occupation, in a fictional space not unlike the montage where Maradona's and the director's lives intersect.

## Maradona as a spectral presence in the arena of justice

It is impossible to do justice to the spectres of Maradona. Critics tried in vain even before his untimely death and have been no more successful since. Neither Maradona's alleged autobiography, nor the semi-fictional accounts, nor the affective narrative and cinematographic texts in which others tried to capture him could ever properly conjure him up. Undisciplined and playful, proud, rebellious, and without humility, creative and spontaneous, arrogant, deceitful when he deemed appropriate, he evades language, either written or visual, because the imagined Maradona is the representation of human desire – and is, as such, spectral and elusive. As he moved the ball, dribbled, and scored goals, he was in some sense besieged not only by the players he routinely outsmarted but also by himself and by all the others that were attracted by his magnetism. Following the example set in his own autobiography, where he often refers to himself in the third person (thus effectively introducing himself as a ghostly other), writers, filmmakers, and sports journalists have persisted in summoning his spectral presence, incorporating him into their stories and situating him in the arena of justice. These authors conjure him up in the genres that are most familiar to them – sports (auto)biographies, novels, films – and keep Maradona-as-apparition, close at hand in the disjunction of times. They talk to him, enable him to talk back to them, and they all, without exception, find joy in projecting their own dreams and desires onto various fantasied versions of the football star. These Argentinians and Serbs seem to share the same perception of injustice and they offer the spectral footballer compassionate, redemptive, and reparative fictional frames in which justice can be enacted. As Alabarces and Rodríguez aptly put it: "We see Maradona as if he were fighting in the Third World's corner against inequality, injustice, and the concentration of power and money in the hands of the few. He is seen as a Father Christmas-type figure, capable of making all our wishes come true" (1996: 46). The narratives analysed in this chapter resonate the idea of justice, somewhat framed, as compromise and negotiation with Maradona as chief executor.

Together, we all make up an emotional community centred around these shared spectres. As for Maradona, he will haunt us all from beyond the portals of death: perhaps from the 1000-peso banknotes, or from the holy pages of his autobiography, or even from the streets of Küstendorf.

## Notes

1  I dedicate this essay to my brother Miško Bilbija, who never tired of explaining to me the invisible intricacies of football.
2  This undue neglect of Dujovne Ortiz's work might be explained by inadequate marketing, but may also point to existing divisions among Argentinian intellectuals over Maradona.
3  Maradona's relationship with the power structure was perennially conflictive and arguably inconsistent in terms of his political orientation. For example, he embraced the free market ideology of the president Menem's (1989–1999) Minister of Economy Domingo Cavallo (1991–1996), while also publicly supporting the socialist politics of Cuban president Fidel Castro. Maradona's relationship with Carlos Menem was equally complex.
4  Dujovne Ortiz is referencing a well-known scandal related to Maradona's televised arrest in his Buenos Aires apartment on April 26, 1991. It was a federal sting operation for the alleged possession and distribution of a pound of cocaine, but the amount was later scaled down to a few ounces, and the judge who was originally in charge of his case was replaced without a plausible explanation. All these unknowns further fuelled the conspiracy theories regarding the reasons for the footballer's arrest.
5  Maradona was suspended in the 1994 World Cup after having tested positive for ephedrine (a medical drug, but not cocaine or similar). Ephedrine was banned at the time but is no longer a forbidden substance for FIFA.
6  In an earlier article on Maradona where I examine reactions of the Argentinian political left to his expulsion from the 1994 World Cup, I argue that he is at once the product, the consumer, and an embodiment of the postmodern (Bilbija, 1995: 205).
7  A fascinating account of Maradona's fall and the way the Argentinian nation experienced it appears in Burgo and Wall's book length account.

8 *Innocent* was prominently featured at the 1995 Buenos Aires Book Fair, one of the most important annual literary events in the Spanish-speaking world. Maradona attended the publisher's book fair promotional event.

9 I am particularly referring to Salazar Sutil's brilliant and timely article (2008) in which he analyses Maradona as a market currency.

10 The book topped the bestseller lists by selling over 200,000 copies per week in each of the first three weeks after publication. Eighteen books (fourteen in Spanish, three in English, and one in Italian) on Maradona's life and career had been published between 1992 and 2002 (Chaván de Matviuk, 2005: 18–19).

11 The entire chapter 7, "Los amigos, los enemigos", from the Spanish original has been omitted in the English version of the book. "Yo soy la voz de los sin voz, la voz de mucha gente que se siente representada por mí, yo tengo un micrófono delante de mí y ellos en su puta vida podrán tenerlo" (82).

12 Maradona did stand up for the football players in fighting the ruling elite of FIFA, organisation he identified with criminal workings of the mafia.

13 See https://www.youtube.com/watch?v=oMBbqvs5PYo. In the book's next paragraph, Maradona mentions River Plate goalkeeper Ubaldo "Pato" Fillol who did refuse to shake hands with Admiral Lacoste (28). It is also worth mentioning here that after the Argentinian team won the 1978 World Cup, their coach César Luis Menotti, along with all the Dutch players, also refused to shake hands with the junta's generals.

14 That we may see Maradona's face and signature – instead of the red ovenbird, designated as a national bird and famous for its strong legs – on the widely circulated Argentinian 1000-peso banknote is telling. Even more curious, if Senator Norma Durango's proposal passes, is that the bill's reverse side would feature an image of one of Maradona's most famous goals. While it is still not clear which one of the two 1986 Mexico World Cup goals against England would be featured, the illegal or the legal one, there are Argentinians who hope it would be the "Hand of God" goal (*Reuters*, 2020). https://thefrontierpost.com/Argentinian-senator-wants-maradona-on-countrys-bank-notes/ [Accessed on January 3, 2021].

15 Dan Rookwood, "Maradona Finishes on a Personal High". *The Guardian*. November 10, 2001. https://www.theguardian.com/football/2001/nov/10/sport.comment [Accessed on January 3, 2021].

16 This was done despite numerous frustrations over the Maradona's engagement with the project.

17 In *Super 8 stories*, Kusturica is introduced as "Sergio Leone on guitar".

## References

Alabarces, Pablo and María Graciela Rodríguez, 1996. *Cuestión de pelotas*. Buenos Aires: Editorial Atuel.

Arfuch, Leonor. 2020. *Memory and Autobiography: Explorations at the Limits*. Cambridge: Polity Press.

Bilbija, Ksenija. 1995. "Maradona's Left: Postmodernity and National Identity in Argentina". *Studies in Latin American Popular Culture* 14: 199–208.

Chaván de Matviuk, Marcela A. 2005. *The Social Influence of Sport's Celebrities: The Case of Diego Maradona* (Unpublished Doctoral Dissertation). Regent University, United States. UMI Number: 3212119.

Dujovne Ortiz, Alicia. 1993. *Maradona soy yo*. Buenos Aires: Emecé.

Freud, Sigmund. 1985 [1904]. "Psychopathic Characters on the Stage". *Pelican Freud Library*, 14. Ed. A. Dickson. Art and Literature London: Penguin.

Giardinelli, Mempo. 1994. "El video del adiós". Buenos Aires: *Noticias de la semana*. July 3, 77–79.

Grondona, Mariano. 1994. "Como un héroe trágico que se autodestruye". *Clarín*. July 1, 40.

Koller, Christian and Fabian Brandle. 2015. "Football and Dictatorship". *Goal! A Cultural and Social History of Modern Football*. Washington, DC: The Catholic University of America Press, 200–237.

Kusturica, Emir. 2008. *Maradona by Kusturica*. Pentagrama Films. 90 min. https://vimeo.com/72205757

Magalhães Britto, Simone. 2014. "The Hand of God, the Hand of the Devil: A Sociological Interpretation of Maradona's Hand Goal". *Soccer & Society* 15.5: 671–684. https://www.tandfonline.com/doi/full/10.1080/14660970.2012.753535

Maradona, Diego. 2005. *The Autobiography of Soccer's Greatest and Most Controversial Star*. New York: Skyhorse Publishing.

N.A. "Maradona". 1996. *El Gráfico*. 4006, March 26, 87.

Niembro, Fernando and Julio Llinás. 1995. *Inocente*. Barcelona: Grijalbo Mondadori.

Nash, Nathaniel. 1994. "Argentina Is Booming but There Is No Rest For Its Tortured Soul". *The New York Times*. July 17, 4.

Nussbaum, Martha C. 1995. *Poetic Justice*. Boston: Beacon Press.

Reuters. 2020. "Argentinian Senator Wants Maradona on Country's Bank Notes". *The Frontier Post*. December 8. https://thefrontierpost.com/Argentinian-senator-wants-maradona-on-countrys-bank-notes/

Rookwood, Dan. 2001. "Maradona Finishes on Personal High". *The Guardian*. November 10. https://www.theguardian.com/football/2001/nov/10/sport.comment

Salazar-Sutil, Nicolás. 2008. "Maradona Inc.: Performance Politics Off the Pitch". *International Journal of Cultural Studies* 11.4: 441–458.

# 10

# THE MARADONA STORY

## Tropes in Biography and Autobiography

*Alan Tomlinson*

### Life writing: Granite and rainbow

Diego Armando Maradona played at four FIFA World Cup tournaments: Spain 1982, Mexico 1986, Italia 1990, and USA 1994. From the second of these, he emerged with a truly enhanced reputation, however, controversial. In 1982, he was sent off for foul play in a game against Brazil; in 1990, he dragged his damaged ankles onto the pitch to help haul an unconvincing Argentinian team to the final match; in 1994, his manic comeback was short-lived when a positive doping test resulted in his expulsion from the competition. But in 1986, his performance scripted a mythology that has dominated the selective memories of generations of football fans and watchers. His tongue-in-cheek yet seriously intended reference to his "Hand of God" goal in the quarter-final game against England, followed by his sublime slalom through the thinning ranks of the English defence for a second goal have shaped the hermeneutic narrative of the man.

Maradona – both on and off the field – has generated responses across the range from positive plaudits to extreme negativity. Writing after the death of Maradona in November 2020, Tim Vickery, the BBC's expert on Latin American football, emphasises the positive side: "Immortalised will be the Maradona of Mexico '86, Diego at the peak of his powers, reaching a level of play in the closing stages of the competition that may never have been seen before or since" (Vickery, 2021: 24). Much earlier, and more negatively, English novelist Martin Amis had referred to what he calls the moral vacuousness of Maradona's "startling inner chaos—acute and chronic flaws of character and judgement, and above all a self-knowledge that remains persistently absentee" (Amis, 2004).

Amis was reviewing the English translation of Maradona's autobiography *El Diego*, which was published in Spanish in 2000, marking the footballer's continuing presence in the public eye at the opening of the new millennium.

DOI: 10.4324/9781003196587-14

Amis adjudged the book to be both "operatically emotional" and "exception-
ally vivid" and conceded that it was a compelling narrative: "the reader is …
wholly seduced by the story and by the turbulent naivety with which Maradona
tells it." *Naiveté* runs throughout the book, culminating in childlike accounts
and reflections on meetings with his idol Fidel Castro, and musings on his hero
Che Guevara, a tattoo of whom decorated his right upper arm. In the book's
last words, Maradona claims that he has always been honest about everything:
"I am the same as always" (Maradona, 2004: 286). This may not be disingenuous,
but it is certainly contestable. Life-writing, in autobiography and biography, is a
matter of selection, balance, and tone. Eduardo Archetti, for instance, prioritises
"the examination of concrete performances" (Archetti, 2001: 154) in his anthro-
pologically insightful analysis of the player's cultural significance as a symbolic
national icon of Argentina, representing the precocious genius of the young kid,
the *pibe*, who is also self-taught in the *potrero* that is seen as a space or territory for
the expression of creativity and freedom (156).

In this chapter, I focus upon two themes in the Maradona narrative: his footballing prowess — what Archetti would call "concrete performances" — at the
Mexico 1986 World Cup; and his need, time and again, to escape the limelight
of his global celebrity in the simple, pastoral setting of his parents' hometown.
In this, I draw primarily upon the autobiography and Jimmy Burns biography
of Maradona's playing days (2010). More generally, I also acknowledge *motifs* in
the Maradona story that have accumulated metaphorical power in the form of
tropes that have shaped interpretations of aspects of and moments in his life. As
appropriate, I draw upon debates concerning life-writing and the distinctive-
ness of autobiography as articulated in the emergent field of the philosophy of
autobiography (Cowley, 2015), and the seminal work of Stephen Greenblatt on
self-fashioning, identity formation, and the projection of the self (1984). My main
analytical framework, nevertheless, is taken from the methodological reflections
of Virginia Woolf.

Woolf, writing in *The New York Herald Tribune* in 1927, distinguished between
the "granite-like" solidarity of established truths – the hard facts of life-writing –
and the "rainbow-like intangibility" of a life as lived and recalled by a particular personality (Woolf, 1958: 149). Woolf points to "voice or laughter … curse
or anger … any trace that this fossil was once a living man" (151) as elements
that must complement established truths. And to achieve "the perpetual marriage of granite and rainbow" the biographer or life-writer must pursue a "queer
amalgamation of dream and reality" (155). There are numerous biographies of
Maradona, including an early insightful account by Rodrigo Fernández and
Denise Nagy, emphasising the Hand of God theme and the godlike genius of his
boots (Fernández and Nagy, 1994); more recently, Guillem Balagué's admirable
analysis of his life (and death) has shown how the subject's "personality, defined
in psychiatric classifications as bipolar, dominated his decisions" (Balagué, 2021:
xviii). The two main sources used in this chapter to consider the earlier years
of the Maradona case are, though, the player's autobiography *El Diego* (2000),

authored with two co-writers, Daniel Arcucci and Ernesto Cherquis Bialo, referred to as *ED* from now on; and Jimmy Burns' *Maradona: The Hand of God* (1996), *MHoG* from now on. These texts represent, respectively, the subjective "truths" of the individual subject, and the objective "truths" of the disinterested investigative journalist/professional writer. Initially, I summarise the content and styles of the two books, referring to complementarities and ruptures in the narrative. I will then be pointing to the granite and the rainbow in each of these accounts *cum* narratives, seeking to identify the balance between reality and fiction that so often shapes the renditions of the life of a sporting celebrity.

## Documenting two ways: Biography and autobiography

Jimmy Burns' book comprises 23 chapters and amounts to more than 100,000 words taking the reader from the poverty-riven origins of Maradona to the turbulent years of his meteoric rise to the apex of world football and global celebrity. The chapters are pithy and focused, anchored in assiduously assembled evidence and testimony from a wide range of figures and sources. From the beginning, Burns emphasises the framework of his study. It is not conceived as an exploration of the subject's footballing qualities:

> My main concern has been to investigate Maradona as a unique social, political and religious phenomenon ... I have tried to go beyond the Maradona of the football screens and to shed some light on the myths and the vested interests that have surrounded him throughout his career, from the superstitions and the political intrigues of his native Argentina to the complicities of doctors and football authorities in the World Cup.
>
> *Burns MHoG (xii)*

To connect the social, political, and religious dimensions of the Maradona story is a mammoth undertaking, and in doing this Burns compiles a full cast list of characters, some even from within the footballer's own circle, whose actions, views, and influences flavour the narrative throughout. Burns seeks evidence of many kinds in looking to link the social and political elements of the narrative.

The depth of analysis in Burns' book allows him to establish themes, return to them and pick up an interpretive narrative as the events and stories about Maradona continue to accumulate. An excellent example is Chapter 16, on his triumphant moment leading Argentina to victory over England in the 1986 World Cup in Mexico: Entitled "Falklands Round Two", it gives a wider socio-cultural context to the Hand of God moment than could any descriptive account of the on-field action in the match itself.

In *ED*, Maradona's 13 chapters are really 11, followed by a twelfth chapter, the longest in the book, entitled "At a Glance - My Loved Ones: the Stars" made up of a list of 100 player vignettes and commentaries on his favourite figures in other sports; also, "not from the world of sport" (277), he opines on the celebrity who most impressed him, Fidel Castro. The book concludes with a pithy self-acclaiming and self-asserting afterwords. The 11 chapter titles are all made up of two words, each one a definite article followed by a single noun. They set the tone of a predictable narrative of rise, fall, and survival, with fluctuating claims of self-justification, victimisation, and self-sacrifice. The Maradona *patois* is prominent. He talks of "vaccinating" football opponents when a goal is scored, with reverberations of sexual domination in some of its uses; he refers to people whom he considers to be in the wrong or stupid as "thermos-heads"; and uses a metaphor to speak of anyone – including himself, in confessional references to his own actions – who does not act decisively or take control of the situation: "letting the tortoise get away". The chapter titles take us on a roller-coaster tour of his life: beginning, explosion, passion, frustration, resurrection, glory, struggle, *vendetta*, comebacks, pain, and farewell. "Comebacks" is the only plural here, amplifying the instances of potential restoration if not rehabilitation in attempts in his later thirties to get back to the glory days of his playing peak. His written farewell in the text is a simple assertion, "I'm me, Maradona. I am El Diego" (286), saying everything and nothing in a final and defiant proclamation.

Incidents and themes covered in both books are recalled in the selected, and selective, detail of the autobiographer and the biographer. In the chapter "Coping with Coke" in the Burns book, Maradona's behavioural excesses during his short spell playing for Spanish side Sevilla are seen to soon alienate the population of the city, generating a magazine exposé of his "leadership" of his team-mates on an excursion to a local brothel after a match in June 1993; Maradona's inability to manage any acceptable level of fitness and performance had led the club manager Carlos Bilardo, his key mentor in earlier years, to substitute him during the match against the Burgos team. The player's response was to jostle Bilardo, call him a "son of a bitch", and in the changing room later the two were said to have exchanged blows. Burns relates how Bilardo – talking somewhat reluctantly about the flare-up – travelled from Sevilla to Madrid, where Maradona had bolted to after the incident, to make peace with his temperamental superstar. Bilardo recalls that they started talking, "said what they wanted to say to each other and then we agreed to put it behind us" (*MHoG*, 212). Maradona has his own version of the encounter: "Bilardo took me off against Burgos and I left the pitch swearing at him. Later we beat the shit out of each other" (*ED*, caption to photograph between 206 and 207). Maradona's account dramatises the encounter, highlighting his rebellious intolerance of authority and his role as protagonist; Burns provides a more widely informed perspective on the incident including, crucially, the voice of the target of the footballer's anger. As Somogy Varga has noted, autobiographical memories are malleable, and self-knowledge can mesh with self-deception in the cycles of recollection of the autobiographer. Unintentional self-deception is likely, Varga adds, where "solid evidence is lacking" (2015: 152). In the account of his spat with his club manager, Maradona could well be deceiving himself on the nature of the dispute; his own selective memory operates as a form of self-deception, even self-denial, both intentionally and unintentionally.

In the following sections, I consider my two selected themes – common to both the Burns and the Maradona narratives – demonstrating how biographical analysis and the autobiographical account respectively balance or portray elements of granite and rainbow in the depiction of Maradona's life.

## The Hand of God

In the quarter-final match between Argentina and England in Mexico in 1986 Maradona scored the two goals that have contributed the most to shape the myth of the man as a global icon in the consciousness of football fans worldwide – and perhaps felt most intensely by those from England. The first goal originated from a series of mishaps. A pass by Maradona was intercepted by English defender Hodge, dangerously hooking the ball back towards his goal. What followed was undeniably a memorable leap by the Argentinian star, his left knee level with the English goalkeeper Shilton's upper thigh, his raised left arm almost at the same height as the flailing arm and clenched fist of the goalkeeper. Maradona, with a flick of the neck, mimed a headed contact as he guided the ball into the net with his left fist. The caption to the photograph of the incident included in *ED* combines deliberate provocation with streetwise arrogance: "The Hand of God, eh … Not even the photographers managed to capture what really happened. And Shilton jumping with his eyes shut was outraged! I like the goal. I almost like it as much as the other one. I felt I was pickpocketing the English" (78–79). This constitutes a disingenuous confession as to his intent and sly opportunism in handling the ball toward the goal (in the Spanish original, Maradona used the phrase *robando la billetera*, or "stealing the wallet" – there is no equivalent in Spanish to the verb "to pickpocket"). On the pitch, he had no intention of owning up to his indiscretion, sprinting over to his teammates to celebrate in a collective euphoric moment. Four minutes on he performed his one-man-show against a shell-shocked English defence for his second and celebrated goal. On Maradona's death, Terry Fenwick, one of the five English defenders that the player had dribbled through, recollected the experience: "Initially I was bitter and twisted" at the Hand of God act, "it was handball, a free kick to England. We thought we had the better 11 players on the field, but they had the world's greatest player. He was the difference. This fella was unbelievable. Give him the ball and he'd destroy you … He was built like you wouldn't believe. He was a pit bull and he came back for more all the time … He knew he was better than the rest. What a player" (PA Staff, 2020).

Maradona's individual motivation before the England game was, in his own account, framed by the Falkland/Malvinas War in April–June 1982, lifting the game to a symbolic level way beyond that of a single football match: "More than defeating a football team it was defeating a country … we knew a lot of Argentinian kids had died there, shot down like little birds. This was revenge.

It was like recovering a little bit of the Malvinas. In the pre-match interviews we had all said that football and politics shouldn't be confused, but that was a lie. We did nothing but think about that. Bollocks was it just another match!" (*ED*, 127–128). Yet in Maradona's reflections on the build-up to the 1982 World Cup in Spain, which coincided with the Malvinas conflict, his preoccupation was his intensifying disillusionment with his fan base in Argentina, and the inappropriate preparatory schedule for the finals: "We believed that we were already there, that it would be easy. But there was something else, something crucial: our physical preparation was terrible … I reached the '82 World Cup tired, overtrained. Dead" (60). There is scant evidence of his concerns about the Malvinas/Falklands conflict at the time, such as its consequences for the national team and the morale and motivation of the players. In the statement about what motivated the players prior to the England game four years later in Mexico, history is not so much embellished as wiped from memory.

Maradona comes clean in *ED* on the Hand of God goal itself: "Now I feel I am able to say what I couldn't then. At the time I called it 'the hand of God'. Bollocks was it the hand of God, it was the hand of Diego!" (130). The player recalls his celebrations, too; the linesman running back to start-up position at the middle of the pitch, and his own rush towards where his father was seated. The scorer was "celebrating with my left fist outstretched and watching what the linesmen were up to out of the corner of my eye. The ref could have cottoned on to that and suspected something was up" (130). With the England players protesting, teammate Valdano "was giving me the *shhh!* with a finger over his lips" (130) and Maradona recalls his relief that the referee appeared not to notice anything suspicious. The following year he could tell a BBC journalist that the controversial first goal was "one hundred per cent legitimate because the referee allowed it and I'm not one to question the honesty of the referee" (130).

In the Burns biography, the Hand of God goal is contextualised in the broader context of the war. During the conflict (early April to mid-June 1982) the Argentinians' military government, and the heavily censored media, broadcast nationalist slogans championing the invasion of the islands and ran these alongside images and scenes of the country's World Cup victory of 1978. Argentinians' intelligence services designed leaflets in the early phase of the war when Argentina played the Soviet Union in a "friendly" fixture in Buenos Aires on April 14, 1982: one such leaflet depicted "a cartoon baby gaucho—not unlike a child Maradona—dressed in football kit and accepting the surrender of an imperial British lion" (*MHoG*, 91). Burns adds that Argentinian journalists were encouraged by the political regime to report on military matters as if they were little more than sporting encounters, so disconnecting "with the reality of war and to confuse soldiers with footballers" (91). In mid-April Maradona walked away from the national World Cup squad after being substituted in the match against the Soviet Union, though in May of 1982 when he re-joined the squad the players posed for a team photograph behind a banner proclaiming:

"LAS MALVINAS SON ARGENTINAS" (89). Whatever the player's claims about not being motivated by political concerns, his actions as closely scruti-nised by Burns were exploited as forms of propaganda by the military dicta-torship. For example, General Leopoldo Galtieri, the country's last military dictator/president from December of 1981 to June the following year, visited the Argentinian World Cup squad on February 21, 1982, singling out and embrac-ing Maradona (85). By mid-1982 though "the government had lost its power to intimidate" and during the World Cup in Spain the Argentinians' squad was, as media reported, "poorly motivated, lacking discipline and leisurely to the point of hedonism" (94). The national team manager, César Luis Menotti, was photographed leaving his "sleeping quarters" with his arm wrapped around a German model (95). Maradona was ensconced in his own set-up in a hotel filled with his girlfriend Claudia Villafañe, his parents, and a group of other relatives and friends – what was labelled the "clan", seen by observers as constraints on Maradona's professional obligations. The World Cup ended in disappointment for the defending champions.

Four years later in Mexico, the sting of the double humiliation of 1982 – ignominy on the pitch for the football team, defeat for the nation in the Falklands conflict – motivated Maradona to lead his team to a World Cup triumph that he justified as a form of "divine intervention" (163). Back in Buenos Aires after the tournament, he rode from the airport to the main bal-cony of the presidential palace, the country's civilian president Raul Alfonsín exploiting the team's success in showing off the trophy to thousands of ecstatic fans gathered in the Plaza de Mayo square (165). Less than a year after his Hand of God moment, Maradona revelled in the fan worship of SSC Napoli's first national championship. After this, it was to be a downward spiral for him in a protracted decline defined by denial, excess, and fantastical self-legitimation over a period of ten years.

The account of the Hand of God moment by Jimmy Burns draws upon a range of sources: government documents produced as political propaganda; interviews with a range of subjects who had contact with Maradona; media cov-erage of the Argentina-England game; players' and coaches' written accounts of the events and achievements that shaped the myth. The accounts in *ED* are the outpourings of a single individual that could also be read as a list of Maradona's character traits: visceral, vulgar, triumphant, cocky, mocking, egotistical, and megalomaniacal in equal measure, a rich and heady mix of emotions, preju-dices, and proclamations serving as a form of self-fashioning – "the fashioning of human identity as a manipulable, artful process" (Greenblatt, 1984: 2).

Burns provides the granite in the Maradona story, facts blended with inter-pretations of material artefacts. The player's autobiography does not deal in facts or evidence; his memories prioritise fantasy and emotion, fuelling the presenta-tion of his personality in an assertion of the power of the self. He creates a world of overlapping actions and aspirations, shooting from the lip and spouting allegations in any direction in which he may be facing, celebrating his dream achievements and sublime moments. Reading *ED* is entertaining, exhausting, exasperating, and emotionally draining. The reader can lose patience with the style, the sheer volume of the Maradona's voice raging inside his/her head in interpretive responses also in part shaped by the expectations of the reader as well as the cultural background of the author(s). Reading *MHoG* we join Jimmy Burns in a narrative that weighs and balances contextual factors and thus lends his account a hermeneutic credibility that the individualised and self-asserting perspectives of *ED* never permit. Yet the respective accounts of the Hand of God are in a way complementary, the Burns book providing the granite (the evidence-based factual material of the biographer), the Maradona life-story embodying the rainbow (the passions and personality of the autobiographer), including self-knowledge and self-deception.

## Home

Maradona's story began early when his precocious skills of ball-juggling attracted not just local talent-spotters and team managers, but the local and regional press and audio-visual media. He was born on October 30, 1960, in Lanús, a working-class area in the greater Buenos Aires urban conurbation, and raised in the nearby poor neighbourhood of Villa Fiorito that was home to many Spanish and Italian descendants. He was the fifth child of his mother, known familiarly as La Tota, and his father Don Diego (nicknamed Chitoro, merging the words for "friend" and "bull"); they had met in their hometown of Esquina, in the Corrientes province, a 604-kilometre drive from Buenos Aires. His father was of mestizo cultural heritage and his mother of Italian ancestry. Esquina – in English, "corner" – was a town of hunters and fishermen with families living in a riverside rural setting. Football was a welcome, cheap, and accessible form of leisure. Lured to the capital city by the persisting promises of the populist regime of Juan and Eva Perón, the couple moved to Buenos Aires in pursuit of a better life described to them by family members who had already moved to the city. Their dream remained elusive, and the young Diego was raised in what was essentially a squatter's shack comprising three box-like rooms separated by sack curtains rather than doors. Maradona's father arrived in Buenos Aires in 1955, forsaking his life as a boatman – and the fishing, barbecues, and football – for work in the big city, for a better-paid job. Maradona commented wryly: "Job is a loose description; he worked in a Tritumol mill pounding cattle bones from four in the morning to three in the afternoon" (*ED*, 5). The job promised to his mother did not last long, and his father traded a life on the river grazing cows in local pastures for a soulless job in the big city, decimating the bodies of the very creatures that he had previously tended. This was home to the precocious football destined to become a star, but it was not to become the "home" to which he fled at the most stressed moments of his adult life.

In such moments, Maradona testifies to the need to leave the world of superstardom and celebrity, to escape to a simpler bucolic past, and that need was fulfilled in his flights to Esquina. Prior to the 1982 World Cup, after a series of international friendly games in which his mediocre performances attracted the hostility of the fans, he explains: "I went to Esquina, the land of my parents, seeking out my roots. I went up the River Corrientes, the Paraná Miní, through the places that only my old man and his mates were capable of wandering into without getting lost" (59). He adds that he was comforted by the company of his girlfriend, Claudia, his brothers, and his friends – "they were my lifelong friends, from Esquina" – travelling the river, sailing, and fishing with them, and spending a lot of time thinking. A phrase "stayed in my soul: 'People have to understand that Maradona isn't a happiness-making machine'. It was time to think about myself, and Spain was calling" (59). Perhaps he was fantasising if not fabricating here; it is difficult to believe that he had any lifelong friends from Esquina given that he was born and grew up in a Buenos Aires suburb. In identifying with such a place, reporting lifelong friendships that are diffi-cult to corroborate, Maradona could emphasise another element also pointed out by Greenblatt as characteristic of his subjects from the English Renaissance: the "profound mobility" (Greenblatt, 1984: 7), both social and economic, that underpinned the construction of their identities. In the player's case, this consti-tuted a trajectory from the parochial, pastoral outpost of his parents' *pueblo* to the urban settings of his own country, life in Spain and Italy, and decades of football celebrity across the world.

Maradona does not hold back from his nostalgic celebrations of the home-town of his parents. Recalling his early days playing for Boca Juniors after his transfer from Argentinos, he reports on the 4-1 victory in his official debut against Talleres de Córdoba at the Bombonera, the stadium a dozen miles or so from his home neighbourhood, the club based in La Boca "where the myth of Maradona as the people's idol has endured the longest … the club he has always claimed as closest to his soul", as Burns notes (*MHoG*, 246). His first competitive game in February of 1981 for Boca was an exceptional event in his career: "I'd been through so much in such a short time that I had started to wonder if this moment would ever arrive: to be at the Bombonera, to win, to score. My par-ents had come down from Esquina to see me and so had my brother Lalo. The only one who missed it was my brother El Turco because he was performing in a *comparsa*, singing and dancing in a street parade" (*ED*, 43). Maradona casually drops this observation into the narrative, implying that his parents were back in Esquina, no doubt thanks to his own success and generosity. This is only a little detail, perhaps even an error of memory. Its effect though is to amplify the family connection with the humble rural township from which his parents had moved years before his birth in Buenos Aires. It reinforces the story of achievement and social mobility underlying the Maradona narrative. He can be both global superstar and local hero, a self-fashioning of identity sustaining his dual role as champion of the people and global celebrity.

In another pivotal moment of his football career, when things turned sour at Napoli in the summer of 1989 and he was agitating for a move to another club and another country, the home crowd turned on him. He claims that SSC Napoli had "forgotten, suddenly, everything I'd given them: the *scudetto*, after sixty years; the Copa Italia; the UEFA Cup, and their first ever European title. It seems they'd also forgotten that they'd paid me just over ten million and they'd already made over a hundred. In truth I was willing to throw grenades at their heads" (*ED*, 98). Maradona's response to what he perceived to be a personal affront was another trip to Esquina. Nonetheless, flights to a mythical past would not hold back the intensifying reports of his alleged connections with the drug trade and with the Camorra, the Neapolitan Mafia.

Esquina features in Burns' book much more extensively than it does in Maradona's autobiography. The Esquina of Maradona's parents is evoked in its cultural and economic characteristics, in the work and leisure lives of Maradona's father Chitoro, and his uncle, Cirilo; and the domestic chores and duties of his mother Tota. Chitoro's work was by all accounts a satisfying way of life but Tota "thought there was little to keep her in Esquina. Her Italian ancestors had come searching for a better life in Argentina, and she had yet to find it" (*MHoG*, 13). Aged twenty-one, Maradona's mother travelled to Buenos Aires in 1950 and got work as a domestic servant in the house of a rich family – "better paid drudgery than the voluntary domesticity of Esquina" (*MHoG*, 13). Two years later, when her husband's work was terminated given that commercial use of river transport was in decline, Tota believed that "survival lay in having her whole family join her in Buenos Aires" (*MHoG*, 13), and a far from enthusiastic Chitoro was persuaded to bring all the family to the city. Thus, the whole Maradona family left Esquina around eight years before the birth of Diego, leaving behind them a place depicted by Alicia Dujovne Ortiz as a community of mixed-race immigrants living pre-modern lives: the Corrientes cowmen are described as at one with their cattle; Maradona's chunky father Chitoro exhibits a bow-legged masculinity, his thick lips conveying African roots; his mother Tota, with Neapolitan roots, felt the humiliation of being a "short, *cabecita negra*" in the house of her "tall, white employers" when taking work in Buenos Aires (Dujovne Ortiz, 1993: 28). Dujovne Ortiz makes it clear that one legacy of his parents that Maradona inherited was the outsider status of his mixed-race (or, pejoratively, *cabecita*) lineage. Maradona would make much of the fact that he could speak on behalf of the marginal, the suppressed and the overlooked as he rose to prominence on the national and international stages. Direct experience of discrimination and poverty would become a powerful tool in his worldview. It allowed him to be perceived by fans as "one of them, yet above them" (Balagué, 335).

The depiction of the rural outpost nevertheless assumes great significance in the Burns biography. Following ecstatic, tense, and draining celebrations of Boca Juniors' championship triumph in August 1981, and relentless demands from both club and country, an injured and unfit Maradona – still only twenty years of age – needed to escape. His visit to Esquina with his parents in that summer is portrayed as a struggle for self-understanding "along the riverbank where his parents had been born, living the uncomplicated rural life" (*MHoG*, 81). Fishing and hunting, camping under the stars, and singing songs with companions around log fires, he sought or at least sampled a simpler way of life. He enjoyed casual kickabouts with locals, for sheer pleasure and with nothing at stake. Burns claims that on this trip "Maradona rediscovered the basic humanity he thought he had lost for ever" (81). In a poignant set of reflections prompted by the request of a local historian Maradona confirmed the attraction of Esquina as a place of solace or refuge from the incessant limelight and expectations of the city, his club, and the national side: "Esquina is beautiful, because I have relatives and friends here, because it is where my parents were born ... I love the river ... and the women are so straightforward and warm" (82). He did not escape completely though; the visit also coincided with the town's annual carnival, and Maradona was the focus of the celebrations.

In the spring of 1982, with World Cup pressures escalating, the footballer sought refuge again in his parents' birthplace. But his time he "acted like a man on the run, limiting his contact with the locals and aggressively rejecting any approaches from the local or national media" (87). He did though confide in one journalist, embittered at his deteriorating relationship with the wider football-following public: "People can't go on pressuring me the way they do in this country ... I'm not going to take the applause the way I did before ... I'm going to score goals for my teammates, for those who love me, and nobody else ... What the people have to understand is that Maradona is not a machine for making them happy. He is not a machine that gives kisses and smiles. I am a normal bloke" (88). Mixing first and third person responses, he berated a public that in fact was shaping his identity, framing his fame, and changing his life course. His third-person reference to the public figure of Maradona strengthens the claim that he is, as an individual, just like the next person. It is a plea to be recognised as such, to be left alone, and understood. His disillusion with his national public, however, did not stop him pursuing ambitions to play in Europe, authorising his manager to put in motion negotiations for the highest profile football transfer of its time, to Barcelona.

As mentioned above in Maradona's own account, the besieged superstar would return to Esquina in the summer of 1989, amid conflicts with Napoli and the once-devoted public now questioning his commitment to its cause. His erratic and aggressive behaviour with journalists and officials – stuffing a piece of newspaper into the mouth of a journalist who had written critically about him, for example, as described by Burns (176) – were alienating his support. Connections with the Camorra were also surfacing, and he hoped "by returning to his roots he could rediscover a sense of self. It was pure escapism, which did little to alleviate the growing tension he had left behind in Naples" (176). Of course, Esquina offered no effective escape and when he returned there once more with his parents in the summer of 1993, after an unsuccessful spell playing in Spain for Sevilla, the fishing, the avoidance of media, and the local kickabouts could not resolve his personal and professional problems. Esquina is a big theme in the Maradona story, a magnet for a romanticised solution to his problems when things got intolerably bad in the professional and public contexts that had made possible his career and reputation. But Esquina offered only the escape to a corner place, an edge, that could not offer any viable alternative to the location of the city and the attractions, trials and demands of metropolitan celebrity life. The town's real significance in the narrative of Maradona allows us to posit it as a trope in his story, a symbolic reference point to an imagined idyll of simpler living – an evocation of a home that never was, a community that for the player himself never existed, a constantly recurring dream of a return to an ideal.

The differences between Maradona's accounts of his returns to Esquina and Burns' take on those returns are telling: they cover common ground but the respective portrayals of the incidents and events take distinctive interpretive directions. In Maradona's version, Esquina provides a form of escape to an off-centre location where he re-imagines his upbringing and background, networks of family and friends, carving out opportunities to show that he is the "normal bloke" despite the profile of his celebrity self. For Burns, drawing upon testimonies and documentation to provide a fuller picture of the nature of Esquina as a community, and of the nature of his parents' early life in this "corner" space so remote from the modern urban setting, "Esquina" is a kind of code for Maradona's recurrent, elusive, and unsatisfied need for solace in a safe and trusted setting. It is a tragic inevitability that such a need cannot be met, as Burns's accounts illustrate so vividly.

## Tropes in search of a narrative

The "Maradona" persona is a multi-accentual source, spawning limitless readings: Maradona the Sublime for instance, brandishing the World Cup trophy in his right hand after the 3-2 defeat of a West Germany side that had levelled the score from a two-goal deficit, only to lose the final to an 85th minute winning goal crafted and assisted by Maradona himself. At the final whistle Maradona celebrated with an outburst of tears, a moment remembered in his autobiography: "I had cried at every moment of my career, and this was the best, the most sublime" (*ED*, 133); "the most sublime moment of my career, the most sublime. When I was there, the World Cup in my hands, I felt I was touching the sky; all my dreams had come true" (caption opposite 79). Maradona even added some reflections on the collective achievement of the team and recalled the modesty of the team's coach Carlos Bilardo. But in the world of Maradona things never keep still. In no time at all, his struggles become the dominant theme of his tales, and Maradona the Sublime seems like a different person, in a long-lost time and place, as the consequences of his professional and social life, and a drug dependency, close in on him. He turns himself at various points into Maradona the Victim, Maradona the Misunderstood, Maradona the Paranoid, Maradona the Rebel. His dreams and his reality coincided to produce his sublime moment in Mexico City on June 29, 1986, also generating other comparable moments of achievement in Argentina and Naples, Italy. But even those spellbinding and sublime moments are blemished by the Hand of God goal, generating Maradona the Cheat as a theme/trope that would also endure.

There are of course other themes that show the multiple balances and imbalances of granite and rainbow in his life story: a focus upon those around him, the money men who sought to profit from any dimension of the Maradona image conducive to marketing across the global economy; the political puppeteers who would present him to a fanatical public, putting him on display like a trophy of war; the hypocrites and hedonists in family and friendship networks who encouraged and indulged his individual excesses. However, and as Raymond Williams so convincingly demonstrated, to perform a cultural analysis we need to work with an awareness of three levels of culture: the "lived culture" of places and times; the recorded culture of a period, embracing "everyday facts"; and the level that connects the first two levels, "the culture of the selective tradition" (Williams, 1965: 66). Thus, this chapter selected two key themes in the Maradona story: his most perfect moment as a footballer, *en route* to winning the World Cup in Mexico in 1986, and the recurrent theme of flight to an imagined home and community, the place his parents had to leave to seek a better life than the marginalised rural township could offer the most high-profile football celebrity in the world.

As Portugal was eliminated from the UEFA's 2020 European Football Championship, Cristiano Ronaldo could nevertheless find some consolation in his continuing profile across global social media. As Barney Ronay (2021) put it, Ronaldo is "top of 'the Instagram rich list', according to a company called HopperHQ'", generating $1.6 million per post. Ronay focused also on absent A-listers who had also been eliminated from the championship arguing that this fact highlighted "a surprising thing about these surprising Euros. There aren't a lot of stars left". Instead, he observed, the players left have represented "collective effort, … chemistry and combinations … teams playing at the edge of their emotions and capacities". Without so many of its superstars in its later stages, Ronay labelled the Euros "a genuinely refreshing spectacle", a stripped-back event undermining the cult of celebrity. This could never be said of Maradona's time on the world football stage. Encouraged by passionate publics, legions of agents and commercial deal makers, politicians, and medical and health personnel of questionable reputation, he was an exhibit for his employers and a gift for a range of sponsors in pursuit of his brand. He was an artefact in himself ready-made for exploitation in an expanding commodification of the game. One way of understanding his career, then, is through a narrative of reciprocal exploitation of his sporting genius, his unapologetic persona, and his headline-grabbing indulgences; reciprocal because in so many ways Maradona was wholly complicit in the marketing of his image, or the demands on his playing time whatever the declining condition of his body. To sustain his bloated clan of close family and slippery sycophants, Maradona constantly needed the financial deals, the flattering entourage, and the media attention which he resented, to anchor his larger-than-life persona and *modus operandum*. On and off the football pitch he propelled himself to the centre of the stage, frequently creating controversies in melodramatic and hysterical fashion, unable or unwilling to hear voices of reason. Reading his claims to be telling it like it is he embodies what Virginia Woolf described as "that inner life of thought and emotion which meanders darkly and obscurely through the hidden channels of the soul" (150). Yet in his own words – and as reaffirmed by a myriad of peers, fans, writers, and commentators – he was undeniably a leading celebrity of his day, a one-off model of superstar celebrity in a globalised and expanding sporting media. Graeme Turner (2004: 137) argues that celebrity "has the potential to operate in ways that one might deplore or applaud, but neither potential is intrinsic". Such potential is also constructed and manipulated by interested parties, and Turner reminds us that celebrity as a component of our public culture is anchored in publicity and promotions, influences often overlooked by academic accounts; Maradona's profile represents a pivotal shift in the emergence of the global superstardom of the footballer, a profile sustained by the cultural economy of sporting celebrity (Smart, 2005).

Maradona's life was anchored in a wide socio-cultural context framed by the expanding parameters of popular culture and modes of consumption whereby people could gain previously available access to the sport spectacle and the stars at the heart of the spectacle. At his most prominent he was incontrovertibly a global superstar for millions of football fans worldwide, an enduring celebrity who could "enjoy a more durable career with the public" (Rojek, 2001: 20) than could the "celetoid", for whom celebrity status is "compressed, concentrated, attributed", and comparatively short-lived.

In the telling of his own story, Maradona negotiates balance between the granite and the rainbow in his life story. The dreams and the reality in the life can become wholly un-aligned, leaving him in a morass of manic allegations, author of a messy *mélange* of reminiscence, accusation, insult, abuse, and self-justification. There are ways of experiencing highs and lows, of balancing dreams and reality. It is a common parlance in stories of aspiration and mobility, and to dream of something and achieve it is to integrate dreams with reality. Without doubt he achieved his dreams in multiple ways; his "dual ambition in life" as expressed as an 11-year-old child prodigy performing his ball skills on a popular Saturday TV show was "to help win the League Cup [with his youth team], and to help win the World Cup" (*MHoG*, 20).

The Maradona story can also be understood, in large part, as an example of the use and exploitation of the celebrity footballer by social, political, and cultural forces beyond the control of the single individual. The celebrity brand of the individual is enhanced in "a close relationship between celebrity and the consumption of commodities" (Turner, 2004: 40). The Burns biography is rich in detail on such forces, tracking the financial and political operators, the cultural intermediaries and drug dealers who wanted their share of the Maradona phenomenon, and Maradona himself in his book is not slow to blame and condemn the politicians, the journalists, the financial advisers, the club managers, and coaches for the excesses for which from time to time he concedes are a matter of personal responsibility.

Woolf recognised the difficulties involved in reconciling or balancing the two core elements of life-writing, the challenge in "welding" solid truths with the intangible dimensions of personality (149); in essence, she observed, this is the primary aim of biography. She selected here a highly appropriate verb, one that evokes an image of a hard scientific process bringing together separate elements, creating a "harmonious unity" of the elements by diluting the core material(s), generating "one seamless whole", as she added. However, creating harmonious wholes of this kind has been an elusive, even impossible, task in biography writing. But there is hope in her analysis, for such wholes are not by any means fixed: "For in order that the light of personality may shine through, facts must be manipulated; some must be brightened; others shaded; yet, in the process, they must never lose their integrity" (150).

The decision whether to brighten or shade is therefore critical. In depictions of an individual biography or analysis of a selected phase of a longer life-course such decisions are frequently made, but there needs to be explicit recognition by the writer, or narrator/autobiographer, that such decisions are anchored in relative "truths" and carefully gathered evidence. Reading *El Diego* there is no room for nuance, no time for reflection; the Maradona voice, in its contradictions, inconsistencies, and tirades against perceived enemies drowns out any other perspective, tone, or presence. In reading *Maradona: The Hand of God* we enter a narrative drawing upon many voices. The lack of balance in the autobiography jeopardises the memory of Maradona's brilliant uniqueness. The Burns biography explains much of this, contextualising the excesses, evasions, and lies. The chaotic interplay of dream and reality in the life of Maradona is shown for what it was – a roller-coaster of celebrity excess alongside unforgettable, sublime moments of performance and achievements, showing us what the shanty-town kid could do in unapologetic torrents of assertion and revelation and unforgettable moments of performative genius, to bring smiles to the faces and memories to the lives of hundreds of millions of football followers throughout the world.

Christopher Cowley notes that narrative arcs shape the telling of life stories with the vicissitudes of success and failure frequently at the heart of the arc; but he adds that in the case of "more poignant" sport celebrities who retire "from competition, perhaps in their mid-twenties" and write an autobiography, many find that "several decades of obscurity await them" (Cowley, 2015: 10). Maradona's passion and ambitions fuelled several decades of sporting precocity and prowess, sustaining a celebrity persona that ensured that he would never be counted among these poignant cases. He himself provided the rainbow – the colour, the beauty, the transience, the unpredictability – that enlivens the granite – the hard truths, the corroborations, the documented evidence, the observable facts – of Burns's more contextually rich telling of the tale.

# References

Amis, Martin. 2004. "In Search of Dieguito". *The Guardian* (online). October 1. [Accessed June 7, 2021].

Archetti, Eduardo. 2001. "The Spectacle of a Heroic Life: The Case of Diego Maradona". *Sport Stars: The Cultural Politics of Sporting Celebrity*. Eds. David Andrews and Steven Jackson. London and New York: Routledge: 151–163.

Balagué, Guillem. 2021. *Maradona: The Boy. The Rebel. The God*. London: Orion.

Burns, Jimmy. 2010 (1st ed. 1996). *Maradona: The Hand of God*. London: Bloomsbury.

Cowley, Christopher, ed. 2015. *The Philosophy of Autobiography*. Chicago and London: The University of Chicago Press.

Dujovne O., Alicia. 1993. *Maradona Soy Yo*. Buenos Aires: Emecé Editores.

Fernández, Rodrigo and Nagy, Denise. 1994. *De las manos de Dios a sus botines. Biografía pública de Diego Maradona no autorizada*. Buenos Aires: Cangrejal Editores.

Greenblatt, Stephen. 1984. *Renaissance Self-fashioning: From More to Shakespeare*. Chicago and London: The University of Chicago Press.

Maradona, Diego A., with Daniel Arcucci and Ernesto C. Bialo. 2000. *Yo soy el Diego*. Buenos Aires: Planeta.

_____. 2004. *El Diego*. London: Yellow Jersey Press.

PA Staff. 2020. "Terry Fenwick: Diego Maradona Ruined my England Career in 90 Minutes". *FourFourTwo*. November 25. https://www.fourfourtwo.com/news/terry-fenwick-diego-maradona-ruined-my-england-career-in-90-minutes-1606336408000. [Accessed June 7, 2021].

Rojek, Chris, 2001. *Celebrity*. London: Reaktion Books.

Ronay, Barnay. 2021. "Stripped-back Euro 2020 Signals Football's Shift Away from Culture of Celebrity". *The Guardian*. July 3. https://www.theguardian.com/football/2021/jul/03/stripped-back-euro-2020-signals-footballs-shift-away-from-cult-of-celebrity. [Accessed July 7, 2021].

Smart, Barry. 2005. *The Sport Star: Modern Sport and the Cultural Economy of Sporting Celebrity*. London: Sage.

Turner, Graeme. 2004. *Understanding Celebrity*. London: Sage.

Varga, Somogy. 2015. "Self-deception, Self-knowledge, and Autobiography". *The Philosophy of Autobiography*. Ed. Christopher Cowley. Chicago and London: The University Chicago Press, 141–155.

Vickery, Tim. 2021. "'The World Cups', Part One of 'Diego: Tributes to Maradona'". *World Soccer*. January, 4–25.

Williams, Raymond. 1965. *The Long Revolution*. Harmondsworth: Penguin Books.

Woolf, Virginia. 1958. *Granite and Rainbow: Essays by Virginia Woolf*. London: The Hogarth Press.

# 11

# ARGENTINIAN FEMINISMS IN THE LIGHT (AND SHADOW) OF MARADONA

*Gabriela Garton and Julia Hang*

## Sport studies and gender studies through Maradona

Football is an essential part of Argentinian popular culture, and women who make this sport the object of their political activism are fighting for the right to enjoy it and play it as much as men, questioning the dominant paradigm of masculinity that has traditionally surrounded it in the country. The death of Diego Armando Maradona on November 25, 2020, interpellated feminist movements in their attempts to reconcile the contradictory meanings that surround his figure with the admiration that many feminist players, critics, and fans feel for him. "Diego is ours too"; "Diego could also be a feminist"; "Diego could never be a feminist"; "Diego was always a feminist, and we never knew it": these statements circulated in the Argentinian media in the aftermath of his death, reviving discussions which had already taken place among feminists involved in football, and who had often carved out spaces in their clubs, either as members or as players, from which and in which to fight towards the eradication of gender inequity in sport.

Maradona's passing inspired a debate which goes beyond academia and activism and has installed itself in the media as a public controversy. Feminist readings of the footballer have come to be grouped into two different positions based on positive or negative attitudes towards him, leading to a so-called feminist rift. In this chapter, we argue that constructing this discussion as a divide between mutually exclusive sides hinders the chance of seeing the heterogeneities within each position. In other words, not everybody who loves or worships Maradona loves or worships him for the same reasons, and the same could be said of those who reject him. To present the dissonance as a rift ignores the fact that conflict is constitutive of feminism, as has been demonstrated by those who have analysed women's and feminist movements in Argentina (Masson, 2007; Angilletta, 2017).

DOI: 10.4324/9781003196587-15

This chapter will first outline the debates around Argentinian feminisms which arose in the media following the death of Maradona, which revolved around the apparent contradiction between being a "feminist" and being, at the same time, a fan, or "Maradonian". Our analysis examines a *corpus* of journalistic articles published in print and digital media, while also considering conversations with feminist activists connected to the world of football, including fans, players, and journalists. The views on this topic express existing tensions between different currents in Argentinian feminism, framed by a context of growing visibility and public impact of national feminist movements: popular feminism and radical feminism. The fluctuation between positions that only give priority to female subordination and those that recognise intersectionality across various dimensions of inequality, such as class and race, is analysed in the context of men's football in Argentina, understood as a central manifestation of popular culture which holds Maradona as a national hero.

In Argentina there is a relatively strong bibliographic tradition which has associated the study of football with the study of masculinities (Archetti, 1994, 2016; Garriga Zucal, 2005; Moreira, 2005; Alabarces, 2014). Eduardo Archetti claimed that "football in Argentina is a privileged arena for the analysis of the formation of a national identity and the construction of masculinities" (1994: 225). In this field, the figure of Maradona has been considered from a gender perspective but always in masculine terms. According to Archetti, Maradona is "*el pibe de oro*" (2008: 271) who, emerging from the *potrero*, embodies the *criollo* playing style and carries virtues such as freedom, creativity, and irreverence. Moreover, the *potrero* is considered an exclusively male space where *pibes* are socialised into the dominant model of masculinity. The work of Pablo Alabarces expands upon this research and asserts that "by working on football and the fatherland, it is clear that we stand before a masculine narrative of the nation that is produced, reproduced, dominated, and administered by men" (2018: 29).

In this context, some researchers aimed to draw attention to the place of women in the hyper-masculine world of football (Binello *et al.*, 2000; Conde and Rodríguez, 2002; Conde, 2008; Janson, 2008) highlighting their presence in the stands and on the field, even while academia and the media tended to ignore them. However, the women who made their way into such a masculine arena were not able to do so on their own terms: male rules and values dictated and regulated their participation and representation (Binello *et al.*, 2000). María Graciela Rodríguez describes the constitution of the field of the social study of sport in Argentina:

> Between 1998 and 1999 we began to have suspicions about the weight of the male sphere on football and the non-hegemonic places to which women were destined, not only in stadiums but also in other social spheres, such as academia. Moreover, these suspicions grew, over time, into certitudes based on situations in which, without prior notice, women who

participated in academic events would be left out of the discussion when it would turn to footballing anecdotes and even to the insignificant details of matches.

*2013: 349; all translations are ours unless otherwise indicated*

Sociocultural studies of sport homologated the concepts "football-fatherland-masculinity" and thus did not consider the experiences of those women who, even in a space which had relegated them to a position of subordination, loved football, admired its idols, and wanted to emulate them on the field. The recent growth and popularisation of feminisms have allowed for many women to share their passion for football, and that which they once believed to be an individual emotion found a collective expression.

In this context, some scholars have begun to pay attention to the experiences of women who play football (Ibarra, 2018; Garton, 2019; Álvarez Litke, 2020) and are also active politically (Hang, 2020). These authors divert the focus from the axis of female subordination (Masson, 2019) and highlight the agency of women in cultural situations marked by gender inequality. In dialogue with both the protagonists and the "subjects" of these studies, this growing literature challenges the view that football can only be a masculine domain. The *potrero* is not an exclusively male space and that it is also significant for many women as well, for whom it represents imagination, dreams, and possibilities.

## Football and feminism(s)

There are almost as many feminisms as ways of thinking about the concept of "women", LGBTQI+ identities, and the struggle against gender inequality. These viewpoints can be problematised further when considering other variables that contribute to social difference and inequality, such as class or race. In Latin America, feminisms make up a vast, heterogeneous, polycentric, multifaceted, and polyphonic field and they have grown rapidly in Argentina, especially after #NiUnaMenos (#NotOne[woman]Less), a national demonstration against gender violence which first took place on June 3, 2015. One of the main consequences of this is that the historic demands of feminism have transcended the specific boundaries of the movement to become part of the agendas emanating from different social sectors (Natalucci and Rey, 2018), reaching spaces previously thought to be inaccessible, such as the world of football. Some authors characterise this moment as the "fourth wave of feminism" highlighting both the extent of the phenomenon and its expansion into the popular sectors of society (Pis Diez, 2018).

Until recently, football and sport in general (whether male or female) were not among the main concerns of feminism (Hargreaves, 2004). In fact, "sportphobia" (Jefferson Lenskyj, 1995) appears as a common trait of feminisms around the world. Mainstream feminism considered other issues such as the pay gap, gender violence, and the lack of women in positions of power to be more pressing items

(Cooky, 2018). However, over the years some feminists, and indeed women who do not perceive themselves as feminists, have battled for female participation in sports (Anderson, 2017). Even though such participation and access have not been debated within the canonical texts of feminism, throughout the last decades, athletes, activists, and academics understood the importance that sports have in the wider struggle against patriarchal power structures and to contribute towards female emancipation (Jefferson Lenskyj, 1995). Mainly, this struggle was centred on taking part of sporting activities, with criticism focused on the restrictions on women's bodies imposed by medical, moral, and political authorities (Hargreaves, 1994; Antúnez and Miranda, 2008). In a male-dominated football culture like the one in Argentina, this debate eventually challenged the widespread idea among fans (and academic scholarship) that only men hold the ability to truly feel footballing passion, which was considered a kind of bodily knowledge from which women were excluded (Conde and Rodríguez, 2002; Conde, 2008). Even so, equality in sport stayed on the fringes of the major concerns of feminism.

While feminisms were growing and becoming more popular, the Argentinian women's national football team began to seek better conditions and wider recognition. Some measures to achieve this included the team's strike in 2017 and the photograph of the players posing with a hand behind one ear during the Copa América Femenina 2018. This ongoing dispute with the Argentinian Football Association (AFA) represented women's wider struggle against patriarchal society and culture (Hang and Hijós, 2018; Garton et al., 2021). Football, the sport that for so many years in the past had not deserved the attention of feminisms because of its highly sexist character, has become a focal point of the struggle against those same trends. Recognising football as one of the remaining strongholds of patriarchy, many feminists have joined the struggle of female footballers and women in football, highlighting how the perceptions of this sport as a male space, historically off-limits for women, should be challenged, leading to a significant transformation of sporting practices in the country (even if, as we will see in the next section, there are different approaches to these aims).

The debate about Maradona takes place in this context, and it goes beyond discussions surrounding his chauvinism and his problematic treatment of the women he was sentimentally involved with (including the children he had or may have had with many of them). The struggle to conceive a national idol who can represent both women and men, the enjoyment and practice of football by women, and the opportunity to join the discussion about arguably the greatest player of all time are at stake. In the prologue to *Todo Diego es político* (2021), an anthology of essays written by women reflecting on the figure of Maradona and published just before his death, Bárbara Pistoia recognises the magnitude of the contribution of a book entirely written by women to a discussion which has been dominated by men: "We wanted to point the GPS of the conversation in a new direction" (2021: 8). Moreover, Pistoia adds that the aim was not only to have women join the discussion about Maradona, but to promote a particular political perspective: "I wanted us all to be women, but not in the way of the contemporary condescension that demands 'more women in' without caring who they are nor what motivations they have or how they see reality" (2021: 7). Anticipating the debate around Maradona and feminisms, Pistoia's book aims to make visible both women's passion for Maradona and their ability to think about him.

The public discussion of Maradona from the above-mentioned perspective has been presented as a "feminist rift", structured according to two apparently opposing views: on the one hand, Maradona and feminism are incompatible; on the other, there is no contradiction in being a feminist and Maradonian at the same time. In the following section, we will analyse the specificities of each position by considering different feminist discourses in Argentinian media. Despite the apparently antinomic relationship between these two positions, each one makes its argument in relation to the other, producing a kind of feedback mechanism through which a dialectic relationship emerges, highlighting the dynamic character of feminism and recognising conflict as intrinsic to the movement rather than a disruptive element.

## Maradona through the lens of radical feminism

The positions that reject the possibility of reconciling feminism with Maradona are based on two arguments. First, Maradona exercised gender-based violence, both psychological and physical, in his relationships with his partners and lovers. Secondly, he engaged in what Micaela Oliva calls "reproductive irresponsibility" (2019), a term that refers to his numerous extramarital affairs, and the children born out of these casual relations, who Maradona refused to acknowledge and support.[1] From a radical feminist perspective, these are convincing grounds to refuse to idolise a person who systematically engages in some of the main chauvinist practices that feminism hopes to erase. Oliva synthesises these two positions in an article asking the Argentinian people to stop idolising Maradona. Brining attention to the multiple demonstrable instances of gender violence towards his ex-partners, her arguments refer to a leaked video in which Maradona verbally abuses his former partner Rocío Oliva [no relation to the article's author], who had previously complained publicly about his aggressive behaviour towards her (Oliva, 2019, n.p.). The article also discusses the charges filed by Claudia Villafañe, Maradona's ex-wife and mother of his two daughters, for "the psychological violence Maradona used against her during their marriage when he justified all of his behaviors and acts of infidelity" (*id.*).

The viewpoints that are most critical of the figure of Maradona do not come from the realm of football but from the traditional stance of mainstream feminism, which, as mentioned, did not consider sport, especially competitive sport, to be an issue worthy of debate because of its close links to capitalist and patriarchal frameworks. This is the case of the feminist group *Mujeres que no fueron tapa* ("Women who were not cover girls"), a collective dedicated to exposing sexist and misogynist messages in the media. Responding to more positive views of Maradona from some feminist groups, the collective published a post on Instagram where they asserted:

> No. We do not believe that Maradona was a feminist or that he could be interpreted as "feminist". We do not believe that one should be silent out of respect for the "popular grief" when "respect for the popular grief" implies validating a discourse which mandates that we adore idols who reproduces the patriarchal order by being violent with women and children ... Our feminism does not celebrate *machitos* or rapists because they are from the left, "confront the powerful", or "represent the people".
>
> *Mujeres que no fueron tapa*

These perspectives are related to a branch of radical feminism that follows the famous formula "the personal is political", expanding feminist demands from public to private spaces, to the point of considering that what happens behind closed doors, even in bed, is also political (Angilletta, 2017: 29). This stance views patriarchy as "an autonomous system of male oppression and identifies it as the primary and common enemy of all women" (Arruzza, 2010: 11). Such ideas have been challenged by popular feminisms for its inability to engage with the realm of popular culture, which it outrightly dismisses instead (Spataro, 2018). For example, Maradonian feminists were attacked for posting positive comments in social media that paid homage to the player after his death. In a *Página 12* article, Mariana Carbajal (2020) responds to this criticism by claiming that *Mujeres que no fueron tapa* acts as a "feministometer" which "aims to cancel whoever does not conform to its unpolluted mirror" and which "cannot accept that we bid farewell to a popular idol who vindicated his *villero* origins, who stood up to the powerful, who stood by the weak, who gave us joy on the pitch, who played the best football" (Carbajal, 2020). This so-called feministometer has moralistic tendencies, which can be observed in Oliva's piece:

> Little do they remember the struggles of the mothers who had to take complete responsibility for his children while he spent his fortune on cars, houses, pleasure trips, and drugs ... The life of Maradona was always surrounded by excess and violence. His drug addiction and treatments are only a part of his character. He has assaulted the press; he has fought with teammates on the pitch.
>
> *Escritura Feminista 2019*

Maradona's behaviour is condemned because of his addictions and for living a lifestyle which did not correspond with his social status: a *villero* spending money on luxury travel, vehicles, and homes. This perspective risks falling into the sort of conservative moral judgement or "preaching" that feminism has struggled with over the last century. Throughout its existence, radical feminism has fought against patriarchal structures, viewed as the principal source of women's oppression, developing revolutionary and liberating ideas around the role of women in society, marriage, sexual relations, prostitution, and politics (Rowland and Klein, 1996). Feminists who question the moralism in these perspectives argue that, ironically, when it comes to Maradona radical feminists adopt a prescriptive and moralising perspective and judge the football star based on very similar arguments to those that were used to justify the oppression of women, arguments that the radical feminists had historically fought. In this sense, Florencia Angilletta, who engaged in the debate through an article entitled "Diego no es de nadie" [Diego belongs to no one], warns: "feminisms cannot act as judges —conflict is part of feminism, not foreign to them—, nor as police —cannibals of the multiplicity of civil society—, nor as priests —the moral arrow always takes aim from both sides" (2020).

Most "anti-Maradonian" feminists come from outside of the sporting world, but it is interesting to note that many of those who do come from football tend to have a different view. For these feminists involved in activism in the sporting world, sport reproduces patriarchal and capitalist structures, and they propose to transform it into a "celebration of physicality and play based on feminist principles of cooperation and inclusion" (Travers, 2008: 86). Some of the feminist groups which do consider Maradona to be compatible with feminism – such as La Nuestra Fútbol Feminista, an organisation of female football in Villa 31, a low-income district in the city of Buenos Aires with high levels of poverty and marginality – share this perspective; however, they differ in their strategies of achieving the goal of replacing the endemic violence and top-down power structures of competitive sport with more inclusive social practices. As Martín Álvarez Litke explains, in these organisations there is a "consensus on whether football can be feminist by maintaining certain characteristics traditionally associated with men's football such as aggression and competitiveness while discarding others" (2020: 17). Maradona, in this case, can be said to represent these principles of cooperation and inclusion of the popular classes and thus is accepted by this branch of feminism.

This dilemma goes well beyond theoretical and scholarly debates. Significantly, it arose for some of the women of the Gender Area of Club de Gimnasia y Esgrima La Plata (GELP) when Maradona was hired as the head coach of GELP's men's first division team in 2019.[2] The Gender Area is a group that gathers club members dedicated to raise consciousness in the club about gender inequality and violence, through a range of activities (seminars, training sessions, workshops). These activities are offered to both athletes and club employees. The group also records and disseminates the life stories of female athletes and members of GELP in relation to gender issues. Micaela Minelli and Emilia De Marziani (2019) state that, at the time Maradona joined GELP, the members of the Gender Area asked themselves: what happens when a violent man and absent father is put forth as an idol or a hero in your institution? The members felt that the presence of Maradona – and his famous entourage – would overshadow the work they had been carrying out, silencing and annihilating voices which showed any kind of dissent. This fear was proven to be justified in the case of footballer Celeste Carlini who, after expressing her discontent with the arrival of the new manager (*Mundo TKM*, 2019), received a warning from the club's directors.[3] The dissatisfaction with Maradona from a feminist perspective, however, has transcended the geographical limits of Argentina, as demonstrated by the protest carried out by Paula Dapena, a female player of the Spanish club Viajes Interrias. In a friendly game after Maradona's death, players observed a minute of silence. Dapena, rather than stand along her silent teammates, opted instead to sit down and face in the opposite direction. She justified her decision by explaining that, since Maradona's victims had not received any tributes, she did not want to participate in any celebration of their abuser (Das, 2020).

## Maradona, champion of popular feminisms?

There is no univocal image of Maradona from a feminist perspective, and the spectrum of views includes some that even regard him as a feminist. According to *villero* football feminist Monica Santino, "Maradona, in what he means for popular sentiment, represents feminism more than what he realized while he lived" (Santino, 2020). Santino, the head coach of La Nuestra (as mentioned above, an organisation that promotes football for women, lesbians, trans, and non-binary people in Villa 31), shows how Maradona is conceived by popular feminisms. She recognises that Maradona was himself a *villero* who was never ashamed of his origins or attempted to disavow them and in fact showed the world what football from the *villa* was like. For her, Maradona is associated with a branch of popular feminism identified as *villero feminism*. The term "villero" refers to someone who lives in a "villa miseria" or a shanty town, but it is almost always laden with a derogatory undertone. However, *villero feminism* turns this meaning around, using the term as a positive identity category. Although *villero feminism* has not been theorised in academic scholarship on feminism, the feminist debate around Maradona provides a good opportunity to discuss this idea. According to Santino (2020), popular and neighbourhood feminism can recover Maradona's "constant vindication of his class, his response to the powerful" (Alabarces, 2005). Maradona was born in extreme poverty in Villa Fiorito and became a perfect example of the rags-to-riches trope, common to footballers in Latin America. In this sense, as Alabarces (2005) argues, Maradona presented himself as the authorised spokesperson for the displaced. And that assumption would provide him with a certain image in the media (especially between 1987 and 1995), which placed Maradona in a political space, steeped in the tradition of progressive populism, and "made him a cultivator of the *clichés* of the alternative and the resistance of popular cultures" (2005: 2). This perspective, which focuses on the subject's popular origins and his irreverence towards elites and the establishment, aligns itself with popular feminism, which "recognizes the need to construct feminisms based on the experiences of organizing of subjects from different subaltern realities" (Pis Diez, 2018: 85).

In Argentina, popular feminism brings together women of diverse backgrounds who fight gender violence while sharing and communicating experiences focused on improving material conditions for the many who live in extreme poverty. Heir to the experiences of resistance and politicisation in the struggles against neoliberalism (Sosa González et al., 2018: 170), popular feminism is framed as a response to the specific problems of women in their communities and territories. It is a feminism that cannot be conceptualised without considering issues of class and race in an intersectional approach which considers multiple facets of oppression. The same scheme would apply to understanding Maradona, the plebeian "hero" of humble origins who constantly exhibited his "plebeianism" (Alabarces, 2020) and was stigmatised as a *negro villero*, an insult used in Argentina to denigrate people from popular sectors. As Malvina Silba explains in "La muerte de nuestro Dios plebeyo", Maradona also "can be taken as inspiration to fight for our rights and for popular celebration in the streets, which is also uncomfortable and dissident" (2020).

In the debate around Maradona, the perspective that aligns with popular feminism is founded on a common passion for football as a sport. Rather than reading football from a feminist perspective, the love of football conditions the ways in which feminism can be put into practice. For women who love football, Maradona represents the possibility of experiencing beauty and freedom. Santino describes Maradona as unifying force for football fans located in the margins: "What unites the most in this sense, in this love for football, is the importance of being a footballer, of having made this role much bigger than what it was" (2020). For many footballers, Maradona was their main sporting idol. Given the lack of visibility of women footballers in Argentina, players did not have the opportunity to have female role models. Yanina Gaitán, a former national team player, describes Maradona as the epitome of football and the nation. Two images illustrate her story: "When I was 14, I went on the pitch at halftime to juggle the ball at the Bombonera [the iconic football stadium home to Club Atlético Boca Juniors] and the crowd was chanting: 'Maradooo, Maradooo!' In the *potrero*, when I would dribble the ball, I would comment my own moves: 'And Maradona takes it, what a goal from Maradona!'" (Pujol, 2020).

Gaitán's reference to the *potrero* harkens back to the idea presented by Archetti (1994) as a space where masculinity was constructed through football. Historically, this had been an exclusively male space where young men could deploy their skills and creativity with the ball, competing without adult supervision, without structures, rules, and regulations. For Gaitán, and for many other women who would join the boys in their neighbourhood potreros for informal games during their childhood and adolescence, Maradona represented not only the *potrero* but also the opportunity to enter this space that was previously off-limits to female footballers. In a way, Maradona was their ticket to the freedom and independence offered by the *potrero*.

Maradonian feminists do not deny that football is a traditionally masculine space historically constituted as a praxis which has excluded and even abused women and dissident genders but still consider the sport to be "beautiful as it is" (Álvarez Litke, 2020). Thinking in terms of Archetti's theorisation of the *potrero* and the freedom that this space represents for young Argentinians growing up playing informal games with family, friends, and neighbours, the beauty of football turns into an aesthetic judgement which refers to its free-flowing nature, the creativity of players, and the movement of bodies around the ball. Moreover, the passion that football generates among people of all social classes is another element of its beauty (Santino, 2020). For Maradonian feminists, Maradona is the ultimate representation of such beauty, as demonstrated by his renowned dribbling feats, in which the ball seems to be tied to his foot as he floats across the pitch (Pujol, 2020). His ability to bring the creativity characteristic of the *potrero* to the highest levels of football, to appear to truly enjoy playing the game, to transform it into "something artistic" (Santino, 2020) are some of the defining aspects of Maradona as a footballer, and Maradonian feminists desire not only to have the right to enjoy them but also to participate in discussions about his on-field talents.

Examining the impact of Maradona on female players and their subjectivity allows us to consider a concept developed by a group of social researchers in Argentina who study mass culture in terms of "affordance" (Spataro, 2013: 203). From this perspective, it is important to note what Maradona has afforded people in their lives.[4] For many women, Maradona acted as an imaginary mirror where they could see themselves beyond the roles that were socially expected of them. Many female players recognise this in their own sporting biographies. Marcela Castro describes Maradona as "the athlete who made us dream and love football" (Pujol, 2020). Victoria Liendro explains that they could be admired for juggling a football and dream of dribbling through an entire team and scoring a goal against England (*id.*) If Maradona not only represented their encounter with the world of football but also with a life plan that can be considered counter to social mandates, this was possible despite not only the prevalent sexism in the sport but also Maradona's own misogyny (shared by most men, and many women, of his generation). Thus, according to Spataro (2018), it is important to question the prevailing prejudices that do not allow us to see how certain mass culture phenomena can at times expand, however unexpectedly, social demands such as, in this instance, the women's movement.

This line of argument is situated within a growing body of literature that calls attention to monolithic, top-down models of cultural enjoyment and considers how they can be reconfigured from a feminist perspective and applied to popular culture (Silba and Spataro, 2017). As Natalia Maderna (2020) writes, for many years, Maradona did not "belong" to women, and it was a male privilege to be able to call oneself Maradonian. Similarly, responding to Maradona's arrival as head coach of GELP, Paula Provenzano states: "Maradona, the social liability with whom we mess up our feminist rulebook, came to coach the most beautiful club in the world. I am not missing out on this party. To a certain extent, I also became a feminist so that partying could also be our own" (2019). These two interventions reveal a privileged access to football and its enjoyment, declaring women's right to appropriate it. Women should occupy this space which was denied to them for so long and in turn should question, as Provenzano suggests, "why men have silently appropriated everything, why we always know the male version of almost everything first" (*id.*).

## Maradona: institution zero for Argentinian feminisms

In an informal conversation following the death of Maradona, Santino told us that "what Diego left us—always so generous, always opening doors—is the opportunity to ask exactly: where will feminisms stand and what will popular feminism be? It's a matter of asking questions to keep moving forward". The controversies among the different feminisms which emerged as a public debate following the death of Maradona contributed to a more complex discussion around one of the sources of tension among feminisms: the issue of intersectionality and how different dimensions of inequality, such as class or skin colour, are interconnected with gender.

Throughout the chapter, we identified tensions between different forms of Argentinian feminisms: a version of feminism that emphasises the violent, misogynistic, and sexist character of Maradona and football in general, and a more popular feminism, which vindicates his figure because of his rebellious anti-establishment character. In the latter view, Maradona invites us to reconsider popular feminism, paying attention to what "enables" the subjective experiences of women, members of the LGBTQI+ collective, and men. Argentinian writer Roberto Fontanarrosa allegedly stated: "I don't care what Diego did with his life; I care about what he did to mine". This point of view offers a space in which Maradona can become an inspiration for women's future sporting dreams as well as a vehicle for emotions relegated by normative masculinities.

Simoni Lahud Guedes (1977) claimed that, in Brazil, football can be explained by the notion of institution zero. Football is a neutral institution without any intrinsic significance that can take on any meaning. Football is then filled with positive or negative qualities by the Brazilian population according to the performance of the men's national football team. We could "read" Maradona from this perspective: he is everything and he is nothing. Meaning depends on the subject who makes a claim about him and on the context in which such expressions are enunciated. He can be sexist and feminist, conformist and defiant. He is the artist who, according to former Argentina manager Marcelo Bielsa, brought beauty to spectators from the popular classes. He subverted the heteronormative order of football by kissing fellow teammates on the lips when celebrating a goal – as he did with Claudio Caniggia when they were both playing for Boca Juniors – a public act that has been read as a challenge to the dominant forms of masculine effect in the world of football (Ramón, 2020; *Olé*, 2021). He was raised by a patriarchal society as a football idol and has been targeted by a society born out of the #NiUnaMenos protests as a legend to be debunked. He is the one who is no longer here, and he is the one who lives on in the dreams of female fans and players who today inhabit a space historically off-limits to them.

Through the light and shadow of Maradona feminisms have been led to re-examine themselves. Activists, academics, football fans, and athletes have broadened their horizons and deepened the way we understand domination. Academic and journalistic articles published after his death continue to reflect on the relationship between Maradona and feminisms.[5] One of the most novel ideas generated by this discussion is that for a large sector of feminism, being Maradonian is a way of being feminist. For these feminists, a communal, shared love of football as a popular sport is a value-building process that allows for the understanding and condemnation of social injustices and inequalities. In addition to a feeling of admiration for the player, Maradonian feminists also emphasise his role as a popular hero who stood up for those who could not, who challenged the established powers, and who symbolised hope for marginalised sectors of society, both in Argentina and around the world (Caparrós and Villoro, 2012). However, Maradona's figure also projects shadows and therefore complexity, as he was not explicitly "feminist" nor was his life free of violence towards women and children.

Understanding the symbolic nature of Maradona provides an opportunity for feminists and for women in general to inhabit and participate in a space which has historically been only accessible to men and almost exclusively narrated by them as well. The aspects of Maradona's life and legacy provide feminists with the opportunity to try to answer complicated questions: what to do with a man as contradictory as this one? On the one hand, he has evaded his paternal responsibilities, engaged in relationships with underage young women, and exerted verbal and potentially physical violence against his partners. On the other, and at the same time, he has stood up for the historically marginalised across the world and inspired innumerable women to dream about the possibility of playing and enjoying the country's most popular sport. The idol and his legacy cannot be neatly pigeonholed into "good" or "bad" categories according to feminist theory.

It is exactly this difficulty in classifying him which will allow feminisms to think through other contradictions of society, particularly those in sport and popular culture, as more and more women begin to engage with them as fans and practitioners. We cannot pick and choose only the aspects of Maradona that we love or hate, he is all (and none) of those things, which represents a challenge for all versions of feminisms as his life, career, and legacy will continue to be examined, analysed, and idolised in the future.

## Notes

1 He eventually recognised his Italian son Diego Maradona Jr. when he was in his late twenties, and his Argentinean daughter Jana when she was 18. There are allegedly several more children of Maradona in Cuba.
2 Gisele Ferreyra's and Julián Barbetti's *La última pasión de Dios* (2021), which chronicles Maradona's stint as a manager for GELP, focuses on the club's performance and fans' adoration but does not mention this episode.
3 Data obtained during fieldwork carried out at GELP in 2019 by Hang.

4 The concept of affordance comes from the sociology of music and refers to an object of study viewed in so far as what it affords, or does not afford, to subjects in terms of practices or appropriations (De Nora 2000; Hennion 2002). In Argentina, Rodolfo Iuliano (2012) applied this concept to the practice of golf to consider how a certain object, in this case a sport, can afford certain actions, career paths, and emotional experiences to those who encounter it.

5 See the testimony of Ayelén Pujol in *Fenomenología de Maradona* (Zabala 2021); the article by María Mónica Sosa Vásquez, "'Las feministas me *bardearon* por maradoniana y las maradonianas por feminista': amores y valores en conflicto a partir de la muerte de 'El Diego' para las futbolistas feministas de la capital argentina" (2021); the section "Gambetas desde los feminismos plebeyos" in *Maradona, un mito plebeyo* (2021); and the ninth chapter of Gabriela Saidón's *Superdios. La construcción de Maradona como santo laico* (2021).

## References

Alabarces, Pablo. 2005. "Maradona, el fútbol, la patria, el peronismo y otros gremios paralelos: un héroe en disponibilidad". *Encrucijadas* 33. Web: http://repositoriouba.sisbi. uba.ar/gsdl/collect/encruci/index/assoc/HWA_529.dir/529.PDF [Accessed April 27, 2021].

———. 2014. *Héroes, machos y patriotas: El fútbol entre la violencia y los medios*. Buenos Aires: Aguilar.

———. 2020. "De Maradona a Messi: viejos y nuevos argumentos sobre el héroe deportivo y la patria". *Im@go. A Journal of the Social Imaginary* 11: 26–43.

Álvarez Litke, Martín. 2020. "'Me paro en la cancha como en la vida': un análisis del fútbol feminista en la Villa 31 desde las teorías de género". *Zona Franca. Revista de Estudios de Género* 28: 79–104.

Anderson, Patricia. 2017. Unedited Chapter from PhD in History. University of Toronto, Canada. Thesis title: "Deportismo! Female Sports and Gender Change in Argentina: 1900-1946". Web: http://www.historiapolitica.com/dossiers/dossier-deporte-educacion-corporalidades/ [Accessed April 27, 2021].

Angilletta, Florencia. 2017. "Feminismos: notas para su historia política". *¿El futuro es feminista?* Eds. Florencia Angilletta, Mercedes D'Alessandro and Marina Mariasch. Buenos Aires: Capital Intelectual, 23–42.

———. 2020. "Diego no es de nadie". *Le Monde Diplomatique*, November. Web: https:// www.eldiplo.org/notas-web/diego-no-es-de-nadie/?fbclid=IwAR3urm9e3flCMRy4p UzHKNZzXJatQAviHMgj-I-mHTzUllD1bQ7z-P28c1M [Accessed April 10, 2021].

Antúnez, Marta Susana and Norah Edith Miranda. 2008. "Mujer y deporte. Una dupla dura en el campo de las ciencias blandas". Paper presented at V Jornadas de Sociología de la Universidad Nacional de La Plata. La Plata, Argentina.

Archetti, Eduardo. 1994. "Masculinity and Football: The Formation of National Identity in Argentina". *Game Without Frontiers: Football, Identity and Modernity*. Eds. Richard Giulianotti and John Williams. Aldershot: Arena, 224–244.

———. 2016. *Masculinidades. Futbol, tango y polo en Argentina*. Buenos Aires: Club House.

Arruzza, Cinzia. 2010. *Las sin parte. Matrimonios y divorcios entre feminismo y marxismo*. Madrid: Crítica & Alternativa.

Binello, Gabriela *et al.* 2000. "Mujeres y fútbol: ¿territorio conquistado o a conquistar?" *Peligro de gol. Estudios sobre deporte y sociedad en América Latina*. Ed. Pablo Alabarces. Buenos Aires: CLACSO, 33–54.

Caparrós, Martín and Juan Villoro. 2012. *Ida y vuelta. Una correspondencia sobre fútbol*. Mexico D.F.: Seix Barral.

Carbajal, Mariana. 2020. "Diego y los feminismos". *Página 12*. November 26. Web: https://www.pagina12.com.ar/308272-diego-y-los-feminismos. [Accessed April 19, 2021].

Conde, Mariana and María Graciela Rodríguez. 2002. "Mujeres en el fútbol argentino: sobre prácticas y representaciones". *Alteridades* 12.23: 93–106. Web: http://www.historiapolitica.com/datos/biblioteca/estudiosdeportes_condeyrodriguez.pdf [Accessed April 19, 2021].

Conde, Mariana. 2008. "El poder de la razón: las mujeres en el fútbol". *Nueva Sociedad* 218: 122–130. Web: http://nuso.org/media/articles/downloads/3575_1.pdf [Accessed August 27, 2021].

Cooky, Cheryl. 2018. "Women, Sports, and Activism." *No Slum Dunk: Gender, Sport and the Unevenness of Social Change*. Eds. Cheryl Cooky and Michael A. Mesner. New Jersey: Rutgers University Press, 70–91.

Das, Ria. 2020. "Spanish Female Footballer Paula Dapena Refuses to Pay Tribute To Maradona, Receives Death Threats". Web: https://www.shethepeople.tv/news/spanish-female-footballer-paula-dapena-refuses-tribute-to-diego-maradona-receives-death-threats/ [Accessed April 19, 2021].

De Nora, Tia. 2000. *Music in Everyday Life*. New York: Cambridge University Press.

Ferreyra, Gisele and Julián Barbetti. 2021. *La última pasión de Dios*. Buenos Aires: Beo.

Garriga Zucal, José. 2005. "Lomo de macho. Cuerpo, masculinidad y violencia de un grupo de simpatizantes del fútbol". *Cuadernos de Antropología Social* 22: 201–216.

Garton, Gabriela. 2019. *Guerreras: fútbol, mujeres y poder*. Buenos Aires: Capital Intelectual.

Garton, Gabriela, María Nemesia Hijós and Pablo Alabarces. 2021. "Playing for Change: (semi-) Professionalization, Social Policy, and Power Struggles in Argentine Women's Football". *Soccer and Society* 22.6: 626–640.

Guedes, Simoni Lahud. 1977. "O Futebol Brasileiro - Instituição Zero". Undergraduate Thesis. Universidade Federal de Rio de Janeiro, Brasil.

Hang, Julia. 2020. "Feministas y triperas. Mujeres y política en el área de género del club Gimnasia y Esgrima La Plata". *Debates en Sociología* 50: 67–90.

Hang, Julia and María Nemesia Hijós. 2018. "Ese juego que las hace felices". *Revista Anfibia*. November 15. Web: http://revistaanfibia.com/ensayo/juego-que-las-hace-felices/ [Accessed August 20, 2021].

Hargreaves, Jennifer. 1994. *Sporting Females: Critical Issues in the History and Sociology of Women's Sport*. London and New York: Routledge.

_____. 2004. "Querying Sport Feminism: Personal or Political". *Sport and Modern Social Theorists*. Ed. Richard Giulianotti. London: Palgrave Macmillan, 187–206.

Hennion, Antoine. 2002. *La pasión musical*. Barcelona: Paidós.

Ibarra, Mariana. 2018. "El aguante: ¿resistencia o masculinidad?" Paper presented at the X Jornadas de Sociología de la Universidad Nacional de La Plata. La Plata, Argentina.

Iuliano, Rodolfo. 2012. "*Mirá el día de golf que me hiciste perder. Emociones y aficiones en torno a la práctica del golf*." In *Actas de las II Jornadas de Antropología*, PPGAS, IFCH-UNICAMP, Campinas, Brazil. Web: http://www.antropologias.org/seminarioppgas/files/2012/06/Rodolfo-Iuliano-2012.pdf [Accessed August 20, 2021].

Janson, Adolfina. 2008. *Se acabó este juego que te hacía feliz. Nuestro fútbol femenino (desde su ingreso a la AFA en 1990, hasta el Mundial de Estados Unidos en 2003)*. Buenos Aires: Aurelia Rivera Grupo Editorial.

Jefferson Lenskyj, Helen. 1995. "What's Sport Got to Do with It?" *Canadian Woman Studies* 15.4: 5–10.

Maderna, Natu. 2020. "Maradona: un amor coherente con un feminismo que abre debates". *Página 12*. November 27. Web: https://www.pagina12.com.ar/308484-maradona-un-amor-coherente-con-un-feminismo-que-abre-debates [Accessed April 7, 2021].

Masson, Laura. 2007. *Feministas en todas partes. Una etnografía de espacios y narrativas feministas en Argentina*. Buenos Aires: Prometeo Libros.

———. 2019. "Aportes de la teoría feminista y de género al conocimiento etnográfico y a las políticas públicas". *Sudamérica: Revista de Ciencias Sociales* 11: 36–52.

Minelli, Micaela and Emilia De Marziani. 2019. "Si yo fuera Maradona". *Escritura Feminista*. Web: https://escriturafeminista.com/2019/09/16/si-yo-fuera-maradona/ [Accessed April 10, 2021].

Moreira, María Verónica. 2005. "Trofeos de guerra y hombres de honor". *Hinchadas*. Ed. Pablo Alabarces. Buenos Aires: Prometeo, 75–89.

Mundo TKM. 2019. "Una jugadora de Gimnasia de la Plata criticó a Maradona: 'Fue violento con su mujer'". Web: https://www.mundotkm.com/genero/2019/09/05/una-jugadora-de-gimnasia-de-la-plata-critico-a-maradona-fue-violento-con-su-mujer/ [Accessed April 10, 2021].

Natalucci, Ana and Rey, Julieta. 2018. "¿Una nueva oleada feminista? Agendas de género, repertorios de acción y colectivos de mujeres (Argentina, 2015–2018)". *Revista de Estudios Políticos y Estratégicos* 6.2: 14–34.

*Olé*. 2021. "El beso de Dios: Maradona, Caniggia y el orgullo LGBT". June 29. Web: https://www.ole.com.ar/maradona/beso-maradona-caniggia-orgullo-lgbt_0_N4LJYqqAI.html [Accessed September 14, 2021].

Oliva, Micaela. 2019. "Y todo el pueblo cantó: dejemos de idolatrar a Maradona". *Escritura Feminista*. Web: https://escriturafeminista.com/2019/03/22/y-todo-el-pueblo-canto-dejemos-de-idolatrar-a-maradona/ [Accessed April 10, 2021].

Pis Diez, Nayla. 2018. "Violencias machistas y resistencia feminista en Argentina: una reconstrucción y algunos elementos históricos para entender la cuarta ola". Graduate Thesis, Faculdade de Serviço Social, Universidade Federal de Juiz de Fora. Web: http://www.memoria.fahce.unlp.edu.ar/tesis/te.1702/te.1702.pdf [Accessed April 10, 2021].

Pistoia, Bárbara. Ed. 2021. *Todo Diego es político*. Buenos Aires: Sincopa.

Provenzano, Paula. 2019. "Maradona, el fútbol y el feminismo. ¿Se puede ser feminista y al mismo tiempo respetar y hasta compartir el amor por Diego? Un intento de respuesta a un interrogante complejo". *Revista Un Caño*. Web: https://uncanio.com.ar/opinion/maradona-el-futbol-y-el-feminismo/ [Accessed April 8, 2021].

Pujol, Ayelén. 2020. "Las futbolistas despiden a Diego: 'Nos hizo amar el fútbol'". *Nuestras Voces*. Web: http://www.nuestrasvoces.com.ar/mujeres-en-lucha/las-futbolistas-despiden-a-diego-nos-hizo-amar-el-futbol/ [Accessed April 10, 2021].

Ramón, María del Mar. 2020. "El hombre que hizo a otros hombres llorar". *El Grito del Sur*. Web: https://elgritodelsur.com.ar/2020/11/el-hombre-que-hizo-otros-hombres-llorar-diego-entre-besos-lagrimas.html [Accessed April 11, 2021].

Rodríguez, María Graciela. 2013. "¿Qué es un campo, y tú me lo preguntas?" *Deporte y ciencias sociales. Claves para pensar las sociedades contemporáneas*. Eds. Juan Branz, José Garriga Zucal and Verónica Moreira. La Plata: EDULP.

Rowland, Robyn and Renate Klein. 1996. "Radical Feminism: History, Politics, Action". *Radically Speaking: Feminism Reclaimed*. Eds. Diane Belle and Renate Klein. Geelong, Australia: Spinifex Press, 9–36.

Santino, Mónica. 2020. "Sin saberlo, Maradona era mucho más feminista de lo que pensamos". *Cosecha Roja*, November 26. Web: http://cosecharoja.org/monica-santino-sin-saberlo-maradona-era-mucho-mas-feminista-de-lo-que-pensamos/ [Accessed April 9, 2021].

Silba, Malvina. 2020. "La muerte de nuestro Dios plebeyo". *Anfibia*. November 26. Web: https://www.revistaanfibia.com/la-muerte-dios-plebeyo/ [Accessed October 11, 2021].

Silba, Malvina and Carolina Spataro. 2017. "Did Cumbia Villera Bother Us? Criticisms on the Academic Representation of the Link between Women and Music". Trans. Federico Álvarez Gandolfi. *Music, Dance, Affect, and Emotions in Latin America*. Ed. Pablo Vila. Lanham, MD: Lexington Books, 140–167.

Sosa González, María Noel, Mariana Menéndez Díaz and Maisa Bascuas. 2018. "Experiencias de feminismo popular en el Cono Sur: reproducción de la vida y relaciones entre mujeres". *Las disputas por lo público en América Latina y el Caribe*. Héctor René Mena Méndez *et al*. Buenos Aires: CLACSO, 159–184.

Sosa Vásquez, María Mónica. 2021. "'Las feministas me *bardearon* por maradoniana y las maradonianas por feminista': amores y valores en conflicto a partir de la muerte de 'El Diego' para las futbolistas feministas de la capital argentina". *Eracle. Journal of Sport and Social Sciences* 4.2: 96–120.

Spataro, Carolina. 2013. "'¿A qué vas a ese lugar?': mujeres, tiempo de placer y cultura de masas". *Papeles de Trabajo* 7.11: 188–206.

_____. 2018. "Abajo el feministómetro". *Bordes* 7. Web: http://revistabordes.com.ar/abajo-el-feministometro/ [Accessed April 10, 2021].

Travers, Ann. 2008. "The Sport Nexus and Gender Injustice." *Studies in Social Justice* 2.1: 79–101.

Zabala, Santiago *et al*. 2021. *Fenomenología Maradona*. España, Altamarea.

# 12

# DEIFYING DIEGO

## The Church of Maradona and Beyond

*Luca Bifulco*

### Football, the sports hero, and the religious experience

Identifying the best player in the history of football may be an impossible and substantially insignificant exercise. It is something different however to understand and analyse those players who have attracted the most public attention, are the object of great devotion, and are embedded in the memory of fans. Diego Armando Maradona has a leading role in this regard. Many years after his retirement from the field, and even after his death, he remains a source of identification and inspiration for many people all over the world. There are several reasons for such devotion: the veneration linked to regional and national identity in Naples, Italy, and in Argentina; the global attraction as he stood as a symbol of social emancipation and struggle against various forms of oppression; up to the institutionalised worship of a real semi-ecclesiastical community, the Maradonian Church, which will be the central subject of this chapter.[1]

Several scholars have emphasised the similarities between sporting and religious experiences in the lexicon they command when they are talked about, in the idea of a sacred space where collective identities can be expressed, and in the narration and representation of human bodies able to reach – at least symbolically – almost supernatural dimensions (Prebish, 1993; Schultz and Sheffer, 2016). The sporting and religious spheres share a similar vocabulary made of words such as sacrifice, devotion, veneration, ritual, and faith (Schultz, 2016). They also share common practices and spaces: ceremonies, gatherings, beliefs, superstitions, consecrated places or "cathedrals", idols, chants, and revered symbols. In addition, sports usually enact an organisational apparatus with actors who seem to take on, at least allegorically, quasi-religious guises: the idolised athletes, the clerics – managers, coaches – the scribes – journalists and storytellers – the worshippers – fans (Sheffer, 2016). Finally, like believers do in most religions, fans seek spaces of liberation, salvation, and joy in

DOI: 10.4324/9781003196587-16

the sports they follow; they suffer and hope and transcend individuality, identifying as part of a community around an individual athlete or a team. Thus, it is no coincidence that sport is full of stories of redemption where we find allegorical paths of purification, sacrifice, and victimisation (Geyerman, 2016).

A footballer can produce something akin to a religious experience because football is a ritualised field where forms of identification take place. In some cases, these give way to real religious fervour, as in the case of the Maradonian Church, which will be explored below. Football competition produces modes of belonging and identity for players and fans, unfolding as a meaningful, exciting, and unpredictable story, with a joyful or sorrowful outcome (Bifulco and Pirone, 2014). Emotions, dreams, objectives, memories, and a common history, together with the creation of a universe of collective meanings, establish a spiritual bond that includes all those involved with a club. This communal experience shares symbols and representative heroes. Both are treated with great respect and affection by fans and are at times defended from real or figurative attacks. Such a spiritual bond is akin to a community of faith. Through these elements, members find identification and a space for belonging. In athletic excellence and sporting merits, fans can project themselves, feel gratified and self-satisfied, and enjoy vicarious glory. The players personify the needs, traits, feelings, values, desires, and ambitions of those who cheer them on; their talent, dedication to the club, charisma, and achievements make them memorable. The construction of pride around this context becomes constant over time, making football heroes not only spokespersons, but also public emblems who establish a sense of collective self-esteem and provide a shared symbolic destiny (Bifulco and Tirino, 2018).

Such is the case with Maradona.

## The invention of the Maradonian Church: Parody and authenticity

Like other champions, Maradona was a sports hero for many social groups and fan communities. But no one before him inspired the birth of a real religious and moral community, established not only in an ironic, yes, but also in a playful and heartfelt way. Any analysis of a religious institution must consider its ideological and experiential dimensions, as well as the type of relationships defined among its members. Based on these three main elements, I will analyse the Maradonian Church to understand to what extent it is similar to and different from traditional Christian religious institutions. We use the word "invention" because we can precisely date it in the contemporary era. Indeed, we are faced with the deliberate creation of an institution founded on a set of beliefs and narratives which imitates Christianity.

There is an official story of the birth of the Maradonian Church.[2] On October 30, 1998, Maradona's birthday, two friends from Rosario, Argentina, Hernán Amez and Héctor Campomar, jokingly wished each other a Merry Christmas, immediately involving Alejandro Verón in their exchange of greetings. This became a ritualised habit in the following years, with an increasing number of

Maradona's fans who, in October of 2001, decided to institutionalise their passion (Caldeira, 2007). One hundred and twenty exuberant and vociferous followers founded a stable and organised creed. In 2014, an unofficial estimate spoke of over 80,000 members in 55 countries (Cusack, 2018), while the Facebook group collects, as of November of 2021, 178,000 fans. The institutionalisation of the worship involves rituals, celebrations, and short liturgical formulas. Such institutionalisation also includes the dissemination of messages among members, through social media, and, in some cases, it even includes organised activism.

We can speak of the Maradonian Church as an invented, fake, fictional, mocking, or parodic religion (Alberts, 2008; Cusack, 2013, 2018). But this definition does not capture the full extent of its significance. On the one hand, the Maradonian Church lacks a reference to life after death and does not provide a tale of the creation of the universe or speak of primordial entities; furthermore, participation does not exclude the coexistence of other religious followings among its base. On the other hand, Maradona takes on evident Christological features in the linguistic, iconic, and value formulations of the institution. Excess, irreverence, and arbitrariness are an essential part of this parody of Christianity. Yet, the playful element does not exclude authentic feelings and beliefs, experienced as solemn and sincere. We move, then, along a fine line that links irony and humour and fiction, on one side, and a genuine symbolic and emotional experience on the other.

A religion is a set of beliefs, rituals, attitudes, and behaviours in a sacred and supernatural sphere, implying a transcendent reality capable of providing a symbolic order. It is also a phenomenon which provides social solidarity, emotional energy, symbolic identification, and moral orientation to its community (Durkheim, 1912; Collins, 1982). In this context, we can first identify an ideological dimension, that is, the ways in which the sacred, the nature of the divine, and its superhuman and otherworldly beings are represented. Then follows the experiential dimension of those who have feelings and emotions related to divinity and the sphere of the sacred. Finally, there is a social sphere which involves meanings, collective values, actions, and relationships that are created within the community.

Based on the concept of the numinous (Otto, 1950), the experience of the Maradonian sacred is characterised by the idea of a sporting superiority, and this is true both for everyone who conceives the *pibe de oro* as a devotional object, and for the Church which has institutionalised it. The Maradonian sacred impresses, almost frightens, and certainly demands respect; fans, in turn, are excited with the possibility of taking part of the experience. These two constitutive elements of the Maradonian sacred – impressive power and magnetic charm – create a bond between the player and his followers, who then derive from it a sense of trust, strength, and support. Maradona's place in the history of the sport involved extraordinary football actions on the pitch, guiding modest teams to victory in competition against stronger, wealthier opponents. These actions are the origin of a portentous, almost supernatural power generating astonishment and passion. This power triggers in his fans not only a sense of obligation but also gratitude, all the while making him worthy of being praised. References to Maradona's allegedly impossible and superhuman acts are accompanied by an outpour of sensations: joy, vicarious glory, and being part of a Maradonian "essence". Fans identify themselves with his greatness and his victories and feed on meanings and values that go beyond the sporting sphere and foster multiple identities.

The Maradonian Church represents then a structured form of this dynamics of sacred dedication. As mentioned, the model followed is the Christian paradigm. The Maradonian Church is based on the deification of a man and a worldliness of "God". The influence of the Christian model is explicit: a divinity is embodied in a man to give a meaning to an earthly, immanent time (Galimberti, 2000). Thus, the manifestation of the divine assumed metaphorically by Maradona – the passage of God into the world – takes on a role of salvation, redemption, and liberation. His figure symbolically opens possibilities of rebirth and regeneration; in his divinity, he can take charge of the human desires of those who find in him a source of satisfaction, pride, and self-esteem. Not surprisingly, the D10S tetragrammaton has accompanied the sporting deeds of the *pibe de oro* from the beginning of his career by virtue of his footballing exceptionality (in Spanish, *god* is written *dios*, so the formula that uses the number 10 in between the letters G and S hint at the divine status of Maradona without explicitly calling him a god). The Maradonian Church is based precisely on the prophetic charisma of its idol and leader and on his advent in the public sphere at a precise historical moment. His rupturing with the consolidated tradition – that of the social and football establishment – showed a new path for many followers, which the Church institutionalises within a system of beliefs and practices.

Meanwhile, ritual participation takes place in real spaces, such as Rosario – a Maradonian equivalent of Vatican City – as well as virtual spaces like those found in social media, where devotees flaunt memories, photographs, and relics simulating Christian phrasing and symbology. The Church thus constructs a sacred territory, in a traditional sense, one separated from daily pagan life profanity and from those who do not share its beliefs and convictions.

The group dimension of this religion implies a devotion to the Argentinian champion. The aim is not to convert, but to welcome enthusiasts to take part in a community made of shared emotions and symbols, and to spread the fundamental messages, passing them on to new generations and thus giving continuity to beliefs. There are at least two forms of participation. One can take part in activities and rituals, affiliating oneself to a real organisation – the Church – or it is also possible to experience a "softer" participation, expressed through social networks.

Religion is a link with divinity based on two dimensions. The interior dimension asks for attention and respect. In this case, this trait encourages feeling and expressing love for the *pibe de oro* and is facilitated by social media's means of communication: posting pictures, images, and symbols associated with the footballer would be examples. The external dimension of the worship includes institutionalised rites and liturgies developed by the Church. The life of this religious movement is marked, in fact, by moments – such as the celebration of the "Maradonian Christmas" – with a procession of the apostles wearing white robes and carrying relics, scarves, votive images, replica world cups, a bloody ball in a crown of thorns, and a rosary with 34 pearls (the number of goals scored by Maradona with the national team).

The liturgical dimension includes prayers borrowed from the Christian tradition (as we shall see), watching videos of the exploits of Maradona, and the sharing of anecdotes related to the Argentinian champion. Another important ritual is the "Maradonian baptism". It marks the official entry of new members into the community and coincides with the "Maradonian Easter", celebrated on June 22nd in reference to the Mexico 1986 World Cup quarterfinal match won by Argentina against England thanks to the two Maradona goals considered the most legendary: the Hand of God goal and the Goal of the Century. These actions are conceived as miracles attesting to the exceptional, the godly, and the impossible. The baptismal ritual requires the new disciple to imitate the famous hand goal scored in that match. The worshipers must also take the oath on the Chuch's sacred scripture: Maradona's autobiography. When sanctioning a "Maradonian marriage", the parties involved can take the oath on that book or on a ball and exchange wedding rings in front of an image of Maradona. These rituals institute social solidarity between community members, establishing relationships among those connected to the figure of Maradona as a symbol and reference of a collective identity.

The core of the religious belief is the passion for football, hence a devotion to the football "god" who is precisely Maradona. After all, as many Argentinians declare, God must be Argentinian, since the country embodies the pivotal location of the community, an "axis mundi", the sacral centre of the world (Eliade, 1968), and of Maradonian cosmology. The bond with the Maradonian divinity is characterised by a common goal shared by all the members of the Church: to keep alive the magic, the joy, and the passion embodied by the player by remembering his actions on the pitch. Another commitment is to share and disseminate the emotions felt thanks to Maradona's football genius. All of this is part of a broader cyclical re-proposition of the divine archetype, and of the epitome of the perfection of the original myth. This relates to the prevalent idea in archaic religions of being allowed into the sacred only by virtue of imitation, repetition, and participation (Eliade, 1949, 1968). The Maradonian hierophanies – his "supernatural" performances; his number 10 shirt; the fight with evil entities (the England of the Malvinas/Falkland Islands) – point to a form of individual and collective redemption and rebirth. Maradona's ever-renewed manifestations are supposedly reflected then in his ubiquitous presence in t-shirts, posters, tattoos, and people's social profiles, turning him into a central and global cultural factor.

Finally, the link with divinity and social belonging has also a moral impact. It is well indicated in the Decalogue of the Maradonian Church:

> 1. *La pelota no se mancha, como dijo D10S en su homenaje.*
> 2. *Amar al fútbol por sobre todas las cosas.*
> 3. *Declarar tu amor incondicional por Diego y el buen fútbol.*
> 4. *Defender la camiseta Argentina, respetando a la gente.*
> 5. *Difundir los milagros de Diego en todo el universo.*

*6. Honrar los templos donde predicó y sus mantos sagrados.*
*7. No proclamar a Diego en nombre de un único club.*
*8. Predicar los principios de la Iglesia Maradoniana.*
*9. Llevar Diego como segundo nombre y ponérselo a tu hijo.*
*10. No ser cabeza de termo y que no se te escape la tortuga.*

[*1. The ball is never soiled.*
*2. Love football above all else.*
*3. Declare unconditional love for Diego and the beauty of football.*
*4. Defend the Argentina shirt.*
*5. Spread the news of Diego's miracles throughout the universe.*
*6. Honour the temples where he played and his sacred shirts.*
*7. Don't proclaim Diego as a member of any single team.*
*8. Preach and spread the principles of the Maradonian Church.*
*9. Make Diego your middle name and name your first son Diego.*
*10. Don't be slow and be awake*].[3]

These rules codify the Maradonian creed, guiding its promotion. As a result of the need to structure worship practices, the whole system of meanings of the Church emerges.

## The Maradonian sacred: Meaning, morality, memory

Any religion systematises meanings and values in a rigorous tradition with symbolic and ethical authority (Berger, 1979). In the case of the Maradonian Church, some aspects of a religious order are amiss, but devotees nonetheless find in Maradona's figure a source of beliefs which they accept in a dimension situated between the ironic and the authentic. The prayers codified by the Church are ultimately calques, witty imitations of Christian prayers and hymns. Nevertheless, explicitly or between the lines, their principles resonate with Maradona's fans and often end up going beyond football. Thus, perhaps in everyday life, the Maradonian example is seen as a great resource of meaning and existential order. Let us consider the following prayers:

*Padre Nuestro (y es nuestro de verdad)*

*Diego nuestro que estás en la tierra,*
*santificada sea tu zurda,*
*Venga a nosotros tu magia,*
*háganse tus goles recordar,*
*así en la tierra como en el cielo.*
*Danos hoy una alegría en este día,*
*y perdona aquellos periodistas*
*así como nosotros perdonamos*
*a la mafia napolitana.*
*No nos dejes manchar la pelota*
*y líbranos de Havelange…*
*Diego.*

[*Holy Father (and it's truly ours)*

*Our Diego who is of this Earth*
*Hallowed be your left foot.*
*Thy magic be done,*
*May we remember your goals,*
*On Earth as it is in Heaven.*
*Give us this day happiness,*
*And forgive those journalists*
*As we forgive*
*The Neapolitan mafia.*
*And lead us into not soiling the ball*
*And delivers us from Havelange…*
*Diego*].

*D10s te Salve.*

*Dios te salve pelota.*
*Llena eres de magia,*
*el Diego es contigo.*
*Bendita tú eres entre todas las demás*
*y bendito es el Diego que no te deja manchar.*
*Santa redonda, madre del gol*
*ruega por nosotros los jugadores*
*ahora y en la hora de nuestro encuentro…*
*Diego.*

[*Hail D10s*

*Hail the ball*
*Full of magic,*
*The Lord is with Thee.*
*Blessed art thou amongst all*
*And blessed is Diego who does not let you get soiled*
*Holy ball, mother of goal*
*Pray for us players*
*Now and at the hour of our meeting…*
*Diego*].

*Creo*

*Creo en Diego.*
*Futbolista todopoderoso,*
*Creador de magia y de pasión.*
*Creo en Pelusa, nuestro D10s, nuestro Señor,*
*Que fue concebido por obra y gracia de Tota y Don Diego.*
*Nació en Villa Fiorito,*
*Padeció bajo el poder de Havelange,*
*Fue crucificado, muerto y mal tratado.*
*Suspendido de las canchas.*
*Le cortaron las piernas.*

*Pero él volvió y resucitó su hechizo.*
*Estará dentro de nuestros corazones,*
*por siempre y en la eternidad.*
*Creo en el espíritu futbolero,*
*La santa Iglesia Maradoniana,*
*El gol a los ingleses,*
*La zurda mágica,*
*La eterna gambeta endiablada,*
*Y en un Diego eterno.*
*Diego.*

[Lord's Prayer

*I believe in Diego.*
*Almighty footballer,*
*Creator of magic and passion,*
*I believe in Pelusa, our God, our Lord,*
*Who was conceived by Doña Tota and don Diego.*
*He was born in Villa Fiorito,*
*Suffered under Havelange,*
*Was crucified, died and mistreated.*
*Suspended from the fields.*
*They cut his legs.*
*But he came back and his spell was renewed.*
*He will be in our hearts,*
*Forever and in eternity.*
*I believe in the Holy Football Spirit,*
*The Holy Maradonian Church,*
*The goal against the English,*
*The magic left foot,*
*The eternal cunning dribble,*
*And in an eternal Diego.*
*Diego].*[4]

We can intertwine the contents of these prayers with elements extracted from Maradona's personal life and also extracted from his fan's opinions, detectable on social media (such as the Church Facebook group). In this sense, the values that the Church advocates often overlap with Maradona's fandom and thus may be merged into a single horizon of meaning. As already mentioned, a self-evident aspect of Maradonian divinity is the supernatural quality of his talent. As such, his intervention was "divine" in as much as it entailed the suspension of the natural order of things, albeit on the football field.

Following Alabarces (2021), Maradona, the superhuman, the one capable of impossible things, defied human limits and crossed boundaries, even to religious territory. Following Archetti (1997, 2001), Maradona was a winner by divine will and himself was a kind of divine gift. His footballing creativity led to a sort of grammar of the impossible and embodied the transgression of rules and limits. In the perception of his supporters, as a footballer and icon, Maradona got transformed into an allegory of the surpassing of the limited condition of human beings. This was the kind of "excess" eventually applicable to his whole life in a very different context. Nonetheless, this divine incarnation and manifestation of the superhuman gives his fans and followers the confidence, strength, and courage needed to face everyday struggles.

When Maradona as divinity be put on this Earth? His task is to create and share joy, happiness, and other pure emotions, even sorrow (Archetti, 1997). The representation of Maradona has always negotiated joy and pain since he indeed brought delight and provided hope, yet his life also included a series of tragic events – some of them were surmounted – which were experienced, in turn, with grief and compassion (Archetti, 2001). The cult of Maradona also implies a resolution for pain, accepted as passion and sacrifice.

The Christological dimension is a natural fit for the Maradonian Church since the devotion also includes the pride of belonging to the subordinate or disenfranchised classes or countries. In the collective imaginary, he stands as the voice of the outcasts. The Maradonian Church creed explains that he suffered on behalf of humanity by facing the corruption of the world – the sporting world, and perhaps the whole world, is contained in this narrative – and then purified it with joy, excellence, and beauty. This sacrifice, which includes self-destructiveness, is accepted by Argentinian, Neapolitan, and many other fans since it ultimately generated bliss and allowed them to foster dreams and find relief. For many, his sacrifice meant assuming the weight of enormous responsibilities, and this often brought him to the breaking point. This transformed the individual guilt of the dishonour and pain felt by the *pibe de oro* into a collective feeling, hence the constant need not only for atonement but also for blaming and attacking Maradona's historical enemies. In these representations we have, on the one hand, a re-proposition of an ethical ideal for symbolic salvation and, on the other, a model that contemplates human suffering and elaborates – through pain – a communal identity.

When the Church had to cope with his death, the community faced a collective mourning, managing the loss of its champion. In some ways, meaning, morality, and memory were enhanced by this painful emotion. Maradona's death reinforced his persistence as a symbol of identity and connectivity for many communities: the Argentinians, the Neapolitans, the dispossessed, the marginalised, and those seeking redemption. In different ways, often through social media, many wanted and still want to display publicly their own bond with Maradona. Traditional religious or secular methods and actions for coping with death find strength in the fellowship of a community, often with references to a nation, a group, or family. At other times, worshipers and fans simply appeal to a personal connection with their hero.

Despite the ideal of immortality borrowed from Christianity, the death of Maradona represented a wound that translated for many into a sense of injustice. This sense can only have a culprit in factual terms: in this case, the medical staff who was caring for him in his final days. Beyond an alleged negligence that fed tabloids and has ultimately turned into a criminal investigation, blaming doctors means blaming the spokesperson for our unconscious desire for immortality. The doctor is a sort of "thanatocrat", a representative of a system which men entrust to challenge death; not only we are aware of the existence of death, but also we try to deny it and believe we could defeat it in some way (Cavicchia Scalamonti, 1991). In this regard, the Maradonian Church acted with purpose by carrying out collective action seeking a legal procedure to hold those responsible for Maradona's death accountable. It was an effective mobilisation process typical of contentious politics (Tilly and Tarrow, 2007), with a repertoire made up of public performances: demonstrations, protests, dissemination of messages and requests, and organising through social media. The campaign brought together fans who spent time and energy united through deep emotions and transformed a shared identity into a political action.[5] Fighting for Maradona meant defending a sacred object whose desecration generated moral anger, collective indignation, and the desire to punish those who allegedly offended the community by violating its highest symbol.

## The beyond: The Maradonian Church, Argentina, Naples, and the Global South

Many aspects of Maradona's life make him a symbol of Argentinian and Neapolitan popular culture, a regional and national hero, and a representative of the collective spirit of Argentina and Napoli. But he reached much farther. Why was a Church enacted in his name?

First, he represents a national style of football, known in Argentina as *la nuestra*, which is linked to identity and a shared memory of the history of the sport in the country. This creole style, opposed to the English, ultimately indicated national autonomy and liberation. This style is not so much represented by power and organisation – the English way – but by speed, creativity, shrewdness, and flashes of genius; dribbling, cunning in finding a winning play. These characteristics defined Maradona's football talent and his achievements (Archetti, 1997, 2001, 2008). Furthermore, it could be said that the *pibe de oro* produced the happiest collective moments in the country's recent history. Alabarces (2021) reminds us that he represents perhaps the last apical moment in which Argentinians were able to be happy and fantasise, at least after the disappearance of Juan Domingo and Evita Perón (political figures beloved by the masses since they rose to power in the mid-1940s). Second, for large parts of his life, his irreverent and pugnacious way of expressing himself made him a spokesperson for the populist demands of some sectors of his country and for the struggle against the powers that be. This had a decisive impact on the public sphere, perhaps weakened only in the historical phase in which Kirchnerista populism wanted to appropriate the image of popular patriotic representatives (Alabarces, 2006, 2014, 2018).

In Naples, Maradona is a football hero and the object of widespread devotion (Bifulco, 2020). In the city, Maradonian effigies, relics, and altars abound, and one can hear his name pronounced in almost every conversation about football. The SSC Napoli stadium was renamed Diego Armando Maradona Stadium only a few days after his death. He represents the memory of a bright and lyrical moment that united the fans of the team and the citizens of Naples. Today he is dogma, doctrine, binding tradition, and a symbol capable of evoking energy, satisfaction, honour, and solace. The relationship between Maradona and the Neapolitans is based on the idealised tale of a footballer coming to give the people much-desired football triumphs, despite the socio-economic difficulties of the city, challenging, in turn, the wealth and arrogance of the north of the country.

When Maradona arrived in Naples, people expected this charismatic character to change their collective destiny, like a *deus ex machina*, providing transcendental help (Pecchinenda, 2014). For this reason, he is seen as the architect of upheavals, of a reversal of football and social power relations, of citizens' redemption, of the struggle against consolidated powers, and of resistance to northern domination. Thus, Maradona allowed many Neapolitans to enjoy a sense of revenge and encouraged a powerful rhetoric of social redemption and symbolic rehabilitation within the framework of a narcissistic identity and local pride (Bifulco, 2020). In addition, Maradona won with a style of play – and attitude – easily relatable to Neapolitans. The *pibe de oro* was an idealised spokesperson for characteristics considered typical of popular Neapolitanism: anarchic, passionate, undisciplined, rebellious, humble, brash, but brilliant, capable of coping with difficulties thanks to his ability, generous with his teammates, shrewd on the pitch, maybe a little less in life.

His formidable sporting performances and his charisma nourish the self-esteem of a community, which even today identifies with his greatness. Many years after his football victories in Naples, the idea of having had the strongest footballer ever, who is represented as unparalleled and unattainable, the one who unified his destiny with the team and the city still provides a sense of pride and strong gratification. Maradona is not considered exemplary in everyday life; the contradictions that characterised him are not denied by Neapolitan fans, but they are put aside, made secondary. Blameworthy behaviours belong to the ordinary, profane, personal life. Instead, the hero lives in a consecrated, separate, and communal world, where his qualities or his triumphs can be idealised into a collective symbol.

Admiration for Maradona's image is widespread, global. Despite his machismo, his ambiguous relationship with money, and many other potentially reprehensible characterisations, his flamboyant style – in football and life – and his irreverent, excessive, and revolutionary actions led many to consider him an emblem of personal or social emancipation and as symbol of the fight against the powerful.[6] The existence of the Maradonian Church institutionalised some important concepts for marginal sections of world population: revenge, action beyond limits, and symbolic salvation. These provided inspiration to those living in conditions of social, economic, or political inferiority. The evidence of the incredible popularity and relevance of the *pibe de oro* in many places around the world was marked by the global mourning that followed his death, providing further support to the idea embedded in the "Lord Prayer" of an eternal Diego.

## Notes

1 At least two books must be taken into consideration for this topic: José Caldeira's *Iglesia Maradoniana* (2007) and Gabriela Saidon's *Superdios. La construcción de Maradona como santo laico* (2021). Also of interest is the article by Carmen Rial (2021), "El Diego de la gente: the most human of the Football Gods".
2 Cf. http://www.iglesiamaradoniana.com.ar/
3 Cf. https://manofmany.com/entertainment/sport/ten-commandments-church-of-maradona
4 Translations by Pablo Brescia.
5 Cf. https://www.theguardian.com/football/2021/mar/11/diego-maradona-argentina-protests-investigation-buenos-aires
6 See, for example, the strong admiration in Kolkata (Mitra and Naha, 2017).

## References

Alabarces, Pablo. 2006. "El mito de Maradona o la superación del peronismo por otros medios". *DeSignis* 9: 211–220.
_____. 2014. "Tra Maradona e Messi. Dal mito parlante all'eroe muto". *Maradona. Sociologia di un mito globale*. Eds. Luca Bifulco and Vittorio Dini. S. Maria C.V., Italy: Ipermedium libri.
_____. 2018. "De Maradona a Messi: viejos y nuevos argumentos sobre el héroe deportivo y la patria". *Im@go. A Journal of the Social Imaginary* VII.11: 26–43.
_____. 2021. "Maradona: mito popular, símbolo peronista, voz plebeya". *Papeles del CEIC* 249.1: 1–11.
Alberts, Thomas. 2008. "Virtually Real: Fake Religions and Problems of Authenticity in Religion". *Culture and Religion: An Interdisciplinary Journal* 9.2: 125–139.
Archetti, Eduardo. 1997. "'And Give Joy to My Heart'. Ideology and Emotions in the Argentinian Cult of Maradona". *Entering the Field: New Perspectives on World Football*. Eds. Gary Armstrong Gary and Richard Giulianotti. Oxford: Berg.
_____. 2008. "El potrero y el pibe. Territorio y pertenencia en el imaginario del fútbol argentino". *Horizontes Antropológicos* 14.30: 259–282.
_____. 2001. "The Spectacle of a Heroic Life. The Case of Diego Maradona". *Sport Stars. The Cultural Politics of Sporting Celebrity*. Eds. David L. Andrews and Steven Jackson. London and New York: Routledge.
Berger, Peter. 1979. *The Heretical Imperative*. Garden City: Doubleday.
Bifulco, Luca. 2020. *Maradona, un héroe deportivo. Tres estudios sociológicos de Italia*. Buenos Aires: Ediciones Godot.
Bifulco, Luca and Francesco Pirone. 2014. *A tutto campo. Il calcio da una prospettiva sociologica*. Napoli: Guida.
Bifulco, Luca and Mario Tirino. 2018. "The Sports Hero in the Social Imaginary. Identity, Community, Ritual and Myth". *Im@go. A Journal of the Social Imaginary* VII.11: 9–25.
Caldeira, José. 2007. *Iglesia Maradoniana*. Mar del Plata, Argentina: Self Published.
Cavicchia Scalamonti, Antonio. 1991. *Tempo e morte*. Napoli: Liguori.

Collins, Randall. 1982. *Sociological Insight. An Introduction to Non-Obvious Sociology.* Oxford: Oxford University Press.

Cusack, Carole. 2013. "Play, Narrative and the Creation of Religion: Extending the Theoretical Base of 'Invented Religions'". *Culture and Religion: An Interdisciplinary Journal* 14.4: 362–377.

Cusack, Carole. 2018. "Mock Religions". *Encyclopedia of Latin American Religions.* Ed. Henri Gooren. Cham, Switzerland: Springer. E-book. DOI : https://doi.org/10.1007/978-3-319-27078-4

Durkheim, Émile. 1912. *Les Formes élémentaires de la vie religieuse.* Paris: Félix Alcan.

Eliade, Mircea. 1949. *Le mythe de l'éternel retour. Archétypes et répétition.* Paris: Gallimard.

———. 1968. *The Sacred and the Profane: The Nature of Religions.* Boston: Houghton Mifflin.

Galimberti, Umberto. 2000. *Orme del sacro. Il cristianesimo e la desacralizzazione del sacro.* Milano: Feltrinelli.

Geyerman, Chris B. 2016. "Biblical Tales in the Sports News: Narrative and the Redemption of Michael Vick". Eds. Brad Schultz and Mary Lou Sheffer. London: Lexington Books.

Mitra, Sarbajit and Souvik Naha. 2017. "Politics and International Fandom in a Fringe Nation: La Albiceleste, Maradona, and Marxist Kolkata". *Sport in Society* 20.5–6: 660–674.

Otto, Rudolf. 1950. *The Idea of the Holy.* Oxford: Oxford University Press.

Pecchinenda, Gianfranco. 2014. "Io l'ho visto! Tracce del sacro nel mito di Maradona". *Maradona. Sociologia di un mito globale.* Eds. Luca Bifulco Luca and Vittorio Dini. S. Maria C.V.: Ipermedium libri.

Prebish, Charles. 1993. *Religion and Sport: The Meeting of Sacred and Profane.* Westport: Greenwood Press.

Rial, Carmen. 2021. "'El Diego de la gente': The Most Human of the Football Gods". *Eracle. Journal of Sport and Social Sciences.* 4.2: 15–36.

Saidon, Gabriela. 2021. *Superdios. La construcción de Maradona como santo laico.* Buenos Aires: Capital Intelectual.

Schultz, Brad. 2016. "Be Not Conformed: The Relationship between Modern Sport and Religion". *Sport and Religion in the Twenty-First Century.* Eds. Brad Schultz and Mary Lou Sheffer. London: Lexington Books.

Schultz, Brad, and Mary Lou Sheffer, eds. 2016. *Sport and Religion in the Twenty-First Century.* London: Lexington Books.

Sheffer, Mary Lou. 2016. "Who's Got the Game: America's New Religion". *Sport and Religion in the Twenty-First Century.* Eds. Brad Schultz and Mary Lou Sheffer. London: Lexington Books.

Tilly, Charles and Sidney Tarrow. 2007. *Contentious Politics.* Boulder: Paradigm Publishers.

# 13

# WRITING MARADONA

## One and All

*Martín Kohan*
*Translated by David Atkinson*

*I*

There is a composite photograph which may be crucial to understand (if it's a question of understanding) what Diego Maradona is, what he represents and what represents him. It's a photograph which shows a line-up of the Argentinian national team, in the usual formation in which players like to pose for photographers: six standing, behind, and five crouching, in front. The peculiarity of this photograph is that the 11 players in the team are all Diego Maradona. An unattainable utopia of the team consisting entirely of genius, consisting wholly of one single genius? No, that isn't what it's about. Firstly, because football doesn't work like that, football works as a collective and the ways in which that collective works together, not as a sum of individuals. But also because, in that photograph, the 11 Maradonas are different from each other. That is, Maradona is shown at different points in his career and with different appearances: with flowing curls, with short hair, dyed blond, dyed blue with a yellow fringe, with a full beard, with a goatee, clean shaven, fat, very fat, thin.

Maradona is many Maradonas and not only because everyone's condition and appearance can change during their lives. Maradona has been especially fickle, he has designed and redesigned himself several times, and each of those images, every time, became a complete emblem: an icon which took root in the Argentinian collective memory. As a result, this dizzying mechanism of being one and being many is not of the usual order of identity and change, of a theme with variations, of

DOI: 10.4324/9781003196587-17

repetition and difference. It's more than that: Maradona, each of those Maradonas, prevailed as an absolute, as an unrepeatable whole, and moved on to the next version to become another absolute, unrepeatable again, another whole.

## II

Is it over the top to call this "God"? Because Maradona had been called that for a long time. And the number is used which symbolises this, the legendary "10" of his successive jerseys, written in this way: "D10S".[1] That's how it's written, "D10S", which is almost like writing "D's", thus respecting the norms of sacredness, which dictate that the name of God may not be written. Maradona is a god in an era of monotheism; he retains, however, something of the gods of antiquity. His divinity is conveyed in this way: resplendent in his uniqueness, but plagued by passions, weaknesses, falls, rages, fanatical expressivity. He is many while being only one; therefore, even among those who adore him, it isn't possible to subscribe to everything that he has said, nor to everything that he's done, not to all the stances which he's taken. He not only has uttered glorious, unforgettable phrases, some of which ("They cut my legs off",[2] "He let the tortoise get away from him"[3]) have become part of the everyday speech of Argentinians; but he has also said other things which are perhaps best forgotten (especially if we wish to admire him). He has associated himself with a number of notorious causes through his personal relationships, not only with Fidel Castro or with Hugo Chávez, but also with neoliberal policies of hunger and subjugation, as in his friendship with Carlos Menem.

A fallible and contradictory god, those who imagine that he is deified because he is idealised are mistaken. It's the other way round: the cult of Maradona is rather a collective decision to sustain, through pure fervour, the almost impossible concept (but one which has become possible) of an ideal plagued by errors and falls, perfection plagued by flaws. Maradona is not a god who has been made profane, but rather a god of the profane, a god who profanes. He is not even a pagan god, he is a god who paganizes, who attains everything which is sacred, appropriates it and spills it onto the lewdness of popular love. He is one and he is many, so, to worship him, one doesn't have to agree with everything, one doesn't even have to consider doing so. He is many but he is one, and for that reason each person chooses one version which subsumes and represents all the others. And my goal, the goal of all goals for me, is not, as it happens, the one he scored against England in the Mexico 1986 World Cup, starting from the middle of the pitch, but rather one which he scored in 1981 against River while playing for Boca: it was raining, it was dark, it was three-nil.

One may of course object that all this veneration is irrational, misplaced and largely without substance, merely an ironclad will to believe, merely a febrile obstinacy of faith. But, is there really any religion about which one might not say the same? At least all those excessive, disconcerting liturgies take on the unique condition of populist carnivalisation, so typical of the popular.

## III

There's that goal which is so famous, the best ever. But before that there was another goal, no less famous and perhaps no less significant: the one he scored with his hand in the same match. At the end of the game, and with the controversy already established, the press in full came along to interrogate Maradona: that goal, had a hand been used? "The hand of god", Maradona replied. In this way, he tried to distance himself from the ruse which he had resorted to, transferring it to the unfathomable sphere of divine will. But since we were all able to verify from the photos and the television replays that the goal had been scored with a hand and that that hand was his, the general conclusion was very different: it was that, therefore, he was God.

Years later, in 1990, Pope John Paul II received him in the Vatican. One had the strong impression that of the two, the one who was most interested in the meeting taking place was Wojtyla. And by the way: on leaving the audience, Maradona complained about the gold in the ceilings and demanded that it be distributed among children living in poverty in Africa, instead of kissing their feet so much. The idolatry of Maradona is rooted, among other possible reasons, in two fundamental bases: the first, naturally, is how he plays; then, although hardly to any lesser extent, his personal charisma.

Maradona played professionally from October 20, 1976 to October 25, 1997. During those years, the marking systems were much harsher, more rigorous, and also more violent, and refereeing was infinitely more lenient, more tolerant of the rough behaviour of defenders. Maradona's feats are incomparable, among other things, because in achieving them he overcame the most oppressive types of individual marking ever (two representative examples: that of Gentile, of the Italian team, in 1982, and that of Reyna, of the Peruvian team, in 1985) and the most brutal kicks of any anthology of horrifying fouls in the history of world football. Maradona's great moves have the beauty of physical prowess (Messi, on the other hand, dazzles with precision and lightning speed), and they become even greater when one considers what he had to overcome. Pelé had to put up with serious fouls primarily in World Cup competitions, and in fact he was injured in two of the four in which he took part; aside from that, almost his whole career was in Brazil. In Messi's case, he has the benefit of an era in which the tactic of zonal marking predominates, with more space and freedom, and full protection of the most talented players by the referee. Maradona's feats on the football pitch must be measured in relation to what he had to fight against in order to achieve them, including, on more than one occasion and in more than one sense, himself; the most demanding obstacles in the most arduous circumstances.

Maradona's charisma also influenced his importance in the game, as it was one of the factors in his leadership capacity, with which he managed to inspire others through his mere presence, or indeed above all through his mere presence. But this is also a key factor to appreciate the singular potency of the idolatry which he arouses. Maradona is charismatic, he is photogenic, he is histrionic, he is epic, he is tragic; he is venerated not only for what he is, but also for what he exudes.

If Maradona is the privileged object of an inexhaustible iconography, it is because he himself is a charismatic machine of iconicity.

## IV

In the 90s, a weekday, in the morning, very early. I saw him. I saw him in the street, on the pavement. Standing still, alone. He was alone. It was a miracle. Not just seeing him (an induced miracle, because I passed by, whenever I could, the school his daughters went to; I passed by and looked), but also, even more, because he was alone. Because Maradona (I think this might explain many things) is never alone. He is never alone. He lives under that pressure; there are always people with him, someone looking at him, someone photographing him, someone filming him, someone greeting him. On that day, miraculously, he was alone, standing on the pavement, looking calmly into the distance. But that state of being alone didn't last, of course. Someone approached him. Who? Me. Why? To worship him.

I greeted him. I hugged him, I told him in a few words how much he meant to me. It would be a lie to say that he wasn't receptive, kind, even welcoming. But at the same time, in some way, he didn't seem to register my presence. He let me embrace and adore him, but at the same time he didn't seem to realise it was happening. Perfectly tangible, within reach of my devotion, but at the same time somewhat remote, somewhat absent. Is there an explanation for that? Of course there is, or is that not exactly how Walter Benjamin defines the concept of aura? The unrepeatable manifestation of a remoteness, however, near something or someone may be.

## V

On the 3rd of November 1985, Maradona, playing for Napoli, scores from a free kick against Juventus. The arc that the ball follows to clear the wall and drop suddenly towards the goal seems to be inexplicable. But there is an explanation; the earth seems to have changed its speed of rotation for an instant, and thus an infallible law, the law of gravity, was subject to a notable exception. But, could something like that really happen, just so that Maradona's shot became a goal?

Of course it could.

## God, the Era, and the Epic

*Ana María Shua*
*Translated by Allison Febo*

A 60-year-old man has been suffering from a serious heart condition for over two decades. This is someone who does not care about his health, not even a little. He has done all sorts of drugs, he is obese and an alcoholic. Having just undergone surgery for a subdural hematoma, he has to remain in hospital because he is suffering from severe withdrawal symptoms. One morning, a few days after being discharged from the clinic, he is found dead in his bed due to cardiac arrest. Had it been anyone else, their death would have been foreseeable, even predictable and there would be no cause for any further investigations. However, this man was Diego Maradona, and no one was willing to accept it, especially the people of Argentina. Someone must be blamed. There is talk of negligence, malpractice, even abandonment. The police raids the offices of the team treating Maradona (nurses, doctors, psychologists). Mobile phones are confiscated, and dangerously irreverent chats are leaked to the press. Gods do not die, they are killed. Gods do not commit suicide, but sometimes they may be crucified.

I try to explain this idea to a friend, but she interrupts me emphasising the importance of an investigation. I try, uselessly it seems, to persuade her that Diego was an adult person who decided how, where, and with whom he did things. A crucifixion requires a traitor. Romans and Jews.

> It is very good that there is a police investigation into Maradona's death because there may be crimes involved: carelessness, mistreatment, or business deals. Personally, I don't trust that doctor!
>
> *Patricia F., 52-year-old, political advisor*

Even after his death, Diego still manages to perform miracles. Fans share memes in which the face of the idol is seen in the shape of clouds, in a spot on the wall, in a shadow. On March 14, 2021, a few months after his death, the classic Boca *vs* River match is to take place. With only 2 minutes remaining, the game at a draw, the ball is on the verge of crossing the line of the Boca goal, when it is mysteriously, almost magically deviated. A rumour begins to unfold on the stands: It was Maradona! It was him; it was Diego! Soon after, more memes appear that display how he could have mediated this divine intervention.

> Everything he gave us, the joy, the excitement, the thrills, making us feel so great; it has no point of comparison. The rest does not matter, what do I care? It was his life.
>
> *Bety R., 65 years old, hairdresser, with eyes full of tears*

It was his life, yet it was everyone's life. All his flounders, his follies, his addictions, his women, his children, he shared everything with everyone as he had shared his goals in the past. We watched at him, we pitied him, we hated him, we loved him. Did he have the right to hurt himself this much?

> I always liked him a lot for his sincerity and in a way for his suffering. It seems that football players, who receive a gift from the gods and go from being poor to being millionaires, are like Freud describes, those who fail with success. It is like a Faustian bargain, to whom am I indebted for the gift I have been given?
>
> *Eduardo C., 55-year-old, psychoanalyst*

The Maradonian church was founded in Argentina, in part jokingly, but mostly seriously. It now has parishioners all over the world. It is not a true religion and in fact it does not compete with other religions its followers may have. They believe in Maradona as their football God. In Scotland, Afghanistan, and Japan, there are official venues where people congregate. There are even couples who have married in some of these venues, in accordance with the Maradonian rites. Most notably, perhaps, is the fact that, unlike other religions, the Church was established well before Maradona's death.

> I have a rational religion, and that is the Catholic Church, and I have a religion in heart, my passion, and that is Diego Maradona.
>
> *Alejandro Verón, one of the founders of the Maradonian Church*

How and why did Diego achieve divinity? Was it only for being an extraordinary player? Yet those who know about football (among whom I do not count myself) say that perhaps he was not as good a player as Messi. Frankly, the comparison is inevitable. Adjectives that are ascribed to either player, either for or against, do not suffice. Messi: machine, robot. Maradona: heart, emotion, feeling. During Maradona's brief reign, no player in the world could be compared to him: you had to think about the historic Pelé. On Messi's long reign, there are other players almost of the same level (Ronaldo for instance). But also (alas!), Messi never won a World Cup with his country. And that cannot be forgiven.

Maradona was not the standard-bearer for the poor. He was the flag itself. All the wealth and the fame in the world were not enough to make him forget even for a moment where he came from, who he was, or for whom he had to win the match. SCC Napoli was a minor club, in a poor region, at a time when the Italian league was the best in the world, dominated by teams from the North (Inter, Juventus, Milan): the big, the powerful, the rich. Napoli was a team like so many when Maradona came in to make everyone play and to bring out the best in each one, to take them to the top.

> Maradona with the ball was like a computer, he calculated everything as if he could see the future. But he was also a poet … He made poetry with the ball.
>
> *Griselda F., 38 years old, commercial employee*

The era: the moment when globalization was rising and football was becoming as globalised as the world, a spectacle for everyone.

The epic: how to raise weaker teams that fought at a disadvantage, with low budgets, and bring down the rich and the powerful.

The epic: Maradona was pure efficiency, like a chess player, like a computer, he was able to intuitively calculate all the possible openings before every move, to map all possible courses of action even before receiving the ball. He had a capacity for prophecy, a talent for strategy. But that wasn't all: he was also a great artist. His goals were lyrical, he jumped like a dancer, and his dancing distracted his rivals, his moves unpredictable.

Pure poetry.

> If one day an alien arrives, an inhabitant of the planet Venus, and wants to know what football is, just show him Maradona's second goal against England in the 1986 World Cup. Everything is there. The goal, the passion, the madness, the football. It was the best goal in history. And always will be.
>
> *Carlos A., 43 years old, architect*

The epic: the two goals against England in 1986, each perfect in its own way: "The hand of God" and the best goal in history.

The era: with Maradona, we beat the English (yes, it was us, all of us, that's what it's all about!) just four years after Argentina lost the Falklands/Malvinas War.

The epic: in the 1990 World Cup, in Italy, Maradona reaches the final fighting against the odds, with a weakened team. Caniggia's goal against Brazil set up by a wonderful pass from Maradona in midfield. In that final game in Rome, the whole stadium was against him, whistling, even the referee was against him. Maradona was crying when Argentina lost to a dubious penalty. Crying, because he was also human. Too human.

The epic: in the 1990 World Cup, in Italy, Maradona playing despite being injured, with a swollen ankle, limping but never giving up.

The epic: the way he confronted the authorities of FIFA, the AFA, the immense courage to challenge those in power by denouncing injustices.

The epic: his attitude when he was disqualified in the 1994 World Cup. "They cut off my legs", he said.

> Maradona was able to turn everything he did into an art form, he was an expressionist without a theoretical framework, he did not seek to do things well, nor only beautifully, he sought to make them his way, leaving his signature at every step. He carried the art in his blood and played football as one more expression of his uncompromising talent. He did things that had been considered impossible before. His magic demanded the constant question: what is he going to do next?
>
> *Gaspar L., 35 years old, journalist*

Skilled like no other with the ball, he was also an intelligent man, with his own judgements, with strong political opinions. He also had a way with words, something unusual in an athlete: he always knew what to say, exactly what we needed to hear. They were perfect phrases, refined and vulgar, with rhetorical figures as sophisticated as they were streetwise. It is not by chance that "the ball does not get stained" is the first commandment of the Maradonian Church. His famous phrases are found on the web and many became part of the language of Argentinians. I wonder how much the rest of the world would have been able to enjoy that verbal wit, so local, so typical. And yet I think they understood and appreciated it. His Nietzschean word ("Say your word and break yourself") was welcomed by all the poor of the world, for the outcasts, the marginalized, those at the bottom of every society. And by many others too because the Maradonian passion cuts across all social classes.

> Maradona was not only great in victory; he also was great in defeat. He was also a genious when falling down, and we Argentinians are very familiar with defeat. He knew how to maintain dignity (or its opposite) in loss, that bliss in failure was pure tango...
>
> *Ricardo B., 73 years old, marketing consultant, his voice shaking as he speaks*

Argentina is just the country of the humble manger where the Lord of Football himself was born. But Maradona transcended domestic fame and the affection of his people to become the incarnation of all the outcasts of the world. Of the underdeveloped countries, of their most disadvantaged inhabitants. In their name, he beat all the rich countries, all the powerful teams. After his death, altars were erected to Maradona in India, in Syria, in Indonesia. He was God and surely still is, but Maradona was, nevertheless, Son of Man. Human and more than human, he fulfilled all the dreams of a *pibe*. Like Peter Pan, he never grew up: he died fighting Captain Hook (whom he also had inside him).

Before the failed ethics and aesthetics of a revolutionary narrative, Maradona was a rebel. He wanted it all, he had it all, he tried everything and fell into all the traps. Above all, he made the mistake of believing to be Maradona. And for being so human, so normal, for making so many mistakes, he was divine. He paid for it all with his health.

> Maradona died for everyone, he died for us, to save us. It was an offering we had to surrender; it was what we had to give in exchange for vaccines against coronavirus.
>
> *Fernando M. 38 years old, building's maintenance man*

## Language and Tears

*Edgardo Scott*
*Translated by Ana Terrazas Calero*

"If they make me play at noon in a searing heat that gives me a splitting head-ache, then I have the right to say it. I'm the one who puts himself on the line in the field. No one pays to see Havelange". Maradona said this at the 1986 Mexico World Cup. Joao Havelange was FIFA president. The subject was the scheduling of the matches for their worldwide broadcasting. If a match was played in Mexico at seven in the evening, when the heat would drop, it would, for example, be two in the morning in Europe. Thus, a terrible timing for advertising business. A World Cup is also business. Playing at noon it was, then. We already know what Maradona did at noon in that World Cup, in that heat, at that altitude.

Maradona always had a key relationship with language which is essential to understanding his epic and the pain of his loss. Once, a television program took him to "La blanqueada", the pizzeria in Pompeya, on the intersection of Sáenz and Roca Avenue, where Diego would eat two slices of pizza when he got off the bus that drove him back from training with Argentinos Junior in La Paternal, before crossing the Riachuelo and taking the train for Fiorito at the Puente Alsina Station. The TV program brings there a boy who plays for Boca Juniors' youth squad, who seems to be good, and who is, in fact, doing all kinds of juggling and freestyling with the ball in that pizzeria. The special surprise is that Maradona shows up, of course. The boy is doing keepie-uppies and Maradona goes in. There is hugging, crying, violin music playing in the background, and then the journalist asks Diego what he thinks. Diego replies: "Now he has to do that in the field". Prior to that, he had told an anecdote about a Hungarian man who wanted to challenge him to see who could do the most keepie-uppies but he had never played with the national team. "You juggle the ball—he had told the Hungarian man—I juggled my life".

Maradona was not only a genius with his left foot; but his tongue was also skilful in all tones and genres. It could go epic: "I made mistakes and paid for them, but ... but the ball does not get stained". It could be more like coarse and spiteful chicanery ("shove it up your ass"), or lean toward tragedy: "they cut my legs off"; gratitude to Bochini, his idol: "Come, Maestro. We've been waiting for you"; or irony: "I'm not allowed into Japan because I did drugs, yet they let in the Yankees, who dropped two atomic bombs on them". It could involve wordplay and Freudian jokes: "I grew up in a private neighborhood ... so private that we were deprived of water, electricity, and telephone".[4] Like Borges, Charly García, Perón, Tita Merello, Federico Peralta Ramos, or Gatica, Maradona's linguistic skill is perfectly connected with the unspeakable truth of being Argentinian.

Perhaps that is why, when Diego heated up, when he brightened up in the field and was ready to run towards goal down the edge of the world and against all the players, and powers, that stood in his way, his tongue would almost always come out. Many photographs have captured it. His tongue was not hanging out, he did not stick it out either. The tongue came out, entered the scene, and made an appearance out of his mouth when Diego enjoyed what he was doing with the ball.

Maradonian language consists of two elements: football language, what Maradona "says" by playing, and verbal language, which is what Maradona says when he speaks. I am using the present tense because his language does not have to die. I suspect that it was not enough at the time to play football extraordinarily well. You had to do extra. You had to be something else, and Diego realized he had to be extraordinary with words as well. The statement of his childhood dreams is famous: play for the national team; be a champion with Argentina.

To master language, one needs to know all its metaphoric and metonymic force, and its ability to synthesize, expand, and suggest. But that is what his football was as well. When Diego says "he let the tortoise get away" or "don't pity anybody", he is making the same use of economy of language as he did with the first goal against Belgium in the 1986 World Cup semifinal, or that indirect free-kick in the box against Juventus. In reality, we should counterpoint football language to Maradona's spoken language in order to discover his total and absolute style in that unlikely synthesis.

That is why it is a mistake to divide Maradona into two. A deliberate mistake, of course. There is no Maradona the football player, and Maradona the man. No good Maradona – the sportsman – and bad Maradona – the insolent, dissolute, irresponsible one. Those are false categories; it is the little finger of power raising up to indicate what is correct and what is not. Maradona is an extraordinary fact in Argentinian history and language. "God is unconscious", Lacan pointed out. "God is Argentinian", we say, and not only us.

Diego cried many times in public. He cried when he lost the 1990 World Cup Final against Germany, when he was disqualified ("they cut my legs off") in the 1994 World Cup, or when he bid farewell to football. He cried over his children and grandchildren, and, in recent times, following the death of his parents, he became emotional and cried often. It is not common to see men who are public figures cry. It is uncommon for politicians to cry, even for artists to cry without an ulterior motive. Why is that?

But peoples cry for their heroes. It has always been that way. They cry and pray. They bring a gift and leave an offering. What would have Diego said at seeing his people cry for him at his funeral like that, mourning him perhaps in a way that people will never mourn anybody else again. It is best that he has not seen it. If he had, he would be so sad that he would have died.

## Saint Diego Maradona?

*María Rosa Lojo*
*Translated by Allison Febo*

In 2007, when the subject was rarely considered by writers, I published a book that merged essay and fiction. In ten chapters, it covered the lives of ten different "saints", fictionalized from different angles. The book, titled *Glowing bodies: Argentinian popular saints* (Lojo, 2007), became popular amongst journalists and intellectuals, curious about the phenomenon of these canonizations that escaped institutional regulation.

After Diego's death, I was constantly bombarded with the same question: could Maradona become a "pagan saint"? Some would go even further and ask if he could become a global saint. Diego evoked expansive emotion in all corners of the planet and in people of all cultures and social classes. Additionally, he is venerated by the "Maradonian Church" (originally founded in Rosario and later expanded to many other countries), with its ritualised commandments and prayers that parody the religious language of Catholicism. Maradona has been commemorated everywhere, both in and outside of Argentina, with flowers, messages, posters, and even candles lit in his name.

However, the permanent promotion of a person to the category of "saint" and, more specifically, of "popular saint", is complex, and above all, requires a specific cultural context. For instance, it was not easy to explain the canonization process of Gauchito Gil (c.1847–1874) in German Universities that were oblivious to catholic traditions. Or even in catholic countries that have become more secular, where the cult of saints is merely folkloric and limited only to the worship of canonical figures.

Latin America, with its anarchic and impoverished societies, with its marginalized masses, has been a particularly fertile space for the development of such devotions that are founded outside of the official Church (Graziano, 2007). It wouldn't be fair to label them "pagan cults" solely under this premise. Although the origin of saints can be traced back to pagan Gods, the centuries of Catholicism created a sufficiently solid framework for its followers to incorporate them naturally to the saints of an already established religion, with liturgical, verbal, and imaginative elements, without subjecting them to the verifications that the Church would require.

The mention of Maradona as a candidate for the status of Saint provokes many contradicting opinions. How can it be possible that an individual denoted for his athletic brilliance and his deficiencies in other areas be deemed worthy of such worship? Apart from his professional talent, what is there to glorify or emulate in a man who disowned some of his own children, who was accused of violence against women, who indulged in his overconsumptions and his addictions?

Frankly, it is the combination of the features described above that make Maradona the ideal candidate for canonization. Primarily, a popular saint does not require moral superiority. He or she could be a notorious sinner, even a lawless delinquent such as the "rural bandits" Gauchito Gil or Santos Guayama in Argentina (both are emblematic examples). Yet there is something in these characters that makes up for their rebellious sides: they show human fullness (in the sense of moral totality, which includes good and bad) and not only their best aspects, like the official saints.

Artist Dany Barreto, author of "Gauchito Gil" and other works drawing on the imagery of popular saints, once trusted me with an illustrative anecdote: a devotee, in love with his sister-in-law, had written Gauchito a letter about such a tormenting situation and asked him for help: "I don't dare tell God, but I'll tell you, because I know you will understand". Partygoer and dancer, cattle raider and lover, Gauchito Gil, that imperfect peasant and deserter of the 19th century, was so relatable that one would confide in him the most unspeakable secrets.

The transgressions of the holy men and women anointed by the people are generally counterbalanced by a premature or tragic death and/or high doses of redemptive suffering. Music stars such as Gilda or Rodrigo had an untimely departure from the world in accidents that took their lives at the peak of success and in the prime of their youth.

However, this was not the case with Maradona. He was already retired as a player and passed away in his sixth decade of life. Many writings described his physical and psychological ailments, his descent into the inferno of drugs and alcohol, his rehabilitation and his relapses, his fight against obesity. The word "calvary", which refers to the Passion of Christ, is repeated in the press with a focus on Maradona the sufferer, a figure no less important than Maradona the footballer.

Maradona's Via Crucis, however, was revealed as even more distressing with the circumstances that surrounded his death. There is already a case open in the San Isidro General Prosecutor's Office for "negligent homicide", which has seven defendants: neurosurgeon Leopoldo Luque, psychiatrist Agustina Cosachov, psychologist Carlos Daniel Díaz, doctor Nancy Forlini, coordinator of Maradona's home hospitalization, nurses Dahiana Gisela Madrid and Ricardo Omar Almirón, and the representative of Medidom (the company that provides medical home care services) Mariano Perroni.[5] All of these people had been tasked with overseeing Maradona's care and well-being.

Negligence, abandonment, malpractice are the accusations being brought by Maradona's former wife Claudia and his daughters, Dalma and Gianina. The voice messages exchanged between some of these characters, distributed widely by media, demonstrate an alarming degree of personal indifference and contempt for the patient. They also show hostility towards Claudia, Dalma, and Gianina. Maradona's lawyers, Matías Morla and Víctor Almirón, do not come out any better in front of the public opinion from all the leaked materials.

Frankly, Morla deserves a separate paragraph. As the sole owner of *Sattvica*, a company established in 2015, he has the rights for "Diego Armando Maradona", "Diego Maradona", "Maradona", "Diegol", "El 10?", "El Diego", and "La Mano de Dios", among other trade names. In December 2020, the lawyer announced that 50% of the proceeds of Sattvica would go to Maradona's sisters, thus fulfilling a protection commitment contracted with the player. Dalma and Gianina sued the lawyer for "fraudulent administration and abuse of power", considering that nothing less than the multimillionaire world exploitation rights of the Maradona name were stolen from their father's estate.[6]

The final days of Maradona evoke, in many respects, scenes from the film *I Care a Lot* (dir. Jonathan Blakeson, 2020, USA), in which elderly men and women, wealthy but vulnerable, are separated from their family members and become prey to "caretakers" (of the medical and legal systems) who operate like a mafia gang with a common objective: to profit as much as they can from the patients.

However, there are also others who think that Dalma and Gianina should share part of the blame. There is no shortage of "fans" (or devotees) who reprimand them for not having fought enough to have closer access to their father and be more personally involved in the treatments he was receiving – even if this was against Maradona's own will.

Maradona, more a victim than a criminal, perhaps "redeemed" by suffering, fragile survivor of his own impulses: that is the image that gains ground in popular thought, and that has been growing for a long time. Who doesn't remember the film *Youth* (2015), directed by Paolo Sorrentino. In a reversal of glory, an incredibly obese Maradona (but still capable of some skilful acts with a ball) appears in a luxury spa, along other famous people (artists, film stars) who are on the decline.

For us, his journey of peaks and valleys exacerbates its most dramatic aspects to the point of blurring with the image of Argentina itself, as psychoanalyst Silvia Bleichmar has argued: "We love what Diego represents as a healer, and also his sense of being incomplete, not totally fulfilled ... He resembles us and our history. We Argentinians are Diego: we can do sublime things and horrible things ... We are a strange mix of talent, brilliance and defeat, and in this is what relates us to him".

Maradona also demolishes the logic of another moral worldview: feminism. A representative of the new generations, Florencia Angilleta, explains why one can easily love the footballer while simultaneously being a modern feminist. Maradona, she says, is "somebody who made men cry, even though they had been raised with the mandate that real men must not cry". Maradona is exceptional and absolute: he "doesn't belong to Peronism, nor to feminism, Diego is Argentina".

That profound, ecumenical representativeness is another reason why Maradona could attain a saintly status, at least among non-canonical saints. Such figures, who tend to come from the lower classes, dedicate their vital time to assisting and serving others. Here, "other" is a truly inclusive term, encompassing everyone, be they poor or wealthy. A popular saint helps not only the poor but also anyone who is in need. The joy of football that Maradona emanated was universal.

Maradona followed a "hero's journey" laden with trials and obstacles. His story of self-improvement takes him from the unpaved streets of Villa Fiorito to the centre of the global stage. In that place he never abandons his family. He lovingly cares for her parents, Don Diego and Doña Tota; he never disowns the humble cradle he came from; and he retains his colourful way of speaking. He does not fear excess or ridicule, nor does he humour the prejudices others have about him and his origins.

Maradona beating the English in the 1986 World Cup in Mexico is like David defeating Goliath. Miraculous on the left (the clandestine "hand of God") and on the right (his masterwork, the "goal of the century"), he is as impeccable as he is stupendous. Now he needs only to perform other miracles in the lives of his faithful followers. Some seem to have happened already, such as the reopening of the legendary bowling alley "Palo's" in Castelar, the Buenos Aires suburbs where I grew up and where I live. One night in 2004, Diego bowled at "Palo's" and signed a Boca replica shirt for the owner's daughter. That treasure will soon go to auction to begin paying off the debts incurred in the pandemic.[7] Maradona, they say, is the only one who can achieve the miracle that Palo's is not forced to close again.

## M and M, to See or Not to See

*Patricio Pron*
*Translated by Emma Byrne*

It is difficult to know whether we tell stories because we cannot sleep, or because we don't want to wake up. Perhaps, for that reason, there are only two types of stories: those designed to help us fall asleep and those that keep us awake. I once had the chance to see Diego Armando Maradona on a playing field, but I let it pass and now I don't know to which of these two types the story belongs to.

Boca Juniors at the time had a goalkeeper who was poor at clearing the ball, but who was an excellent shot-stopper and very confident at the goal, an experienced defence, an illustrious and creative midfield revolving around Maradona, and dizzying attackers. Rosario Central suffered from a very poor defence line, a volatile goalkeeper, a limited midfield strengthened by the presence of a veteran player and static forwards. In contrast to Carlos Salvador Bilardo, a diligent coach and a perfectionist through and through, Rosario Central was coached by Ángel Tulio Zof, who reclaimed *potrero* football, from which, until some time ago, the great Argentinian football players had emerged. Zof's intervention in matches was usually limited to asking his players to play "the way they knew how".

The scales were clearly tipped, and I, at the time, being a member of Rosario Central, had a season ticket that included all the home games. I had discovered football recently thanks to my friend C. G. but I deplored the feeling of emptiness that gripped me after every match, as Sunday and its anticipation began to slide irretrievably towards Monday and its predictable weariness. So I decided to stay at home, in safety, and listen to the match on the radio, which has always been – for some reason that I now know is an alternation of narrative and analysis that has become, among other things, the dominant style of the books I write – my favourite way of "watching" football, with my eyes squeezed tightly shut.

The year 1996 could have been good, I don't remember. At that time, the country was showing signs of each of the circumstances that would lead to the days of December 2001, but most of us preferred to look the other way. A single feeling united us, and Maradona was both a product and a manifestation of it: that the good times were behind us, not so far away as to evoke nostalgia, but not so close that we could benefit from the remnants of goodness that had survived. Watching it again, I have the impression that Boca's victory was more laborious than I remembered. Hernán "Rifle" Castellano saved a penalty taken by Maradona and then tackled him. Boca won 1-0 in what was the only victory of Maradona in his four matches against Rosario Central. Despite this, the 1986 World Cup hero exited to a standing ovation. He had returned to football the previous year after his suspension at the United States 1994 World Cup. He had a yellow streak in his hair and had gained a few extra pounds, but in essence, we noted that he was the same man we had always known. However, he wasn't the same. He had gained a desire for revenge that made him larger than life and a tragic character. Maradona's glory was made up of failures of one kind or another, and his ascension to the footballing altars consisted only of a lengthy descent; his fate was predictable and yet inevitable.

Lionel Messi, like many Argentinians, may have wanted to be like Maradona. Unlike all of us, however, he may have realised the impossibility of being so. Time and again, in the wake of Messi's successes, accolades, his best games for the Argentinian national football team, as well as his worst ones – and more recently, after Maradona's death (see: https://bit.ly/3sJMoed) – the comparisons between Messi and the 1986 World Cup champion have moved from the comparison of dates and statistics to personal preferences, and from there to the messianic thinking which underlies the way in we Argentinians are moving through the "post-Maradona" era, awaiting a Second Coming in which the appearance of each new player who is attributed the status of heir is a reason to hope briefly and be disappointed almost immediately. It is also a burden which, at least for the moment, only Messi seems to have been able to carry without succumbing to its weight.

Beyond both the similarities and differences in results, venues, times, and styles, what would the main distinction between Maradona and Messi be? For the Argentinian population, its significance is closely linked to the eras in which both players lived. For Argentinians, Messi does not symbolise what Maradona did. Unlike Maradona, whose talent was natural and emerged in circumstances of particularly adverse poverty and vulnerability, Messi was trained in the best football academy in the world, a fact which rendered him fake and disconnected in the eyes of certain Argentinians. Moreover, his lack of verbal innovation, the fact that his private life was not characterised by ups and downs, his lack of anxiety, and that what appears to be a certain conformism in the face of social and political events, makes him difficult for Argentinians to relate to. His image does not reflect what we Argentinians want to believe we are (but are not): creative despite adversity, spontaneous, heroic, and passionate. Argentina loves its "stars", but stars are, by definition, those who possess an innate talent which does not require any effort on their part and which will ultimately doom them. Regarding Messi, it is evident that he has put too much work, too much effort, and too much commitment into his profession for Argentinians to seriously consider him a "star". In addition, he possesses a stable personality that not only keeps him out of danger of ending up like Maradona but also prevents him from taking the step that would elevate his personal history into myth and myth into a narrative that underpins the vision that society has of itself.

Perhaps that is the problem. After all, we Argentinians love Maradona because we see ourselves in his overindulgences, setbacks, and outbursts. Or at least we see what we want to believe; that the possession of a talent leads to the condemnation of the subject who possesses it, and that it is therefore better not to strive, it is better not to desire to have a gift, it is better to contemplate those who possess it in the hope that they too will fall. Through Maradona's highs and lows – arrests, injuries, suspensions, comebacks, even his death, which for a few hours allowed the Plaza de Mayo in Buenos Aires and the Casa Rosada to regain a sense of history and significance – he reflected the many ups and downs of Argentina in the 1980s. Messi, on the contrary, is the product of a period which, with its inevitable turbulences, is one of the most "ordinary" (in a positive sense) in the last 60 years of Argentinian history. Maradona was worthy of the creation of a religion to worship him, not least for his goals against England (which some still consider to be revenge for the Argentinian defeat in the Malvinas/Falklands War), for having given Argentina a World Cup title, for having embodied the exceptional nature of an exceptional country like no other. Messi may not even succeed in getting someone to erect a small chapel for him at a crossroads, even though his achievements well surpass those of Maradona at this point (not counting his performances at the World Cup, something that Argentinians are not willing to forget). As I write this, Messi is the top scorer in the Spanish football league and seems to be able to single-handedly revive a poorly constructed team. He is now 33 years, 8 months, and 3 days old; the same age Maradona was when he was banned from the World Cup in the United States for testing positive for ephedrine after playing Nigeria. Messi is only two days older than Maradona was at that defining moment in his career, the moment of yet another failure. To be the best in history, you need to have been the best not for three or four years, but throughout the years and competitions. Messi, who has won 36 titles and 6 Ballon d'Ors in 15 seasons as a professional, is still active. He will never be a banner of reconciliation or a pledge of unity among all Argentinians, but he is proof that excellence in a discipline does not have to be paid for at the price of personal destruction.

It is not a matter of individual talent or personal merit. It is the result of the fact that times have changed, as they always do, and that Argentina is much more "normal" now than it was in Maradona's time. This means it also exhibits the same signs of inefficiency and corruption and the same problems of poverty and marginality that are common in the region. Furthermore, their best player is also normal, which is something we should celebrate, despite everything. I watch Messi play at least once a week; sometimes to do so is to share in his powerlessness. More commonly, however, it is an exercise in intelligence and calculation that restores football to its status as an intellectual sport. But Messi lacks a sense of epic, even when it is necessary to turn a game around, when the opposition is a historic rival, or when there is a medal at stake. I have also seen him playing live on a couple of occasions, but none of these has left such an indelible mark on me as that time when I preferred not to watch Maradona.

Sometimes I think that the reason I preferred not to see Maradona in person – the reason I gave up an opportunity that seemed historic and, needless to say, was never to be repeated – is that I was afraid. I feared that I would be disappointed by this man, who was already in free fall at the time. I refused to see him for fear that seeing the hero would destroy what the "hero" was for me and for others: the incarnation of a complex ideal, the protagonist of one of those stories whose perfection – in the symmetries that establish the dizzying ascent and the plummeting fall – forces us to continue telling them, even though we no longer know whether to hold on to the dream we once had or to wake up from it, to embrace the daylight that is not as blinding as the glow of the bonfire and the myth.

## Number Ten in Ten

*Pedro Angel Palou*

1. Many football players have an impact outside the field. Some influence the youth and become role models – Pelé, Cristiano Ronaldo, Messi; many of them are also a significant source of revenue for their clubs. There is only one who went beyond the field and also had such economic impact. A player who was also a point of reference for a generation of fans in Latin America and the world. A player that became a cultural phenomenon: Diego Armando Maradona. He is, in all senses, larger than life.

2. He has a religion, a temple, a shrine, and thousands of believers. For them, Diego is God. Period. The maradonistas worship their idol and go to Sunday services in their memory. If a football player is capable of such fanaticism is because his figure goes way beyond the grass, the ball, the goals he scored. He was even able to speak with God. In the Mexico World Cup in 1986, he scored one of his immortal goals with "The hand of God" and the referee could not see the infraction to the rule.

3. Once, in a taxicab in Buenos Aires, the driver told me that he wanted to baptize her newborn daughter as Diega Armanda. Apparently, there is a law in Argentina that prevents parents from picking names that don't exist. He came up with another, irrefutable: Mara Dona. The girl bears that name, and her identity is linked to Maradona's. There are, of course, thousands of Diegos in Argentina because of the same reason. You want your kids to be named after your Patron Saint.

4. Football is the only truly democratic sport. It can not only be played in the streets or the beach with a coconut seed – or so says Pelé's myth – but it can also be played by someone without the athletic attributes needed in many competitive sports. Hugo Sánchez had to sculpt his body to overcome the insults of the Spanish fans calling him "indio" while playing for the first time in Atlético de Madrid. He worked countless hours in the gym and became a sort of gymnast at Real Madrid, able to win five "pichichis" as the best scorer in la Liga. Maradona did not need that. He was a kind of Sancho Panza of the field. He was short, with a big build, his legs curved; he had sometimes a prominent belly. But he also, had "duende", a demon made of grace and street smarts according to Spanish poet Federico García Lorca. Few poets achieve "duende" in Lorca's view. Maradona's duende had no parallel. Not then, not now.

5. Football is a sport that must be played with the help of others; it is a team effort. In recent times, some clubs play with a star-centred system. Barca with Messi, Real Madrid with Ronaldo. Maradona was, of course, the

centre of his teams but also played along with others, sometimes dancing, almost levitating. In the national team, with Ardiles, Kempes, Burruchaga, or Goycochea, in Boca with Brindisi, in Barca with Schuster, in Napoli with Careca. Sometimes you forgot that you were watching a match and thought were attending a sublime ballet. He was, of course, the prima ballerina.

6. In Napoli, he meddled with the *mafiosi*, the Camorra. It changed his career and his health. Maradona had strong political opinions and was a leftist. He became friends with Fidel Castro and later with Hugo Chávez. He knew he was watched all the time, and he endured the gossip of the tabloids. At times, he seemed to be the Princess Di of football players. The paparazzi and the unscrupulous journalists did not understand him. They messed up and tried to destroy his reputation. But he was – is – an antihero, a character of Shakespearian strength and scope. Every article, every photograph that tried to assassinate his character only contributed to his aura.

7. During the 1990 World Cup, he played hobbled with an ankle injury. The team's doctor did not want to administer him any more injections for the pain. He injected himself. He was a leader. He also had a lot of superstitious rites and, during World Cups, had his father bring meat for *asados*, or traditional Argentinian barbecue. His teammates said that he only wanted to compete, to win. Argentina was able to beat Brazil – thanks to a beautiful pass from Maradona to Caniggia – but was defeated by Germany 1-0. He even played another World Cup in 1994. He announced his retirement in the eve of his birthday in 1997. He did not die young and with a beautiful body, as James Dean. He endured many injuries and years of hard life, like all antiheroes do.

8. Many phrases of his became part of a sort of "Maradonian" language. "I am Maradona, who scores goals, who makes mistakes. I can take it all". Or this one: "Messi scores a goal and celebrates. Cristiano scores a goal and poses like he's in a shampoo commercial." He praised Messi many times for being a true heir, a teammate, a leader. He said many times that he did not like money and had a Ferrari in a time when no one in the sport had one. He liked to show off, and to get under people's skins.

9. He was always a supporter of social causes and used football to advance his ideas – football's Robin Hood. He did not need to steal and already had more money that he could have ever dreamed of. He was a man of politics, not a politician. A poor kid from any country in Latin America saw him and thought of possibilities, of dreams realized. His final days were dark, but those shadows were not sins, only a reminder he was of this Earth.

10. He was 60 when he died. Thousands were present to say goodbye in the Casa Rosada – the Argentinian house of government. A line of people 25 blocks long. After many hours, the police shut place down so the body could be moved to the cemetery. People were angry; there were arrests. The poor kid from Villa Florito could never rest in peace. One of the *cabecitas negras*, one of the mestizos, while alive had become a living legend, a myth. Now he

was becoming a God, a "dirty" god as Eduardo Galeano wrote. The most human of the gods.

## Children of Maradona

*Beatriz Sarlo*
*Translated by Ana Terrazas Calero*

A few years ago, a Chilean winery launched a wine branded "Divine" (Divino). The label on the bottle showed a light blue and white shirt with a disproportionate number 10, which was the number that corresponded to the divine Maradona.

It is impossible to think about Maradona without exploring the dangerous triviality of the common place. Both his friendship with Fidel Castro and his appearance in every popular place that had a television camera on demonstrate that his world was a heap of celebrities; or, rather, that in his world even Castro would become a showbiz celebrity.

His excesses were exaggerated and overacted. His loquacity was predictable in the face of sociological interpretation. He was too narcissistic to be listened to with interest, and the combination of drama and orgies that streaked his life had the banality of a telefilm. Maradona was too petty-bourgeois when he whimpered, thinking of his family, for such excesses to be considered Dionysian. He was too cunning to elicit sympathy in the face of his decadence. He was too "noveau rich" not to come across as irritating in a continent where millions of impoverished people will continue to idolize him. However, Maradona is an unattainable goal, a genius, and a myth.

### *Mythology*

Myth carries both a promising and poisoned chalice. I would not want to say that it only illustrates the potential decadence of a country like Argentina, which nowadays only finds some recognition in the Great Dead, like a Borges, the revival of Tango thanks to Broadway, which led to the opening of dance patios in Buenos Aires, and the miraculous transmutation of Eva Perón into Madonna after having passed through the purgatory of rock-opera.

The myth of Maradona, like all myths, induces and rejects interpretation. I would venture only one hypothesis: Maradona's life (like that of Argentinian rock idol Charly García) was an epic tale of transgression. On this level, Maradona may be interpreted in the same way as the support Carlos Saúl Menem received during his first five years as President of Argentina, or the popularity that Alberto Fujimori and Abdalá Bucaram enjoyed when they rose to in Peru and Ecuador, respectively. In Menem's case, people admired the grace with which he bent petty-bourgeois moral standards. He kicked his wife out of the presidential palace, having an aide throw her clothes out on the street as if she were a second-rate lover who was suddenly being replaced. He would drive the most extravagant cars and speed down the highway at 200 km/h. He never slept, driven by an energy that put him in the most unlikely places and supplied him with dozens of women. "He stole but he also made the economy work" was an accepted cynical mantra by the same people who nowadays remember that past with outrage and, perhaps, with regret, scandalized for its lack of morality and the nefarious economic consequences it brought about.

Like Maradona, Menem used the word transgressive in relation to himself until it lost all meaning. For a time, both Menem and Maradona belonged to a "party culture", where excesses were seen as a sign of quality. Both felt they were ethically and practically exceptional. Both put themselves beyond limits that they perceived as legitimate when applied to the rest of society. Nevertheless, Menem was not the only politician to do that. Almost a dozen other former Latin American presidents were or currently are incarcerated, prosecuted, or have absconded. Unlike Lula, not all of them are paying for the progressive nature of their government measures. This is not a minor fact, and it shows that the 1990s were the decade of "anything goes". The new century is still dealing with its consequences.

Naturally, Maradona's transgressions were not disastrous like Menem's were for Argentina, Bucaram's for Ecuador, or Fujimori's for Peru. That is the reason why his mythical aura remained intact. He could do anything (his hand was finally the hand of God, as it was said of a cheating goal against England). Besides, he was only a poor, enriched, and stammering boy. The promise of his myth continued to be fulfilled every time Maradona, hardly an elusive god, appeared before his faithful followers like the deity that simply expects the veneration of his Jupiterian lightning every time it cuts through a clear sky. And we honoured that divinity for the last time in 2020, in the fitting setting of the Presidential Palace, with the crowd filling iconic the Plaza de Mayo square like they did when they mourned former President Néstor Kirchner.

## Theology

Theologians will continue to discuss whether God was present in that game, not only pushing the ball into the goal of the perfidious English, but also blinding the linesman for a millisecond and placing the referee at an angle from which he could not see the Maradonian hand. Without wanting to add to this debate, it is difficult for me to believe that God was not watching the 1986 World Cup and, knowing that the English are thieves and colonialists, did not intercede a little bit for Argentina. God certainly inspired Diego when, to end his account of the goal with lesson of high moral caliber, he stated that "it is no crime to steal from a thief". God, who knows the past just as well as the future, leveled the field so that our national history would also be leveled.

Maradona was a walking miracle. The believers in the hand of God always knew that that was the hand of our Argentinian god, and we were simply waiting for his mouth to speak the truth in the form of that modest public confession that acknowledged the handball. Diego touched the ball with his hand because there was no other way to score the goal. What was needed at the time was a goal and not a stupid player who would hesitate to touch the ball with his hand, who would just stay still before the open goal and deprive us of stealing from the thieves (the English). That goal needed to be immediately celebrated and the linesman's fleeting and timely blindness had to be attributed to God because, as illustrated in Greek mythology and tragedy, gods blind those who wish to lose.

Maradona was a genius but I believe God's involvement in our team's controversial goal should not be forgotten. If God had wanted it, the linesman would have called Maradona's hand and that would have been it: goal disallowed. We would have had to wait for the truly inspired second scoring that came a few moments later. The one we always enjoy because it does not steal anything from anybody, which precludes it from being inscribed into the national epic evoked by Diego's phrase: the English stole the Malvinas/Falklands from us and may have stolen a football game or two, so too bad, let them deal with it.

If the English printed press, which likes to extend the belief that the English are good losers, were upset, it was because they are in fact resentful. Why make such a fuss about something they had been denouncing from the beginning? They never believed God to be Argentinian, nor did they think that goal was a miracle. They always stated it had been a cheat. When Maradona admitted this, instead of everybody agreeing and moving on, the English were outraged. They always pretended to be the genteel, fair-playing ones. What truly happened was that they hate to lose, and Diego told them to their face: I cheated. Let bygones be bygones. Sporting miracles are complex. Diego's statement should not have been broadcast during daytime. Any children watching it could have become confused or be ensnared.

### Maradona and French philosophy

Given Maradona's dedication to unproductive spending, Georges Bataille would have found him of interest. According to Bataille, wars, luxury, gaming, and perverse sexuality fall into the category of unproductivity. Unconditional expenditure is what Bataille termed those acts which do not adhere to the economic principle of preserving wealth or life. Expenditures which burn up a fortune not because of carelessness, but deliberately, like an excess that is part religious, part beauty, and part eroticism. Unproductive spending is the stuff of princes and powerful people who imaginarily maintain their power with the decision to do whatever they please with the goods as the rest of the wretched mortals meticulously looks after.

Maradona was, indeed, a squanderer who travelled the world with the financial reserves he had accumulated during his magical football-playing years. At the same time, his capital as myth became symbolically endless. That is why he could do and say whatever he pleased. He visited Menem and Fidel Castro and adopted multiple discourses: that of the marginalized, that of the devout father, that of the player who brings out to light the dark schemes of international soccer. The discourse of a cynic and of a sincere person. However, nobody could have said that he was fake. He was situated, simply, beyond the norm and objectivity.

It was the discourse of a privileged and indestructible body – as indestructible as the memory of his movements across the field, as long as those memories, or the tapes in which they are recorded, endure. Maradona's body, both compact and ethereal, was an immense, dilapidated capital which, precisely because he wasted it without rhyme or reason, remains intact, infinite, untouched by time, guarded only by death.

The overweight, stammering, emotional, and truculent middle-aged man the screens showed did not manage to vanish the figure of the heroic myth. To his faithful followers (almost everyone), Maradona continued to be a mirror image of the happiness that challenged the lying narrowness of capitalism with obscene luxury and unending squandering.

Maradona was undoubtedly an unassailable Jupiter. He had impunity and magnetism. Charismatic and plebeian, he cannot be subjected to judgment for his actions because, in the face of reckless personal excesses, such judgment would fall into a moralistic trap. How could anybody criticize Maradona without immediately thinking about mean, petty-bourgeois scandals that other petty-bourgeois members are the first to denounce?

## Notes

1 The form D10S, containing the number 10, closely resembles DIOS, the Spanish word for "god".
2 Maradona made this remark after his expulsion from the United States 1994 World Cup.
3 This is a comment that Maradona made in relation to an incident in which a search was carried out for a "lost" pet tortoise which belonged to the son of the American ambassador to Argentina at the time. Maradona highlighted the fact that it would seem very difficult for a tortoise to become "lost" due to its slow speed, and the phrase subsequently became an expression in Argentinian everyday speech to refer to missing easy opportunities.
4 Maradona's original quotation ("Yo crecí en un barrio privado… privado de luz, de agua, de teléfono") is a wordplay around the Spanish adjective *privado,* which translates to English *private,* and *privado de* ("deprived of").
5 *Clarín.* "Investigación judicial: Uno por uno, los siete imputados en la causa por la muerte de Diego Maradona". March 10, 2021. Web: https://www.clarin.com/policiales/imputados-causa-muerte-diego-maradona_0_KuW8VYbWj.html [Accessed March 23, 2021].
6 *Télam.* "Dalma y Gianinna denunciaron a Matías Morla por apropiarse de la marca de su padre". March 12, 2021. Web: https://www.telam.com.ar/notas/202103/547285-dalma-y-gianinna-denunciaron-a-matias-morla-por-apropiarse-de-la-marca-de-su-padre.html [Accessed March 28, 2021].
7 *BAE Negocios.* "Rematan una camiseta firmada por Maradona para salvar al bowling de Castelar". March 26, 2021. Web: https://www.baenegocios.com/negocios/Rematan-una-camiseta-firmada-por-Maradona-para-salvar-al-bowling-de-Castelar-20210326-0197.html [Accessed March 30, 2021].

# References

Angilletta, Florencia. (no date). "Maradona y los feminismos. Diego no es de nadie". *Le Monde Diplomatique*. Web: https://www.eldiplo.org/notas-web/diego-no-es-de-nadie/ [accessed March 28, 2021].

Graziano, Frank. 2007. *Cultures of Devotion. Folk Saints of Spanish America*. Oxford: Oxford University Press.

Lojo, María Rosa. 2007. *Cuerpos resplandecientes. Santos populares argentinos*. Buenos Aires: Sudamericana.

# BIBLIOGRAPHY ON DIEGO MARADONA IN CHRONOLOGICAL ORDER*

## Books by Maradona

1. Maradona, Diego Armando. *Yo soy el Diego*. 2000. Buenos Aires: Planeta [translated as *Maradona. The Autobiography of Soccer's Greatest and Most Controversial Star*. 2004. Trans. Marcela Mora y Araujo. New York: Skyhorse].
2. Maradona, Diego Armando and Daniel Arcucci. *México 86. Mi mundial. Mi verdad. Así ganamos la copa*. 2016. Buenos Aires: Sudamericana. [translated as *Touched by God. How We Won the Mexico '86 World Cup*. 2017. Trans. Jane Brodie and Wendy Gosselin. London: Constable].

## Biographies and miscellanies

1. Acampora, Romolo and Sergio Troise. 1985. *Maradona. L'oro di Napoli*. Milan: Siad Edizioni.
2. Blanco, Guillermo. 1986. *Maradona. L'uomo, il mito, il campione*. Italy: Editrice Ediservice.
3. Dini, Vittorio and Nicolaus Oscar. Eds. 1991. *Te Diegum: genio, sregolatezza e bacchettoni*. Milano: Leonardo editore [translated to Spanish as *Te Diegum. Maradona: genio y transgresión*. 2001. Trad. Roberto Raschella. Buenos Aires: Editorial Sudamericana].
4. Lombardi, Armando. 1992. *Maradona. Pies mágicos... Pies de arcilla*. Buenos Aires: Marymar Ediciones.
5. Dujovne Ortiz, Alicia. 1993 (1st ed. in French 1992). *Maradona soy yo*. Buenos Aires: Emecé.
6. Pasarelli, Bruno. 1993. *La caída de un ídolo. Maradona al desnudo*. Barcelona: Ediciones B.
7. Fernández, Rodrigo and Denise Nagy. 1994. *De las manos de Dios a sus botines. Biografía pública de Diego Maradona no autorizada*. Buenos Aires: Cangrejal Editores.
8. Burns, Jimmy. 1996. *Hand of God. The Life of Diego Maradona*. New York: The Lyons Press.

---

* Essayistic or journalistic pieces are not included.

9. Levinsky, Sergio. 1996. *Maradona, rebelde con causa*. Buenos Aires: Corregidor.

10. Bernstein, Gustavo. 1997. *Maradona. Iconografía de la patria*. Buenos Aires: Biblos.

11. Nélida Khaled. 1997. *Maradona te amo. Maradona te odio*. Buenos Aires: Author edition.

12. Besa Camprubi, Ramón. 1998. *Maradona: historia de un desencuentro*. Barcelona: Barcanova.

13. Arcucci, Daniel. 2001. *Conocer al Diego. Relatos de fascinación maradoniana*. Buenos Aires: Prometeo.

14. Cornejo, Francisco. 2001. *Cebollita Maradona*. Buenos Aires: Sudamericana.

15. *Clarín*. 2001. Special Edition: *El 10: Vida y Magia de Diego Maradona*.

16. D'Orta, Marcello. 2002. *Maradona é meglio e Pelé*. Napoli: Limina Edizioni.

17. de Calò, Alessandro. 2002. *Maradona e la macchina per la felicità*. Milan: La Gazzetta dello Sport.

18. Algore, Cipriano. 2004. *Diego Armando Maradona. Fango, oro e polvere*. Milano: Bevivino Editore.

19. Gatman, Marcelo and Andrés Burgo. 2005. *Diego dijo. Las mejores 1000 frases de toda la carrera del 10*. Buenos Aires: Distal.

20. Zanoni, Leandro. 2006. *Vivir en los medios. Maradona off the record*. Buenos Aires: Marea.

21. Caldeira, José. 2007. *Iglesia Maradoniana*. Mar del Plata: Author edition.

22. Ciriello, Marco. 2008. *Maradona è Amico Mio*. Rome: 66thand2nd Editore.

23. Sapegno, Claudia. 2009. *Il romanzo di Maradona*. Italy: Aliberti.

24. Magdic, Zvonimir. 2008. *Maradona, Mali Zeleni*. Zagreb: Naklada, Ztih.

25. Juillard, Alexandre. 2010. *Maradona*. Paris: Hugodocument.

26. Guanella, Emiliano. 2010. *50 Volte Diego*. Rome: Author Edition.

27. Bellinazzo, Marco and Gigi Garanzini 2012. *Il Napoli di Maradona*. Segrate: Mondadori.

28. Burgo, Andrés and Alejandro Wall. 2014. *El último Maradona: cuando a Diego le cortaron las piernas*. Buenos Aires: Aguilar.

29. Maradona, Dalma. 2014. *Hija de D10S. No es el Diego, es mi papá*. Buenos Aires: Sudamericana.

30. Ludden, John. 2014. *Maradona in Barcelona*. South Carolina: Author edition.

31. Ludden, John. 2014. *Maradona. Once Upon a Time in Naples*. South Carolina: Author edition.

32. Burgo, Andrés. 2016. *El partido. Argentina-Inglaterra 1986*. Buenos Aires: Tusquets.

33. Mora, Angelo. 2018. *Maradona. 101 Pillole di saggezza*. Italia: Agenzia Alcatraz.

34. De Amicis, Igor and Paola Luciani. 2019. *Maradona. El pibe de oro*. Trieste: Edizioni El.

35. Masso, Elisabetta and Carla Reschia. 2019. *La spia di Dios. I segretti di una citá*. Italy: Rogiosi Editore.

36. Barceló Larran, Diego. 2019. *10 Gracias Maradona. La persona, el jugador, la leyenda. Reflexiones para entender el mito del fútbol mundial*. Sevilla: Samarcanda.

37. Domínguez, Sergio, ed. 2019. *Maradona 365 historias*. Buenos Aires: Librofútbol.com.

38. Schiavone, Alberto, ed. 2020. *Diego Armando Maradona. La mano de Dios*. Firenze: Clichy.

39. Siano, Sergio. 2020. *Maradona*. Napoli: Intra Moenia.

40. Sapegno, Claudia. 2020. *Diego da Buenos Aires*. Italy: Aliberti.

41. Ferrara, Ciro. 2020. *Ho visto Diego. E dico o vero*. Milan: Cairo.

42. Carratelli, Mimmo. 2020. *Elogio di Maradona*. Naples: Tullio Pironte Editore.

43. Lanzetta, Peppe. 2020. *Il Dio Inquieto. Elogio di Diego Armando Maradona*. Napoli: Colonosse Editore.

44. Botti, Claudio, Flavio Tranquillo and Antonio Salvati. 2020. *Processo a Diego Armando Maradona. La mano de Dios*. Milano: Edizioni Le Lucerne.

45. Pistoia, Bárbara, ed. 2020. *Todo Diego es político*. Buenos Aires: Síncopa.

46. Ferrer, Julio, ed. 2020. *D10S. Miradas sobre el mito Maradona.* Buenos Aires: Octubre.
47. Eduardo Bolaños y Sergio Barbieri. 2020. *Lo quería Barcelona… Lo quería River Plei. Diego, Boca y la mágica tarde del 22 de febrero de 1981.* Buenos Aires: Reduerco.
48. Ferrero, César. 2021. *Maradona. Obras completas. Un viaje a través del fútbol.* Torino: Bradipolibri.
49. Duchini, Alejandro. 2021. *Mi Diego. Crónica sentimental de una gambeta que desafió al mundo.* Barcelona: Lince.
50. Zabala, Santiago *et al.* 2021. *Fenomenología Maradona.* Madrid: Altamarea.
51. Villar, Antonio Gómez, ed. 2021. *Maradona, un mito plebeyo.* Madrid: Ned.
52. Biazzo, Salvatore. 2021. *60 d.D. dopo Diego.* Napoli: Guida Editori.
53. Altamura, Marcello. 2021. *L'idolo infranto. Chi ha incastrato Maradona?* Italy: Ponte Alle Grazie.
54. Crosetti, Maurizio. 2021. *Quando ucissero Maradona. L'incredibile morte del piu grande calciatore di tutti tempi.* Italy: Edizione Piemme.
55. Mina, Gianni. 2021. *Maradona: "Non saro mai un uomo commune". Il calcio al tempo de Diego.* Roma: Edizioni Mínimum Fax.
56. Beretta, Enzo. 2021. *Il re degli ultimi. I sette anni meravigliosi e folli di Maradona a Napoli.* Roma: Lit Edizioni.
57. Sollazzo, Boris. 2021. *Non avremo un altro D10S. Diego Armando Maradona: una vita da cinema.* Milan: Bietti Fotogrammi.
58. Mangoni, Fabrizio and Oscar Nicolaus. 2021. *A tavola con Maradona. Da Napoli a Buenos Aires, ricette e azione straordinarie del pibe di oro.* Torino: Il Leone Verde.
59. Galullo, Roberto and Angelo Mincuzzi. 2021. *Il tesoro de Maradona.* Italy: Il Sole 24 Ore.
60. Grune, Hardy and Dietrich Schulze-Marmeling, eds. 2021. *D10S. Maradona. Ein Leben Zwischen Himmel Un Holle.* Bielefeld, Germany: Verlag Die Wekstatt.
61. *So Foot.* 2021. Special Edition: *Hasta siempre.*
62. Balagué, Guillem. 2021. *Maradona. The Boy. The Rebel. The God.* UK: Orion.
63. Chaveztoon. 2021. *Maradona. Con unas cuantas líneas.* United States: La Pereza Ediciones.
64. Ludden, John. 2021. *Maradona. The Kid from Villa Fiorito.* South Carolina: Author edition.
65. Ludden, John. 2021. *Duende. Diego Maradona's Lost Season at Sevilla.* South Carolina: Author edition.
66. Ludden, John. 2021. *Maradona. Give My Regards to Hope Street.* South Carolina: Author edition.
67. Ludden, John. 2021. *Maradona: Adiós Diego. A Naples Wall of Fire.* South Carolina: Author edition.
68. Domínguez Prost, Micaela. 2021. *La mano de Diego.* Montevideo: Editorial Tajante.
69. Saidon, Gabriela. 2021. *Superdios. La construcción de Maradona como santo laico.* Buenos Aires: Capital Intelectual.
70. Ferrer, Julio. 2021. *Maradona. Fútbol y política.* Buenos Aires: Punto de encuentro.
71. Castro, Nelson. 2021. *La salud de Diego.* Buenos Aires: Sudamericana
72. Rep, Miguel. 2021. *Diego. Nacido para molestar.* Buenos Aires: Planeta.
73. Ferreyra, Gisele and Julián Barbetti. 2021. *La última pasión de Dios.* Buenos Aires: Beo.
74. Signorini, Fernando, Luciano Wernicke and Fernando Molina. 2021. *Diego desde adentro. Cómo el mejor futbolista del mundo se convirtió en el mejor futbolista de la historia.* Buenos Aires: Planeta.
75. *Crónicas maradonianas.* 2021 (Lástima a nadie maestro, blog). Buenos Aires: Milena Cacerola.

76. Surra, Roberto *et al.* 2021. *El fútbol te da vida. Homenaje a Diego Armando Maradona.* Buenos Aires: Ediciones Fabro.
77. Almada, Lucas, ed. 2021. *La palabra de D10S. Maradona desde sus frases.* Buenos Aires: Librofutbol.com.
78. Cukierkorn, Damián and Sebastián Schor. 2021. *Proyecto Pelusa. La vida del más grande a través de los ojos de la gente.*
79. Moores, Ezequiel Fernández, Wall, Alejandro and Burgo, Andrés, eds. 2021. *Rey de Fiorito. Crónicas políticas y sociales de la vida de Diego Maradona.* Buenos Aires: Ediciones Carrascosa-SiPreBa.

## Films/Documentaries/TV Series

1. *¡Qué linda es mi familia!* 1980. Directed by Ramón "Palito" Ortega. Argentina.
2. *Te rompo el rating,* 1981. Directed by Hugo Sofóvich. Argentina.
3. *Hero. The Official Film of the 1986 FIFA World Cup.* 1986. Directed by Tony Maylam. UK.
4. *Napoli Corner: Maradona y el Nápoli.* 1987. Directed by Bernard Bloch. Canal +, Spain.
5. *El día que Maradona conoció a Gardel.* 1996. Directed by Rodolfo Pagliere. Argentina
6. *Maradona, Il miti dello sport.* 2002. Directed by Ciro Capone. Italy.
7. *La noche del diez.* 2005. Canal 13. Argentina.
8. *Amando a Maradona.* 2005. Directed by Javier Vásquez. Argentina.
9. *Maradona, un gamín en or.* 2006. Directed by Jean Christophe Rosé. France.
10. *El camino de San Diego.* 2006. Directed by Carlos Sorín. Argentina.
11. *In the Hands of the Gods.* 2007. Directed by Benjamin Turner and Gabe Turner. UK.
12. *Maradona, la mano de dios.* 2007. Directed by Marco Risi. Italy, Argentina.
13. *Maradona by Kusturica.* 2008. Directed by Emir Kusturica. Spain, France, Serbia.
14. *El representante de Dios: Guillermo Cóppola.* 2010. Directed by Matías y Nicolás Gueilburt. Canal Infinito, Argentina.
15. *D10S: The Story of Diego Armando Maradona.* 2012. History Channel. UK.
16. *Destino Fútbol: Ciudad Diego.* 2013. ESPN. Argentina.
17. *Youth.* 2015. Directed by Paolo Sorrentino. Italy, France, Switzerland, UK.
18. *Informe Robinson: Los años felices.* 2016. Canal+. Spain.
19. *Maradona, el pibe de oro.* 2016. Directed by Jean-Christophe Rosé. France.
20. *Maradonapoli.* 2017. Directed by Alesso Maria Federici. Italy.
21. *Bring Me the Head of Diego Maradona.* 2018. Directed by Ed Davies and Joe Pearlman. History Channel. UK.
22. *Maradona confidencial.* 2018. Directed by Jovica Nonkovic. National Geographic Channel. Italy.
23. *Maradona en Sinaloa.* 2018. Netflix. Mexico/United States.
24. *Diego Maradona.* 2019. Directed by Asif Kapadia. UK.
25. *Maradona's Legs.* 2019. Directed by Firas Khoury. Palestine.
26. *Fútbol Club Maradona.* 2019. Movistarplus. Spain.
27. *Informe Robinson: Maradona en Sevilla.* 2020. Canal+. Spain.
28. *El bueno, el malo y el Diego.* 2020. History Channel. Argentina.
29. *Yo jugué con Dios.* 2021. Directed by Raúl Papalardo. Argentina.
30. *Maradona, sueño bendito.* 2021. Amazon Prime Video. Argentina, Italy, Spain.
31. *Maradona: La muerte de Dios.* 2021. Directed by Ivan Kasanzew. Argentina.
32. *The Hand of God.* 2021. Directed by Paolo Sorrentino. Italy.
33. *El Diego. El pueblo no olvida.* 2021. DEPORTV. Argentina. https://www.youtube.com/watch?v=E-7qjUOZRSg

## Fiction and Creative Works

### Poems

1. Benedetti, Mario. 2008. "Maradona". *Un balón envenenado. Poesía y fútbol.* Eds. Luis García Montero y Jesús García Sánchez. Madrid: Visor, 2012, p. 52.
2. Picardo, Osvaldo. 2012. "La mano de Dios". *Un balón envenenado. Poesía y fútbol.* Eds. Luis García Montero y Jesús García Sánchez. Madrid: Visor, p. 188.

### Novels

1. Niembro, Fernando and Julio Llinás. 1995. *Inocente.* Barcelona: Grijalbo Mondadori.
2. Castaldi, Paolo. 2012. *Diego Armando Maradona. La vita e le imprese di Diego Armando Maradona raccontate a fumetti.* Padova: BeccoGiallo [*La mano de Dios.* Madrid: Diábolo Ediciones, 2014]. ★Graphic novel
3. Ahmadi, Amhed. 2013. *Strange and Incredible Story of Maradona [the correct title is Maradona, Plastic Goalkeepers, And That Decisive Penalty... Did He Score It? Or Not? What Happened?* [in Farsi]. London: H&S Media.
4. Bartoletti, Marino. 2021. *Il retorno degli Dei.* Rome: Galucci.

### Short stories

#### Anthologies

1. *El 10 Maradona.* 2021. Comp. Reinaldo Marchant. Santiago de Chile: Mago. [anthology]
2. *Maradona, uno de los nuestros.* 2021. Sevilla: Peña Sevillista Coke Andújar. [anthology]

#### Single stories

3. Medina, Enrique. 1984. "Yo fui Maradona". *El Gráfico* https://www.elgrafico.com.ar/articulo/1088/35645/yo-fui-maradona-por-enrique-medina.
4. Soriano, Osvaldo. 1987. "Maradona sí, Galtieri no". *Rebeldes, soñadores y fugitivos.* Buenos Aires: Editora 12.
5. Fontanarrosa, Roberto. 1996. "Aquel gol de Maradona a los ingleses". *Página 12.* April 30.
6. Saccheri, Eduardo. 2000. "Me van a tener que disculpar". *Esperándolo a Tito y otros cuentos de fútbol.* Buenos Aires: Galerna, 2005, 35–42.
7. Vargas, Walter. 2004. "Bautismos". *Del diario íntimo de un chico rubio y otras historias futboleras.* Buenos Aires: Ediciones al Arco, 103–109.
8. Casciari, Hernán. 2005. "Vivir para contarlo". *Más respeto que soy tu madre.* Buenos Aires: Ediciones Orsai, 203–205.
9. Braceli, Rodolfo. 2009. "Recomendaciones para parir un hijo que salga Maradona". *Perfume de gol.* Buenos Aires: Planeta.
10. Casciari Hernán. 2013. "10.6 segundos", *Orsai,* 11, 36–49.
11. Feinmann, José Pablo. 2014. "Dieguito". *Bongo. Infancia en Belgrano R y otros cuentos y nouvelles.* Buenos Aires: Planeta, pp. 21–51 (first published in shorter version in 1997 and included in *Cuentos de fútbol argentino.* Buenos Aires: Alfaguara, 2003, 47-53).
12. Scher, Ariel. 2018. "Todo mientras Diego". *Todos mientras Diego y otros cuentos mundiales.* Buenos Aires: Grupo Editorial Sur, 9–11.

13. Scher, Ariel. 2018. "1990. A llorar se aprende". *Todos mientras Diego y otros cuentos mundiales*. Buenos Aires: Grupo Editorial Sur, 92–93.
14. Pecchinenda, Gianfranco. 2020. *Quel Tal Maradona*. Napoli: Amigdala Edizioni.
15. Brescia, Pablo. 2022. "Dos tiempos distintos". *Olfato de gol. Nuevos cuentos de fútbol*. Eds. Antonio Sánchez Jiménez and José Domínguez Búrdalo. Madrid: Reino de Cordelia, 65–75.

## Books, journal articles and book chapters

1. Dini, Vittorio. 1994. "Maradona: Héros Napolitain". *Actes de la recherche en sciences sociales* 103: 75–78.
2. Bilbija, Ksenija. 1995. "Maradona's Left: Postmodernity and National Identity in Argentina". *Studies in Latin American Popular Culture* 14: 199–208.
3. Alabarces, Pablo and María Graciela Rodríguez. 1996. "'El fútbol no es la patria' (pero se le parece)" y "Maradona revisitado. Apostillas a 'El fútbol no es la patria'". *Cuestión de pelotas. Fútbol, deporte, sociedad, cultura*. Buenos Aires: Atuel, 37–57.
4. Archetti, Eduardo. 1997. "'And Give Joy to my Heart: Ideology and Emotions in the Argentinean Cult of Maradona". *Entering the Field. New Perspectives on World Football*. Eds. Gary Amstrong and Richard Giulianotti. Berg: Oxford; New York, 31–51.
5. Sebreli, Juan José. 1998. "El mito Maradona". *La era del fútbol*. Buenos Aires: Sudamericana, 119–153.
6. Archetti, Eduardo. 1998. "The Potrero and the Pibe. Territory and Belonging in the Mythical Account of Argentinean Football". *Locality and Belonging*. Ed. Nadia Lovell. Routledge: London and New York, 189–210.
7. Alabarces, Pablo and María Graciela Rodríguez. 1999. "Football and Fatherland: The Crisis of National Representation in Argentinean Soccer". *Sport in Society* 2.3: 118–133.
8. Archetti, Eduardo. 1999. "The Masculine Imagery of Freedom: The World of Pibes and Maradona". *Masculinities. Football, Polo and Tango in Argentina*. Oxford: Berg, 180–189.
9. Archetti, Eduardo. 2001. "The Spectacle of a Heroic Life: The Case of Diego Maradona". *Sport Stars: The Cultural Politics of Cultural Celebrity*. Eds. David L. Andrews and Steven J. Jackson. London; New York: Routledge, 151–164.
10. Tobin, Jeffrey. 2002. "Soccer Conspiracies: Maradona, the CIA, and Populist Critique". *Sport in Latin America and the Caribbean*. Eds. Joseph L. Arbena and David G. LaFrance. London: Eurospan, 51–73.
11. Archetti, Eduardo. 2003. "The Spectacle of Identities. Football in Latin America". *Contemporary Latin American Cultural Studies*. Eds. Stephen Hart and Richard Young. UK: Routledge, 116–126.
12. Rodríguez, María Graciela. 2003. "Los días en que Maradona usó kilt: intersección de identidades profundas con representaciones massmediáticas". *Futbologías. Fútbol, identidad y violencia en América Latina*. Comp. Pablo Alabarces. Buenos Aires: CLACSO, 181–197.
13. Alabarces, Pablo. 2005. "Santa Maradona, ascenso y caída de un mito futbolístico". *Delirios de grandeza, Los mitos argentinos: memoria, identidad, cultura*. Comps. María Cristina Pons and Claudia Soria. Rosario: Beatriz Viterbo, 41–53.
14. Alabarces, Pablo. 2005. "Maradona, el fútbol, la patria, el peronismo y otros gremios paralelos. Un héroe en disponibilidad". *Encrucijadas* 33.
15. Alabarces, Pablo. 2007. "Maradonismo, o la superación del peronismo por otros medios". *Fútbol y patria: el fútbol y las narrativas de la nación en la Argentina*. Buenos Aires: Prometeo, 133–161.

16. Sebreli, Juan José. 2008. "Maradona". *Comediantes y mártires. Ensayos contra los mitos.* Barcelona: Debates, 165–202.

17. Salazar Sutil, Nicolás. 2008. "Maradona Inc.: Performance Politics off the Pitch". *International Journal of Cultural Studies* 11.4: 441–458.

18. Brown, William J. and Marcela Alejandra Chaván de Matviuk. 2010. "Sports Celebrities and Public Health: Diego Maradona's Influence on Drug Use". *Prevention. Journal of Health Communication* 15.4: 358–373.

19. Sedda, Franciscu. 2010. "Maradona e l'esplosione. Dalla Mano di Dio al Poema di gol". *Mitologie dello sport. 40 saggi brevi.* Roma: Edizioni Nuova Cultura, 292–302.

20. Brach, Bartlomiej. 2011. "Who is Lionel Messi? A Comparative Study of Diego Maradona and Lionel Messi". *International Journal of Cultural Studies* 15.4: 415–428.

21. Bellinazzo, Marco and Gigi Garanzini. 2012. *Il Napoli di Maradona.* Milano: Mondadori.

22. Janssen, Steve, David C. Rubin and Martin A. Conway. 2012. "The Reminiscence Bump in the Temporal Distribution of the Best Football Players of All Time: Pelé, Cruijff or Maradona? *The Quarterly Journal of Experimental Psychology* 65.1: 165–178.

23. Hughson, John and Kevin Moore. 2012. "'Hand of God', Shirt of the Man: The Materiality of Diego Maradona". *Costume* 46.2: 212–225.

24. Acker, Ana María. 2012. "Construções de poder no documentário Maradona, de Emir Kusturica". *Verso e reverso* 26.63: 135–143.

25. Segura M. Trejo, Fernando. 2013. "Diego Armando Maradona. Vers una inter-prétation de sa trajectoire". *Questions de Communication, Série Actes: Spectacles Sportifs, Dispositifs d'Ecriture.* Ed. J. F Diana. Lorraine: Université de Lorraine, 123–136.

26. Magalhães Brittoa, Simone, Jorge Ventura de Moraisb and Túlio Velho Barretoc. 2014. "The Hand of God, the Hand of the Devil: A Sociological Interpretation of Maradona's Hand Goal". *Soccer and Society* 15.5: 671–684.

27. Bifulco, Luca and Vittorio Dini. Eds. 2014. *Maradona: sociología di un mito globale.* Ipermedium libri [translated to Spanish as *Maradona, un héroe deportivo. Tres estudios sociológicos de Italia.* 2020. Buenos Aires: Ediciones Godot].

28. Sibaja, Rwany and Charles Parrish. 2014. "*Pibes, Cracks* and *Caudillos*: Argentina, the World Cup and Identity Politics". *Soccer & Society* 15.5: 655–670.

29. Free, Marcus. 2014. "Diego Maradona and the Psychodynamics of Football Fandom in International Cinema". *Celebrity Studies* 5.1–1: 197–212.

30. Alabarces, Pablo. 2014. "La patria, Maradona y Messi: variaciones sobre el ser nacional". *Héroes, machos y patriotas. El fútbol entre la violencia y los medios.* Buenos Aires: Aguilar, 103–132.

31. Levinsky, Sergio. 2014. "Maradona y Messi, ensayo sobre la continuidad y la rup-tura". *Istor* 15.57: 111–117.

32. Serra, Marcello. 2015. "Maradona entra la tierra y el cielo". *Cuadernos de información y comunicación* 20: 13–25.

33. Ahl, Frederick. 2015. "The Hand of God. Diego Maradona and the Divine Nature of Cheating in Classical Antiquity". *Archai: Revista de Estudos sobre as Origens do Pensamento Ocidental* 14: 11–19.

34. Korstanje, Maximiliano. 2016. "Sacrificio y ejemplaridad. Comprendiendo los fenómenos de Leonel Messi y Diego A. Maradona". *Nómadas. Revista Crítica de Ciencias Sociales y Jurídicas* 48: 259–265.

35. Garton, Gabriela. 2016/17. "Un relato futbolero de viaje: el mito de Maradona en las 'idas y vueltas' de Caparrós y Villoro". *Letras* 74–75: 103–114.

36. Sarbajit, Mitra and Souvik Naha. 2017. "Politics and International Fandom in a Fringe Nation: La Albiceleste, Maradona, and Marxist Kolkata". *Sport in Society* 20.5–6: 660–674.

37. García Cames, David. 2018. "El gol y el héroe. Aproximación mítica a Maradona en tres cuentos argentinos". *Pasavento. Revista de Estudios Hispánicos* 6.2: 413–431.

38. Segura M. Trejo, Fernando. 2018. "Diego Armando Maradona: los mundiales y la política". *Istor* 72: 227–236.

39. Alabarces, Pablo. 2018. "De Maradona a Messi: viejos y nuevos argumentos sobre el héroe deportivo y la patria". *Imago. A Journal of the Social Imaginary* 11: 26–43.

40. Silveira Dantas Junior, Hamilcar, Zoboli, Elder Silva Correia and Cristiano Mezzaroba. 2018. "Identidade e alteridade na publicisva televisiva brasileira: o endere Çamento de Maradona durante a copa do mundo de 2014". *Conhecimento online* 1: 39–53.

41. Bauer, Thomas. 2018. "From Maradona to Jude Law: Sport in Paolo Sorrentino's Movies". *Studies in European Cinema* 18.1: 60–75.

42. Genschow, Oliver, Davide Rigoni and Macel Brass. 2019. "The Hand of God or The Hand of Maradona? Believing in Free Will Increases Perceived Intentionality of Other's Behavior". *Consciousness and Cognition* 70: 80–87.

43. Silva Garcés, José and María Mare. 2020. "Acerca de la creatividad. *El Diego* y el lenguaje humano". *Quintú Quimun, Revista de Lingüística* 4: 1–9.

44. Bavassi, Luz Laura Kaczer and Rodrigo S. Fernández. 2020. "Maradona in Our Minds: The FIFA World Cup as a Way to Address Collective Memory Properties". *Memory and Cognition* 48: 469–480.

45. López Medel, Ismael. 2020. "Diego Maradona". *Athletes Breaking Bad. Essays on Transgressive Sports Figures*. Eds. John C. Lamothe and Donna J. Barbie. Jefferson, North Carolina: McFarland & Co, 80–95.

46. Alabarces, Pablo. 2021. "Maradona: mito popular, símbolo peronista, voz plebeya". *Papeles del CEIC* 249.1: 1–11.

47. Saposnik, Gustavo, Florencia Saposnik and Pedro Saposnik. 2021. "Rethinking Adherence to Home Care in Heart Failure: The Lessons Learned from Diego Maradona's Death". *Home Heatlh Care Services Quarterly* 4.3: 192–203.

48. *Funes Journal of Narratives and Social Sciences*. Special Issue: *Global Maradona: man, athlete, celebrity, idol, hero, myth*. 2021. 5.

49. *Eracle. Journal of Sports and Social Sciences*. Special Issue: *Global Maradona: man, athlete, celebrity, idol, hero, myth*. 2021. 4.2.

# INDEX